So Great a Proffit

So Great a Proffit

HOW THE EAST INDIES TRADE

TRANSFORMED

ANGLO-AMERICAN CAPITALISM

JAMES R. FICHTER

HARVARD UNIVERSITY PRESS
Cambridge, Massachusetts & London, England   2010

Library of Congress Cataloging-in-Publication Data

Fichter, James R.
    So great a proffit : how the East Indies trade transformed
Anglo-American capitalism / James R. Fichter.
       p. cm.
    Includes bibliographical references and index.
    ISBN 978-0-674-05057-0 (alk. paper)
    1. United States—Commerce—Asia.
    2. Asia—Commerce—United States.
    3. United States—Foreign economic relations—Great Britain.
    4. Great Britain—Foreign economic relations—United States.
    5. Capitalism—United States—History.   I. Title.
HF3118.F53 2010
382.0973'05—dc22   2009050549

Dedicated to my father,
the wisest man I know

The American commerce to the East,
will ere long rival England.

—Independent Chronicle,
Boston, MA, 1796

Contents

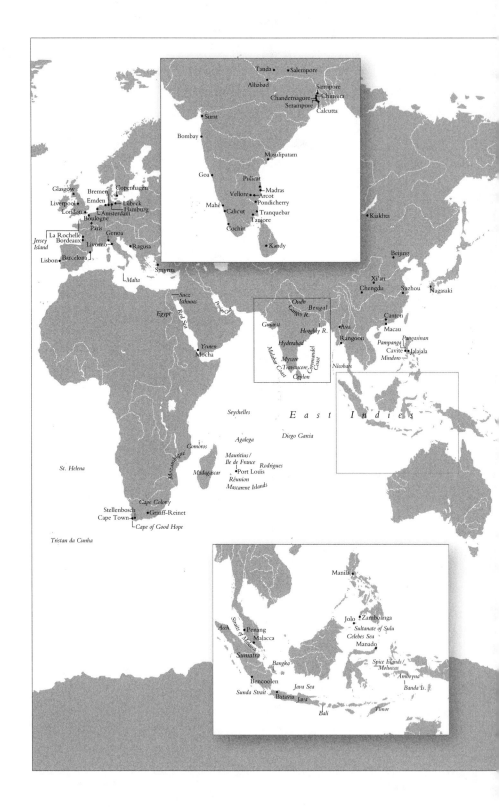

Tanda
Salempore
Alliabad
Sanupore
Chinsura
Chandernagore
Serampore
Calcutta
Surat
Bombay
Masulipatam
Goa
Pulicat
Vellore
Madras
Arcot
Mahé
Pondicherry
Calicut
Tranquebar
Cochin
Tanjore
Kandy

Glasgow
Bremen
Copenhagen
Liverpool
Emden
Lübeck
London
Amsterdam
Hamburg
Boulogne
Paris
La Rochelle
Genoa
Bordeaux
Jersey
Island
Livorno
Ragusa
Lisbon
Barcelona
Smyrna
Malta

Kiakhta

Beijing

Xi'an
Chengdu
Suzhou
Nagasaki

Suez
Isthmus
Persian Gulf
Egypt
Red Sea

Oudh
Ganges R.
Bengal
Gujarat
Hooghly R.
Hyderabad
Ava
Canton
Macau
Rangoon
Pampanga
Pangasinan
Cavite
Jalajala
Malabar Coast
Mysore
Travancore
Coromandel Coast
Mindoro
Ceylon
Nicobars

Yemen
Mocha

Seychelles
East Indies

Agalega
Diego Garcia

Comoros
Mauritius/
Ile de France
Rodrigues
St. Helena
Madagascar
Port Louis
Réunion
Mascarene Islands

Cape Colony
Stellenbosch
Graaff-Reinet
Cape Town
Cape of Good Hope

Tristan da Cunha

Manila

Jolo
Zamboanga
Sultanate of Sulu
Acch
Penang
Celebes Sea
Malacca
Manado
Sumatra
Bangka
Spice Islands/
Moluccas
Amboyna
Bencoolen
Banda Is.
Java Sea
Sunda Strait
Batavia
Java
Bali
Timor

Bering Sea

Alaska

chatka

Sitka

Unalaska

Pacific Northwest

Nootka Sound

Astoria
Columbia R.

California

Hawaii

Hudson Bay

Rupert's Land

*Lower
Canada*
Québec
*Upper
Canada*
Montréal
Salem
Boston
Baltimore New York City
Philadelphia

New
Brunswick
Nova Scotia

Great Lakes

Charles Town

New Orleans

Veracruz
Acapulco

Cuba
Jamaica

Spanish Main

Cumaná
Demerara River
Berbice River
Cayenne

La Guaira

Essequibo River

Surinam

South Seas

Nuka Hiva

Marquesas Is.

Fiji

P o l y n e s i a

Potosí

Juan Fernandez

Valparaiso

Buenos Aires
Montevideo

Falklands

Tierra del Fuego
Cape Horn

South
Georgia
Island

Cap Français   Monte Cristi

Hispaniola

Port-au-
Prince
Léogane
Saint Domingue

SantoDomingo

St. Thomas

Puerto
Rico

St. Martin   St. Bartholomew

St. John

St. Eustatius
St. Croix

Guadeloupe
Marie-Galante

Martinique

St. Lucia

St. Vincent

Grenada
Tobago

Curaçao

Trinidad

So Great a Proffit

Introduction

In 1784 the first U.S. merchantman reached Asia. For such a new nation it was a fittingly small start. Less than three decades later, U.S. trade with Asia was greater than that of any other Western nation on earth, save Britain. How could this happen? Europeans had bought tea on the China coast for centuries, and now Americans were not simply appearing among the mix of Western traders in China but enjoying precipitous commercial success. Between 1793 and 1812, French, Dutch, and Danish merchants soon found themselves sailing in American wakes.

At first glance this seems incredible. But the trade raises questions that can tantalize the imagination. The trade grew quickly, only to be set back on its heels just as quickly again. Was this a twenty-year blip in history, or did this trade have long-term effects? Did it influence the development of the United States? Did the shifts in global trade achieved by American merchants influence the rest of the world?

The simplest explanation for the growth of American trade in Asia credits the French Revolutionary and Napoleonic Wars—termed here the French Wars—for American commercial success. British warships kept French and French-allied merchants from the sea, and neutral traders from the United States took up the Continentals' trade. U.S. merchantmen trafficked between the Caribbean and Europe in an old and well-known story; surely developments in Asia were echoes of the same phenomenon—no more, no less.

Americans sailed to more places in Asia than China alone, and the French Wars can help explain the growing U.S. trade with these other parts of Asia as well. If Americans sailed so far to take up France's trade with China, they might be willing to take up the carrying trade between French Europe and the French, Dutch, and Spanish colonies in Asia. Indeed, American trade in the French Indian Ocean colonies of the Mascarenes (roughly 500 miles east of Madagascar), in Dutch Java, in Dutch Southern Africa, and in Spanish Manila boomed during the French Wars. The boom was remarkable—quite so in some cases—and gives credence to the neutral-trade thesis.

American trade also flourished in British Bengal, in the very heart of the British Empire in Asia. This success, too, could at least partly be credited to the French Wars—the East India Company certainly explained the Americans' trade this way—with the Americans simply meeting French demand for Indian goods. And yet in Bengal the French Wars are a necessary but not sufficient explanation, for the U.S. trade in Bengal was intimately connected with British merchants in Calcutta and in London. These connections, which the French Wars do little to explain, make it difficult to conceive of a discretely American trade with India as much as of an American trade abetted by British merchants, who were ostensibly the Americans' competitors. U.S. merchants in India, and in Asia more generally, competed with the English East India Company for the carriage of goods between Asia and the Atlantic. Yet they worked with British merchants—Company directors, shareholders, and employees among them—to do so. How does one explain the bizarrely competitive and cooperative connections between the Americans so recently departed from the British Empire and the British traders now remaking that empire in Asia?

Through these connections, U.S. trade to Asia between 1783 and 1815 transformed both the British Empire and the United States. Because of these connections it is difficult to consider American trade to Asia without its British counterpart, and so this book is not a history of American trade to Asia but of Anglo-American capitalism there. The far-reaching consequences of the trade suggest the deep links between the United States and the rest of the world from that country's inception. They also yield a new understanding of the American relationship with the British Empire after American independence as well as new avenues of inquiry into the "great divergence" between east and west.

China, India, the Mascarenes, and Southeast Asia constitute a vast array of ports and countries, each meriting study in its own right. And yet examining them together is essential because that was how early modern Americans and Europeans saw them: of a piece and as part of the great expanse of the world's shore stretching from the Cape of Good Hope eastward to the Straits of Magellan and referred to as the East Indies. By the eighteenth century the East Indies included the Indian Ocean and the East Asian littoral, fading into the South Seas somewhere over what we would call the Western Pacific. "East Indies" was a vague term and made sense only from an Atlantic perspective—that is, Western and maritime—whereby however far Calcutta and Canton were from each other they seemed still infinitely closer to each other than to home, whether that home was London or Brest or New York. Eighteenth-century European empires were primarily Atlantic in focus, and Western governments regarded the Indies as a realm beyond. "Distant" had once meant "beyond the pale" or "beyond the line." In the eighteenth-century Atlantic it meant "beyond the Capes," and to Atlantic men in the east, a term like "East Indies" thus made sense. In the minds of the American, British, and European merchants who traded to the Indies, China, Bengal, and the Mascarenes were all East Indian destinations.

The East Indies were more than an abstract formulation. Each European East India Company had its own patent, making that Company the exclusive national merchant between the East Indies and the Atlantic and giving the East Indies economic definition. As American independence ended British rule in one part of the world, it brought American merchants into competition with the English East India Company in another. Americans were not new to Asia: colonial American merchants had smuggled and pirated their way across the Indian Ocean in the early eighteenth century, and others had gone east legally with the East India Company. But after 1783 Americans went east as U.S. citizens, not British subjects.

This new U.S. commercial presence was greater, more sustained, and spread across more of the Indies than anything that had emanated from North America before. It also occurred in tandem with the recentering of the British Empire on the east. As a result, the English East India Company found itself with a new and vigorous competitor in Asia just as the Company itself was coming under greater scrutiny as the custodian not of a remote imperial backwater but of a growing imperial heartland. The rivalry was consequential: when Parliament revoked the Company's monopoly on Indian trade at the end of the French Wars, many Members of Parliament pointed to the Company's failure to deal with its American competition.

Thus the American trade to the East Indies as a whole had repercussions for society, economies, and politics on both sides of the Atlantic. In Britain it helped end the East India Company's monopoly on British trade to India and helped begin Britain's nineteenth-century free-trade empire there. In the United States it abetted the accumulation of wealth and financial capital in the hands of the wealthiest Americans, creating financiers who would profoundly alter the shape of American business. British merchants gained free trade, becoming more like their American counterparts, and American merchants gained capital and became more like their opposite numbers in Britain. Convergence between British and American trades to the east led to convergence between Britain and America at home.

Thus the need to examine the East India trade in a global context. The convergence between British and American East India merchants occurred while the center of global economic activity was shifting from Asia to the North Atlantic. This shift was known as the "great divergence." Historians offer various reasons for the divergence, including markets, European property rights, industrialization, and colonialism.[1] Of these, industrialization is usually taken as the main cause of the North Atlantic's rise, leaving capital to a supporting role at best.[2] But capital was key. Capital, often in the form of specie (silver coin), was fundamental to American and British trade in Asia and to east-west interaction generally. The U.S. East Indies trade had effects out of proportion to its size, in part because of the role of capital. Recent scholars of the great divergence have missed this point by misunderstanding capital, failing to distinguish between paper money and fixed capital on the one hand and gold and specie—which were fungible and globally accepted—on the other.[3]

The early U.S. East Indies trade encouraged the capitalization that reoriented New England and the mid-Atlantic states in the world economy; it served as a marker for those who had specie in the early national U.S. economy; and it spurred reforms in British and, to a lesser extent, European trade links to the Indies, so that the global North was broader, more uniform, and more directly linked to the Indies, a region that was not yet but would soon become a center of the global South. The U.S. East Indies trade had diverse effects because it intersected at various points with European countries' trade (and the financing thereof) in Asia, particularly Britain's. Despite the East India Company's formal monopoly, British and American trade in Asia were, though fundamentally distinct, financially interconnected: the global flow of capital and global Anglo-American commercial networks could not help but link them. Likewise, the economic transformations of the nineteenth-century Atlantic and of nineteenth-century Asia are distinct but related. Yet not just any characterization of their relationship will do. Though the great divergence occurred just as the Anglo-American east-west trade opened to well-capitalized private merchants, there is little evidence that these merchants opened trade to Asia solely or even primarily to export industrial goods. Once the east-west trade had been liberalized, however, it was certainly easier for merchants subsequently to export the industrial products of the North Atlantic. Capital is key here as well, since liberalization of east-west trade in Britain and capital accumulation in the United States (and perhaps also in British outports) allowed merchants to exploit this divergence better.

The ties among world history, U.S. history, and British imperial history are fundamental to understanding the transformation of the Anglo-American trades to the Indies. Therefore this book covers an array of subjects; British policymakers, American merchants, and corrupt French officials all play their part. So, too, do creole society in Java, Qing Chinese governance, and British policy in India.

In passing among the histories of the United States, the British Empire, and the world, this book uses new and familiar sources. Shipping records from South Africa, Mauritius, India, Indonesia, the Philippines, St. Helena, and the United States; American and British merchants' papers; French imperial correspondence; and less thoroughly examined portions of English East India Company records join the *American State Papers* series and more-familiar Company correspondence. Taken together, these sources reveal transformations in disparate places that were deeply interrelated.

This book is arranged around the French Wars, which catalyzed the changes wrought by expanding Anglo-American connections. Chapters 1 and 2 consider the development of American trade to the Indies in the years 1783–1793, explaining how it functioned before the French Wars began. Chapters 3–8 examine the booming U.S. trade to the Indies during the period of the French Wars, 1793–1812, each chapter covering a different aspect of the U.S. East India trade in this period. The remaining chapters look at the longer-term effects of the U.S. East India trade after 1812 in both the British Empire and the United States.

But before 1813, before these dual transformations, before the great divergence, and before the nineteenth-century convergence of British and American free-trade liberalism in Asia, there was an eighteenth-century separation between the two nations: the American Revolution. And so it is with the American Revolution, and with the Asian tea that was the source of so much trouble, that this story begins.

CHAPTER ONE

Revolution — the significance of the tea boycott — anti-monopoly, which breeds tyranny, oppression, famine etc.

Some time after one in the morning, a "violent knocking at the Street-door" startled Benjamin Fanueil and his family from bed. Fanueil opened the bedroom window to ask what was the matter. A man answered back that he carried a "letter of great consequence," something that could not wait for morning. He slipped it under the door.[1]

At "about one o'Clock" the same morning, Richard Clarke also woke to a "violent knocking at the door." By moonlight he and his brother made out two men in the courtyard below. One held "a letter from the Country." Clarke sent his servant to fetch it.

Elisha Hutchinson woke to fists on his door that night, too. We have a letter, the callers told him, urgent.

Fanueil, Clarke, and Hutchinson read:

> Boston Nov[r] 1, 1773
>
> The Freemen of this Province understand from good Authority that there is a Quantity of Tea Consigned to your house by the East India Company which is Distructive to the Happiness of every well wisher to his Country[;] it is therefore expected that you personally appear at Liberty Tree on Wednesday next at 12 o'Clock at noon day, to make a publick resignation of your Commission agreeable to a Notification of this day for that purpose.
>
> Fail not upon your Peril.[2]

This was the first in a series of events in which tea, though an Asian commodity, helped bring about American independence.

As a consequence, global trade would link the United States from its very beginning to the trade with Asia and, somewhat paradoxically, to the fate of Britain's Asian empire.

The next morning, a Tuesday, the Hutchinsons, Clarkes, and Fanueils ventured "abroad" and found "Printed Notifications" all over town, calling local residents to witness their resignations at the Liberty Tree on Boston Common. The notices implied, as Richard Clarke later complained, that they had given up their part in the tea consignment, even though they had agreed to nothing of the sort. But their nemeses had no patience for details like that.[3]

At eleven o'clock on Wednesday, church bells across Boston began to toll and continued until noon. The town crier walked the streets, summoning people to the Liberty Tree. And they came. Some estimated 500 people, others guessed even more. Meanwhile, the merchants involved in selling the East India Company's tea met at Clarke's warehouse on King Street. No one there "entertained the least thought of obeying the Summons" to the Liberty Tree. One did not obey "people of the lowest rank," as Clarke termed the crowd. Instead, the merchants opposed "the Mob" and decided to force *them* to obey, and in this they were pleased to have "a number of Gentlemen of the first Rank" join them.[4]

At one o'clock that afternoon, an angry crowd marched from the Liberty Tree down to the warehouses to seek out the merchants who had ignored their summons. Massed at the warehouse door, the crowd sent a deputation inside asking the merchants to give up selling the Company's tea and to agree to send the tea ships back to Britain once they arrived. The merchants "firmly refused" and gave the request its "proper contempt." The response stirred the already angry mob outside. "Irritated with the haughty manner with which the answer was . . . given," the people charged the warehouse door.[5]

The merchants set their servant to shut the outer doors before the mob could break in. Nathaniel Hatch, a local justice of the peace with them in the warehouse, rushed to help. They made "all possible exertions to stem the torrent of the Mob." Hatch shouted out again and again to the people outside. He was a magistrate. In the king's name, he commanded them to disperse. Outside, the crowd shouted back all sorts of "insulting and reproachful words," and, with so few people holding the doors from within, the mob ripped them clean off their hinges.[6]

Inside, the merchants and their "first Rank" friends fled upstairs to the counting house. The staircase was narrow; a hatch at the top opened into the upper story. On the staircase the merchants made their most "vigorous efforts" to fight back the crowd below before fleeing into the counting room and throwing down the hatch. There they sat. After an hour and a half, the throng, bored, was mostly "drawn off." And the merchants, surrounded by a pack of friends, made their way home in relative safety.[7]

That was hardly the end of it, however. The next night Benjamin Fanueil found another "menacing Letter" addressed to all the tea merchants "thrust under" his door. It tried to "intimidate them from executing their Trust," in Clarke's phrase.[8]

> Gentlemen,
>
> It is currently reported, that you are in the extremest anxiety respecting your standing with the good people of this Town . . . as Commissioners for the sale of the Monopolized and Dutied Tea, we do not wonder in the least that your apprehensions are terrible . . . long have this people been irreconcilable to the Idea of spilling human blood, but . . . this is the last warning you are ever to expect.
>
> Thursday evening 9 O'clock November 4th, 1773[9]

Similar threats and plenty of rumors circulated in the days that followed. Then, mid-month, the Fanueils began to hear stories that "a number of picked men" were going "to break into our house one night." "I can hardly believe it," Benjamin Fanueil wrote, but in his words a sense of fear belied his disbelief.[10]

The Clarkes, too, heard the rumors of "an Assault" on their home. On November 17, as the Clarkes gathered for a family celebration, the rumors proved true. Suddenly they were "alarmed with the sounding of Horns, whistling and shouting, and a violent Beating at the Doors." The Clarkes moved the "women into the safest Part of the House," while the men tried to secure the doors and windows on the bottom story as best they could. From the front of the house the mob "huzzaed," and the Clarkes feared the crowd would break in.[11]

Then one of the Clarke men lost his head, drew a firearm, and shot toward the crowd. The mob responded with "Showers of Stones and Brickbats, and soon beat in all the lower Windows." They pelted the house for almost an hour, when eventually "a worthy Gentleman of the Town" stopped the fracas and encouraged the Clarkes and the crowd to calm down. As at the warehouse, the pause broke the energy of the mob. Eventually, people wandered off.[12]

By now, the merchants feared for their safety in Boston. The next mob might not be drawn off so easily. The merchants began spending their nights in outlying towns.[13]

At the end of November the tea finally arrived, and the conflict worsened. On November 29 a 5,000-strong gathering at the Old South Meeting House repeated the demand made over the past month that the tea be sent back to Britain. The merchants refused. But they feared what would follow and fled to Castle William, an island fortress in the city harbor. There they stayed all winter.[14]

On their flight to Castle William, the merchants wrote the governor to beg for his protection. They recalled the past month bitterly. They had been "cruelly insulted in their persons and property." They had found "incendiary Letters . . . thrown into their Houses in the night." A "large body of Men" had "repeatedly attack'd" them. One of their homes was "assaulted in the night." And they remained constantly "threatned in their persons and property and further with the destruction of the said Tea in its arrival in Port." But they stubbornly clung to their precious tea and still somehow imagined it could be sold. Even now they asked the governor to protect it until they would "be at liberty openly and safely to dispose of the same." They believed—or wanted to believe—that the whole affair would just go away.[15]

Samuel Adams and John Hancock led the forces arranged against the tea. They organized a night guard to keep it from being unloaded and sold. They left the tea and the ships intact for the time being, and so for the next several weeks a standoff endured, the tea guarded by its enemies, and its owners holed up in the harbor castle.

rebellious symbolism

Then on the night of December 16 a crowd with several men "dressed as Indians" at its head gathered at the docks by the tea ships. The Customs officer had required that the tea be unloaded the next morning. The crowd moved "dexterously" and quickly to prevent the landing, hatcheting every chest open and dumping the tea into the harbor mud. When the tide rose, it washed the shattered chests and tea around South Boston and Dorchester Neck, tossing bits on shore. The tea was completely ruined, an unmitigated disaster for the merchants.[16]

To many Americans, this all seemed exhilaratingly patriotic. John Adams certainly thought so. In his diary the next day he wrote, in a passage often repeated in American high school textbooks,

> this is the most magnificent Movement of all. There is a Dignity, a Majesty a Sublimity, in this last Effort of the Patriots, that I greatly admire. The People should never rise, without doing something to be remembered—something notable And striking. This Destruction of the Tea is so bold, so daring, so firm, intrepid and inflexible, and it must have so important Consequences, and so lasting, that I cant but consider it as an Epocha in History.[17]

Three years had passed since the Boston Massacre, the last major "Epocha" of the imperial crisis developing in Boston. Patriotic fervor was waning. Samuel Adams knew he needed another incident to reignite Boston's ardor, and he had found it in the Boston Tea Party.[18] But his success, brilliant as it was, owed much to Governor Hutchinson and the tea merchants. By being so high-handed and unyielding, they reinflamed the Patriot cause more than Adams could have done on his own. The East India Company had shipped tea to buyers in New York, Philadelphia, and Charles Town, South Carolina as well as to Boston. The tea met with resistance everywhere, but only the Boston merchants refused to back down. Only the Boston merchants took such an ominous tone, and only in Boston was the tea destroyed. It was the merchants' stubbornness, more than the Company's bad planning or the Patriots' organization, that made an issue out of tea. John Adams noted that even "the Tories blame the Consignees" for the trouble.[19]

It is impressive that Thomas and Elisha Hutchinson, descendants of a century and a half of supposedly hard-nosed New England merchants, could ruin a business so thoroughly. But they had reason to think they could sell their tea, even as merchants in other ports buckled. Colonial customs records show that since 1770 nearly two-thirds of legally imported tea had entered the thirteen colonies via Boston. Boston merchants—the Hutchinsons included—had found retailers willing to take this tea, whereas merchants in other, larger ports had not. Instead, those merchants acquired tea brought from China by the Dutch East India Company and smuggled to America from the Netherlands. Between 1770 and 1772, Roanoke, North Carolina—hardly a metropolis—imported as much legal tea as New York City, while Wynyaw, South Carolina, imported nearly as much as Philadelphia. But then again, there was one year when Philadelphia, the largest city in the British Atlantic after London, imported not a single pound of legal tea at all.[20] (See Table 1.1 below.) The Tea Act, passed in 1773, had sought to change this. Parliament lowered the tea tax, making a prohibitive tax into a more affordable one. It also extended the Company's remit to include direct sales to merchants in the colonies. The Company had previously auctioned its tea in London, where wholesalers bought it; direct sales to America cut out London middlemen and lowered the price. These measures were intended to push Dutch tea out of the colonial market.

In the face of the Patriot campaign, taking a shipment of Company tea was, for the merchants of New York and Philadelphia,

Table 1.1 Legal Tea Imported into Major Ports and the Thirteen Colonies, 1770–1772 (weight in pounds)

	Philadelphia	New York	Boston	Thirteen colonies
1770	65	147	48,070	99,498
1771	0	344	265,884	342,092
1772	128	530	107,193	237,062

Source: PRO CUST 16/1 f 8, 41, 71, 127, 129, 185, 231. "Thirteen colonies" includes all ports listed in the North American customs records from Piscataqua, New Hampshire, through Sunbury, Georgia. Data for Newfoundland, Quebec, Nova Scotia, St. Augustine, Pensacola, Mobile, the Bahamas, and Bermuda are not counted here.

too risky. Since they already sold smuggled Dutch tea, they could afford to give up their contracts with the Company. The Hutchinsons, by contrast, stood to lose much more by renouncing their links to the Company. They had been finding buyers for Company tea who were willing to pay Parliament's taxes and the charges of a London middleman for years; they seem to have assumed that it would take little effort to find buyers for a cheaper version of the same. This made Adams and Hancock's timing all the more significant: strike the tea now and destroy some of the most powerful Loyalists (and rival merchants) in Massachusetts, or let the tea sell enough to become commonplace and lose the initiative altogether. As the Patriot effort showed, the tea was both a commercial and a political affair. This was the Hutchinsons' failing: commercial greed left them politically tone-deaf. *(note colen - consumer-cities)*

The Hutchinsons were not alone. They had won their share of the tea business through their father, the departing and hated Governor Thomas Hutchinson Sr. Though it could hardly have helped their public personae, all three also owned shares of East India Company stock. There was also Richard Clarke, the younger Thomas's father-in-law, who, with his sons Jonathan and Isaac, had been one of the major tea importers in Boston in the 1760s. The third consignee consisted of a partnership between Fanueil and Joshua Winslow. Fanueil and Winslow, perhaps sensing their inferior position in a group of men who cared deeply about hierarchy, left the decisions to the Clarkes and Hutchinsons.[21] Winslow in particular laid low. Though he was probably at the meeting at Clarke's warehouse when it was mobbed by the crowd from the Liberty Tree, Winslow alone seems to have had the sense to realize that forcing the tea issue was bad business.[22]

For the rest, not sending the tea back to Britain was the worst decision of their careers, all of which collapsed. The Hutchinsons fled the city the next spring. The governor had hoped his sons might stay behind to resurrect their business, just as the sons had vainly hoped to sell their tea the previous winter. In the end it all proved impossible.[23] From Britain, they entertained hopes of returning but never did. In 1779 Elisha and Thomas Jr., along with their father, were proscribed from returning to Massachusetts for being "conspirators against the liberties of the people." The state of Massachusetts seized their property in America, and the Hutchinsons died in Britain. The Clarkes also fled to Britain, moving to London with their in-law, the painter John Singleton Copley. They were proscribed in abstentia, their property seized.[24] Benjamin Fanueil left in March 1776, evacuating to Halifax during the Siege of Boston. Later he moved to Britain, where along with the rest of the tea consignees he received an annuity of £150 from Parliament. Living on the Strand during the war, Fanueil dreamed of returning. "When we shall be able to return to Boston I cannot say, but hope and believe it will not exceed one year, for sooner or later America will be conquered, that you may depend on." He died in Britain too.[25] Loyalists all, they did not find happiness in the land where their loyalties lay. The upper classes there grimaced at the émigré provincials who, as Bernard Bailyn notes, "when people of fashion were mentioned, did not know to what country they belonged, or with what families they were connected; who had never in their lives amused themselves on a Sunday, and not much on any day of the week; who were easily shocked, and whose purses were slender."[26] It was a bitter ending.

Most of the other tea sellers in Boston had more sense than the Hutchinsons. The day after the Boston Tea Party, "some of the principal Venders of Teas in Boston"—probably the retailers to whom the Hutchinsons hoped to sell—met and agreed to stop selling the commodity.[27] Toward the end of December a larger group, including "the principal Dealers in Teas in Boston," boycotted tea as well. The group was probably made up mostly of shopkeepers, for whom tea was but one of many goods sold.[28] They complained that the East India Company's plan to sell tea in America was a "flagrant attempt against our Liberties." Had it succeeded, it "would have drained the Colonies of the greater Part of their Specie" and "would have been construed an acquiescence in the right assumed by the British Parliament to tax [us]." These merchants, unlike the Hutchinsons, had the sense to approve of and voice such sentiments in public. What was more, they agreed to boycott all tea, Company and Dutch, anticipating widespread support in "suppressing its use." With popular backing, they planned to eliminate "this destructive herb from the Province." In Boston, in Lexington, in Charlestown, and across Massachusetts, local residents agreed and began destroying their tea in public tea burnings.[29]

With Boston's tea to the bonfire, most New England towns followed suit and destroyed all tea—British or Dutch—outright. Shrewsbury "Indians" mugged a peddler to strip him of his tea. New England innkeepers, merchants, and traders who kept tea fell to the mercy of angry, violent mobs. Ipswich, Brookfield, and Medway, Massachusetts banned the use of tea. In Bedford, Massachusetts a man caught with tea was forced to surrender the contraband or face punishment from the town ladies.

Bostonians asked the colonists in the small town of Windham, Connecticut to join the tea boycott. The town—perhaps already radicalized, as one of the signers of the Declaration of Independence hailed from there—pledged to "discourage and discountenance to the utmost of our power the excessive use of all foreign teas, china ware, spices and black pepper," as well as British manufactures." The Virginia House of Burgesses concurred, passing the Virginia Non-Importation Agreement in the summer after the Boston Tea Party. "We view it with horror," the burgesses declaimed, "and therefore resolve that we will not, from this day, either import tea of any kind whatever, nor will we use or suffer, even such of it as is now at hand, to be used in any of our families."[30] Tea became a "political evil" throughout the colonies, as Americans swore allegiance to the Solemn League and Covenant to boycott British goods.[31]

Indeed, in the year after the Boston Tea Party, mobs held copycat tea parties across the colonies. In Charles Town, South Carolina, long after the Company's ships had been sent back, colonists emptied their own tea chests into the Cooper River. Student Patriots at Princeton—perhaps already fixing for a riot and most likely drunk—jubilantly destroyed all tea on the college grounds. In New Jersey and Maryland, whole shiploads of tea were burned. In the former state the mob, as in Boston, dressed as "Indians." Boston held a second tea party in 1774, this time with the colonists playing Narragansetts.[32] Patriot actions were widespread.

After the Boston Tea Party, the colonists leaped from opposition to the Company's tea to opposition to any tea at all. This was due at least in part to a not wholly unreasonable fear that if Dutch tea were allowed, the newly affordable Company tea would be smuggled under the same name. But the campaign against tea, waged by mobs, policed by committees of safety (the revolutionary euphemisms which assumed authority for the Patriots), and propagandized by radical newspapers, became more than protest. Through its enforcement, it became part of the Patriot experience in organizing the extralegal governments on which a more-sustained action would depend. It was this political groundswell that the tea dealers had been so quick to join: better to lose their tea and keep their shops than risk both.

It was well they did. Tea became a measure of Patriotism in the colonies. Americans who continued to own and consume it were often making a deliberate point of their loyalty to Britain. Americans who destroyed or burned it made a public point of their Patriotism. Tea was, in Breen's phrasing, a "major article in the development" of colonial consumer society, and it was one of the few goods with which nearly every American could show his or her colors because it was consumed, to varying degrees, at many levels of American society. Even the inmates of Philadelphia's poorhouse took tea, though they were given only low-grade bohea. Because of the prevalence of tea in the colonies, the tea burnings had a wide reach, drawing the attention of colonists who before 1773 might not have cared about politics so fervently. By participating, many Americans made Boston's resistance to tea their own. And so, unsurprisingly, public tea parties proliferated. In the place of tea, some Patriot Americans drank coffee as well as home-grown infusions of local herbs, including "Labradore" and chicory.[33]

Yet, though the tea protests were broadly accessible to many segments of American society, it is not clear that the protests made for a deep or long-lasting commitment to drink coffee over tea. Anecdotal evidence suggests that any fall in tea consumption may not have been by much. John Adams was careful to serve coffee, not tea, to his guests on the way to the First Continental Congress, but only after having been corrected on the same journey when he ordered tea.[34] Later, en route to serve as ambassador to France in the midst of the war, he recommended tea to a seasick French friend and "told him he must learn to drink Tea in America in order to please the Ladies, who all drank Tea." American ladies, Adams insisted proudly, "shone at the Tea Table." Adams was not being impolitic— Congress had lifted the ban on tea in 1776—and Americans appear to have returned to the drink as avidly as wartime shortage permitted. In 1781, despite the ongoing war, the Abbé Robin thought Americans did "use much tea." "The greatest mark of civility and welcome they can show you," he wrote, "is to invite you to drink it with them."[35] The revolutionary committees no longer needed to boycott tea to oppose Parliament—the Patriots had an army for that—but, as Adams's slip of the pen shows, how effective the boycott ever was is anyone's guess.

The American Revolution did not end Americans' taste for Chinese tea, Indian cloth, or Asian spice. Instead, the creation of the United States freed American merchants to seek out these commodities for themselves. Sentiment against the Company's tea was strong enough to contribute to the separation of the American colonies from Britain, but it was not strong enough to dissuade Americans from drinking tea permanently. This begs the question, why tea?

For Patriots, tea signified monopoly as much as anything else—the monopoly of the East India Company, which engrossed all of British trade with Asia. And to them monopoly meant tyranny, cruelty, and oppression; it was a tool of a dangerous state. Consequently, when the American Revolution ended, American trade with Asia assumed a distinctive form: it was a trade, as the tea in Boston Harbor had made clear, with Revolutionary roots.

Historians have noted the pre-Revolutionary controversy over taxation but not the equally important issue of monopoly. And it was monopoly, not just taxation, that came to the fore in December 1773. As Governor William Tryon of New York explained, "if the tea comes free of every duty, I understand it is then to be considered as a Monopoly of the East India Company in America; a monopoly of dangerous tendency, it is said, to American liberties . . . let the Tea appear free or not free of Duty"; in the end it was the monopoly that mattered most.[36] Taxation addressed matters between the thirteen colonies and London, but the monopoly issue was broader; it encompassed the entire empire and helped ensure that the American Revolution would be economic as well as political. In 1600, the Crown had granted the East India Company the exclusive right to import from Asia to England. The Company bought Indian cloth and spices, but most importantly, by the late eighteenth century it bought Chinese tea. The Company sold its tea at auction in London; private merchants then reshipped the tea to America. Because the Company had no legal competition, and because the tea tax was prohibitively expensive, prices remained high. Thus, before the Boston Tea Party took place most Americans, rather than buy Company tea, bought Dutch. Governor Hutchinson estimated that three-quarters of the tea in Boston (excluding that thrown into the harbor) and nine-tenths of the tea in New York and Philadelphia was Dutch.[37]

Parliament repealed the Townsend duties on paint, lead, glass, and paper in 1770, but it left a tax on tea. Colonists did not rise up against this tea tax, for the tax—unpaid on smuggled tea—affected few. And those whom the tax did affect hardly blanched at paying it. Those who disliked Parliament's tax, for reasons of politics or purse, bought smuggled tea instead. Thus in 1770 tea was not yet a defining issue. How else could a Patriot like John Adams dine at John Hancock's in 1771 and record in his diary equivocally that they drank "Green Tea, from Holland I hope, but dont know"?[38]

It was only when the Tea Act was passed in 1773 that Patriots cried foul. In Boston, "Reclusus" wrote, "tho' the first Teas may be sold at a low Rate to make a popular Entry, yet when this mode of receiving Tea is well established, they, as all other Monopolists do, will meditate a greater profit on their Goods, and set them up at what Price they please."[39]

The objection was not simply about price. It was about principle. There was a strong anti-monopoly tradition in Britain, one that conflated the powers of state-granted monopolies with the overwhelming authority of despots and slave masters. In America, this was quickly absorbed into the republican emphasis on the right to liberty. Another and more liberal strain of anti-monopolism emphasized the right to property. (Motivated by this liberal respect for property, the mob's care not to damage any other cargoes in Boston Harbor seems less surprising.) Parliament had granted business privileges to a few and thus violated the property rights of other Britons who might wish to invest their wealth in the tea trade. Government, in the liberal phrasing, should not tell people what to do with their money. After the American Revolution, this second strain would be restated in more democratic form: equal rights for all meant exclusive rights for none.[40]

These strains were often intertwined and usually indistinguishable, and many Americans offered only generic anti-monopoly objections. In the *New York Journal,* "A Citizen" lamented in 1773 that the monopoly was "a monster, too powerful for us to control, or contend with, and too rapacious and destructive, to be trusted, or even seen without horror." Here was plain antipathy with no discernible pedigree, a sign perhaps of how widespread anti-monopoly sentiment had become among the general public. The staunchly Patriot *Massachusetts Spy* was more specific: "The very establishment of exclusive trading companies" is "an infringement" against the "free Briton" and his "right to a free trade." Indeed, a year after the Boston Tea Party, the First Continental Congress—more restrained than "A Citizen" had been—still felt the need to reiterate the Patriots' grievance that the "Administration [had] . . . entered into a monopolizing combination with the East India Company."[41]

John Dickinson put the republican equation between monopoly and tyranny best when, writing as Rusticus in late 1773 at the height of the tea drama, he penned a broadside that appeared in several colonies. Dickinson complained that the problem was not just the Company's monopoly per se, but what the Company had done with its monopoly before. "Their conduct in *Asia,*" he wrote, "had given ample Proof, how little they regard the Laws of Nations, the Rights, Liberties, or Lives of Men. They have levied War, excited Rebellions, dethroned Princes, and sacrificed Millions. . . . They have, by the most unparalleled Barbarities, Extortions, and Monopolies, stripped the miserable Inhabitants of their Property, and reduced whole Provinces to Indigence and Ruin." "Are we," he asked, "to be given up to the disposal of the *East-India Company,* who have now the Assurance to step forth in Aid of the Minister, to execute his Plan of enslaving America?" Dickinson then turned to the Company's role in the 1770 Bengal famine, at the time infamous across the English-speaking world. Famine, he implied, would follow the Company to America. For now, having starved India, the Company

> cast their Eyes on *America,* as a new Theatre, whereon to exercise their Talents of Rapine, Oppression and Cruelty. The Monopoly of Tea is, I dare say, but a small Part of the Plan they have formed to strip us of our Property. But thank God, we are not Sea Poys, nor Marattas, but *British Subjects,* who are born to Liberty, who know its Worth, and who prize it high.[42]

Dickinson was not the only one who prized his liberty this way. Others equated monopoly with monarchy and slavery, linking the Company's iron rule in Bengal to its supposed future tyranny in America.[43] Patriot organizers in Philadelphia, writing upon the arrival of the Company's tea—"That worst of Plagues"—made just that point. "We are determined not to be *enslaved* by any Power on Earth," wrote Philadelphia's Patriots. "The East India Company," wrote "A Mechanic," "if once they get Footing in this (once) happy Country, will leave no Stone unturned to become your Masters." "They have a designing, depraved, and despotic Ministry to assist and support them. They themselves are well versed in Tyranny, Plunder, Oppression, and Bloodshed. Whole Provinces, labouring under the Distresses of Oppression, Slavery, Famine, and the Sword, are familiar to them." "Thus," he went on, "they are become the most powerful Trading Company in the Universe."[44] Other writers compared the Company's conduct in India to Spain's in the New World. Compared with the Company, even the Black Legend paled.[45]

These sentiments were common. In response to the Boston Tea Party, Patriots in Windham, Connecticut passed a town resolution against the Company's "murder" of "millions by sword and baleful famine." "Let the Spanish barbarities in Mexico . . . sink in everlasting oblivion" when compared with "such more recent superior cruelties," they added. In resisting the tea, American Patriots could save their country from "thralldom and slavery." Thomas Paine gave such sentiments even wider notice in his pamphlet *The Crisis*

(1776), in which he argued that "through the East India article tea" the Company "hoped to' transfer their rapine from that quarter of the world to this."[46] In Patriot reasoning, the Company's monopoly was just as much a means to enslavement as were Parliament's taxes.[47]

The anti-monopoly tradition owed much to the role of corporations as defined by English law. Early modern corporations were not, as their current descendents are, mutually competitive enterprises. They were, inherently, monopolies. Businessmen sought corporate charters from the Crown not to attain limited liability (a later addition to corporate law) but for the right to be rid of competition. A chartered corporation also received the authority, as historian Pauline Maier has shown, to "make binding rules for its self-government, to function in law as a single person with the right to hold property and to sue and to be sued—and so to protect its assets—and to persist after the lifetimes of its founding members." Towns, churches, and universities, as well as business organizations, valued these privileges and incorporated for them. Most eighteenth-century English corporations were thus not businesses but devolved instruments of the state. They served civic needs: building wharves, installing public sewers, and maintaining bridges and roads, all in exchange for the right to charge a toll or fee for use. Towns were one of the most common corporations. When the Crown granted a town charter, it expected order, stability, and law to be maintained on the local level; in turn, the town received the right to levy some taxes and fees of its own and, in Britain, freedom from the demands of local nobles. The Crown thus subcontracted government.

It is hardly surprising, then, that Sir William Blackstone, whose *Commentaries on the Laws of England* (1765) was the first comprehensive treatment of the common law, found no distinction among universities, towns, and incorporated businesses. In his estimation they were all corporations, with charters granting them similar privileges.[48] English trading companies were thus cartels granted by the Crown for an exclusive right of trade. Just as two towns could not be granted authority over the same land, so two trading companies could not have overlapping patents. The South Sea

Company, the Hudson Bay Company, the Levant Company, and the Royal African Company, as well as the companies that had encouraged the original settlement of British America (the Virginia and Plymouth Companies), were monopolies just as the East India Company was. So too was the colony of Massachusetts, which held, as did every town within it, a corporate charter.[49]

In keeping with other corporations, the East India Company had a quasi-government character. In Asia, it taxed, ruled, and judged whatever subjects were in its territories. It made wars and signed treaties. It maintained a large army and raised a navy in Asia as well—in all, an expensive undertaking.[50] At the end of the eighteenth century, it was the largest corporation in the world: the decision of the "Mechanic" to call the East India Company "the most powerful Trading Company in the Universe" was not far off the mark.

But it was the Company's business monopoly that particularly upset American colonists. In their assessment, monopolies like the Company's were pernicious because they enforced business aristocracy in the place of business meritocracy; they granted rights to some that others, earning them, might better use. This was an echo of English anti-corporate sentiment, a body of ideas that had been part of the resistance to corporate monopolies since at least Elizabethan times. Historians have dubbed this the anti-charter tradition.[51] In America, Revolutionary ideology absorbed this tradition.[52] In the decades following the Revolution, Americans continued to oppose monopolies—particularly business monopolies—by rephrasing English anti-monopoly sentiment in American terms. The opponents of the Bank of North America in Pennsylvania objected to "granting peculiar privileges to any body of men." Opponents of Alexander Hamilton's Society for Useful Manufactures in New Jersey—"friends of equal liberty," they called themselves—feared that "corporations with exclusive privileges" violated their "favorite republican principles." In 1792 Massachusetts's Attorney General explained that the people had "a just cause of complaint" "whenever the laws . . . give to one man, or one order of men, an exclusive right to acquire property, or a greater and more advantageous opportunity to improve his, or their talents, than is given to all."[53]

The attorney general would have had many kindred thinkers in Boston twenty years earlier. Indeed, anti-monopolism endured long after the end of the Revolutionary era. It was, after all, what lurked behind President Andrew Jackson's veto of the Bank of the United States. The Bank's "exclusive privilege" and "monopoly," Jackson explained in 1832, was "granted at the expense of the public." Congress, doubling the problem, had not even allowed for "competition in the purchase of this monopoly."[54]

Adam Smith best captured the spirit of eighteenth-century anti-monopolism. Britain had long maintained a strong tradition of property rights and, alongside the myriad monopolies, many Britons maintained a near-mystical adherence to the principles of free trade. One of the most articulate proponents of these liberal ideas, Smith was finishing *The Wealth of Nations* even as Boston's "Mohawks" held their tea party.[55] Published in 1776, his book quickly became a free-trader's bible, putting in their best form many of the sentiments merchants had held for years. Smith's study argued that government too often encumbered the small merchant with bad policy. He spoke for the small to middling merchants of outport towns who lacked proximity to power, influence, and great wealth—advantages big-city London merchants had in spades. He was an ardent opponent of the East India Company. "Monopolies of this kind," he wrote,

> are properly established against the very nation which erects them. The greater part of that nation are thereby not only excluded from a trade to which it might be convenient for them to turn some part of their stock, but are obliged to buy the goods which that trade deals somewhat dearer than if it was open and free to all their countrymen.[56]

When it came to trade and manufacturing, Smith complained that joint-stock companies "scarce ever fail to do more harm than good."[57]

Smith would not become widely read in the United States until the nineteenth century, but he stood on the shoulders of English writers who had advertised free trade since the seventeenth century, and those writers were certainly influential in America. Liberal English writers expounded a core set of ideas. They espoused the idea of progress—a neologism in the eighteenth century—in opposition to the notion that societies must either stabilize or die. (In 1776, Edward Gibbon's *Decline and Fall of the Roman Empire* played on just this sense of inevitable social decay.) For liberals, this new thing called progress was chaotic and disorderly. Man pursued his self-interest in competition with his peers, and out of the hodge-podge of discordant self-interests came the direction and order of the market—the "invisible hand," as Smith would later call it. With time, the controlling power of the market became a moral imperative in itself, as liberals sought to attack government monopolies, such as lotteries, which they argued were poorly run and could not be improved as long as government prevented competition (and hence better lotteries) from coming along.[58]

Smith defined a moral sentiment behind liberalism: the business classes' yearning to be free of economically oppressive government. He was not an advocate of a desolate, impersonal, atomized world ruled by economic imperative, as he is so often made out to be; nor was *Wealth of Nations* a conservative document. (The association of laissez-faire policy and conservatism with Smithian thought was to be a post-Napoleonic construction.)[59] Rather, Smith believed that interference with economic freedom was a form of oppression that could affect anyone. And if it stretches the modern imagination to take the vexations of businessmen as truly oppressive, one must remember that in the eighteenth century economics and politics were not taken separately: thus philosophers such as Smith wrote of "political economy," not of politics or economics individually. John Burgoyne, a Member of Parliament before he fought the Americans at Saratoga, noted that "chaos" surrounded the debate on the Tea Act, "where every element and principle of government, and charters, and firmauns, and the rights of conquests, and the rights of subjects, and the different functions and interests of merchants, and statesmen, and lawyers, and kings are huddled together into one promiscuous tumult and confusion."[60]

Small wonder that for Smith and the American Patriots, economic tyranny bled into political tyranny—and in this sense the republican and liberal objections to monopolies were not all that different from one another. As historian Emma Rothschild has noted, Smith's reaction to interference in the right to buy, sell, and work was "intense and emotional," just as the Patriot reaction to tea was.[61] The original corporate charters were economic privileges granted for reasons of state; for anyone opposing them—whether Smith or the American Patriots—the advocacy of free trade gave economic affairs a political and often emotional dimension.

For the free-trade ethic to work, men had to have control of their property and be free to risk it in whatever way they desired. Restrictions on property rights—and especially the laws barring ordinary Britons from trading to the Indies—did not so much protect the Company from unbearable harm as they prevented better men from doing any good. American Patriots absorbed this absolute interpretation of property rights. Thus in the 1760s the leader of Charleston's Sons of Liberty, Christopher Gadsden, pointed out the difference between "a free and open trade" and the imperial policy of "discontented monopolizing selfish Great Britain." "What a boundless & alluring prospect of advantage must even the most distant Idea of an open Trade to all . . . the World be to the Americans," he went on. Patrick Henry, the Virginia Patriot, concurred. "Why should we fetter commerce?" he wondered. "Fetter not commerce"—"let her be as free as the air."[62]

Colonists like Henry saw the Tea Act as "a threat to free enterprise." Once the monopoly on tea had been established firmly, Americans feared the creeping power of the Company would establish monopolies on spices, silks, and other goods—hence the fear of incipient tyranny. It would at once drive American merchants out of business and, as Dickinson argued, impoverish the continent in the process. Colonists' property rights would be supplanted by the Company's. "What the Parliament could not Fleece from us by Taxes," exclaimed one New York paper, "the Crown will by Monopoly."[63]

In what was to become the United States, the Boston Tea Party helped expand free trade—the freedom of every citizen to invest or spend his wealth as he wished. It also led to the enshrinement of the "right to property," which, in the Declaration of Independence, Jefferson rephrased as the "pursuit of happiness." American government would not set aside some trades as the exclusive domain of a picked few. This did not mean the new American governments would be laissez-faire; they regulated the economy and attended to public welfare.[64] These governments also assumed the role of protecting their citizens' trade and property rights. Free trade under the rubric of "neutral trade" remained the centerpiece of diplomacy for the first half of the country's existence, from the Napoleonic Wars through the Open Door Policy to World War I.

But the American Revolution did more than provide a venue for liberal thought. It provided the reality of free trade, especially to Asia, something no Western government had ever before tried on such a scale. Britain, France, the Netherlands, Sweden, Denmark, Scotland, Prussia, Austria, and even Estonia chartered an East India Company. Spain had its Philippines Company, Portugal had its crown monopoly, and the Czar had his Russian-American Company. The English Company showed just how expensive this sort of trade could be: flotillas of massive, heavily armed ships ("Indiamen") to carry the valuable commodities home; tens of offices ("establishments"), some fortified or with armies occupying hinterlands, stretched across Africa, Asia, and various islands to manage business with local merchants; and above all, capital (the "investment") shipped annually to Asia. Between 1786 and 1800 the East India Company exported, on average, more than £450,000 in silver to Asia per year.[65]

After 1783 American merchants sailed to the east without large or heavily armed ships, without any establishments, with little assistance from their government, and with much less capital than the Company had. They began slowly, but their numbers grew, profiting from the nonimperial nature of their ventures. They also profited from the wars of the French Revolution and of Napoleon (1793–1815), commonly known as the French Wars, which boosted trade, as ships shuttled from French-aligned ports in Asia to the United States and then re-exported their goods to French-aligned ports in Europe. Some even sailed between Asia and Europe direct. Americans were invaluable middlemen, and for French and French-aligned colonies in the east they were often the principal link to the Atlantic world. In the first decade of the nineteenth century,

American shipping to and across the East Indies—in China, India, the Indian Ocean, and Southeast Asia—was second only to Britain's. In many ports it was second to none. True to the anti-monopolism of the American Revolution, the government formed no East India Company to conduct this trade, permitting a free and competitive trade east, open to all who could afford to engage in it. This trade to the Indies occasioned two transformations, one in the United States and one in the British Empire, and both with far-reaching results.

In America, the new East Indies trade's most important effect was on the division of wealth, as the particular freight-renting system American merchants used in the Indies facilitated capital accumulation among a new group of rich American investors with an especially hard-money ethic.[66] These men, in turn, used their wealth to finance, and coordinated the financing of, the most heavily capitalized sectors of early American business. The Lowell Mills, icons of early American industrial and corporate history, were founded, funded, and managed to a significant extent by American East India investors. The Second Bank of the United States—killed by Jackson for its monopoly—was funded, in part, by East India capital. So too did the Astor fortune, later invested in New York real estate, have its initial fluorescence in the East India trade.[67] As important as any individual investment, however, was the simple existence, for the first time in American history, of American investors with capital at their disposal to rival (or cooperate with) investors in the City of London.

Back in Britain, the American East India trade helped destroy the English East India Company. When free trade to the Indies remained untried, Company officials had been able to dismiss it as a risky and unproven theory—albeit one with which professors like Adam Smith were enamored. But Americans' mutual competition and more-effective organization made their trade faster, better, and cheaper than the Company's. Their speed and affordability gave them markets for East Indian goods abroad in places Companies had once served: the West Indies, Canada, South America and Europe all became markets for U.S. East India re-exports. Americans success became a tool for British free traders itching to ship to Asia themselves. In 1813, these propagandists and merchants deprived the Company of its India-trade monopoly; the Americans' example was an important part of their argument that free trade to the east was possible, and even better than the Company's, and American competition added another layer of economic self-interest to their demands. In place of the Company's monopoly rose the free trade between Britain and Asia that would indelibly mark Britain's nineteenth-century empire. Thus, ironically, the British Empire's turn to the east began and ended with the Company's American problems, and in this sense British liberalism fed the Boston Tea Party and was also deeply affected by it, having in what has been termed an "Age of Revolution" a truly transatlantic career.[68] In the long run, the Company lost a lot more than tea in Boston harbor.

The creation of the second British Empire was crucial to the changes in the Company's fortunes, however the "creation" is today much contested. The "swing to the east" describing this creation was first coined by V. T. Harlow, doyen of British imperial history, whose *The Founding of the Second British Empire, 1763–1793* was a manual to a generation. Debate on the "swing" has continued ever since. Did the shift occur in the Battle of Plassey (1757) or in the recognition of the United States (1783), or at some later time, or perhaps not at all? Most historians assume that whatever shift did occur must have happened in 1784—but this is in most cases a fairly unexamined assumption, coming from a sense among many Americans that their Revolution must have had global importance and from an assumption among Britons (looking back from the nineteenth and twentieth centuries) that India naturally became the center of the empire. And so "swing to the east" has become one of those hoary saws, like "salutary neglect," that historians cannot seem to extirpate from the textbooks, no matter how many monographs they write.[69]

The Second British Empire was created in the period between 1793 and 1815 as an empire emphasizing trade, especially trade eastward to Asia. During William Pitt's administration (1783–1801, 1804–1806), conceptualization and execution of this fell to one man: Henry Dundas. Dundas was Pitt's close friend and cabinet minister, and he encompassed in his person and his offices imperial decision making for the Pitt administration. After the India Act with which Pitt began his administration was passed, Pitt set Dundas in charge of overseeing Indian affairs. Dundas was a Smithian free-trade advocate for empire, but his was an eighteenth-century understanding of the term "free trade," by which he meant the freedom to trade, not the abolition of tariffs. (Revolutionaries such as Thomas Paine and James Madison used "free trade" in this sense as well.) Dundas and others fully advocated discriminatory tariffs to encourage commerce to flow in one channel or another; what he opposed was that Parliament forbade certain individuals to trade to certain places at all. Pitt, William Wyndham Grenville, and Dundas were all such Smithians free traders.[70] Their successors were the anvil upon which British opponents of the Company monopoly struck their hammers in 1813, constituting a political establishment warmly disposed to Smithian principles.

Such developments, though, were hardly apparent from Whitehall in the placid years of the mid-1780s, the last gasp of the ancien régime. In 1784 Britain began to lay the groundwork for the second empire, turning a mostly transatlantic imperium into an increasingly eastern one. This in part compensated for the loss of the American colonies, but there were pressing Indian affairs in any case. Sweeping into office the previous year on a platform of Indian reform, the new prime minister, William Pitt the Younger, pushed the India Act through Parliament. The act created a government office overseeing Company rule in India, which had formerly been conducted without input from Whitehall. Pitt wanted to keep the Company's foreign policy in India and its relations with other European powers there compatible with British diplomacy in Europe, though he was also concerned about Company maladministration. The same year, Pitt passed the Commutation Act, which lowered the prohibitively high tax on tea in Britain. It made legally imported Company tea cheap enough to drive out the tea smuggled in from Continental Europe, which is what Frederick Lord North had tried to do in America with the Tea Act ten years earlier. Pitt, unlike North, succeeded. Swedish, Prussian, and Austrian shipping to the Indies fell after Pitt's tax cut made Company prices more competitive. The lower taxes in the subsequent boom were paid so much more often than the older, higher taxes had been that tea-tax revenues increased. This left a rejuvenated Company free to focus on its core businesses, tea and Indian government, while its monopoly went unchanged. In a final move to cement his reforms and strengthen the British presence in India, Pitt sent out a new governor-general to head the Company's government there: Charles Lord Cornwallis, fresh from losing the American Revolutionary War at Yorktown.

CHAPTER TWO

America Sails East

American merchants muddled toward a basis for financing their trade to the Indies in the first years of their trade there. Some men favored an American East India Company—despite the popular distaste for monopolies—but the several proposals made in the 1780s all failed. Others, more distantly affected by Company logic, tried to attach to their private trade to Asia some of the public pretense East India Companies so often employed, but these efforts did little to improve their profits. Traders with no national purpose and no aim of state behind their profits did well. They tramped British, French, and Dutch imperial routes and traded across imperial bounds. Since they had no Asian establishments, American traders appeared imperially inoffensive, inviting none of the military attention and imperial rivalry of formal Company establishments. In this first decade they were not always as successful as they hoped, but their work positioned them uncannily well for the long war no one could have known lay ahead. For in this first decade, the most crucial aspect of American-Asian trade was hidden from public view: the accumulation and reorganization of U.S. merchants' capital, which ameliorated their lack of it, that is, their silver problem.

The World Silver Economy

At the end of the eighteenth century, the world economy was silver based. From 1555 to 1810, Spanish mines in Mexico and South

America yielded 3 billion to 3.5 billion ounces—approximately 90,000 metric tons—of silver.[1] Between Columbus's first voyage and the American Revolution, 85 percent of the world's silver came from Latin America.[2] Potosí, the main mine in Peru, was nearly three miles high and a two-and-a-half month donkey trek to Lima, and yet so great was the demand for silver that Potosí was exploited as the greatest silver lode in the world. Overnight, the mines made Spain the wealthiest country in Europe. They financed its wars, trade deficit, and inflation, with Spain bleeding ever-greater amounts of silver to the rest of Europe to support its high cost of living. Europeans packed that silver by the crate, box, and keg and shipped it to Asia, first to pay for Southeast Asian spices, then for Indian cloth, and finally, by the eighteenth century, for Chinese tea.[3] Europeans tried to find other commodities to sell, but they found that Indian and Chinese merchants wanted little they could offer, save silver.

So they shipped it. In the decades before 1765, the net *annual* flow of silver from Britain to India was several hundred thousand pounds sterling.[4] In India, Europeans bought locally manufactured cloths— the ginghams, calicoes, and kerchiefs whose names come down to us today, as well as lesser-known weaves. Cloth from India also financed the eighteenth-century slave trade. Measured by value, fully one-third of the goods English slavers traded for African slaves and half the goods French slavers traded in Africa consisted of India cloth.[5] The slaves they bought, in turn, were the key labor source for the plantation economies from the Caribbean to Virginia.

From India as well as from Europe, silver traveled to China. Estimates vary as to how much, but even conservative estimates put the Chinese silver stock at approximately 20,000 metric tons by 1800. More-generous estimates put that stock growing from 7,000 to 8,000 metric tons in 1680 to anywhere from 27,000 to 31,000 metric tons by 1830. Much of the silver inflow occurred over the course of the eighteenth century, as silver travelled not only from India but also from Europe on to China. Between 1760 and 1821 the English East India Company alone exported roughly £150,000 in silver a year to China—over half a million ounces—the level varying annually.[6]

At the same time, Spain shipped yet more silver to Asia via the Pacific Ocean, sending galleons from the Americas to the Philippines, where the silver was transshipped to China. This was the most direct link between the Spanish American mines and the Chinese merchants who bought their silver, since Spain still followed an agreement with Portugal that gave the latter Brazil and the route around Africa, whereas Spain traded to China via the Pacific and the Philippines. This Pacific trade was equivalent, in some estimates, to the silver sales to Asia of the British, Dutch, and Portuguese combined.[7]

Though early modern economists saw the outflow of silver as a trade deficit, scholars now consider silver a good that Europeans sold in exchange for other commodities. When China's stream of silver began to reverse in the 1820s, it was largely because Westerners had finally found another good to sell: opium.[8] In the meantime, they transported silver to China because of its relatively high sale value there. Buoyant Chinese silver demand meant that ten to twelve ounces of silver bought an ounce of gold in China, whereas it took fourteen or fifteen ounces of silver to buy an ounce of gold in Europe. The East Indies, noted Adam Smith, was a "market for the produce of the silver mines of America, and a market which, from the time of the first discovery of those mines, has been continually taking off a greater and a greater quantity of silver."[9] Silver, then, was a commodity that, like all others, had its price, and the buyers—in this case Chinese—who were willing to pay most got it.

American merchants were somewhat cut out of this flow. Late-colonial-era traders accepted "country-produce" rather than silver for tea.[10] The mid-eighteenth-century Boston merchant Thomas Hancock, conducting business in a colony with few coins in circulation, bought and sold on credit rather than in cash. He paid his tailor for breeches with credit at his store, redeemable when the tailor bought tea and paper later. In this way, the two could go on for years keeping account of mutual credits and obligations, the balance swinging from side to side on the ledger, but with hardly a penny passing between them. Hancock usually took payment in corn or pork or lumber instead of cash, marked down as credit for future purchases or against past debts. This system of barter-credit—or "bookkeeping barter," as one historian has called it—was common in the American colonies but ill adapted for trade beyond them. For transatlantic transactions merchants used bills of exchange, written orders to a merchant bank with which the writer held an account, often in London. These ordered the bank to pay a sum to the recipient at a future date. Such bills functioned like postdated checks and worked as long as the recipient trusted that the writer of the bill had enough money—he might have drawn down his account after issuing the bills—and that the bank was sound. The bill itself could be endorsed by the recipient, just as a check is today, and paid over to another party. Even in the Atlantic bills sold at discounts, with the rate depending on a merchant's reputation. It was a system Asian merchants were loathe to engage in with Westerners, relative strangers from half a world away, whose solvency they had no means to assess and against whose collapse they had little recourse. The goods and credit Thomas Hancock traded in were things neither he nor his more famous nephew John could sell in Asia.[11]

America was not, however, cashless. Though merchants constantly complained about the dearth of silver, "it is difficult," one economic historian declaimed, "to take the colonists' complaints at face value."[12] As colonists and citizens, Americans were part of the international commercial system, albeit peripherally. Trade with the Caribbean and the Spanish Main could bring in specie, as could trade with Europe. Moreover, the Revolutionary War itself, especially the provisioning of British and French armies, left further specie in America.[13]

But access to that silver was limited. Certainly the farmers and fishermen who made up most of the U.S. population had little. Merchants, on the other hand, along with shopkeepers and small businessmen, had some. But even among these, only an established merchant had enough silver to outfit a ship to Asia. Smaller merchants, who in colonial times might have traded to the Caribbean on their own, had to hire freight space on other merchants' vessels if they wanted to trade to Asia with what little silver they possessed. Thus the pressing need for silver subverted lesser merchants (who were often little more than storekeepers with ambition) beneath greater ones, the latter dealing in larger volumes and having access to greater amounts of specie.

In the 1780s, the United States suffered a severe depression. Price series—our best measure of economic well-being for this period—show an economic decline lasting until 1789. For the smaller merchants this made a bad situation worse, deepening lines between the "silver haves" and the "silver have-nots." The difficulties of some silver have-nots are well known. Burdened by debt, some western Massachusetts farmers thought armed uprising their only hope. But coastal merchants suffered too. Bankruptcies ruined some, and the subsequent auctions of their assets concentrated property in the hands of others. Many merchants lost on bad loans to western farmers, who, if dragged into court, simply could not pay. Shipping was particularly hard hit. On average, 125 vessels per year were launched in Massachusetts before the Revolution, yet only forty-five were launched in 1784 and fifteen to twenty between 1785 and 1787. Cod fishing, whaling, and mercantile shipping all suffered. It was only in 1788 and 1789 that shipping began to recover. The merchants who survived had more capital and sounder credit.[14] Unsurprisingly, between 1783 and 1789 Massachusetts merchants sent only a handful of ships to the East Indies.[15] By 1790, however, New England's merchants and the U.S. economy as a whole were rebounding, with earnings from mercantile ventures returning to pre-Revolutionary levels. And by 1792 New England and the northern states generally possessed a greater share of the export market than they had before the Revolution.[16]

The View from the Cape

Fragmentary American customs records make measuring the 1780s American East Indies trade difficult, but reliable data for this period do exist in the Dutch records of vessels passing Cape Town. The Cape was a popular waypoint to the Indies; sailors called it the "tavern of the two seas." There, ships exchanged news and letters, and captains provisioned and watered their vessels from the jetty reaching out from the beach by the Castle of Good Hope. African and Chinese hawkers paddled out to the ship anchorages and bartered produce to the ships' crews. On shore, everyone took a holiday from the months at sea. Crewmen found lodging in crowded, cut-rate rooms that skirted the boundaries between lodging house, *taphuis,* and brothel. Tavern-whorehouses, with names like the "Bottle and Glass" or the suitably maritime "Speedy Cutter," were so commonplace that sailors and soldiers were routinely passing each other syphilis by the prostitutes. The ensuing disease at one point incapacitated so many members of the Cape garrison that army medics compiled an index of "Houses of Resort for Loose Women" to try to curb disease.[17] (One wonders how this was researched.) After whores, the *taphuis* or bar, was the favored entertainment for sailors, soldiers, slaves, and free laborers. Some had billiard tables; one offered opium. Most had fights, too.

Outside, the streets were no more than dirt channels between housing blocks, which ran with mud in winter and dust in summer. The sidewalks, such as they were, were privately maintained by each house, leaving a jumble of heights and widths for drunk crewmen to clamber over at night. In the daytime, farm animals roamed about.[18]

There were refined pursuits as well. Table Mountain provided a stunning 3,000-foot backdrop to the town and was already, by the eighteenth century, a "must climb" for visitors. John Ledyard, the American sailor and traveler, marveled at its ability to inspire "wonder" when he climbed it. At the end of the century, during the first British occupation of the colony, Lady Anne Barnard, the Cape's new "first lady," began organizing outings to the mountaintop. With cold meats and wine hauled up by slaves, the trips were popular with local society and visiting officers. Then there were the Company Gardens, watered by the streams condensing on Table Mountain (the water was then piped to ships in the harbor). In the Gardens the Dutch Company had conducted botanical research into its lines of fruits and spices, but by the late eighteenth century, with its trade secrets long revealed, the Company opened the gardens to amblers seeking a shady path.[19]

Visitors made trips inland as well. Constantia, a wine estate on the back slopes of Table Mountain and an hour's walk from the port, was particularly popular. Its Cape Dutch architecture and its sprawling fields of vines drew many, including Ledyard, who tried the wine pure rather than in punch as it was usually served in Europe and America. On one visit to the Cape, Captain James Cook managed a trip to Stellenbosch, a farm town further inland famed for its vineyards and bucolic setting.[20]

The *Harriet* was the first U.S. ship to reach the Indies, touching at the Cape of Good Hope in April 1784 with a cargo of American ginseng. April was the end of the Cape summer and also the end of the shipping season. The abundant harvest was coming in. Later American captains gawked at the "delicious grapes" from Stellenbosch and Franschhoek in this season and relished the "Water & Musk Melons, Apples, Pears, Peaches & Figs" from nearby farms.[21] For Captain Allen Malet and the crew of the *Harriet,* the fruit must have been welcome refreshment from the long months at sea and the Yankee winter behind.

But the *Harriet* went no further than the Cape, for its captain was able to purchase tea from European vessels returning from China and then in port. Presumably, the *Harriet* returned to the United States, certainly it remained comparatively anonymous. American "firsts" in the East Indies trade inspired poems, paintings, even medallions in their honor. Stations aboard such vessels were hard sought. Men paraded upon their return. Like the East India Company's, these vessels tended to generate more notice than profit. But the *Harriet* was not famous. It left little behind—a single entry in a Boston newspaper, a line in the Cape Town shipping register, and a few shipping papers—yet it signaled the way to come. No fanfare, no delay, no Company, it was easily lost in the comings and goings at the Cape. An American first might be painted on canvas, stamped on medallions and considered notable, and even if such a first were a losing concern these appurtenances of fame might—for some egos—be worth the loss. But while there could be only so many firsts, there could be a hundred quiet *Harriets,* enough for a business revolution.[22]

Yet such a transformation of the East Indies trade is hardly apparent in the *Harriet's* arrival, not least because the rest of the Cape's

shipping nearly buried the *Harriet*. Cape Town drew in 200 ships
between July 1783 and May 1784—this, in a town of no more than
a few thousand Dutch colonists and with little more than fresh
vegetables to offer.[23] Such a volume put it on a par with ports in
Europe. The Cape was not a major trading destination in its own
right, but for captains of many nations, concern about water, food,
and scurvy made the Cape a major port of call. Britain and France,
which in addition to the Netherlands were the major trading powers of the day, had large numbers of ships calling at the Cape. Significant numbers of Austrian, Danish, Prussian, Swedish, and American vessels stopped at Cape Town, too. This makes the Cape a good
place to observe the general rhythm of trade between Asia and the
West. For smaller trading nations like the United States, with no
post of their own in the southern hemisphere, the Cape Colony
was particularly important, and the Dutch maintained the Cape as
a supply point open to all.[24]

Table 2.1 Number of Likely East Indiamen at Cape Town

	American	Danish	Dutch	English	French	Other
1783–1784	1	23	33	12	41	35
1784–1785	3	26	55	10	26	17
1785–1786	5	19	39	10	22	14
1786–1787	9	10	53	11	20	4
1787–1788	5	6	N.A.	13	14	12
1788–1789	16	9	61	6	26	9
1789–1790	19	5	63	6	29	6
1790–1791	18	8	54	34	14	9
1791–1792	8	4	25	6	14	5
1792–1793	29	9	57	17	19	11

Notes: Dutch data for 1787–1788 are missing; no data are available for the quarter
from February 1 through May 1, 1788. "Other" includes vessels labeled "Folcaans,"
Imperial, Portuguese, Prussian, Russian, Spanish, Swedish, "Tortcaans," Sardinian, and
Genoese. N.A.=not available.

Sources: Neth VOC 4307, Reel 1395-2, No. 538, Ships' lijst, July 1, 1783–May 5, 1784;
VOC 4311, Reel 1398-1, No. 324, Ships' Roll, May 9, 1784–May 11, 1785; VOC 4315,
Reel 1401-1, No. 753, Ships' Roll, May 16, 1785–April 30, 1786; VOC 4320, No. 13,
Scheeps Rolle, May 2, 1786–April 24, 1787; VOC 4324, No. 6, 37–40, Ships List, April
25, 1787–November 1, 1787; VOC 4325, No. 10, 521–523, November 3, 1787–February
1, 1788; VOC 4332, 850–865; VOC 4339, 875–892; VOC 4350, 170–191; VOC 4351,
820–821; VOC 4538, 245–258.

There were never, in the first decade of American independence, hundreds of *Harriets*. By the last year for which there are Dutch records—covering the winter of 1792 to the winter of 1793—thirty-one U.S. vessels called at the Cape; twenty-nine of those were trading to the East Indies. Table 2.1 shows the American mercantile presence at the Cape.[25] Though the American East Indies trade continued to grow during the young nation's depression, it remained relatively small compared with, say, Dutch trade with Asia. U.S. trade was, after all, starting from zero. But the depression and recovery strikingly coincided with the expansion of the East Indies trade. The average annual number of ships (15.25) passing the Cape in the post-depression years between 1788 and 1792 is nearly triple the average (5.5) during in the 1784 to 1788 depression; these numbers confirm that the U.S. East Indies trade shared in post-1788 growth.[26]

An American East India Company?

In late 1785 John Wingrove, an Englishman, appeared in New York bearing a letter from John Adams, then American minister in London. Wingrove proposed to form and lead an American East India Company. It was an unlikely proposal: the inlet-studded U.S. coastline made any monopoly unenforceable, and anti-monopoly sentiment was still strong. Congress turned him down.[27] Rufus King informed Adams of the result, noting with approval "that the commercial intercourse between the United States and India would be more prosperous if left unfettered in the hands of private adventurers, than if regulated by any system of a national complexion." "Mr. Wingrove," he concluded, had been "frustrated in his project of an India Establishment."[28]

Many Britons attempted to use American trade in India to remit their Asian funds to Britain away from the East India Company's sight. The Company charged a fee on funds shipped in its own vessels' bottoms to Britain. If Wingrove's American company was intended as an offshore vehicle for British capital transfers, Captain John O'Donnell was the sort of Briton who might have patronized it. O'Donnell had originally served with the Company in Bombay and afterward lived as a merchant in Calcutta before moving to the United States. There he asked to be made consul to India, hoping to funnel funds from India to the United States and then on to Britain, but he was turned down, perhaps in part so as not overly to irritate Company authorities in India.[29] O'Donnell owned a ship that the Company claimed was "navigated chiefly by British Born Subjects," but it was registered as American, and O'Donnell himself had become a naturalized U.S. citizen. Thus when he returned to Calcutta in 1787, Company employees chose to consider him as American and not British (or else he might be in violation of the Company's monopoly). They likely loaded his ship full of their most valuable goods. O'Donnell returned to the United States with his cargo.[30]

Unlike O'Donnell, John Adams had not seen Wingrove's efforts as, in effect, establishing an offshore British company. Rather, he saw in Wingrove a means to create an American establishment in India. Adams thought the United States needed a stronger presence in Asia—if not a Company, then *something*, and he pressed on others his wish for a link to Asia of a national complexion. In London in 1785 Adams urged upon Richard Henry Lee that the "United States must establish a factory of their own" alongside the "French, English, Dutch, Danes, Swedes &c." in Asia. "Why," he asked, "should we come to Europe for East India goods?"[31] In November he urged John Jay that Americans "push their commerce to the East Indies as fast and as far as it will go." "The stronger footing we obtain in those countries," the more important "will our friendship be to the powers of Europe who have large connections there." Yet, as Jay explained, Congress, "for want of Power to regulate Trade by their own Acts" under the Articles of Confederation, could do nothing about this. That power still lay with the states. So too did the power to set duties and regulations for Asian trade.[32]

One of the central debates at the 1787 Constitutional Convention centered on corporations and trade.[33] James Madison, who wrote the commerce clause, saw his creation as a means to address not only the regulation of foreign trade, but also to permit the granting of federal corporate charters, largely considered inherent monopolies—a point he twice pressed upon his fellow delegates. Similar proposals appeared in the New Jersey plan and in suggestions brokered by Charles Pinkney, Edmund Randolph, and John Rutledge.[34] These invited familiar objections. Elbridge Gerry complained that "the Power given respectg. Commerce will enable the Legislature to create corporations and monopolies."[35] George Mason cited the Convention's own interpretation of the U.S. Constitution as giving Congress the right to "grant monopolies in trade and commerce" as one of his reasons for opposing the new Constitution.[36] King objected that "it would be referred, in some states, to the power to grant a bank monopoly, in others to mercantile monopolies."[37] These objections were forceful enough that Madison feared a vote against the commerce clause either in the Convention itself or in the subsequent ratification process, when anti-federalists, boycotting the Convention, were stronger. So he left the commerce clause ambiguous. The final wording—that Congress have the authority "to regulate commerce with foreign nations, and among the several States"[38]—ruled monopolies neither in nor out.

[margin note: debate over commerce in US gov't]

Fear that the clause would give Congress power to erect monopolies persisted in the state debates over ratification.[39] Virginian Richard Henry Lee worried that the commerce clause might give northern states a way to monopolize the commerce of southern states.[40] Writing from Paris, Thomas Jefferson told Alexander Donald that he wished the Constitution would include a bill of rights guaranteeing, among other freedoms, "freedom of commerce against monopolies."[41] James Winthrop, writing in Massachusetts as Agrippa, objected that the "unlimited right to regulate trade, includes the right of granting exclusive charters," and noted the damage the East India and other chartered companies had done to British outports by confining their commerce to London. Would Philadelphia be similarly advantaged?[42] Yet even in Philadelphia, Samuel Bryan worried in the *Independent Gazetteer* that merchants in favor of the commerce clause were misperceiving their long-term interest. Congress would have the power to "institute injurious monopolies and shackle commerce with every device of avarice," he warned, meaning "property of every species will be held at the will and pleasure of rulers."[43]

It was Winthrop who made the connection to the East Indies trade most explicit. "Exclusive companies" threatened the "freedom that every man, whether his capital is large or small" enjoys in commerce. Before independence Americans had purchased their India goods "through the medium of an exclusive company." But now American commerce in India had reached a "respectable" amount— a dozen vessels just from Massachusetts, he thought—with no company at all and India goods coming "at about half the former price." Yet now Congress was to have the nebulous authority to regulate commerce? "It has been so much the practice of European nations to farm out this branch of trade, that we ought to be exceedingly jealous of our right,"[44] Winthrop warned.

Ultimately the Massachusetts convention approved the Constitution but wanted it amended such "that Congress erect no company with exclusive advantages of commerce." Rhode Island, New York, New Hampshire, and North Carolina voted for similar bans on the right of Congress to create monopolies.[45]

The concern continued after ratification: when Congress debated the Bank of the United States, monopoly opponents worried that "the bank would be a precedent for the granting of monopolies of the East and West India trade."[46] Thus in 1791 Jefferson advised the president that the bank was "against the laws of monopoly." In 1815 even Madison had his concerns, vetoing a new bank charter on the grounds that it "monopolized profits."[47] The federal power to charter corporations was not firmly established until Chief Justice John Marshall's ruling in McCullough v. Maryland (1819). Yet fear that such corporations would be monopolies did not die even then. As William Gouge opined in 1833, "the very existence of monied corporations is incompatible with equality of rights . . . they can never succeed, except when the laws or circumstances given them a monopoly."[48]

In 1789—long before Marshall's ruling—Thomas Randall proposed his own American East India Company to Alexander Hamilton, then secretary of the treasury. Randall was a long-time, if occasional, correspondent of Hamilton. Contrary to Winthrop, he insisted that the meager amount of U.S. shipping to the Indies vindicated the Company model: only a monopolied company could conduct Asian trade on a large scale.[49] But the Treasury was less keen than Randall on the idea of an East India monopoly, busy as it was with Hamilton's already controversial economic agenda and aware of the objections to monopolies in the Convention and in states, such as North Carolina, that had yet to even ratify the Constitution. Randall never got a reply.

Randall wrote from experience. He had been to China twice and was a partner in the early China-trading firm Shaw & Russell. And he had a taste for monopolies, whatever others thought of them. He had pushed for the completion of the Charles River Bridge in 1785: the company owning it would become famous for the eponymous Supreme Court case, in which it argued that corporate charters were implied monopolies (the court struck this argument down in 1837).[50] Randall was a director of the Massachusetts Bank and later of the Boston Branch of the Bank of the United States, an institution that, as noted, inspired heartfelt cries against monopoly from anti-federalists, Jeffersonian republicans, and Jacksonian Democrats alike.[51]

Shaw and Randall built what may have been intended as the first ship for Randall's abortive American East India Company, and it was an instructive case. The *Massachusetts* was finished in 1789 and sailed the following year. Though built "expressly for the Canton trade,"[52] it was more than just another China trader. It was built for stateliness. At 820 tons, it was the largest ship built in America.[53] Its "model and dimensions," wrote maritime historian Samuel Eliot Morison, "were taken from a British East-Indiaman." And it was beautiful, pleasing all who saw it, just as English Company ships were meant to do. Docked at Boston, "parties of people in every rank of society frequently came on board to gratify their curiosity and express their admiration."[54] Teas and soirees were held on its decks. British and French naval commanders, purports Shaw's biographer, Josiah Quincy, "expressed their admiration" of the ship's form.[55] When on its first voyage the *Massachusetts* arrived at Batavia and Canton, commanders of the European ships in port "were continually coming on board to examine her, and to admire the model and the work." In part because of the ship's majesty and because of the newness of its trade, there was a cachet to joining the *Massachusetts*. "A station on board her . . . was an object of consequence," wrote the second mate (not too humbly, having gained that station for himself). He assured posterity that, in addition to his own, "hundreds of applications were made by persons of the best character."[56] This was not simply braggery. Congress had sold its wartime navy, and the *Massachusetts* may have appealed to the sort of men who would otherwise have been seeking naval commissions. Indeed, when Congress sold its last ship, the *Alliance,* in 1785, that ship sailed into private use as a China trader. The U.S. Navy and the East Indies trade exchanged both ships and men. The *Massachusetts* was larger than any ship the U.S. Navy had had. It carried two full decks, a large armament of cannons, and a crew of the "best" men. In the prestige vacuum created by the lack of a proper navy, the merchantman *Massachusetts* appeared to fulfill a half-public, or at least half-naval, role.

Yet for all its trim the ship was a complete disaster. It sailed with no chronometer (in 1790 these were still expensive; the Royal Navy did not put them into general use until 1825) and neither a sextant nor an officer skilled in lunar observations. Though the *Massachusetts* carried a compass, the device was little help in determining longitude, which the crew half-guessed at.[57] What was worse, the ship was built of bad wood and was half rotten when it reached Canton. Without proper navigation the voyage took longer than necessary, and in that time the mold grew so rank that the air in the hold snuffed out the candles of those who went below to investigate the stench.[58] The cargo was ruined. The captain sold the *Massachusetts* to the Danish Asiatic Company at Canton, abandoning the officers and crew in China to make their own way home.[59]

Poor management was the root of these problems. The captain should have seen to the equipment. The owners should have kept a closer eye on the vessel's construction. With both owners absentee, and a shipping boom taxing his time, the builder had used green, unseasoned oak, known to decay in the tropics, a poor material for a ship that had to cross the equator four times in a single voyage.[60] Worse, the ship dallied in Boston for months after construction, waiting to be laded and manned.[61] On-the-spot owners could manage this. But Shaw, arriving late, had not. Stateliness was no substitute for profitability.

From Political Economy to Public Economy: The *Empress of China*

Many early voyages around the Capes, as that of the *Massachusetts,* had a quasi-public character. Poetry ushered the ships to sea; parades welcomed them home. Under the Articles of Confederation, Congress could not promulgate a national economic program or pursue a national political economy, but the political-economic functions unfulfilled by Congress—what one might call the public economy—remained. These included the regulation of overseas and interstate commerce and were, as noted, a subject of intense public interest. Owners of early voyages to the Indies often cast their ventures opening new lines of trade and thus fulfilling a certain public utility. Individual merchants and private partnerships such as Shaw and Randall's cast themselves in a role similar to that of the quasi-public corporations that met aims of state with private funds. They portrayed themselves as virtuous republicans offering themselves for the national good—a sincere reflection of their patriotic sentiment and also a way to sell product on their ships' return. As they rallied popular attention to their ventures, those ventures took on a national, semipolitical hue.

One such venture was the *Empress of China,* the first American ship to reach Asia. Save for the North Atlantic passage, it followed the same route hundreds of European vessels had followed for centuries. But contemporary Americans considered the voyage a feat anyway. The *Empress* left with newspaper encomiums and thirteen-gun salutes. Later, Philip Freneau captured the pride of the moment in his rather unpoetically titled poem, "On the First American Ship That explored the Rout to China and the East-Indies after the

Revolution," in which he recounted the ship's sailing in verse only slightly more poetic:

> With clearance from Bellona won
> She spreads her wings to meet the sun
> Those golden regions to explore
> Where George forbade to sail before.

As Freneau pointed out, the *Empress* was another emblem of American independence.[62] But Freneau was a poet, not a businessman, and he seemed to forget that the real point of the *Empress* was to make money. It was well to sail "without the leave of Britain's king"—a point he made several times—but profit, king or no, was better. He would not be the last to make that mistake.

Samuel Shaw was the *Empress*'s supercargo. Supercargoes supervised a ship's business affairs and did the trading in port. Shaw was later Randall's partner in the *Massachusetts*. He had a keen sense of patriotism and of his voyage's importance. In the war he held firm against the mutiny of the Pennsylvania Line in 1781 and the Newburgh conspiracy in 1783, and he became an active member of the Society of the Cincinnati at war's end.[63] It was in this service-oriented mind that he wrote John Jay and Congress after his return from China, "for the information of the Fathers of the Country." Jay soon wrote back, beaming over Congress's "particular satisfaction" with the voyage.[64]

Jay's offer of a consulship to China soon followed. Shaw was unpaid; "consul" meant little more than a head merchant, and he was, like the other merchants there, expected to support himself with his business. But Shaw considered the appointment an opportunity to serve. He asked Jay to convey to Congress his "favorable and grateful" acceptance of the offer and the chance to do a "public benefit." Perhaps a little absorbed with the importance of his post, he recommended creating a vice consul under him and giving his partner, Thomas Randall, the job. Congress agreed.[65] Unfortunately, Shaw's interest in distinction and status could get in the way of business. His wait for the renewal of his consulship was what held up the *Massachusetts*'s departure—a very uncommercial reason for not sailing.

Captain Malet and the *Harriet,* by contrast, left hardly a trace. Malet and the *Harriet's* owners seemed to be less interested in public spectacle than in private profit. They may have believed that advertising their plans could only hinder their getting their ginseng to China first. Certainly it would have hindered their landing tea in America ahead of the competition. And though the *Empress*'s first touching at China was a notable accomplishment, profit was the accomplishment that mattered. The *Empress* managed both, but falteringly. The gap between what its owners and what the public found notable would be more difficult for later voyages to bridge.

From Political Economy to Public Economy: The *Columbia*

The *Empress* and the *Massachusetts* sailed under the public eye. The semistate role of East India Companies and their philosophy of corporate statism, which assumed that Companies contributed to national grandeur and impressed the popular mind, had rubbed off. The *Columbia* was another such public voyage. Joseph Barrell, the *Columbia*'s owner, hoped to avoid shipping much silver. The *Empress* attempted this by carrying a cargo of ginseng, but since Western demand for Chinese tea outstripped Chinese demand for American ginseng, one still had to send specie. (Likewise, European East India Companies, which had been exporting North American ginseng for decades, still needed to send specie as well.)[66] So Barrell sought a new product, sea otter pelts, that might sell in China instead.

The idea of selling furs was no secret. Russians merchants had sold pelts to China for years. With the Russian empire extending across the north of China to Alaska, Russians were the only Westerners to sell fur in China before the 1780s. They were also the only Europeans that had equal treaty relations with China.[67] Most of their fur was Siberian, though some might have come from the Russian outposts in North America. Indeed, so firmly associated were Russia and furs to Qing dynasty officials that when war broke out between the Russian and Qing empires in the late 1780s, Qing officials closed down not only the fur trade at the Kiakhta land crossing, but briefly halted other Europeans' fur trade at Canton, assuming those furs must have been Russian.[68]

The Russian stranglehold on furs ended in 1784 when the official account of James Cook's third and final voyage hit London bookshops. "At this Island of Nawanalaska [Unalaska]," Cook's surgeon Samwell wrote, "are about 60 Russians . . . they have small Settlements . . . for the Purpose of buying Skins from the Indians, the chief of which are those of the Sea Beaver which has a beautiful & very valuable Furr. These are sent to . . . China where they bear a high price."[69] Second Lieutenant King, another one of Cook's officers, described Nootka Sound, in present-day British Columbia, as having a "grand supply" of "seals" and "Sea Beaver," "the skin of which is so valuable at China."[70] Here was a potential solution to the silver problem.

These were not the first accounts to reach the press. John Ledyard, the American traveler who had climbed Table Mountain, also served as a marine with Cook and published his own story in 1783.[71] Ledyard recalled the winter of 1778, when Cook was anchored off Unalaska and gave Ledyard a special assignment. Some of the islanders were wearing waistcoats and breeches, Western clothes completely alien to Unalaska, which suggested that Russians might live there. Cook sent Ledyard ashore with a native guide, two servants, and some rum, wine, and porter for gifts. After a rainy first day by land, the party pressed on the next morning by kayak—with Ledyard stowed as luggage in the hold—and paddled right into the Russian camp. The Russians were friendly; not too many visitors made it to Alaska in winter. And with rum in hand, Ledyard was able to dispel any lingering doubts. He returned to the ships with three Russians to answer Cook's inquiries about the islands and the Bering Sea. British officers spent the next two weeks getting the Russians drunk and plying them for information about that trade.[72]

In his journal Ledyard noticed "the variety of [Alaska's] animals, and the richness of their furr." The skin of one animal (he called it a "glutton")

> was sold at Kamchalka, a Russian factory on the Asiatic coast for sixty rubles, which is near 12 guineas, and had it been sold in China it would have been worth 30 guineas. We purchased while here about 1500 beaver, besides other skins, . . . but it afterwards happened that skins which did not cost the purchaser six-pence sterling sold in China for 100 dollars. Neither did we purchase a quarter of the beaver and other furrskins we might have done, and most certainly should have done has we known of meeting the opportunity of disposing of them to such an astonishing profit.[73]

Back in the United States, Ledyard sought financial support for a voyage to meet that opportunity for profit. He nearly convinced the owners of the *Empress of China*. But to merchants, as one New England captain later recalled, Ledyard seemed "sanguine" and his enterprise "doubtful."[74] He came off as an adventurer, not a businessman. (In a later century, he probably would have been a backpacker.) He was not used to handling large sums of money, which made it hard for the *Empress*'s owners to trust him with much. When published British accounts of Cook's voyage put these doubts to rest the next year, the *Empress* had already sailed.

Official news of Cook's last voyage warmed American merchants to the fur trade. On September 30, 1787, Joseph Barrell, along with five other investors, sent the *Columbia* and the *Lady Washington* from Boston with orders to round South America and make the fur-hunting grounds of the Pacific Northwest. There, Barrell planned for the smaller *Washington* to ply the coast and tender the larger *Columbia* with furs, as Cook had suggested.[75] Once full, the two vessels were to proceed to Canton, sell their cargoes, and return via southern Africa. The ships would be the first American-owned vessels to reach the Northwest Coast.

The most attractive part of the business plan was the cost: $50,000 purchased and outfitted both vessels, and by far most of the cost consisted of the vessels' purchase, something that could be paid for in kind or with barter-credit. By contrast, buying tea with specie would cost from $50,000 to well over $100,000 in silver. Barrell managed to outfit a subsequent voyage to the coast with £Ma 1,500 of cargo: trinkets and cheap trade goods along with sheet metal, which the ship's blacksmith could fashion into whatever local Indians fancied—it was not a cargo that particularly taxed a Yankee peddler's ability to assemble it.[76] The small cargo occupied so little space on the *Columbia* that Barrell managed to wedge the frame of the *Lady Washington* into the *Columbia*'s hold, to be brought out and assembled on the coast.

But Barrell did not want his ships to slip away in the night. He made the impending voyage an open affair, heightening interest in the teas the vessels would bring home, and, just as importantly for Barrell, heightening national pride. Barrell was a patriot without a national government. In an earlier proposal for an East India voyage, he had urged Jeremiah Wadsworth to join him in a venture to the "Pacifick Ocean & China" on the grounds that "tis for Americans to find out new Traits and for such Public Spirited Men as you to engage in them."[77] Wadsworth, perhaps less public spirited with his money, demurred.

The state of Massachusetts finished work on a new mint before the *Columbia* made sail. Barrell was well connected and had commemorative coins for the *Lady Washington* and *Columbia* struck (the first die-struck coins made in the United States) before the state began striking any of its own coins. Barrell made silver, copper, and pewter pieces. The last took to the die readily, but the machine was untried (perhaps this was why the state let him use it first), and it took considerable time to get the silver and copper coins right: "The *Medals*, the *Medals!*" a frustrated Barrell wrote to his brother-in-law when the first die broke.[78]

At least 300 commemorative pewter coins were struck.[79] These were intended for use on the voyage. Barrell instructed the captains to reserve them until after rounding Cape Horn, "to be distributed amongst the Natives on the North West Coast of America, and to commemorate the first American Adventure to the Pacific Ocean."[80] On the obverse, the coins read "Columbia and Lady Washington commanded by J. Kendrick," and on the reverse, "fitted at Boston in America for the Pacific Ocean." The news spread quickly; little more than a week after the *Columbia* and *Washington* departed, the *Pennsylvania Packet* reported news of the voyage to its readers and wrote glowingly of the medals "to be distributed among the natives of the Indian Isles."[81]

Silver and copper medals, on the other hand, were meant to pique the interest of—and curry favor with—men of national political significance. Massachusetts Historian Anne Bentley estimates that Barrell produced only a dozen such medals, giving them to Thomas Jefferson, George Washington, and John Adams, among others, as well as possibly to General Lafayette. Barrell sent one to his brother Nathaniel, elected to the Massachusetts convention then debating whether to ratify the Constitution. The vote in Massachusetts was close, and Nathaniel, elected as an anti-federalist, eventually changed his mind and voted for the Constitution. The medal, Barrell explained to Nathaniel, was "to commemorate the first American Enterprize to the Pacific Ocean." "If you are Federal," he needled his brother, "you will be pleased, but to the Antifederalists, the man of Enterprize must be disgusting, nor can he wish him success . . . for what is property without good government?" Barrell hoped the voyage would have national importance. He imagined it might inspire his brother to vote for the Constitution. He thought the medals tied national figures to his effort. (Cook's example inspired the medals as much as the voyage itself: the Royal Society had already commemorated Cooks' explorations with two different medals. Barrell, perhaps more interested in advertising than the Royal Society, produced his medals before the voyage rather than after.)[82]

When the *Columbia* and *Lady Washington* reached Nootka Sound, they found the British building a trading settlement. The British had with them "a number of Chinese carpenters" as well. The head of the British effort had, as he later recalled, already "obtained a plot of ground at Friendly Cove . . . erected a house, surrounded it with breastwork and mounted a cannon."[83] The Spanish claimed Nootka Sound and sent a force to retake possession and expel the British. In front of the *Columbia*, the Spanish commander seized all four British vessels, imprisoned the Chinese settlers, and sent two vessels to Mexico for condemnation. The incident nearly began a war.

The Spanish commander took notable pains to be cordial with the Americans. The third mate of the *Columbia* remarked that the Spanish commander "endevoured to do everything to serve us" and "made Captain [G]ray [of the *Columbia*] presents of Brandy wine hams sugar and in short every thing he thought would be acceptable." Robert Gray assured Barrell that "we are now in good friendship with the Spanish Commodore." By contrast, hearing of a nearby British vessel from the officers of the *Columbia,* the Spanish commander remarked that "it would make him a good prize." Having his own, and now four British vessels, at his disposal, the Spanish commander easily could have taken the Americans as well, had he thought they were trying to make a similar claim. He did not.[84]

Americans understood that Nootka was Spanish, and by the time Gray and the *Columbia* reached home again, Spain appeared to have established its claim to the Pacific Northwest by right of conquest. Boston newspapers universally applauded Gray's success in commanding "the protection and respect of the European *Lords of the soil,* to the American flag," all the "while that of another nation hath been forbidden to be unfurled on the coast."[85]

In a second voyage, Gray returned and charted the Columbia River, named for his ship. The discovery of the river, considered by some a basis for the U.S. claim to Oregon, was feted then and has been since, and therefore historians have seen national significance in the *Columbia* voyages. Barrell may have wanted to claim Oregon, Gray probably did make such a claim, and in the end Oregon became American. But that was not because of Gray or the *Columbia.* The real basis for U.S. possession of Oregon came later: the settlement at Astoria (1811) as well as diplomatic agreements between Britain and the United States. In 1790 the Pacific Northwest was, as far as the United States was concerned, Spanish.[86] Certainly no one in 1790 or 1792 considered the Northwest Coast American.[87]

Barrell rallied public opinion well. The *Columbian Centinel* reported "with real pleasure" the *Columbia*'s return in 1790. To the shipowners, "their country is indebted, for this experiment in a branch of Commerce before unessayed by Americans." "On the Columbia's arriving opposite the Castle," the paper beamed, "she saluted the flag of the United States with 13 guns; which was immediately returned therefrom—and on coming to her moorings in the harbour fired a federal salute—which a great concourse of citizens assembled on the several wharfs, returned with three huzzas, and a hearty welcome."[88] The Columbia—to everyone's constant comment—was the first U.S. vessel to round the globe. It was no feat—Magellan's crew had done that in 1522—but, as with the Empress of China, it fed a young nation's pride. Nor were the Columbia's navigational achievements crucial to its business plan; the African route was simply a shorter and well-plied route from China. But circumnavigation did attain fame for the Columbia and Barrell. Later historians recollected that after the "huzzas" on the docks, "General Lincoln, the collector of the port, went on board with a party of friends; and Governor Hancock gave a reception to the owners and officers, which was largely attended. Captain Gray walked up State Street in the procession by the side of a young Hawaiian chief whom he had brought with him."[89] The Boston Gazette added that the Hawaiian paraded "in the war dress of his own country."[90] Newspapers up and down the coast ran the story, noting not so much the business, profit, or loss of the Columbia, but its public role. In the 1790s a series of paintings was commissioned, with cheaper prints for popular distribution, portraying various stages in the voyages of the Columbia and the Lady Washington. This was perhaps the most striking testament to the Columbia's enduring meaning to the new nation.

In the end, it was well the papers did not mention the business side of the Columbia, for it made no profit. After leaving the Lady Washington in the Pacific Northwest and proceeding in advance to China, Gray found a rotten market for furs. (Because of the war with Russia, Chinese authorities were clamping down on fur trading.) Captain Kendrick and the Lady Washington caught up just as Gray was preparing to leave Canton. Gray urged Kendrick to remain at Macau and sell his cargo there. "You will not receive one third of the Value for your Skins" in Canton, he wrote.[91] Gray's own furs had sold so badly that "Mr. Randall to whom we consign'd the Ship positively declines transacting the business of your Sloop."[92] Randall had written to Barrell to "solicit" "the consignment of this vessel to our house" upon first hearing of the *Columbia*'s voyage, and promising "fullest assurances" of his "capacity to do the business of any vessel" Barrell sent. But now he could not, and would not, sell its cargo.[93]

Despite the losses, neither Barrell nor Gray was deterred. After a six-week turnaround in Boston, Gray and the *Columbia* were out again. They did not wait for commemorative coins or consular commissions. And with less fanfare than the previous voyage, they also turned a profit.

Yet while the *Columbia* sailed back out of Boston, Barrell had another concern: Kendrick and the *Lady Washington* had not returned. After reaching China, Kendrick went rogue. He made a "sham sale" of the *Lady Washington,* signing it over to himself— which is to say, he stole it. For several years he labored to amass his own fur trading fortune, all the while promising to give the owners their ship back. He did neither.[94]

The divergent stories of these two captains doubtlessly underlined the wisdom of choosing captains carefully. Hoping to avoid future Kendricks, merchants tapped sons, brothers, and in-laws for the job—family who would be less tempted to strike out on their own half a world away and beyond the reach of the law. The *Columbia*'s voyages taught that the public value of a venture could come at the expense of profit. So too did the *Massachusetts*'s and *Empress of China*'s. But it took only a few bad voyages for American merchants to dispense with the notion that they were working for some fuzzy idea of national glory rather than their own profit. Later voyages were more anodyne, without their owners wasting attention on medallions or money on woodwork or time waiting for commissions. They were also more successful. Perhaps it was easier to concentrate on money with all the "firsts" out of the way, as there was considerably less distinction in being second. Rather, merchants could concentrate on the humdrum job of making millions. It helped that a general European war was soon to break out. American merchants would spend a generation supplying European markets cut off from the produce of Asia and the Pacific. With no more firsts and plenty of markets, voyages to the Indies became both more common and more profitable.

CHAPTER THREE

Commerce in a World at War

French wars

"In the establishment of the French republic," lamented William Wyndham Grenville, the British foreign minister, "is included the overthrow of all the other governments of Europe."[1] As if to agree, France declared war against Britain and the Netherlands in February 1793. Eight years passed before a peace, twenty-two years before peace lasted. These wars, collectively called the French Wars, spanned Europe, Asia, and the Americas and created vast trading opportunities for American merchants, including East Indies traders. But Americans were far from the only ones interested in Asia; using the French Wars as a cover, the British Empire took the Asian colonies of France and her allies and swung itself east. British ministers expanded their trading empire partly to compensate for loss of trade with Europe (though that trade was by no means completely gone) and partly to encourage the re-exportation of foreign commodities and, as Henry Dundas, Prime Minister William Pitt's secretary of state for war, put it, to make London the "Emporium of the Trade of Asia." Dundas and Pitt pushed a radical agenda linking trade and colonial expansion. In Dundas's view, trade and colonial war went hand in hand: "We are contending for colonial interest with France," he explained.[2] As they did so, the U.S. East Indies trade became their principal competition.

The French Wars in Europe, 1793–1814

The French Republic fought Britain, Austria, the Netherla
Prussia, Sardinia, Spain, Portugal, and the Two Sicilies. The comb
ants encompassed much of Western Europe and many of the se
ports engaged in transatlantic trade, giving the wars considerable
commercial significance. The consequent French conquests along
the European shore—for France defeated or allied with almost all
of the powers mentioned—particularly affected U.S. trade.

By 1802 almost the entire coastline of Western Europe was allied with France or was under direct French control, leaving Americans with the only large neutral merchant fleet. France annexed
Savoy (1792), Monaco and Nice (1793), and the Austrian Netherlands (1795). A Patriot revolution in the Netherlands proper
(1795) turned that state into a French satellite; Prussia withdrew
from the war and Spain switched to the French side the same year.
France extended its control over northern Italy in 1797. Russia
(1800) and Austria (1801) eventually deserted Britain's anti-French
coalition (its second), and in 1801 Britain attacked neutral Denmark, pushing that country into France's arms. By 1802 Portugal
leaned French, and even Sweden and Hamburg could not remain
neutral.[3]

American merchants profited handsomely from the destruction
and relegation to port of so much shipping. The Netherlands had
been a major European trading center, but with the Dutch allied
to France, the British Navy blocked Dutch shipping and ports,
leaving the Netherlands, like France, dependent on neutral and
American shipping for sugar, coffee, tea, spices, and cloth. As major
entrepôts—including Livorno, Genoa, Emden, and Hamburg—lost
their neutrality, the remaining neutral merchants supplied those
ports too. With each neutral port's entry into the war there were
fewer neutrals remaining to supply the increased demand for neutral trade.[4]

The eighteen-month Peace of Amiens between Britain and France
(1802–1803), along with the subsidiary treaties of Lunéville and
Montfortaine between France and other powers,[5] provided a general,

if short, respite from hostilities. But war resumed. Napoleon established a new fleet-works at Boulogne and prepared to invade England (1803–1805), until the covering fleet was destroyed at Trafalgar (1805). He then marched east, defeating Austria and Russia at Ulm and Austerlitz (1805) and Prussia at Jena (1806). These victories turned over Prussian Friesland to the Netherlands and Venice, Illyria, and the ports of the Papal States (Ancona, Civita Vecchia, Rimini) to direct French control or occupation. Britain attacked Copenhagen in 1807, forcing Denmark to rejoin France. Despite Spanish resistance to French rule after 1808 and Austria's brief, failed fight in 1809 (after which Napoleon annexed the North German coast and the Papal States), Napoleon remained dominant in Europe between 1806 and 1812. Indeed, in 1809 he concluded a dynastic alliance with Austria's Habsburgs and in 1810 one of his marshals, Jean-Baptiste Bernadotte, was elected Crown Prince of Sweden. Napoleonic rule was weakened by the Russia campaign (1812) and jeopardized by Bonaparte's defeat at the Battle of Leipzig (1813), but not overthrown until 1814.[6]

European trade overseas suffered during the wars. Major French and French-aligned ports endured the worst.[7] Bordeaux had been an important exportation point for wine and an important import and re-export point for Caribbean products under the ancien régime. Now this previously French-carried traffic was replaced by neutral and American shipping. Even in 1802, a peacetime year, so much of the French merchant fleet had been destroyed that a third of Bordeaux's trade with the Caribbean remained in foreign vessel bottoms. As Ernest Labrousse explains, after war resumed, "the indirect commerce by neutral intermediaries, Americans most of all, maintained itself: in 1805 201 American vessels entered Bordeaux, being 23 percent of its foreign traffic."[8] In 1808 when the United States, nearly drawn in to the French Wars, embargoed overseas trade, Bordeaux lost even this (the embargo was lifted in 1809, and U.S. trade rebounded). As the American consul in Bordeaux reported, "from the Baltic to the Archipelago nothing but despair and misery is to be seen. Grass is growing in the streets of this city. Its beautiful port is deserted except by two Marblehead fishing schooners and three or four empty vessels which still swing to the tide."[9]

French merchants at La Rochelle scarcely fared better; from 1794 to mid-1797 a dozen French vessels arrived in that port. Over the same period more than 200 neutrals arrived. Americans were prominent among them, many bringing cloth from Britain. Daniel Garesché, a major merchant in La Rochelle, went as far as to settle some of his family in the United States to handle the traffic.[10]

Shipping in neutral ports such as Hamburg, Bremen, Lübeck, Ragusa, and Lisbon prospered between 1801 and 1805, but this prosperity was short-lived. Of these, Hanse towns traded for longer than most because of their importance as centers of credit and commerce. Between 1806 and 1810 these ports, still under only indirect French rule, were permitted to handle neutral trade and hence British goods onboard neutral ships, a privilege denied to French or Dutch cities. Still, after 1806 the British Navy kept Hanse shipping from the seas. In 1807 a French force "cleansed" British goods from Livorno, confiscating and burning whatever it could find. Bonaparte later transferred the cleansings to the Netherlands, North Germany, and beyond.[11] Lisbon also became a major smuggling center, one of the reasons Bonaparte occupied Portugal in 1807 (the occupation lasted only six months but was quite destructive). Denmark, perhaps the most significant neutral in Europe, fared just as badly. Britain attacked preemptively in 1807, fearing a potential Danish-French-Russian alignment. A third of Copenhagen's buildings were destroyed, hundreds of civilians were killed, and Britain captured fifteen Danish ships of the line and fifteen Danish frigates. One British naval historian noted that "this apparently unprovoked British attack on an inoffensive neutral aroused widespread disgust in Europe, and indeed among British officers." Even in Parliament, some called it a great "fleet robbery."[12] As each of these neutral shipping fleets was removed from the sea, American merchants tried to take its place.

The French Wars at Sea, 1793–1815

While France fought in Europe during this period, Britain fought overseas, where its navy could be most useful. The British army was simply too small at the outset of the war—only 50,000 men in 1789 as opposed to France's 255,000—and too ill-organized to make a difference against France.[13] Yet the British Navy was already half again as large as the French at the start of the war, despite Louis XVI's shipbuilding efforts; by 1810 the British Navy was larger than the navies of all other Western powers combined. In 1812, at the French Empire's height, Britain controlled every French or allied colony overseas. British ministers had not set out to do this; their conquests were ad hoc responses to events, much as the British imperial accretion of previous eras had been. After all, how could anyone have planned such an expansion when the French allies of 1812 were the British allies of 1793? Still, as territories accrued, British ministers sought to order them into a coherent empire. The unifying rationale, if not always the result, was trade. From Pitt through Liverpool, British governments took advantage of the French Wars to foster an economically self-sustaining empire of trade which they hoped to keep—at least in part—after the war. Initially Pitt's government sought colonial and mercantile success in the Caribbean, but this soon proved inadequate, encouraging a "swing to the east" in an attempt to make London the "Emporium of the Trade of Asia"—and hence render Asia another source of trade.[14]

The Caribbean, locus of more British and European trade in the 1790s than the east, was the "first point to make perfectly certain" in securing the world from France.[15] In 1790, an estimated £37 to £70 million of British trade and capital were invested in the Caribbean, whereas only £18 million were invested in the East India trade.[16] (This imbalance was fast changing. British imports from the Caribbean were valued at £8.6 million for the years between 1794 and 1796, while imports from Asia came close to £7.3 million in the same period and Asian trade offered greater room for growth.)[17] Caribbean trade, especially in sugar, had been at the center of Europe's foreign trade for some time. So rich was the Caribbean sugar economy that the French part of Saint Domingue—a pinnacle of sugar monoculture—maintained an overseas trade greater than that of the entire United States.[18] For Britain, increased Caribbean trade would generate increased cus-

toms revenue, which might help finance the war in the short term
(though British ministries took care not to count on such increases
for their budgets), with the plantations serving as a basis for further commercial expansion in peace. All the most valuable French
colonies were in the Caribbean, making victory there the most accessible way to punish France, and as France was Britain's only
adversary in 1793, there were at first few conquests to be had in
Asia.

In 1794 British forces swiftly captured the islands of Martinique,
St. Lucia, and Guadeloupe as well as Port-au-Prince, the capital and
main port of Saint Domingue. Though a French squadron retook
Guadeloupe late that same year, encouraged slave uprisings on
Grenada and St. Vincent in March 1795, and recovered St. Lucia in
June 1795, British reinforcements recaptured St. Lucia and put
down the slave revolts on Grenada and St. Vincent in 1796, also
taking the Dutch South American colonies, Demerara, Essequibo,
and Berbice. Spanish Trinidad fell in 1797, and British forces attempted Puerto Rico in the same year. Then, with Britain's plans in
Asia growing, its ambitions in the Caribbean diminished. In 1798
Britain reached an understanding with Toussaint l'Ouverture, leader
of the black revolutionary forces on Saint Domingue; later plans to
conquer Cuba and New Orleans (1800) were scuttled. New acquisitions came from local garrisons only, including Surinam (1799) and
Curaçao (1800) from the Dutch, St. Martin's (1801) from the
French, St. Bartholomew (1801) from Sweden, and St. Thomas and
St. Croix (1801) from Denmark.[19]

During the Peace of Amiens, all these colonies except Trinidad
were returned by a dovish Addington ministry eager to end the war.
They were taken a second time when the war resumed: Tobago and
Santa Lucia (1803) from France; Demerara, Essequibo, Berbice
(1803), Surinam (1804), and Curaçao (1807) from the Netherlands; the Danish islands (1807); French Cayenne (1809); Martinique (1809); and Guadeloupe (1810). With this last went the final
French foothold in the New World. British forces also attacked, but
could not hold, Buenos Aires (1806) and Montevideo (1807).[20]
Arthur Wellesley was slated to follow up with a landing in Central
America, but was redirected to Iberia once the Spanish insurrection

broke out. British forces occupied Danish St. Thomas and St. John in 1807 as well.

As British conquests in the Americas continued, the East India Company took the French posts in India: Chandernagore in Bengal, Pondicherry on the Coromandel Coast,[21] and Mahé in Malabar, along with the French factories at Surat, Masulipatam, and Calicut in 1793.[22] These posts were little more than docks and warehouses and did not add much to the Company's territory or commerce, though their occupation did eliminate a rival trader. The French, shorn of their Indian possessions, urged the Dutch to join their fight, warning, "Your most important Establishments, the Cape of Good Hope, the Island of Ceylon, and all your commerce with the Indies. . . . Do you believe that the English, insatiable for power and lucre, would never take these important places from you, which would assure them of their Indian Empire?"[23]

Indeed, the British lost no time in taking these after 1795. After the Netherlands turned to France, the English Company immediately attacked the Dutch Company's posts: Cochin on the Malabar Coast, Pulicat on the Coromandel, and Chinsura in Bengal. As Company troops stormed the Indian factories, Crown forces seized additional Dutch posts to the east: the Cape Colony in Southern Africa (1795), Malacca (1795), and the littoral of Ceylon (1796). British forces arrived with letters from the stadholder-in-exile ordering Dutch governors to stand down and turn over their colonies to "protect" the colonies from rapacious France. But Pitt and Dundas did not intend to return them. Pitt considered the Cape and Ceylon the bare minimum they would retain in a peace settlement.[24] Dundas urged him never to return them, threatening to resign if he did. These were large territories. The Cape Colony covered at least 64,000 square miles.[25] Ceylon, a coastal ring surrounding the Kingdom of Kandy in the interior, was another major landed acquisition. Robert Lord Hobart, Governor of Madras and an early proponent of a muscular British policy overseas, personally led the conquest of Malacca, which complemented the existing British post at Penang and helped Britain control traffic passing through the Straits of Malacca to China.[26]

Meanwhile, a combined Crown and Company force attacked Amboyna and the Banda Islands (1796) in the Netherlands East Indies (present-day Indonesia). In 1797 British forces destroyed the French settlement in Madagascar and launched an abortive attack on Manila. Operations continued against the Dutch East Indies; by 1799 most of the Dutch fortresses and islands outside the main strongholds in the Java Sea had fallen, and some began to think Britain might maintain permanent interests there as well, prompting Sir John Dalrymple to expect "a free trade to the Spice Islands" and any other Eastern islands the Dutch might be suffered to keep in a general peace.[27] That same year Company forces attacked Mysore, an Indian state allegedly allied with France; the French "threat" to India was used to draw the Indian states of Hyderabad, Arcot, Oudh, and Tanjore more firmly into the British orbit as well. The British governor-general in Bengal considered attacking the French Indian Ocean base at Mauritius (also known as Ile de France) and the Dutch stronghold on Java—the latter twice—but decided against both in order to assist operations against the French in Egypt in 1801.[28] That same year, the Company seized the last neutral ports in India, the Danish posts of Serampore in Bengal and Tranquebar on the Coromandel Coast. In 1802, the Company occupied Portuguese Goa and attacked Macau.[29] By 1802 Britain controlled every European port in the Subcontinent and almost every colonial port in the broader Indo-Pacific region, keeping French and French-allied ships out of every one.

Henry Addington returned all British conquests in Asia, save Ceylon[30] in 1802, but as in the Caribbean, these were retaken once war resumed. By 1807 Britain had regained the Cape of Good Hope, Malacca, and Bangka from the Dutch and Tranquebar and Serampore from the Danish. It began blockading the French Mascarenes and sending sorties toward Batavia as well. British Indian forces prevented a French squadron, as well as troops dispatched by Napoleon during the peace, from investing themselves in Pondicherry (1803). The Company made a second failed attempt on Macau (1808) and considered another Manila expedition before taking French Mauritius and Réunion (1810) and Dutch Batavia (1811).[31]

Such global maneuvers—attempts to "redivide the world," in Lenin's phrase and in Gillray's famous print—spawned a mania for fantastic schemes, as Europeans were thinking globally for the first time. Among the numerous plans and schemes and phobias, perhaps the most fantastic was the letter of one half-pay British captain to the First Lord of the Admiralty, warning of naval attacks on India from Siberia, staged from a Russian-occupied Japan. French imaginations were also robust; several unpursued projects to reassert French influence in the Indian Subcontinent rested on the assumption that the Spanish might willingly give up part of the Philippines. The unsolicited advice both governments received made even the most ambitious projects they did pursue—the French invasion of Egypt and the British attacks on Macau among them—seem sober. (Wisely, the British scuttled a proposal to attack the Pacific coast of Spanish America from India.) Dundas himself was particularly innovative in this regard.[32] As a scheme-weary French naval minister wrote in 1797 after having just received yet another plan to "menace English commerce in the China seas," "I always receive the views of my Constituents with pleasure.... I thank you for your offer, but I must tell you that the moment is not opportune for the execution of a project so vast. There is already in the Offices of the Navy a great number of memorials and reports" on this.[33] And into the back of the file cabinet it went.

Henry Dundas and the "Emporium of the Trade of Asia"

Henry Dundas was, as an earlier generation of imperial historians have described him, the "presiding genius of the new empire."[34] He commanded the Crown and Company war efforts, serving doubly as British secretary of war (1794–1801) and president of the Board of Control, the government body charged with overseeing the East India Company's affairs (1793–1801). He served briefly in Pitt's second administration (1804–1806) as First Lord of the Admiralty (1804–1805). He was, along with William Wyndham Grenville, Prime Minister Pitt's closest advisor, even serving as Home

Secretary for a time. One inside observer noted that "the efficient ministry is Pitt, Dundas and Grenville."[35] Dundas's electoral machine returned Scotland for Pitt, supporting the government and guaranteeing the Scotsman influence in Whitehall. He enjoyed considerable control over British foreign policy in particular; Pitt's remark, "every act of his being as much mine as his," was apt.[36] Pitt and Dundas were friends as well as political allies, and the two were often inseparable, repairing to the latter's estate at Wimbledon or drinking in London. Relieved to have action after months of indecision and tension, the pair celebrated France's declaration of war in 1793 with a binge; their wobbly return to Parliament provoked a telling ditty: "I cannot see the Speaker, Hal, can you? / What! cannot see the Speaker, I see two!"[37]

British imperial historians have only recently recalled Dundas's significance, thanks to the biographical efforts of Michael Fry.[38] Britain's new empire was largely Dundas's vision. He limited army commitments to Europe, where he feared the British Army was too small to make a significant contribution. He could not, he explained to Pitt,

> assent to appropriate any such share of the force of this country to any expedition on the coast of France as would interfere with the objects which naturally present themselves in the West or East Indies. Success in those quarters I consider of infinite moment, both in the view of humbling the power of France, and with the view of enlarging our national wealth and security.

Operations overseas were thus as important as operations on the French coast.[39] Admiralty's concentration of naval forces along the French shore, boxing in the enemy, left the rest of Britain's possessions defenseless should a French fleet escape, as one did in 1794. "I have always differed in opinion from those who have thought that everything was to be sacrificed to a strong Channel fleet," Dundas explained to George John Spencer, First Lord of the Admiralty, in 1796. "Home will take care of itself . . . in the present war . . . there can be no real injury done to this country but in its distant possessions," meaning "the Eastern World is their only rational object."[40]

Spencer and Grenville were less sure home would take care of itself. No one knew whether their blockade would work; at times Britons feared French invasion. These concerns were reasonable, but blockade, and the endless pirouetting in the Channel this entailed, would not end the war. Dundas was one of the few with the sang-froid to pursue colonial objectives in the midst of fears about the invasion of home. Confining the British fleet to Europe allowed the French Navy—purged of officers by the French Revolution and long since maligned by historians—to tie up a British naval force twice its size. Colonial conquest, by contrast, allowed the navy to contribute material gains rather than merely protect against loss.

Dundas supported efforts to check France in Europe, such as the 1799 den Helder campaign, and maintained a considerable and direct correspondence with Philippe d'Auvergne, the British naval officer (born on Jersey, he was adopted into the d'Auvergne French ducal line) and spymaster for the French Coast and the Channel Islands. D'Auvergne distributed money and arms to royalists (and later anti-Bonapartists) in France and relayed information on French naval movements back to Britain from 1792 until 1808, when he took command of the Channel Island flotilla.[41] Dundas understood that it was in Europe where ultimate victory was to be won, and he worked for victory there but not at the expense of surer or more-immediate prospects elsewhere. He urged that colonial conquests contribute to the "national wealth" needed for a long-term conflict and that enemy colonies be exploited for this as opportunities appeared. As he explained in 1799, "Great Britain can at no time propose to maintain an extensive and complicated war but by destroying the colonial resources of our enemies and adding proportionately to our own commercial resources, which are, and must ever be, the sole basis of our maritime strength."[42] Dundas had held since the beginning of the war that "all wars are a contention of purse,"[43] and he fully dispatched the navy and army to the colonies to hurt French trade and augment Britain's. The Dutch Patriot revolution (1795) gave him the opportunity to pursue wars of the purse in Asia, and Richard Lord Mornington's Governor-Generalcy in Bengal (1797) gave him the reliable agent and army in India that he needed to do the job.

Mornington and Dundas did not agree on everything, but they shared an expansionist view of the empire and wished to bring as much of the West's East India trade to London as possible. Mornington often bypassed his immediate superiors at the Company's Court of Directors and corresponded directly with Dundas, under whom he had served a political apprenticeship of sorts at the Board of Control.[44] With Pitt's ear, Mornington's hand, and two cabinet posts, Dundas centered imperial decision making in one man for the first time. In the 1800s his son, Robert, exerted a similar influence. Naval deployments, too, were better coordinated with overall strategic needs, since both Henry and Robert Dundas served in the Admiralty over the course of their careers. Dundas's own expertise on India (he was Pitt's India hand) meant that in Asian policy he had particularly free reign. Dundas envisioned a global, maritime empire of trade, with Asian commerce run by the East India Company and Atlantic and Caribbean commerce by private traders. For Dundas, expanding the empire meant expanding this worldwide system of trade.[45]

Dundas would make London "Emporium of the Trade of Asia" by drawing French Europe's Asiatic trade to Britain, thus building on London's existing role as the main distribution point for East Indian goods in Britain and the British Atlantic.[46] This had been a lingering goal for some time; in 1786 one correspondent had urged Dundas to make London the sole "Emporium of the Asiatic Trade to the western world."[47] Now Dundas could act on the idea. He ordered the taking of French and French-allied possessions in the east, drove their trade from Asia, blockaded their ports, destroyed their fleets, and drove their shipping from the sea. He tried to force France, Spain, the Netherlands, and other French allies to buy their East Indian goods—Chinese tea, Indian cloth, Asian spice—from the English East India Company's London auctions, or via British smugglers who supplied Europe from there. He did not order those conquests solely to achieve this result, however. Colonial theaters, naval patrols, and privateers were normal parts of late-eighteenth-century British warfare; Dundas would have pursued these regardless. But once these places had been denied France, they were accorded Britain; the emporium idea became a unifying rationale for Britain's new possessions—a rationale that, once created, lingered after the war.

To make London an Asian re-export hub to an armed and hostile Europe was not so far-fetched. France imported from Britain throughout the Revolutionary and Napoleonic Wars, despite French strictures and British concerns to the contrary. Dundas wished to take further advantage of this smuggling. Britain ensured that France and its allies had little connection to their colonies; now Dundas tried to force Europeans to buy British-carried colonial goods instead. In the first three-quarters of the eighteenth century, re-exports had made up a third of British exports. Imperial trade had been more firmly Atlantic then; now that the empire was shifting east it made sense to encourage the re-export of Asian goods as well.[48]

Rerouting Continental Europe's Asian trade through Britain would bring capital to Britain and deprive France of the same. In the last years of the ancien régime, though the French establishments in India were never, as one writer claimed, among "the principle sources of the prosperity of the [French] State," they were certainly lucrative.[49] After the collapse of the French East India Company, the French king granted licenses for trade with Asia on an ad hoc basis, usually to the men with the largest douceurs. Now this was lost. Dundas's emporium policy was a means to profit from the enemy's trade, and merely one of many economic measures the Smithian Dundas might have expected to benefit the empire broadly.

The English Company was thus assigned a monopoly not just of British trade with Asia, but of French Europe's as well. Dundas's 1799 Warehousing Act made such re-exports even easier. But while this furthered Dundas's goal of making London *the* emporium of Indian goods, it left the Company as the only stumbling block to blame if that emporium failed. This higher standard of success was eventually disastrous for the Company, and Pitt's successors would accuse the Company of failing to carry the preponderance of east-west global trade. But initially, rerouting French Europe's trade through London and the Company seemed to Dundas like a sensible means for binding the new empire together.[50]

The "Swing to the East"

As Dundas explained in 1799, "the way to defeat France is to take all her colonies and to destroy her trade."[51] (Napoleon, invading Egypt, said much the same of Britain.) Early efforts in the Caribbean yielded valuable conquests: the sheer devastation of the war in Saint Domingue boosted the value of the surviving (and increasing) sugar plantations in British hands, and Sir Francis Baring took pains to ensure that the trade of Toussaint l'Ouverture's regime passed through Britain and not just the United States.[52] Meanwhile the more stable colonies taken in Dutch Guiana attracted, by some estimates, £18 million of British investing capital between 1796 and 1802, when they were returned to the Dutch. Subsequently recaptured, by 1805 they produced more cotton for British mills than the whole of the British West Indies.[53] Still, Britain already was the major re-export hub for Caribbean products by 1795; though there was room for an absolute growth in trade, there was less room for growth in market share.

Meanwhile, the political economy of Caribbean sugar was precarious. William Wilberforce's efforts to abolish the slave trade threatened the viability of those plantations as they were then constituted, since they relied on slave imports to sustain their labor force. Wilberforce's measures lost in Parliament by only the slimmest of margins in 1797 and 1799, and Pitt considered including a general abolition in the terms of the Amiens peace settlement. The Fox and Grenville ministries backed Wilberforce's abolition bill in 1806 and 1807. Thus, though Britain had expelled the French and Dutch from their most valuable Caribbean colonies by 1798, it was at the same time unclear how durable or profitable Caribbean trade would soon be. Meanwhile, the prospect for future trade growth shone bright in Asia (not least because of the relative availability of Indian and Chinese labor; as early as 1810, the East India Company began importing several hundred Chinese indentured servants to its South Atlantic island of St. Helena, supplying labor the African slave trade could no longer meet).[54]

Lord Mornington obliged Dundas his vision, unleashing the Company on the Subcontinent. His conquest of Mysore in 1799 earned his creation the First Marquis Wellesley. But Wellesley's campaigns provided little benefit to the Company's trade and did not always advance London's position as an Asian emporium. His most costly wars established British supremacy in the Indian interior, not the coast, as with his campaign against the Marathas. The Danish and Portuguese ports in India he did seize saw only minor trade compared with French Mauritius and Dutch Java, which he spared to invade Egypt, of no economic value at all. By not attacking the main Dutch and French ports, Wellesley left important centers of Asian trade shut to Britons and delivered to neutral hands, which undermined Dundas's goal of concentrating Europe's Asian trade in London. Even most trade-related conquests were redundant of existing British ports. Such conquests excluded rivals from trade but failed to penetrate new markets. The exceptions—Ceylon for cinnamon, Amboyna for cloves, and Banda for nutmeg—represented commodities that did not comprise a large share of east-west trade.[55] The conquests of Chinsura in India and Malacca on the Malay Peninsula excluded the Dutch from these areas but duplicated the British posts at Calcutta and Penang. These conquests did nothing to weaken the Dutch hold on Java, where American merchants could still trade. Wellesley's real animus, as he confessed to Dundas, was their mutual and "voracious appetite for land and fortresses," for which the goal of trade was often a flimsy rationale.[56] During his tenure the East India Company's debt tripled while American trade in India boomed free of such debt. The "Emporium" idea and the economic swing it represented covered the development of a new, landed empire in the east. Some saw under the covers, including many French, one of whom remarked that "it is doubtlessly in Britain's interest to retain the possessions of other nations in India and prevent them from trading there." This remark encapsulated the marriage of landed empire and trade inherent in Dundas's vision. One British admiral worried along similar lines: "I fear we are aggrandizing in this Country full as much as your friend Bony at home."[57]

Since the Americans' first arrival in Asia it had been the Company's standing practice to permit U.S. merchantmen to trade with British India—better that a British India port get their business than a French or Dutch one—but now, as the Company took enemy ports and had less reason to welcome American shipping, U.S. vessels were permitted into the British East Indies by black-letter law. After 1794 the Jay Treaty accorded Americans most-favored-nation status in Company possessions. Anywhere a Company vessel could go, an American vessel could follow, but in some places (e.g., Mauritius, Batavia, and Manila) British ships were still barred. Meanwhile, in Calcutta the Company had to compete with neutral Americans on equal terms (something the Company abhorred) while still having to absorb the cost of Wellesley's wars.[58]

Company operations in Asia under Wellesley's tenure (1797–1805) were aggressive and successful, if costly. There were more Indian troops in the Company's army than British troops under Crown control in Europe or the Caribbean, meaning the greatest opportunities for British arms—until an army large enough to contend with France in Europe could be developed—were in Asia. Subcontinental wars provided battle experience for British commanders, including Wellesley's younger brother, the future Duke of Wellington. Indian sepoys began to be deployed around the Indian Ocean and remained a constant feature of the imperial presence in that region for the next century. The Company's army was so reliable that by the end of the war only 30,000 Europeans "stiffened" and supervised over 200,000 native troops.[59]

British commercial dominance in the east finally came with the arrival of another energetic governor-general in Bengal, Gilbert Lord Minto, and of Robert Dundas at the Board of Control.[60] Politically, they did not see eye to eye: Minto had been sent out by Grenville under the Ministry of all the Talents, and Dundas was a firm Pittite, receiving the Presidency of the Board of Control from Portland. Dundas was sometimes displeased with Minto, and contemplated replacing him with Arthur Lord Wellington if British forces were to be "expelled from Portugal (an event which certainly *may* take place)," he informed Liverpool in 1810. Dundas also complained that Minto "writes a great deal more than is necessary" and "does not produce efficient measures."[61] Nor did Minto have much initial political success in the Subcontinent. He seemed to deal with the Vellore uprising (1806) inefficiently, and he made a hash of Persia (1807–1808). But he sent Company forces to battle with vigor, which ultimately was enough for Dundas: he attacked Macau in 1808 and took the Moluccas and Mauritius in 1810 and Batavia in 1811. After 1811, no enemy colony in Asia remained unattacked.

The Orders in Council, the Continental System, and the "Emporium of the Trade of Asia"

After 1806 peace seemed impossible to both the British and French sides. European disillusion with Napoleon—Beethoven being the famous avatar—became widespread. Even Talleyrand resigned in disgust in 1807, seeing no hope for a negotiated peace. Meanwhile, in Britain, the death of Charles James Fox (1806) carried off the last Member of Parliament of any significance who was willing to negotiate with France. Eradication of Bonaparte's regime, not peaceful coexistence with it, became a goal for successive governments. By 1807 war had lasted so long that a seventeen-year-old conscript could remember only fourteen months of peace in his lifetime, and it was so widespread that not a single neutral state survived in Europe.

With Britain as unable to defeat France on land as France was unable to defeat Britain at sea, the war seemed unending, and the Dutch, Spaniards, and Danes seemed like permanent additions to the French coalition. Collaboration of the Spanish (twelve years), Dutch (eighteen years), and Danish (six years) governments with France in this period was long-lasting, much longer than, for example, Vichy France's collaboration with Germany in World War II. Faced with military stalemate, Bonaparte instead sought economic victory against Britain with his Continental System; Britain's new Orders in Council heightened the economic war against France in response. Meanwhile, Britain took an increasingly annexationist approach to the French, Dutch, Spanish, and Danish colonies it ruled.

The first move had been Britain's: a formal blockade was declared in May 1806. Napoleon responded in November 1806 with the Berlin Decree, banning British imports on British ships. Prussia also agreed to follow Napoleon's system. Britain then banned shipping between neutral and enemy ports (such as between New York and Seville) in January 1807 and began to restrict shipping between neutral ports that November. At the end of the year Bonaparte's Milan Decree banned all British imports, even on neutral ships. Russia joined Napoleon's Continental System that same year. In the autumn of 1807 the HMS *Leopard* bombarded and boarded the *Chesapeake*, a U.S. naval vessel, and impressed four seamen. The incident nearly started a war. President Jefferson averted this with his embargo on overseas trade. Bonaparte's St. Cloud and Trianon Decrees further strengthened his blockade in 1810. Britain and France each squeezed neutral shipping to punish the other; this made American trade in East Indian goods to Europe both more difficult and—should U.S. traders find a loophole in the Continental System, such as Danish Tonningen—more lucrative.[62]

East Indian re-exports took on greater significance during this commercial warfare. Yet as war removed European rivals from Asia and from the sea, it was unclear whether the Company had made good use of its re-export opportunities. In 1807 and 1808 the East India Company's directors debated how to make London an Asian emporium. The chairmen of the Court of Directors, Edward Parry and Charles Grant, agreed "it clearly for the Interest of this Country to bring as large a proportion of the Indian Exports to the mart of London."[63] "The object of the present arrangement," they wrote in 1808, citing Henry Dundas's words of 1793, "is to extend the trade to and from India, through the medium of the Company, by every possible means, to make London the great Emporium for Indian Commodities."[64] Here Dundas had finessed an important point: one could not extend the trade solely through the Company and also by *every* means.

Now Robert Dundas and his new ally Sir Francis Baring worried that extending Indian trade through the Company alone might be impossible.[65] The Company seemed incapable of supporting a reliable re-export trade to Continental Europe while the commercial war with France continued. Smuggling was possible, but U.S. merchants had the advantage: they could smuggle as Britons did, and they could also bring their own Indian goods to the edge of the French Empire legally. Even in the midst of Jefferson's embargo, Baring thought U.S. merchants would return to India and sell to Europe once the ban was lifted. The Company's Court of Directors thought U.S.-India trade should be constrained by the Company's Indian government, but Dundas and Baring were more tolerant of American trade in India. American trade has its benefits, including the specie brought by U.S vessels. Minor concessions on Indian trade—allowing Americans to pay the 5 percent tariff for Britons rather than the 10 percent rate for foreigners—were worthwhile if they kept the U.S. government, a minor if troublesome neutral, out of the general war.[66] Grant and Parry disagreed, finding U.S. re-export of Indian cloth "manifestly to the prejudice of our own Commerce."[67]

Baring, a Company director, thought that the Company's failures in sustaining re-exports set it up for disaster. Its monopoly, a "disability of the Company's constitution," meant it could not "stand the competition with Foreigners. The only way to give British subjects a fair chance is to lay the Trade open, and *commercially* speaking," Baring added, "this conclusion is unanswerable."[68] Concerned that "stagnation in the Company's Sales" be "urged against us," the chairmen assumed the role of the aggrieved and demanded that the Americans "supply *their wants for their own Markets* from thence, leaving the rest of the supply of Europe to the Emporium of London." They proposed to return tariffs on Americans in India to 10 percent to make the prices of their own Indian goods more competitive in Europe. The debate got heated: Grant suggested Baring was a traitor, and Baring resorted to equally ungentlemanly outbursts (in his notes, at least) and grumbled at Grant's "lofty dictatorial" and "irritable" tone.

He "has not a mind fit to preside over a great commercial establishment, still less, over the general interests of a great Empire."
Neither side gave way.[69]

Baring had hit upon Grant's real fear: that Dundas would con-
clude that the Company was *unable* to make London the emporium of the trade of Asia, and that this inability could not be rem-
edied without altering the nature of the Company itself.
Re-exporting risked this conclusion, since British and American
performance in European markets could be compared directly—a
comparison that could not be drawn in their respective domestic
markets. Thus when the chairmen admitted that sales of goods
from India to Europe were "supplanted or reduced in their value"
by goods "supplied in our Indian ports" and brought "to foreign
Europe, nay to the British Colonies in the West Indies and North
America" by Americans, they vociferously blamed American neutrality, lest Dundas suspect Company deficiency. Yet perhaps without realizing its implication, they admitted in the same letter that
the phenomenon of U.S. sales to Europe, which "forestal[l] our
Market and render the resort less to London for Indian commodities," began "when the Continental Ports were not shut against us."
And just how had the Company failed, then? The directors papered
over this, and argued that a return to the 10 percent tariff on
American trade in India would counter the presumed neutral
advantage.[70]

This modest tax increase did not price American-carried India
goods out of Europe. Robert Dundas, taking up the Smithian
principles of his father and of Pitt, grew convinced of the Company's deficiency and opposed the India-trade monopoly in 1813,
arguing that British free traders could succeed where the Company had not. Dundas's cipher and fellow lord, Lord Buckinghamshire, remarked quite pointedly on the success of American
free trade in Asia. In 1806–1807, he noted, the United States and
the European nations bought "nearly 1,600,000£" worth of
goods from India, "whereas the imports of the Company for that
year had been only 1,200,000£." Would not the £1.6 million
"carried on as it was by Americans . . . have been a considerable

object to British subjects?"[71] It was a good question, and a damning one, since for Dundas making "London the Emporium of the Trade of Asia" was more important than preserving the Company's monopoly.

By 1813, British politics had reached a strange point: sales to an enemy abroad in a time of war were the generally accepted measure of success, and a Tory government was trying to abolish part of the East India Company's monopoly, citing *American* free trade—of all things—as its example. All this raises the question of just how much British re-exports had fallen.

British Smuggling to French Europe

During the blockade British exporters to French Europe relied on smuggling. British farms and factories produced much of the food and many of the textiles found in the residences of high French officials; British colonies fed the elite of France with tropical luxuries, and no matter how badly the war went, Bonaparte always seemed to have a supply of British goods.[72] Smuggling was common on the French coast and rampant in the Netherlands, where the Dutch chafed under the Bonaparte yoke. Napoleon sent his brother Louis to rule the new Kingdom of Holland (established on the ruins of the Batavian Republic, with formerly Prussian East Friesland appended) to shore up French control in 1806, but the new king identified with his people over his brother and made little effort to stop smugglers.

British smugglers also operated in the German states. Hamburg was a notorious transshipment point, despite the dispatch there of Napoleon's former personal secretary, Louis-Antoine Fauvelet de Bourrienne, as minister plenipotentiary in 1804. Bourrienne so enriched himself with bribes (not itself uncommon) that Napoleon recalled him in 1810. "Commerce forms a level field by the strongest of all connections—common interest—commercial correspondents offer a frequent and abundant source of precious funds," Bourrienne explained. "I've profited greatly in that." He scoffed at the Berlin Decree. "It was not a decree . . . without boats, without a navy, it was ridiculous to declare Britain in a state of blockade, all the while English vessels were in fact blockading every port in France." And so British goods came in with fake Swedish, Danish, or Russian certificates of origin, with Bourrienne's knowledge. Meanwhile the port of Altona, a Danish enclave abutting Hamburg, was still separate, undermining France's control of the city. Also with Bourrienne's knowledge, Altonans smuggled "sugar, coffee, vanilla, indigo" and other colonial imports inside coffins, some Altona residents having the right to be buried in the Hamburg cemetery. Funeral processions grew strangely frequent.[73]

Then there was the island of Helgoland, all of 2 kilometers wide, which Britain seized from Denmark in 1807. In the North Sea off the mouth of the Elbe, Helgoland had a good harbor only 70 kilometers from the German mainland and stood close to Denmark, Hamburg, Bremen, and the Netherlands; it was a perfect smuggler's den. British re-exports to Helgoland soon reached over £1 million a year, most going on to Continental Europe. In 1809, British re-exports to France, the Netherlands, Germany, and Helgoland totaled £6 million sterling, much of it in coffee and sugar, a quadrupling from the previous year.[74]

Elsewhere, similar practices prevailed. Smuggling was so rampant in the Illyrian provinces—craggy, mountainous places perfectly suited for the business—that the region was removed from the French imperial customs system altogether. The Illyrian possessions were supposed to strengthen the Continental System, but their customs service became, as one scholar of Illyrian administration explains, "defeated" and an "overall failure" in "the Emperor's economic war against Great Britain."[75]

Fed up with the weak adherence of the Netherlands and the German states to his Continental System, in 1810 Bonaparte annexed the whole of the Atlantic coast from the Netherlands through Hamburg and Hanover and on to Lübeck on the Baltic Sea, and with it the whole of Spain north of the Ebro. British re-exports to northwestern Europe fell from the previous year's high, but British re-exporters to French Europe were still able to undermine

French customs regulations. From Bonaparte's perspective, this must have been maddening (see Figure 3.1).

After 1809 British exports to France dwindled, partly compensated for with trade to the periphery of the French Empire. Exports to France were still valued at over £1 million in 1812, but were significantly less than exports elsewhere. Hamburg, even as a French province, remained a smuggling haven. The city's legal sugar imports were abnormally low after the French takeover; historians suspect the difference was smuggled. Meanwhile traffic with Altona continued apace. Ridiculously, Hamburg remained "placed at the extreme frontier of the Empire, touching so close to foreign lands that," as one French official remarked, "at low tide one must disembark in Denmark to arrive at French Hamburg." Up to 10,000 people passed through the Altona-Hamburg customs frontier in an hour, hardly the stuff of rigorous inspections.[76]

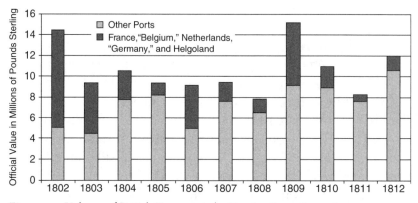

Figure 3.1 Volume of British Re-exports by Destination, 1802–1812

Source: François Crouzet, *L'économie britannique et le blocus continental (1806–1813)*, vol. 2 (Paris: Presses Universitaires de France, 1958), 887, table 5. The terms "Belgium" and "Germany" are Crouzet's; they are in quotes because they do not refer to any state then in existence. Helgoland was British from 1807 onward. "Other ports" refers to all other destinations: Russia, Sweden, Denmark, Norway, Prussia, Portugal, Spain, "Italy," Malta, the Ottoman Empire, Ireland, Asia, Africa, and the Americas. Data portray official values. These were fixed and did not fluctuate with the market. Official values in this chart should be read for relative changes in *volume*.

British East Indian Re-exports to French Europe

Though re-exports were significant to the East India trade and though general re-exports remained strong, re-exports of East Indian goods—despite Dundas's hopes—were a small part of overall British re-exports when compared with re-exports from the Caribbean. As determined by official values, tea constituted less than 6 percent of the goods re-exported from Britain; Indian cloth was less than 15 percent for the Napoleonic decade (and after 1807, less than 10 percent). Coffee, a largely Caribbean product, made up more than 27 percent of British re-exports; sugar and rum, 17 percent (see Figure 3.2).[77]

Of the two major East India goods, tea and Indian cloth, tea was particularly unresponsive to changes in the export market. One way to measure the responsiveness is the use of standard deviation, which accounts for how much one year's tea re-exports

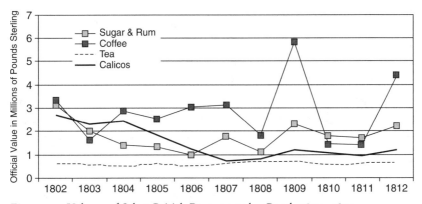

Figure 3.2 Volume of Select British Re-exports by Good, 1802–1812

Source: François Crouzet, *L'économie britannique et le blocus continental (1806–1813)*, vol. 2 (Paris: Presses Universitaires de France, 1958), 890, table 9. What is given here as calicos is given by Crouzet as as "indiennes." The French term "indienne" refers to printed calicos, but it does not refer to calicos printed only in India. The term could have been used to describe British- or Indian-made prints. The source describes British re-exports, however, meaning British-made cloth is excluded, though a few "indiennes" from other, non-Indian sources might be present in the calicos given here. Data portray official values; this chart should be read for relative changes in *volume*.

vary from the average for re-exports over several years. The figure is small, the standard deviation being only 11 percent of average tea exports for the decade between 1802 and 1812. This indicates a relatively low level of variation. The standard deviation of all re-exports was higher (22 percent of the yearly average), with sugar and rum (34 percent) and coffee (47 percent) much higher. One would expect re-exports to fluctuate with the war, as ports changed hands and British and European economies were affected. But though exports of sugar and coffee were duly volatile, exports of Chinese tea were not. And while at first blush re-exports of Indian cloth seem to vary wildly (a standard deviation of 47 percent of the annual average), this variation is explained by the falloff in Indian *imports* between 1805 and 1806. With the Indian-cloth data divided in two (1802–1805 and 1806–1812), the standard deviation falls to 15 percent and 19 percent of the respective yearly averages within those two periods.[78]

The weak response of Indian cloth and Chinese tea to changes in European demand suggests that the East India Company monopoly was less responsive to the re-export market than were the private merchants who brought coffee and sugar to Britain. It also suggests that the European market did not take much of the English Company's tea or cloth, and that most of the Company's sales, despite Dundas's goal to create Europe as the "Emporium of the Trade of Asia," ultimately met home demand. Company officials protested that the Continental System prevented them from placing much tea or cloth in Europe, but the rampant smuggling suggests it was not prohibitively difficult to transfer goods from Britain to the Continent. The Company kept a year's supply of tea in reserve—it was, after all, vital to the British diet—and so decreases in tea imports were unlikely to affect tea re-exportation. The stability of tea re-exports in this period suggests a relatively calm market—probably Canada, Ireland, and the British Atlantic rather than Europe. Conversely, Indian cloth re-exports mirrored their import so closely that it is difficult to see any correlation between Indian cloth re-exports and re-exportation generally.

It was hard for British policymakers to miss their merchants' inability to sell India goods on the Continent. The falloff in Indian imports, the escalation of the economic war with France, and the ascension of Robert Dundas to the head of the Board of Control all roughly coincided, fixing debate in Company and government circles on whether and how British policy on Asian trade should be altered as a result of the war.

London did not become *the* emporium of Asia, as Buckinghamshire noted. Ironically, this was the result of British war policy—Henry and Robert Dundas's policy. Dundas permitted U.S. merchants to trade with British India while he delayed the conquest of Dutch, French, and Spanish colonial possessions until 1811, in the meantime surrendering the carriage of those colonies' cargoes to neutral traders. As a consequence, U.S. re-exports of Asian goods were large enough to deny the East India Company dominance in east-west traffic. To understand how this occurred, to understand just how anxious the Company directors were, and to understand how U.S.-Asian trade could have affected British imperial policy, we must consider the American trade itself.

CHAPTER FOUR

America's Re-export Boom

Wartime Europe created a boom market for American-shipped goods, East Indian and otherwise. The effect, as one U.S. writer has commented, "was to throw into our hands the greater part of the colonial carrying trade of the world—an economic prize for which European nations had been fiercely struggling for nearly two centuries." Timothy Pitkin, a compiler of American trade figures writing in the 1830s, elaborated that

> valuable articles of colonial produce, such as sugar, coffee, spirits, cocoa, indigo, pepper, and spices of all kind, were carried by [American merchants], either directly to Europe, or brought to the United States, and from thence exported in American vessels. . . . The manufactures of Europe, and particularly those of Great Britain, as well as the manufactures and produce of the East Indies and China, were, also, imported, and again exported in large quantities, to the West Indies, South America, and elsewhere.[1]

American consumption of these goods increased as well. If there was a commercial revolution in the 1790s and early 1800s, as some historians suspect, the East India boom was certainly a part of it. U.S. customs data track this commerce, and the comparison of U.S. and British re-exports reveals the extent to which the East India Company's empire did—and did not—make London the emporium of Asia.[2]

Re-exportation was a significant part of U.S. trade. During the French Wars, between 20 and 50 percent of all goods (the share varying by year) imported into the United States were resold abroad, particularly to Europe and the Caribbean. The economic historian Cathy Matson has pointed out that

> England and France were forced to suspend their mercantile regulations against American trade in order to take advantage of American merchants' services in transporting Caribbean and East Indies goods to trans-Atlantic ports. Pepper, salt, tea, coffee, and sugar were among American merchants' reexports to England and France; however, the same commodities also figured more significantly in the northern states' pattern of consumption as well.[3]

Indeed, between 1790 and 1815 U.S. re-exports averaged $23 million per year, a third of total imports.[4] East Indian goods made up but a small portion of these re-exports; sales of Caribbean sugar and coffee in Europe and of European manufactures in the Americas made up the bulk of U.S. re-exports, just as they made up much of British re-exports. But within the East Indies trade itself, the re-export boom was quite significant, and this is by far the greater point, for it allowed U.S.-sold East India goods to begin to compete with British-sold ones. U.S. customs records do not permit a comparison across the different commodities re-exported. U.S. import and export of pepper, tea, Indian cloth, and Chinese manufactures (nankeens and porcelain) are notable in this. Several commodities less commonly considered by economic historians as "Asian" but that had East Indian sources illustrate the general character of the East Indies re-export trade as well: sugar, coffee, indigo, and cotton.

Pepper

In Magellan's time pepper had been an important global commodity, but by 1800 it had lost its former importance in favor of more valuable goods. Most of the commercially important spices (cinnamon, nutmeg, cloves) were not harvested wild but cultivated on plantations that had long concentrated Dutch interests in Ceylon (cinnamon) and the Banda Islands (cloves). By contrast, pepper was a cheap spice that no one tried to monopolize in the late eighteenth century, that grew abundantly, and that the British raised on plantations only for ease of access and not for want of it. Beyond Sumatra, Travancore and Mysore in southwestern India and Penang in Malaya produced commercially significant supplies of pepper.

Most pepper reached the United States from Sumatra, the large island in the west of the Indonesian archipelago. The region was nominally Dutch, though the British maintained a trading post there at Bencoolen (during the Revolutionary War, some American prisoners of war were put to work picking peppers on Bencoolen plantations). Most of the island littoral and almost all its interior were controlled by local potentates, and though sometimes a lone Dutch official was there to keep watch on Sumatran trade, more often one was not. Nathaniel Bowditch, master of the *Putnam,* was there in 1803. Bowditch was a careful man with facts and figures, an amateur statistician as well as a captain and supercargo; his attention to detail seems to have endeared him to the *Putnam*'s owners. He recalled the cutthroat bargaining of the Sumatran coast in some detail. Captains contracted with the "Datoo," or local ruler, for pepper on arrival. If a second vessel arrived the Datoo might split between them the pepper that was brought down daily to the beach or, for a price, load one vessel first and leave the other waiting (for some time, if the supply ran out). Thus American captains preferred to take on pepper alone, lest their compatriots pay to deny them a supply. There was no trust lost between the Americans and the Sumatrans, either. The Americans weighed the pepper with their own scales (which, others noted, were sometimes rigged), while the Sumatrans demanded payment for the day's weight each evening, "being unwilling to trust their property in the hands of those they deal with." Bowditch also recommended against prepayment, "as it could often be difficult to get either pepper or money" for it afterward.[5]

American purchases on the Sumatra coast were large enough to move the local market. In 1803 the price was "10 to 11 dollars per pecul," an increase from a low of eight in earlier years; with "near 30 sail of American vessels on the coast," Bowditch judged "demand for [pepper] had risen the price considerably." He noticed that "several of the Natives" spoke English well enough to transact business. As usual in the Indies, silver dollars were the "current coin." If an American could buy no pepper for his silver, he would sail along the coast until he found somewhere he could. With so many local entities there was almost always a supply of pepper and a demand for silver somewhere.[6]

In the 1790s, U.S. merchants worked their way into the world pepper market: by the end of the decade they routinely brought in several million pounds of pepper a year from Asia. In the years for which import data are available (October 1, 1789–September 30, 1791, and October 1, 1794–September 30, 1815), U.S. merchants imported 54 million pounds of pepper in U.S. vessels, more than 97 percent of which came from the East Indies. By seeking their own supply, American merchants not only cut out the European middleman, but, given a chance, stood to become middleman to Europe.[7]

Most pepper brought from Asia was not consumed in the United States but re-exported to Europe. In the years for which both import and export records are available (1790–1791, 1794/1795–1814/1815), the United States imported 62 million pounds of pepper and re-exported 56 million pounds of it—more than 90 percent of the pepper brought in (see Figure 4.1). Some European vessels transshipped pepper through the United States as well; and the import figure here includes 8 million pounds of pepper arrived in foreign-owned vessels over the same years. Much of this 8 million may have been "laundered" through U.S. customs for re-export to Europe, perhaps by British or French merchants evading the other country's commercial restrictions. Since the goods imported on foreign vessels were more likely to be foreign-owned than goods imported on U.S. vessels, only importations on U.S. vessels are considered as the trade of U.S. merchants (U.S. cargoes on foreign vessels and foreign cargoes on U.S vessels are presumed to cancel one another out, roughly).[8] However, since export data do not distinguish between U.S. and foreign-owned shipping, total U.S. imports on both American and foreign-owned vessels are the necessary basis of comparison when comparing imports to exports.[9]

Where did these millions of pounds of pepper go? Mostly to France, to French-occupied Europe, and to the neutral ports nearby (even in a Federalist era American merchants were quite catholic about their trading partners). In the years for which export data show destination (October 1, 1790–September 30, 1799), 31 percent of U.S. pepper exports went to France. The Hanseatic towns, neutrals on the periphery of the French Wars, took 17 percent, likely redistributing it into Germany and the French-controlled Rhineland. Such volumes were significant enough to make the United States, according to one historian of U.S.-German trade in this period, Europe's "most important neutral marketplace."[10] Spain took 16 percent, almost all of which came after the Spanish had switched to the French side in 1796. "Italy," still merely a geographic expression, took a further 10 percent.

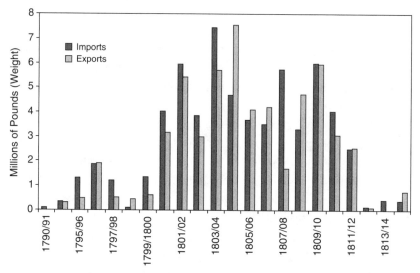

Figure 4.1 U.S. Pepper Imports and Exports, 1790/1791, 1794/1795–1814/1815

Source: ASP, passim. Each year given here represent the twelve- month period prior to Septemeber 30 of the year indicated.

Although specific Italian ports or states are not named, the peninsula's political alignments—partially neutral and partially allied
with France—would suggest a variety of ports capable of shipping
goods onward to French zones nearby. The Netherlands imported
an additional 9 percent, almost all coming (as in Spain) after the
Dutch had allied with France. Smaller shares went to the Caribbean. In all, 56 percent of U.S. pepper re-exports went to France
and its allies, with another 27 percent distributed to neighboring
neutral states.[11] U.S. exports to France of pepper or any other
good were not uniformly easy; individual merchants were liable to
fall afoul of a capriciously enforced edict or an overbearing bu-
reaucrat. Americans, as British merchants, paid off officials, as did
the U.S. captain in Trieste who "paid the French Consul, a Bribe
for Certifying that the above Coffee (w[hi]ch was imported from
Jamaica & Demerara/is the production of a French Colony)." The
Quasi-War, the undeclared shooting match that emerged between
the United States and France between 1798 and 1800, certainly
cut into the U.S. re-export trade as well, but U.S. re-exporters
faced no more difficulties than British smugglers did.[12]

Seeing the American pepper trade in action, Bencoolen officials
increased their purchases of pepper from native Sumatrans. After a
trial run in 1799, in 1801 the Bencoolen commissioner proposed to
Henry Dundas expanding pepper purchases so as "to take the pepper trade out of the hands of the Americans, & to transport the
foreign pepper to London."[13] Bencoolen bought a stock of Sumatran pepper in 1804, sending it to London invoiced at 9 pence a
pound.[14] This was supposed to "exclude" Americans from Sumatran trade, thereby protecting "the interests of the Company and
the nation."[15] But continued American trade with Sumatra increased
the Atlantic pepper supply and drove down the price. By 1806 U.S.
traders were underselling the Company in Europe, with London
pepper prices falling to less than what Bencoolen had invoiced.[16]
The directors ordered that "no more of this pepper be purchased
on any terms or conditions whatever [for] Europe,"[17] and blamed
the Bencoolen commissioner for the loss and a "total disregard to
the interests of the Company."[18] The Company simply could not
get pepper to London cheaply enough.[19] "Europe having been for

some years past supplied with pepper by the Americans," the Court explained in 1806, "our warehouses in London are filled with pepper, and the price of which is low beyond all former example."[20] By 1810 there were 17 million pounds of pepper stocked in its London warehouses.[21] Americans were probably not as successful re-exporting Chinese tea and Indian cloth as they were re-exporting Sumatran pepper. Yet Americans did re-export Chinese tea and Indian cloth around the Atlantic in competition with the English East India Company—and they did so enough to prevent the Company from dominating east-west trade.

Tea

Before the 1830s, the tea consumed in the West was grown in China, much of it in the hills of Anhui and Fujian provinces. From these places it was shipped by riverboat to Canton, and there sold to Westerners for silver.[22] In the years for which import data are available (October 1, 1789–September 30, 1791, and October 1, 1794–September 30, 1815), U.S. merchants imported more than 84 million pounds of tea, over 96 percent of which came directly from China.[23] The United States imported only 1 million pounds of foreign-carried tea beyond this, suggesting that few foreign merchants were interested in "laundering" tea through the United States to Europe. Thus the effect of the American tea trade on the political economy of British re-exports was, at least initially, more muted than the effects of other East Indian goods.

In the 1790s U.S. tea importers focused on the American domestic market. Little tea was re-exported to Europe until 1800, and between October 1, 1795, and September 30, 1815, only 27 percent of U.S. tea imports were resold abroad. The difference—nearly three-quarters of U.S. tea imports—went into American teacups (see Figure 4.2a). Americans reverted to their old colonial taste for tea; even Thomas Paine, a man of impeccable Revolutionary credentials, drank it. Visitors to his farm in New Rochelle, New York noted that the old radical dried the leaves and thriftily reused them. Indeed, the beverage and the customs around it—a visitor paying a call, a host serving tea—enjoyed a revival in American society, even in the nation's capital. Thomas Twining, whose father ran the eponymic tea firm, visited Philadelphia in 1796 and found tea drinking common even at breakfast. He sipped a cup with Quakers immediately after his arrival and noticed "several members of both Houses of Congress" taking it in their rooming house after dinner.[24]

U.S. customs records reveal nothing about where tea re-exported after 1799 went. Customs do, however, note what sorts of tea were re-exported—showing a pronounced emphasis on black teas, with bohea re-exports spiking in 1800 and again in 1803 and with souchong re-exports remaining strong for the remainder of the Napoleonic Wars. Whoever these overseas consumers were, they preferred their tea black. Anecdotal evidence, at least, supports the suspicion that re-exports flowed to France and the Continent. Thus one French memorialist, having visited Macau, reported to Napoleon that Americans, "just as active and even greedier than the British," not only purchased tea in China for "their own luxury" but also exported "the surplus to less-active nations, or to those whom circumstances did not permit to take a direct part in this commerce." Indeed, it seemed "the better part of their [the Americans'] Chinese teas, nankeens and sugar candies are consumed in [our] colonies and in France."[25]

The comparative volatilities of British and American tea re-exports provide another clue to where American teas were headed. While British tea re-export levels remained largely unchanged in the early 1800s, barely responding to changes in British tea importation or to the European war, U.S. tea re-exports varied wildly, first growing with tea imports and then falling with the embargo and the War of 1812 (see Figure 4.2b). The standard deviation of British tea re-exports was 11 percent of average annual tea re-exports in the decade between 1802 and 1812. In the same period U.S. tea re-exports had a more volatile standard deviation of 54 percent. U.S. tea re-exports evinced a variability akin to that of U.S. coffee re-exports (60 percent of average annual exports) or British coffee re-exports (47 percent). British tea re-exports, by contrast, varied little because they were hemmed in by the East

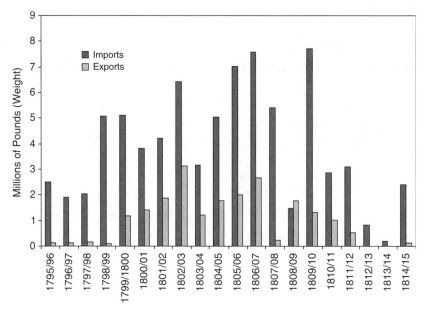

Figure 4.2a U.S. Tea Imports and Exports, 1795/1796–1814/1815

Source: ASP, passim. Each year given here represent the twelve- month period prior to Septemeber 30 of the second year indicated.

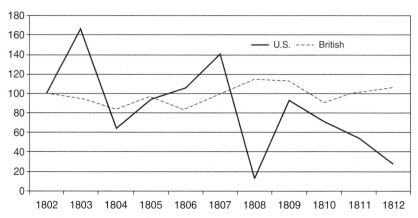

Figure 4.2b Comparative Volatility in U.S. and British Tea Re-exports, 1802–1812 (1802 = 100)

Sources: François Crouzet, *L'économie britannique et le blocus continental (1806–1813),* vol. 2 (Paris: Presses Universitaires de France, 1958), 890; *ASP*, passim. British data (denoted as value in pounds sterling) represent calendar years; U.S. data (denoted as mass in pounds weight) represent a twelve-month period ending September 30 of the year indicated.

India Company.[26] Company dirigistes regarded this stabilization of tea re-exports as beneficial—a mark of superior business structure, rather than of opportunities missed.

By the 1820s U.S. merchants were re-exporting tea to Canada as well, undermining the Company monopoly there. American tea sales to Canada became something of a scandal. "Three fourths of the Teas consumed in the Canadas are supplied by Smuggling from the United States," claimed one Canadian legislator in 1822.[27] Many Canadians urged legalization either of a private Canada-China trade or of tea imports from the United States, or at minimum that the Company send ships from China to Canada direct. The East India Company sent its own Captain Weltden to Canada in 1820 and again in 1823 to investigate the illicit U.S.-Canadian tea trade. Weltden claimed that the "American merchants supply the Colonies with Teas, and the manufactures of China at half the price a regular dealer can procure them from in England."[28] The Montreal Committee of Trade added that teas and silks were "sold in Canada 50 per cent under the cost and charges of similar articles imported from Great Britain."[29] Imports from Britain were kept up simply to mask the much larger tea trade with the United States; tea merchants, Weltden argued, imported Company tea only so they could sell American tea from the same tin. From Boston, tea was smuggled into New Brunswick by the St. John River. From New York, tea went up the "grand Western Canal" to Buffalo and Rochester, where, perhaps hyperbolically, Weltden thought "every store is a Tea Warehouse, and every Storekeeper a Smuggler supplying the British Coast of Lake Erie with Contraband Goods, whence they are forwarded to the remotest parts of Upper Canada." He estimated that between two-thirds and three-quarters of the tea in Nova Scotia, New Brunswick, and Upper and Lower Canada were imported from the United States. Thus, though Canadians were brewing tea "two or even three times a day,"[30] their taste for tea benefited the Company but little. Smuggling between the U.S. and Canada had been going on since the French Wars, all parties agreed, and the extensive U.S.-Canadian boundary made interdiction all but impossible. In the port of Quebec alone, legal tea imports from Britain fell by over 70 percent between 1814 and 1822, even though both the Canadian population and per capita tea consumption (the latter according to anecdotal evidence) increased.[31] This suggests significant importation of tea from the United States (barring a sudden Canadian revulsion toward tea), but there are few comprehensive customs sources to verify a general re-export of East Indian goods from the United States to Canada or the British Caribbean.

All this tea being re-exported and consumed was hardly monolithic: there were different types with different markets. The finest black tea in American customs registers, Souchong, was made of large, thick leaves plucked from prime bushes at just the right time (midday) and in the right weather (fine). The first picking of the season commanded a premium. The leaves fermented in the open air and, once red marks of fermentation appeared, were roasted. Workers rolled them to extract liquid, and the roast-and-roll process was repeated several times. Finally, the leaves dried over a fire. Congou, a lower grade, had thinner leaves and was rolled fewer times. Bohea, the lowest-grade black tea, was slashed off the shrubs in bunches (the stems, though dross, adding to the weight), briefly fermented in the sun, and then roasted and dried in one operation. Bohea had its uses: milk and sugar buried its taste well enough (an admixture ill suited for the smokier Souchong), and no one could tell from which kind of tea punch was made. But to the Western connoisseur, Souchong was better. Chinese tea drinkers went further, valuing a tea whose flavor could retain a taste through multiple steepings, as opposed to Bohea, which did not take reuse well and, like most low-grade black tea today, imparted most of its flavor within the first thirty seconds after wetting. Green teas exhibited a similar range, from Fine Hyson to Hyson Skin to Gunpowder and Twankay. These teas remained green because they were not fermented before roasting.[32]

American consumers had access to all these grades of tea. Their tastes in this regard suggest one reason why the American tea market was distinct from Europe's: initially, American drinkers preferred Bohea. This preference dated at least as far back as the 1760s, when American colonists drank smuggled Dutch Bohea in place of finer, English Company grades, and lasted at least through the early republic. Bohea was cheap, a sort of people's tea. By contrast, British consumers preferred higher-grade teas such as Congou or Souchong. The East India Company prided itself on the quality of its teas and routinely denigrated American-purchased teas as trash unfit for Britons (though British teas preferences were likely affected by the Company's selection).

In the two decades between October 1, 1795, and September 30, 1815, high-grade teas (Hyson and Souchong) constituted only 31 percent of American net tea imports by volume. Meanwhile, the lower-grade Bohea and "other green"—an inexact but hardly flattering designation—occupied the remaining two-thirds of the domestic market. However, within these two decades there were considerable changes in the teas Americans chose to consume. Increasingly, early nineteenth-century Americans eschewed Bohea for Souchong and Hyson for generic green; that is, they moved upmarket in black tea and down-market in green, simultaneously. Whereas in 1795 and 1796 Bohea represented more than 90 percent of net black tea imports, by 1814 and 1815, it made up less than 10 percent. At the same time a down-market shift occurred among green teas as American tea drinkers abandoned Hyson, which occupied over 50 percent of the green tea market in 1795 and 1796, for other green teas, which occupied over 85 percent of the market by 1814 and 1815. In general, American preference in this period shifted from black to green tea and particularly to those "other greens," and therefore remained down-market overall.

Asian Manufactures

U.S. merchants also imported East Indian manufactures. This included Chinese porcelain and nankeens, a form of cloth used to make breeches, and Indian piece goods, a term for various weaves sold by the piece or set length. Porcelain remained part of upper-class American tea drinking. Not everyone could afford such finery—Bohea drinkers especially—but a greater proportion of the population may have been able to afford porcelain over time. Benjamin Franklin's dismay at his wife's purchase of a porcelain set (he thought it extravagant) suggests the extent of the population which, in the late colonial era, had yet to purchase fine china.

Of the various merchandise, as the customs collectors generically termed all these goods, the largest amount by value was British Indian cloth. In the years between October 1, 1794, and September 30, 1815, American merchants purchased $43.7 million worth of "merchandise" from India, most of it cloth from Bengal, along with $31 million of merchandise (nankeens and porcelain) from China. The next largest source of such goods, the Dutch East Indies, provided only $0.6 million worth over the same period (pepper, tea, and other groceries priced by the pound were enumerated separately).[33]

Catch-all terms such as "merchandise" and "piece goods," though frustrating, suggest the complexity of the Indian cloth market. The cloth came in all varieties of patterns and colors, from blue handkerchiefs to long bolts of red cottons and light, white muslins. Each bolt came one to two yards wide and twenty to thirty yards long, ready to take whatever form a seamstress or tailor could give it. The weavers were spread out across the towns and districts of the Indian east coast, and the local variety of their products deterred U.S. customs collectors from grading or classifying them. Labeling all such cloth "merchandise" and charging a tariff based on its purchase price was easier. Even merchants found the profusion of names daunting, many calling them after the towns they had come from: "Salempore" this or "Pulicat" that, as a way to denote the pattern. "Bengal requires a very correct knowledge of the markets & of piece goods which is a 'sine qua non' & a work of time," one merchant explained.[34] But supercargoes who wished to familiarize themselves with the Indian market were wise not to fixate on terms: "It often happens that the names of the Cotton goods change & therefore they are not always distinguishable by their names," another merchant wrote.[35] It was better to distinguish a cloth by its weave and its prospective market.

It is impossible to determine how much of these manufactures were consumed in the United States or resold abroad, since the "merchandise" that U.S. customs registers saw re-exported included more than East Indian goods.[36] In all likelihood, Indian cloth met a ready market both in the United States and abroad. American textile manufacturing was still in its infancy in 1800. Those mills that did exist made cotton yarn, not cloth. Most U.S. cloth was woven at home, some was produced through the "putting out" system, and the remainder was imported. This last was a high-end product, and among imported fabrics Americans found Indian cloth particularly fine (especially white muslins, which were better weaves and, being blank, could be stamped or painted according to the desired taste back in the United States). Even in Britain industrialists were only beginning to match the complexity and fineness of Indian weaves. U.S. re-exports of cloth were likely common, too. At least one British merchant traveling in the United States remarked on the increasing re-exports of Indian cloth to the Caribbean.[37] It is not hard to imagine that the lighter Indian weaves held appeal there.

Crown and Company officials were concerned that U.S. East India goods would reach the remaining British American colonies and corrode the re-export of the Company's goods from London. As early as 1789, Phineas Bond, British Consul in Philadelphia, argued that "as the Quantity of India Goods imported into North America, so far surpasses the ordinary Consumption of the Inhabitants, it is very clear that a Vent is found to Europe, as well as to the West India Islands, for whatever Articles do not command a ready sale here." Yet Bond conceded that he lacked "precise Information" on the subject, Philadelphia merchants being surprisingly reticent with their trade secrets.[38] The British Board of Trade likewise lacked precise information, but still urged that American smugglers in the Caribbean be prevented from colluding with British planters, "hovering" offshore, or coming in from Dutch St. Eustatius.[39] The Board later found that "the supply of the Islands from the States of America of East India Goods is highly injurious of the Revenue as well to the Navigation of this Country, and to the Interests of the East India Company." The Board was particularly upset by reports from Barbados that Americans were smuggling liquors and "even Nankeens, Muslins, and other East India Goods" onto the island, though all the Board could do was admonish the Admiralty and the islanders to try harder to stop it.[40] In 1808

Company directors complained that U.S. sales of India goods abroad caused "evident interference with our own exports of Indian Goods from London to foreign Europe and our American and West Indian Colonies."[41] The following year, Americans were said to be selling Indian goods in British-occupied Curaçao as well.[42] Reliable figures for U.S. re-exports of Indian cottons to the Caribbean are lacking, but, nevertheless, show that re-export trade did exist, and merchants' papers reveal how that trade functioned. The papers of one merchant in particular are an immensely detailed and previously untapped source.

Israel Thorndike

Born in 1757, Israel Thorndike, son of a Beverly farmer-mariner, turned out to be a very successful and lucky man. In 1772, when he was seventeen years old, he already owned more than six vessels. Most were fishing boats, but two were engaged in international trade. During the American Revolution he captained several privateering vessels, and soon after the war went into partnership with a few local merchants; as happened so often, they were his in-laws (Thorndike married three times). By 1800 he was trading independently.[43]

Thorndike's concerns were "chiefly to the East Indies," as he explained to one Spanish correspondent, though he expanded his business into re-exporting Indian cargoes to Europe, too. Both aspects of his business thrived, and his neighbors joked, half-bitterly perhaps, that "if he put a pebble on a shingle and sent it out to sea, it would come back in the shape of a dollar."[44] Thorndike did sell some imported textiles domestically, but this took time, as retailers bought up his stock only gradually. A single cargo could take almost a year to sell off, as with the cargo of Indian textiles from the *Mary*, which sold from March 1798 to February 1799 in more than a dozen transactions with nine different buyers. At the end of that time, Thorndike grossed $22,756.[45] The next year, when he was instructing the captain of the *Cyrus* for a voyage to Calcutta, Thorndike specified that his goal was to buy goods "best suited for this

Market," but added the latest prices at Livorno and suggested that the captain buy goods for Italy if he found them selling cheaply enough in Calcutta.[46] When the *Cyrus* returned, Thorndike hired his son-in-law, Bostonian Ebenezer Francis, to wholesale the goods, paying him a 1.25 percent commission. The sales, as with those of the *Mary*, took several months (July to November 1801), during which period Francis sold the goods to fifteen buyers. After commission and charges, Thorndike received $24,419 for the fifty-eight bales Francis sold. Thorndike shipped additional consignments to other addresses: to Beverly, Massachusetts (28 bales), across the Atlantic to Bordeaux (31) and Genoa (8), and down the coast to New York (11), Philadelphia (21), and Norfolk, Virginia (9).[47]

The shipment to France had specific instructions: sell immediately and for as much as possible. Take "specie or good bills well Endorsed on London + by no means sell them for paper money or on Credit," Thorndike wrote in 1801. Lastly, the proceeds were to be remitted to Thorndike's London friend, merchant Thomas Dickason, a silent British investor in many of Thorndike's Indian voyages.[48] Dickason's son resided in the Boston area to attend to the father's American mercantile connections.[49] The French consignment was valued at over $12,000.[50]

Thorndike re-exported to Italy as well. On the *Mary* he sent a cargo of salt cod and Indian cloth worth about $35,000 to Genoa.[51] As usual, he wrote ahead, asking commission houses in Spain and on the Italian coast to advise his captain on local markets and to forward advice to Barcelona and Genoa. In January 1802 Captain Thissel and the *Mary* arrived in Genoa and found information from Thorndike's Livorno correspondents indicating the latest Italian fashions (black, of course) and apprising him of the market for fish.[52] Thissel looked for buyers and in mid-February received another letter, this time from correspondents in Barcelona apprising him of the market there. But, they warned, "East Indian Cotton Stuffs and every other like Stuffs white or printed are not admitted here."[53]

By then the fish had spoiled. Thorndike had tried to pawn off a few barrels of old fish by mixing them in with a newer salting, but they had all rotted and the cloth stank of it. What was more, the cloth was substandard even without the smell. Thorndike's Genoan correspondents complained that the "quantity of Ginghams, Chintz, and other coloured articles dishearten them more than the quality of the white goods, that are inferior to what comes from the English East India company & the finer assortments would command a more ready & advantageous sale here . . . in future."[54] Yet even though the Genoan merchants panned Thorndike's goods, they still bought them; by the start of March Thissel had sold all sixty-nine bales of Indian cloth for a net profit of 94,811.14 Genoan pounds, and the fish for another 71,000-odd more.[55] And this was a *difficult* voyage.

Tarbox Moulton was master for another re-export voyage. He departed Salem in December 1801 and spent that winter and spring peddling Thorndike's East Indian goods throughout the Caribbean. His cargo included a bewildering assortment of Indian cloth (handkerchiefs mostly), cheaper cloth than the long bolts of muslin that the Company specialized in, sorted by color and origin—"Red Madras," "Ventipoliam Washed Red," "Brown Red Pulicat," "Brown & Blue." In addition he packed ginghams, chintz, and nankeens, slightly higher-market fabrics. To that Thorndike added tea and nutmeg, along with duck, Russian sheeting, cordage, fish, and a few bottles of Bordeaux—all things Caribbean plantations did not produce. Taking care that the *Two Friends* not be stopped by privateers, the schooner's manifest certified that its owners were all Americans.[56]

By December 1801, prices in most Atlantic markets were depressed, as merchants, on hearing news of European peace negotiations, were unwilling to pay wartime prices for goods they thought they could get more cheaply in a few months' time. Thorndike consequently was less sanguine about Moulton's voyage than he had been about earlier ones. He was more interested in selling "at saving prices," "at tolerable prices," or even simply "without loss" than in making a killing. But he still instructed Moulton to tramp the Caribbean, stopping at every port and peddling whatever answered well:

> Proceed to Guadaloupe . . . from thence to Trinidad . . . & if you should not sell the whole there you will go to Cumina [Cumana,

in Sucre Province, present-day Venezuela] or Laguira [La Guaira,
near to Caracas, present-day Venezuela] . . . or to any other Port
on the Spanish Main . . . then proceed to Hispaniola calling first
at the citty of St. Domingo & from that down that Island into the
Bite of Leagan [Léogane, near Port-au-Prince] touching at all the
Ports to try the markets untill you can sell the whole or the greatest Part of the outward cargo.[57]

Captain Moulton followed the instructions to the letter. At Marie-
Galante, an out-island of Guadeloupe, he started peddling.[58] On
Guadeloupe proper he sold off a bit more of his cargo and with
the proceeds shipped back two vessels laden with coffee and sugar.
The rest of the voyage was a comedy of errors, but it is a testament
to the value of an East Indian cargo that, despite all his setbacks,
Moulton managed to send home as much as he did.

The Best Fishing Is in Troubled Waters

In the winter of 1801–1802, as Moulton sailed for the Caribbean,
Bonaparte sent General Charles Leclerc to Saint Domingue with
troops to reassert French control. Leclerc ordered that any American ship trading with Toussaint's forces be confiscated. But Leclerc
controlled only the ports of Cap Français and Port-au-Prince.[59]
Moulton did not go to either, but the French still stopped him at
Monte Cristi, demanding that he deliver up his provisions and
cargo for their government and their war effort, which was not
going well. Moulton would have to sail to Cap Français for payment, "if they see fit to pay me" at all, he wrote Thorndike. So he
refused to deliver up anything until he was paid, and in cash, "in
Consequence of which I Lay their twelve Days with a gard on
Board and not being admitted to Sell a Single Article." On the thir-
teenth day the French stormed the vessel and took what they
wanted by force. They told Moulton to "go to the Cape and to the
Ordernater and he would Emform me what he was agoing to give
me for it and When to be Paid." They took the "only Saleable articles" left and then magnanimously told him he could sell the rest to
whomever he saw fit.[60] He sailed to Cap Français in mid-February

but could not get payment, so he began peddling the remainders as best he could.

At Trinidad, held by the British, he managed enough sales to send a vessel laden with sugar and money to the United States. But he found all the neighboring Spanish ports "shut to Americans."[61] He left at the start of April for Santo Domingo, the main port on the eastern side of Saint Domingue.[62] He arrived on April 12 and "to my Great Surprise find there is an Imbargo on." Still, perhaps after a few bribes, he could write that he had "Sold Some Part of my Cargo here, and Rather Expect to Sell the Remainder, to Say that is if I Can git the first Cost."[63] But, to his unwarranted surprise, the same thing that had happened at Monte Cristi happened at Santo Domingo. At the end of April he wrote Thorndike that the

> government hase Prevented me of that for they have taken it without money or Price But They Say they will give me a Receit, that they have Received it, and that I must go to the Cape and make an agrement with the Commesary their, But what it will be I dont know, and weather they will Pay any thing, it is all unsartain.[64]

More cautious men might not have gone back to Saint Domingue, but Moulton had because the profits seemed worth the risk. As the American consul to Guadeloupe explained on news of a slave revolt there, the best fishing is in troubled waters.[65]

By the start of June Moulton had straightened things out enough with the local authorities to make up a shipment of mahogany to send along to Salem, which he purchased from a local Spanish merchant house with 2,740 pesos worth of Madras handkerchiefs.[66]

In July, he headed over to Cap Français, where he made no note of receiving any payment for the seized goods, but where he did sell off the sundry remaining East India goods (tea, handkerchiefs, ginghams, and Luddalore dimity), along with some other goods, to the French garrison there and loaded up on coffee for the return voyage to Salem.[67] The French seemed desperate for every sort of good at Cap Français. Their invasion had wreaked havoc on the region, and a note of Moulton's from mid-March made special mention of the "India, China and English Goods" in demand there.[68]

All told, and despite having his cargo twice seized without payment, Moulton's sales came somewhere between $33,000 and $38,000, all of which he spent on local produce to be shipped up north to New York and New England.[69]

American merchants like Thorndike thus acted as centrifugal forces, redistributing East Indian cargoes around the Atlantic world and across imperial boundaries, sometimes successfully, sometimes less so, undermining authorities who sought to control or limit the flow of their cargoes at every turn. From Salem Thorndike was only a few weeks' sailing time behind the latest news from Europe and the Caribbean, and yet he remained so unsure of the conditions his captains would find on arrival that he asked them to try every port they could—British, French, Spanish, or otherwise. His instructions amounted to little more than a preferred order in which the command "to every port" was to be executed. Thorndike had to leave to his captains the decisions about where to trade, what to trade, and for how much to trade it because the warfare and slave uprisings wracking the Caribbean made anything but the vaguest planning difficult. How, then, could the East India Company with all its committees and boards and meetings and bureaucracy keep up with demand in the British Caribbean (the political boundaries of which were constantly changing) for East Indian goods? In war, such planning was simply impossible, with the British Navy taking French, Dutch, Spanish, Danish, and Swedish islands; with French counterinvasions appearing from the sea; with both sides spread too thin; and with slave revolts arising as a result in Saint Domingue, Guadeloupe, and Grenada, to name only the most prominent uprisings.

Thorndike compensated for this by stocking his Caribbean-bound ships with a little of everything. Americans had been selling generalized cargoes to Caribbean planters for centuries; that part of U.S.-Caribbean trade had not changed with the general war, and it was easy enough to add a few India goods to diversify the outbound cargo further.[70] This also had the effect of spreading East Indian cargoes across as many re-export voyages as possible, so that if some fell into the hands of a confiscatory "Order-nater" or were tainted by the stink of rotten fish, the rest were not. This was a very different tact from the Company's, which concentrated investments in Asia trade in a few ships, saw none of the profits of the further re-export of its East India goods, and consequently had less direct information about what goods might sell abroad.

Unlikely Cargoes

Many typically "Caribbean" crops grew in Asia as well. As the Caribbean wars and slave rebellions escalated, and because Americans could not always obtain enough of the produce of Saint Domingue and other islands to meet demand, U.S. merchants began turning to Asia for raw cotton, indigo, coffee, and brown sugar. Of these, sugar and coffee became quite prominent. Sugar (especially that coming from Bengal) served as a ballast for Indian textiles, and Javan coffee developed its own place in the U.S. market. In the United States sugar and coffee were for the most part Caribbean in origin, but in the 1790s an important minority of both goods came from Asia. With U.S. sugar and coffee imports plummeting to half or a third of earlier levels because of the wars and revolts in the Caribbean, ventures to Asia for such goods became increasingly attractive.

Of all American imports, brown sugar was far and away the most voluminous; on average, 81.7 million pounds a year arrived on U.S. vessels, dwarfing the 1 to 5 million pounds of pepper and tea that came in annually. Over 1.5 *billion* pounds of brown sugar were imported between 1789 and 1810. Most was Caribbean; between October 1, 1789, and September 30, 1815, only 9 percent of the American-carried U.S. sugar supply came from Asia.[71] Much of this was produced and promoted at the behest of the East India Company's employees in India, who were looking for additional products to export to Britain even if, as some believed, sugar-planting in Bengal flew directly in the face of the interests of Britain's Caribbean planters. Sir Francis Baring, East India Company director and financial advisor to the government, thought Bengali sugar could never be shipped back to Europe at a profit. It was "too soft to be used for the extensive purpose of general consumption, like that of the West Indies," he wrote.[72] Still, Company employees oversaw a massive expansion of sugar culture in Bengal, expanding the sugar plantocracy from the Caribbean to India. Britons would later carry it to Mauritius as well.

Coffee was the other major "Caribbean" commodity Americans imported from Asia. Between 1789 and 1815 an average of 41.7 million pounds entered the United States annually; 19 percent of the U.S.-carried supply came from Java, Bourbon, and Mocha.[73] Even greater shares of U.S. indigo and raw cotton imports came from Asia, though these products, particularly cotton, were also grown within the United States, so that imports represented a fairly small share of overall U.S. demand.[74] Nevertheless, Asian sugar and coffee provided a notable supplement to the tea, spice, and cloth more commonly considered East Indian.

There were more whimsical cargoes as well. Consider that of Jacob Crowninshield, who belonged to a family of India traders. Jacob, at age twenty-four, captained a ship that by November 1795 reached Calcutta, where he bought an elephant. He explained to his brothers that

> We take home a fine young elephant two years old, at $450. It is almost as large as a very large ox, and I dare say we shall get it home safe, if so it will bring at least $5000. We shall at first be obliged to keep it in the southern states until it becomes hardened to the climate. I suppose you will laugh at the scheme, but I do not mind that, will turn elephant driver. We have plenty of water at the Cape and St. Helena. This was my plan. Ben [Jacob's brother] did not come into it, so if it succeeds, I ought to have the whole credit and honor, too. Of course you know it will be a great thing to carry the first elephant to America.[75]

Miraculously, the animal survived. Crowninshield worried that his 3,500-gallon water supply might not suffice and made watering stops at Mauritius and St. Helena on the return. It was well he did: the elephant drank as much as the entire crew. At St. Helena, Nathaniel Hathorne, first mate (and father to Nathaniel Hawthorne, the author), noted that they brought on board "greens for the Elephant" as well.

By April 1796 the elephant had made it to New York. The *New York Argus* reported:

> The *America* has brought home an elephant from Bengal, in perfect health. It is the first ever seen in America, and a very great curiosity. It is a female, two years old, and of the species that grow to an enormous size. The animal is sold for $10,000, being supposed to be the greatest price ever given for an animal in Europe or America.[76]

The $10,000 elephant went on tour up and down the American coast, from Savannah to Salem. It was a first-rate curiosity and living, breathing proof of the strange things that came out of the East Indies. When the elephant made it to Salem in the summer of 1797—having acclimated, perhaps, to the climate—the Reverend William Bentley tried to sneak a peak but found "the crowd of spectators forbad me any but a general & superficial view of him." The keeper kept the elephant oiled. The animal was already over six feet high, and perhaps not too pleased with his master. It "could not be persuaded to lie down," Bentley noted.

> The Keeper repeatedly mounted him but he persisted in shaking him off. Bread & Hay were given him and he took bread out of the pockets of the Spectators. He also drank porter & drew the cork, conveying the liquor from his trunk into his throat. His Tusks were just to be seen beyond the flesh, & it was said had been broken. We say *his* because of the common language. It is a female & teats appeared just behind the fore-legs.[77]

She was a curiosity; her own traveling, alcoholic circus; and a part of a pattern of Americans experiencing exciting, different, and new things (as well as people and animals) from the east. P. T. Barnum's circus followed in this tradition, and by the 1830s it included not just elephants in its show, but even Chinese men.[78]

The elephant was not the only thing Crowninshield brought back. He carried a cargo of coffee and piece goods, too. (One wonders whether the cloth took on an elephant smell.) Yet these piece goods, like the elephant, were listed simply as "merchandise" by U.S. customs officials. It was these piece goods—along with teapots, shawls, and handkerchiefs, the material goods of the Indies—that made the idea of Asia seem real to individual Americans. Thus, two days before seeing the elephant, Reverend Bentley noted "the funeral of a young Black," at which the mourners "were dressed from common life up to the highest fashions": they wore everything from "plain homespun [to] rich Indian Muslins."[79] To Bentley, it was a sure sign of how demotic and widespread the taste for eastern luxuries had become.

Some merchants took to maintaining Chinese or Indian servants. Their households were stocked with exotica—a Qing vase, fine tea, silk robes, an Indian umbrella, an aboriginal weapon. Andreas Everard Van Braam Houckgeest, the Dutch Ambassador to China, after being turned out by the Chinese court and finding that his Orangist politics made him unwelcome in Patriot Netherlands, set up a house in Philadelphia in the late 1790s complete with five Chinese servants, a Malay *amah,* a massive oriental garden, and a whole collection of Asiana with which to awe his American friends.[80] Thomas Twining was equally thrilled to show off his Indian "curiosities" in the city, including the skin of the goat from which cashmere was made (settling a dispute about whether the wool came from sheep or goats); a "Cabul sheep" that grazed on William Bingham's lawn; a "Bengal cow" already attracting "numerous visitors" to its stable; and the 100-pound bottom shell of a massive oyster, which he had collected from "a heap of oyster-shells at Madras." This last he donated to the "National Museum."[81] Such whimsy and exotica were window dressing for the boom in U.S.-Asian trade, but it was the sort of window dressing that could convince merchants that perhaps they, too, should get involved in the India or China trade to get a slice of the profits from those muslins that everyone seemed to be wearing.

Twining noticed as much. On April 12, 1796, he "Breakfasted" in his boarding house

> as usual, with the Members of Congress, with whom I was now upon easy terms. As we stood round the fire, one of these

gentlemen, Mr. Gallatin [later Jefferson's Secretary of the Treasury], examined the ends of my muslin neckcloth, and much surprise was expressed when I mentioned the cost at Santipore. Many questions were asked me respecting the qualities and prices of the fabrics of India, and it is not impossible that the lowness of the latter suggested the idea of a profitable speculation, the object of almost every American at this period.

Indeed, the low price of Indian cloth in India, and its high price and status in America, compelled many a trader to try sending a parcel of silver to the Indies. Twining found himself in Baltimore later that year, being quizzed on "the information I had collected in different parts of India, respecting the manufactures and commerce of that country." "American merchants," he recalled,

had their attention at this time very much directed to this new and promising branch of commerce; and Mr. Gilmore, one of the principal merchants of Baltimore, and already holding a share in the *India*, was glad to be informed of the names, qualities, prices, and places of manufacture of such fabrics of the interior of India as were suited to the American market. Mr. Gilmore was surprised to find so great a difference between the original cost of many sorts of goods, and the prices exacted from the inexperience of American captains and supercargoes at Calcutta.

Despite, as Twining suggests, sometimes overpaying in India, U.S. merchants could still sell their India goods profitably back home.[82]

As much as East India investments held cachet among American capitalists for their returns and as much as East India goods had a cachet among American consumers for their exoticism, so an eastern voyage held cachet for its crew. As Richard Henry Dana, the Harvard-student-cum-seaman whose account of his skin-and-tallow voyage to the California coast became a best seller, explained,

The style and gentility of a ship and her crew depended upon the length and character of the voyage. An India or China voyage always is *the thing*, and a voyage to the Northwest coast (the Columbia River or Russian America) for furs is romantic and mysterious, and if it takes the ship round the world, by way of the Islands [Hawaii] and China, it out-ranks them all.[83]

Herman Melville explained it much the same way in *Moby Dick*. Compared to a whaling voyage—his ultimate measure—only the prestige of an East Indian voyage came close.

Correspondence Partners

Many U.S. merchants coordinated their re-exports from the United States to Continental Europe with London. Merchants in a given region—called corresponding partners—would receive advance notice of U.S. ships heading to the area. Hence when Thorndike sent a vessel to northern Italy, advices were sent to various merchant houses in the western Mediterranean, allowing the vessel captain, if he sensed a better market nearby, to try another port. Corresponding houses provided the captain with the latest prices and brokered any deals he made in port on commission. Most such merchants were British expatriates (though there were some Americans), brothers or sons in a London firm. American captains, usually monoglots barely out of their teens, would have found much to commend such merchants. If the sale was not paid in specie, the brokering firm might facilitate payment by using a bill of exchange to deposit proceeds from a U.S. sale in Europe into the American merchant's London bank account. Thorndike and any other American merchant of significance maintained an account with a London merchant bank so that, by credit and debit, the London banker could manage the American's transactions with European correspondents. This gave London bankers special prominence in financing American sales to Europe: Dickason did this for Thorndike; the Baring family as well as John Kirwan & Sons did similarly for other American merchants.[84] As Henry Dundas was warned in 1800, American East Indian merchants "were powerfully supported by most eminent houses in London."[85] International financing was potentially corrosive to a country's trading controls and beyond the understanding of all but a few government ministers, so much so that Sir Francis Baring bragged he could have financed Bonaparte's wars from London without Pitt's notice.[86]

The Philadelphia merchant Stephen Girard accumulated vast sums this way, despite a precarious start as a merchant. By early 1810 his account with the Barings held over £100,000 sterling, from which he withdrew heavily and which was replenished by deposits from Hamburg, Denmark, Russia, and the Netherlands—the last of these reaching well over £100,000.[87] In such merchant banking, the book credits of an early generation transformed into capital, which could be deposited, transferred, and withdrawn at will. Debits from these accounts were accounted for as withdrawals from existing funds, as modern bank checks rather than as the "credit" that Thorndike so disparaged and that was little more than an IOU counted against future, theoretical business. Deposits of silver into London bank accounts from sales in Europe helped American merchants move from barter-credit to cash-debit, making their accounts with British banks both more sound and more liquid than previously. American merchants could also trade with each other with greater confidence that debited funds did, in fact, exist.

Such paper was also sold to Western merchants trading to China, but the practice did little to lessen the need for silver since such debits were stronger when backed by silver. They were less liquid than silver (not everyone would accept them), and more "lumpy" (a bill could not be broken up and sold in pieces). On a China voyage large bills had to be saved until reaching China and often were used only if the silver ran out. Any trades made while tramping en route required silver as well. Debit's cumbersome nature (not to mention the discount at which it sold) meant that many captains usually sailed with a full stock of silver, keeping "checks" drawn on the shipowners' accounts only as a reserve.

Men like Baring and Dickason took a central role in directing U.S. re-exports to the Continent. London merchants were well informed of market prices throughout Europe and could suggest various places to sell a cargo. Thus Thorndike's captains often returned to London from a peddling voyage in Europe for new instructions, rather than make the several-week-longer voyage across the Atlantic to Salem. Some even started new voyages to the Indies directly from the River Thames, though the East India Company was hardly pleased. For ventures from London (of which we have no firm number, since they were of doubtful legality), Thorndike and Dickason would be joint investors, Thorndike investing a portion of the silver Dickason held for him and Dickason adding his own. For these voyages, Thorndike's instructions were ridiculously vague, often advising trips to Europe, Asia, or Latin America for a single voyage, leaving the real decisions about cargo and destination with Dickason. On their return from the Indies, these vessels stopped at Dover for instructions and the latest market conditions before peddling their wares in Europe.[88] Business along these lines continued well after the Orders in Council and the Continental Blockade. Stephen Girard did not wind up his business on the Continent and withdraw his funds from London until 1811.

With a portion of U.S. re-exports to the Netherlands, Hamburg, Denmark, and the Baltic funded by London merchant bankers and brokers and British expatriates on the Continent, it is hard to believe that merchants in Britain would have had a difficult time re-exporting their own East Indian goods to Europe if they had goods worth selling. Such American re-exports were hardly secret: even the chairmen of the East India Company's Court of Directors knew that remittances were "made to London on American Account for sales [of India goods] on the Continent."[89] No British law prevented Dickason from buying Indian piece goods at the East India Company's auctions and selling them to France on Thorndike's ship. That both he and Thorndike thought it better to send an American ship docked in the Thames around the world to Bengal and back for East India goods—a trip that might take a year— rather than buying India goods at the Company's auctions and selling them in a few weeks surely testifies to their assumption that the Company could not supply the right goods at the right prices for Europe. Testifying before the House of Lords, the British merchant John Bainbridge agreed that the Mediterranean was "more cheaply supplied with East India and China commodities by the

Americans, than" it could be from London. British smugglers saddled with Company goods could not drive Americans from the European market for Asian goods. Their failure to do so cannot be entirely blamed on the perfidy—real or imagined—of the average British merchant.[90]

CHAPTER FIVE

Merchant Millionaires

During the French Wars, U.S. East India merchants became part of a newly wealthy investing class. This handful of northern merchants became the first millionaires in American history—men rich enough to engage in business on a scale unknown in colonial America. Their wealth, grown in the silver-rich trade to Asia, allowed them access to banking, credit, and trade as business leaders. The growing division of wealth within the merchant class, between the well-capitalized few and the greater number of middling merchants (both sides being among the wealthiest 1 percent of the population), is the subject of this chapter.

Most of this money was business capital, not personal wealth. U.S. merchants traded singly or in partnerships, and entirely at their own risk (there was no limited liability). Thus early national merchants did not live as extravagantly as the term "millionaire" might imply today. And though they certainly accumulated greater fortunes than their late-colonial merchant forbearers, comparisons to contemporary elites elsewhere in the Anglo-Atlantic are harder to draw. Observers drew such comparisons anyway, and certainly some West Indian planters and London bankers lived more extravagantly than American merchants. Opulence is an imperfect measure of wealth, and merchants struggled with this as they attempted to determine what was an appropriate level of expenditure—a pliable and culturally contingent notion that suggested who was a worthy business risk. This was important because, despite their newfound wealth, U.S. merchants still did not have as much operating capital as they might have wished and often invested together. These collaborative enterprises are at the root of the modern competitive American business corporation.

The Early Republic Economy in the North

One is tempted to look for the effects of U.S. re-export and carrying trade not in the wallets of a few rich men, but in economic growth as a whole. And yet U.S. economic growth from 1793 to 1807 has been estimated at 1.08 percent, a third of which is attributable to the carrying trade. One percent is not bad for early modern economic growth, but it is not the rate one might expect from a re-export trade that sold a third of all U.S. imports (East Indian and otherwise) abroad. This has perplexed economic historians: where did the effects of the re-export trade go?[1]

The re-export trade affected the U.S. economy unevenly, benefiting general economic growth less than it enriched the already well-off. The labor and produce of New England and the mid-Atlantic region, where much of this commerce was based, had little to do with re-exporters who traded with foreign markets. As long as the French Wars lasted, it made sense for re-exporters to reinvest their money in additional cargoes profitably kept at sea. Investment in new businesses—whether banking, insurance, or wharves—usually supported these ships. Indeed, one of the re-exporters' greatest contributions to economic growth was likely their patronage of the shipbuilding industry. They did not invest much in factories, though some did speculate in land, with varying degrees of success. Merchants' personal spending focused on imported manufactures and luxury goods, which gave little boost to the largely agricultural domestic economy. In other words, because there was a decreasing marginal utility for their wealth, there was no "trickle down." The result was not economic growth, but wealth accumulation among those who already were the wealthiest men.[2]

But not all wealth was equal. Most merchants' wealth was denominated in coffee and sugar shipped back from the Caribbean and sent on to Europe. This trade had low barriers to entry for U.S. merchants, most of whom were little more that shopkeepers with ambition. Their business focused largely on local farmers of the "middling sort" who acted as a drag on the merchants, ensnaring them in the local barter-credit economy and, with little silver of their own, preventing them from accumulating reserves of specie. Merchants like these lacked the investing capital to develop other sectors, such as industry or finance, on a large scale.

Those few U.S. merchants who already had enough specie to invest in the East India trade were the partial exceptions. Their silver was largely from Spanish America, even after the United States began minting its own coins. Spanish silver was legal tender in the United States and constituted about 80 percent of the circulating specie in 1800 (the U.S. Mint did not have enough silver for minting). The U.S. coins were rarely exported. By U.S. law they stood at par with Spanish coins as long as they circulated within the United States, but U.S. dollars contained slightly less silver than Spanish ones. Abroad, U.S. coins were discounted based on their silver content and were usually worth 1 to 5 percent less than the Spanish coins. U.S.-minted coins valued at $100,000 in New York might thus be worth only $95,000 in China. U.S. merchants were loath to take such a loss on their money and sought out Spanish silver instead.[3] Because Spanish coins were worth more, and because there were more of them, the importance of obtaining silver from Spanish America continued.

The French Wars gave U.S. merchants better access to the Spanish silver supply. East India merchants such as Israel Thorndike demanded specie in payment for their re-exports. After Spain's entry into the war, Spanish American demand for neutral trade rose and U.S. merchants also acquired silver via the Spanish carrying trade. Stephen Girard obtained silver directly from South America during the Peninsular War (1808–1814), when Spain's energies were turned inward and the Spanish American colonies began their struggle for independence. Edward Carrington, a Providence China trader, also traded to South America for specie en route to China. Collecting on a loan to the Spanish government, the Dutch firm Hope & Co. obtained permission to take millions in silver directly from Veracruz. Hope & Co. was resident in Britain, and lending to Britain's Spanish enemy was politically risky, so the firm arranged to launder its silver through American middlemen, including Robert Oliver of Baltimore. Even in the British trade with Spanish America U.S. merchants prospered. All these measures helped merchants recoup specie outlays for East India ventures, monetizing accounts previously full of bartered goods and IOUs.[4] The growing stacks of silver coins in American counting houses spurred commercialization and the development of an emergent U.S. financial sector by providing merchants and financiers with a sound basis for trade and lending. This silver accumulated in the hands of a few financiers, while the U.S. economy as a whole hardly grew at all.

For the economy, such newfound unevenness was good. This is counterintuitive to economic historians who look to U.S. growth in the nineteenth century as a model for postcolonial societies of the twentieth century. In many modern developing economies, the gaping division of wealth between rich and poor leaves almost no middle class. These economies struggle to develop modern basics; the lack of literacy, numeracy, immunization, sanitation, and a relatively corruption-free government make it hard, if not impossible, for the poor to lift themselves up by their labor.

Early modern New England and the mid-Atlantic states were the opposites of this. New England had one of the world's highest literacy rates by 1790, with 90 percent of adult men capable of signing their name—a measure historians correlate with reading ability.[5] Only lowland Scotland, Sweden, and parts of north Germany attained similar levels of literacy by the end of the eighteenth century. Northeastern France approached 70 percent adult male literacy at this time, while old England and the rest of the United States maintained a literacy rate at 60 percent of the adult male population. (By contrast, New England's literacy rate *began* at 60 percent of adult men in the mid-1600s, when English rates were at 40 percent).[6] On the eve of the American Revolution, there were as many colleges in colonial America as in all of the British Isles; all but one of these were north of the Mason-Dixon line. The northern colonies were such a high-literacy environment that reading, from the individual's standpoint, was probably more necessary to prevent social decline than it was to facilitate advancement.[7]

Demographically, New England and the Middle Atlantic were distinct as well. White and black inhabitants could generally look forward to a long life and a merciful disease environment which, along with other factors, encouraged high population growth (2.4 percent per annum in New England, just shy of doubling every twenty-five years, and 3.4 percent in the Middle Atlantic, this due in part to immigration).[8] The availability of land staved off any Malthusian problems that might emerge from this. At the end of the eighteenth century, the average free male in the northern states was a literate, long-lived farmer, who could expect to sell some of his annual crop to the local merchant in exchange for trade goods from that merchant's general store. Few towns exceeded this stage of development. With so much land available on the frontier, Americans formed new towns in the West (especially Ohio, Vermont, Kentucky, and Tennessee) along the lines of old ones. There was no radically new way of organizing economic life, just more people living as their parents had.[9]

American growth, then, was extensive rather than intensive. The rise in population sent more farmers to the merchant's store, but those farmers dealt in barter-credit, entailing an equal expansion of small-scale merchant-shopkeepers with little access to specie. With this geographic and demographic expansion, merchants and urbanites in the main northern ports remained a small, even dwindling, fraction of the population. In 1770 2.7 percent of New Englanders lived in Boston's Suffolk County, while in the same year 6.7 percent of the inhabitants of the Middle Colonies lived in Philadelphia and New York Counties.[10] By 1810 these numbers had changed only slightly: 2.3 percent of New Englanders lived in Suffolk County, and 9.9 percent of the population of the mid-Atlantic states could be found in New York and Philadelphia.[11] Together these cities represented only 3.4 percent of the national population. With such a landed people, only a landed boom could create significant overall economic growth (which was just what happened with cotton and the cotton textile industry).

Silver in the early republic remained rare: the specie supply oscillated between slightly less that three and slightly more than four dollars per capita. A shopkeeper would be hard pressed to accumulate several thousand dollars in specie by trading with the average farmers around him. A merchant's best hope for gathering silver came from abroad: the overseas trades with Latin America, the Caribbean, and Europe and the overland trade with Mexico. For though the New England and mid-Atlantic economies were well structured to create a "middle class" of prosperous farmers and small-scale grocers, they were poorly structured to create a wealthy, specie-holding class above that.[12]

In the late colonial period, the wealthiest colonies were not in New England and the Middle Atlantic: they were southern. In *Wealth of a Nation to Be,* Alice Hanson Jones reveals that in 1774 New England controlled only 20 percent of American wealth (25 percent if slaves and indentured servants are excluded), while the Middle Colonies controlled another 24 percent (29 percent without slaves). The remaining 46 percent to 56 percent of American wealth was in the south, despite the fact that the population legally entitled to hold wealth was distributed evenly among the three regions. In New England, what wealth existed was concentrated at the top of the economic ladder; the wealthiest decile controlled nearly half (47 percent) of the region's physical wealth. In 1774, a New Englander needed £401 sterling in physical wealth to be among that group.[13] The south was similarly stratified, but it took a lot more wealth to join the highest stratum:[14] over £1,100 sterling to join the highest decile there. Likewise, although the richest 1 percent of the population owned £1,175 in New England and £1,087 in New York, New Jersey, and Delaware, it owned £2,647 in the south. Among the ten men with the greatest physical wealth Jones studied, nine were southern. Eight were planters. One was a northern merchant.[15] On the eve of the American Revolution, the wealth of America was southern, and even the wealthiest merchants of New England and the Middle Colonies failed to rival the southern plantocracy. Knowing this, it is perhaps less surprising that northern merchants coming into their own during the Revolution or shortly afterward, men like Thorndike and Girard, needed to collaborate with others to amass the silver needed to make up a venture to India.[16]

The Name of Wealth

Among the words Americans sought to describe these different levels of wealth and status, two stand out: "competence" and "affluence." Competence denoted sufficiency. As Daniel Vickers has explained, it "was tied not to a logic of endless accumulation, but to the limited" aim of possessing enough to live comfortably.[17] It meant "sufficiency, without superfluity, of the means of life," "sufficient income, easy circumstances":[18] enough money not to need to work, enough to retire on, but not enough to be rich. The association with "retirement" in our modern sense was common—a state one entered, notes the Oxford English Dictionary, "after having made a competence or earned a pension." In this "squirearchical" sense, Jane Austen—who had a better eye for class than she?—described in 1815 "an easy competence" as "enough to secure the purchase of a little estate." Richard Lord Wellesley, in 1803, likewise wrote of "a state of dignity, competency, and comfort."[19] Competency implied financial independence and a gentlemanly disinterestedness in money and whatever age one attained it. To this ideal of competence, retirement, and gentlemanly rank Benjamin Franklin aspired in his lifetime of labors, and it was for a lack of it that Alexander Hamilton had to quit the government for his law practice.

This sense of the word "competence" appears often in early American literature, usually described as "moderate," the sort of thing one "scraped together" and differing from "comparative wealth" or "riches." It was sometimes associated with sober, gentlemanly professions like the law, medicine, and the cloth. Susanna Rowson, author most famously of *Charlotte Temple* (1791), emerged as a lesser, American Jane Austen by penning a slew of marriage-, money-, and seduction-themed tracts in the early republic, in which "competence" appears widely. While sensible men and women, she explained in *The Inquisitor,* were content with "only a bare competence," the "luxurious or avaricious wretch" asked for "but a competence," wanted more, and was never happy.[20] In *Mosses from an Old Manse,* Nathaniel Hawthorne, son to an East India captain, described a stolid woodcarver who worked "industriously for many years, acquired a competence," and eventually became a deacon. Alexander Baring, British banking scion, was shocked to encounter deacon-sized competencies among Boston families in the 1790s. They spent no more than £1,000 a year, and a $2,000 income was enough to "set up with, and the young ones of the best families begin in this manner." In part, this meant it was cheap to be rich, but Baring took it to mean that the rich were cheap.[21]

Baring thought so because he was used to affluence: profuse wealth and a liberality toward others commensurate with noble station (and in America's untitled society, such wealth soon replaced titled rank); it was more than ease, comfort, and gentry living. Few were competent; fewer still enjoyed affluence. And in early America, affluence meant millions.

Didactic nineteenth-century novelists equated affluence with "Crœsus." "Blessed, by a large inheritance and the income of his lucrative profession"—the inheritance making work a pastime, not a need—wealth on this scale meant "affluence without the necessity of economy" and all the "delights of extravagance."[22] Susanna Rowson's characters linked "grandeur, affluence, and numerous attendants, to the possession of a title."[23] In her prescriptive writing Lydia Maria Francis Child described "affluence" as a level to which a "thrifty man," "left with a small patrimony,"—that is, a competence—might aspire.[24] Nathaniel Parker Willis illustrated the difference in his description of a dowry, "a portion large enough . . . [for] a situation not only of independence but affluence."[25] Though colonial American society had many competent men, no northerner before the East India and carrying-trade merchants of the 1790s and 1810s had been truly affluent.

The New Business Model

Affluent merchants owned the ships plying the routes to the Indies. But they did not own all the cargoes on board. Instead they rented out freight space to other (often merely competent) merchants to send their own cargoes east. This gave merchants who could not afford to outfit an entire ship access to the Indies. It also allowed affluent merchants to diversify their capitals over more ships.

This model was adapted from past practice in Atlantic shipping, where various collaborative commercial arrangements, including joint ownership of cargoes and vessels and the renting of freight space, were common.[26] But such collaborative efforts took on new significance when the cargo was as fungible and easy to value as silver. During the French Wars the renting of freight space and the investment of the shipped specie began evolving into something distinct from early modern shipping as it was normally conducted, possessing some of the formative elements and capital structures of the modern business corporation. Thus the American East Indies trade altered the structure, if not the growth, of the American economy. "Competence" and "affluence," as markers of wealth, were crucial in this transformation.

In 1800, Israel Thorndike fitted out the *Cyrus* for a trip from Salem to Calcutta. He loaded it with kegs of his own silver, with which he planned to buy Indian cloth. He shipped other men's silver, too: 5,000 Spanish milled dollars belonging to Thomas Winthrop; 2,000 belonging to John Lowell; and 6,000 belonging to Daniel Gilman & Co. This $13,000 was treated as cargo, with Thorndike receiving a 2.5 percent commission and, as the cost of freight, "one third part *of the nett profits* which this adventure may produce after deducting all charges except insurance & the premium paid here for the dollars."[27] Small investors could thus enter the East Indies trade with only modest charge to their principal, since the one-third was charged only on the profits. This fee structure (if not the fees) resembled the two-and-twenty of modern-day hedge funds. With the silver shipped to Asia running from 50,000 to 100,000 or even 200,000 Spanish dollars on a single ship, supplying all the silver on board was beyond the means of all but the wealthiest merchants. To sail with less was, as the East India supercargo Thomas Truxton lamented, quite difficult. But finding a berth for a smaller sum was not difficult: even the wealthiest merchant preferred to spread his silver across several ships to protect his cargoes, making up the difference with other men's silver and the prospect of a tidy cut from its successful management.[28]

Smaller shipments such as these were common. William Gray, another Salem East India trader, followed the same pattern. His business was extensive enough that some considered him the "largest shipowner in Salem" and "the greatest merchant in Massachusetts"— this last, it seems, a statement of his capitalization.

Gray shipped cash to the Indies for his friends, such as Fisher Ames, the staunch Connecticut Federalist (both Ames and their common friend Benjamin Goodhue were charter members of the Essex Junto). Ames began small, shipping 1,500 Spanish dollars on board one of Gray's ships to India in 1794. Gray's captain invested the funds in Alliabad and Tanda "cossas," handkerchiefs, and two bales of a cloth called "Mahurazgunzu": in all, six bales of piece goods and a box of handkerchiefs. Back in the United States, the cargo sold for $2,866.60. Deducting duties, the captain's and retailer's commissions, and the original investment gave $1,076.79; with the shipowner's third, and insurance subtracted as well, Ames had made $529.11 profit on $1,500 over eighteen months—a 23 percent annual return. Ames was so encouraged that he left the funds with Gray to reinvest, adding $5,000 more, and yet another $5,000 from his father-in-law by late 1796. Gray divided the money up among several vessels and sent it all to India. By March 1799, Ames had recovered his $13,457.95 in principal and another $4,714.23 in profit as well. By then Ames was already investing another $5,000 in a China-trade venture, on which the *profit*—after duties, fees, and Grays' third—was $9,800, 130 percent a year. In all, he made twelve shipments of silver dollars to Asia.[29]

The need to ship specie made it difficult to invest in the Indies trade on credit; unlike other investments Asian merchants' demand for silver meant East India investments *had* to be cash. Ames was forced to sell some of his stock in the Bank of the United States to fund his India investments. He could not ship the stock certificates themselves, for however safe U.S. merchants considered Bank stock, their Asian counterparts did not necessarily agree. The silver requirement stabilized the East India trade by restricting the funds that could be invested. In other trades, speculators traded on margins in multimillion-dollar loans, creating bubbles. But these speculators could not invest in India goods without paying in cash up front. East India merchants might pass on their cargoes to other retail or wholesale merchants, but always with an eye to the end-market. U.S. merchants did not exchange East India goods among themselves to any great degree—certainly not to the degree that they traded in land. There were still plenty of risks: pirates, shipwreck, market collapse. But the East India market could never be a bubble in the way the land or paper markets were.

To be a consignee, that is to receive a cargo consigned to and invested for him by Gray's supercargo, was an excellent investment for Ames. To be sure, renting out an East Indiaman might have been yet more profitable, but that took more capital than Ames could afford. "I see no better way of employing my small capital than the India trade," Ames wrote Gray in 1797 in a series of letters which sound like an investor's consulting a financial advisor. Considering his returning China-trade venture in 1799, Ames explained his ship's "arrival would be truly fortunate for me, as it would mend my circumstances a good deal, and tho' I should be placed many thousands below *affluence,* I should be so near to a *competence,* tho' short of it, as with frugality to abate the most uncomfortable exertions in my profession."[30]

Competence was the consignee's prospect. Ames never became a merchant-capitalist, but his investments netted him enough to retire. Ames trusted his money to Gray because Gray's much more substantial funds were at stake, and Gray took no risk with Ames's money that he did not take with his own. In this way, merchants adapted an old commercial form—the renting of freight space—to new use. It provided the large investor with both diversification and profits, and it provided the small investor better access to the risks and profits of the India trade than buying shares of East India Company stock ever could.

The combination of competent and affluent investments in a single venture was distinctive to the East Indies trade. East India ventures were costly, and their costliness necessitated complexity (i.e., more investors) to fund them. That complexity gave the East Indies trade a deeper significance by restructuring merchant capital. A shipping venture's complexity can be measured in the number of separately owned properties on board. Each cargo was a discrete property, owned by the vessel owner or by merchants renting freight space on board. Since each cargo represented a different investor or group of investors, it had to be accounted for separately. A cargo—also called a consignment—might be of any value, might consist of one or several goods, and might have one or several owners (e.g., two partners might jointly own a load of sugar and coffee). This was common in all trades and might be considered something of a wash among them. But after all this has been considered, East India ventures carried a significantly larger number of cargoes than other ventures did.

Consider Salem, Massachusetts, a midsize New England port, and the mid-Atlantic city of Philadelphia, the largest in the United States. In both, most vessels arriving from abroad came from the Caribbean, the region dominating early American overseas trade. In 1790, 96 of the 145 vessels entering Salem from abroad came from the Caribbean. That same year, 408 out of Philadelphia's 635 overseas entries came from the Caribbean. These vessels carried few consignments. To Salem, they brought, on average, 1.16 separate consignments. By comparison, there was an average of 1.47 consignments per vessel in Salem across all vessels in from abroad. To Philadelphia, Caribbean vessels carried an average of 3.14 consignments, whereas overseas vessels in general brought 6.22. The vast majority of overseas arrivals in both ports came from the Caribbean, thus weighting average consignments for all overseas vessels heavily in their favor. In both ports, Caribbean vessels generally had fewer consignments than an average vessel from abroad. At Salem the average number of consignments for Caribbean vessels was extremely low, especially considering that vessels with less than one cargo (i.e., in ballast) are not counted. So few Salem vessels carried more than one cargo back from the Caribbean that the average number of consignments barely moved above one. Certainly, Caribbean vessels were smaller and less expensive than East Indiamen. Petty shopkeepers and businessmen sailed to the Caribbean themselves. One man might own the entire vessel and cargo, sailing it himself and selling his own farm goods for sugar and molasses in the Caribbean. Larger merchants might own whole fleets. The affordability of Caribbean cargoes and vessels, when compared to that of other voyages, kept barriers to entry low and left little need to rent freight space. Merchants who were less well capitalized simply owned one Caribbean schooner instead of ten. Caribbean voyages were common, frequent, and cheap.[31]

Yet if Caribbean vessels predominated, and if they had so few consignments, what was inflating the average number of consignments on vessels in from abroad? Most of the other overseas arrivals in Salem in 1790 (37 of 145) came from Europe. Most of these, too, had only one cargo, with an average of 1.14 properties per vessel. In Philadelphia, 203 vessels arrived from Europe out of a total of 635 foreign arrivals. They were larger and carried more cargoes than their Salem counterparts; there were, on average, 12.36 separate consignments on board. Salem was not a major hub for European manufactures, and so one should not read too much into the Salem number. Philadelphia, however, was a hub for trade with Europe. Some vessels in from London and Liverpool carried 100, even 150, separately owned cargoes; these raise the average number of consignments per vessel from Europe significantly. These cargoes represented U.S. shopkeepers' orders, paid for by barter-credit or money of account. U.S. and London merchants decided what was to be shipped in their correspondence, the vessel captain having little to do with selecting cargoes. He merely delivered them. Thus though the cargo arrangements on European voyages were more complex than on Caribbean voyages, the London merchant dealt with the complications. This was Thomas Hancock's trade, one that American merchants had been conducting since early colonial days.

The East Indies trade was less common and qualitatively different, such that change in degree became change in kind. In Salem, only 8 of 145 vessels came from the East Indies in 1790. In Philadelphia 5 of 635 did. Salem East India vessels carried an average of 6.88 discrete cargoes; the five Philadelphia vessels carried an average of 22.20.[32] These denominators merely hint at the rarity of East India voyages, since they include only arrivals from foreign ports: they exclude fishing, whaling, and coasting voyages. A small portion of the international shipping fleet, East India vessels were an even more rarified portion of the combined international and domestic trades. East India venture were few because of their cost. The need to ship silver to buy a cargo from Asia prevented many merchants from attempting the venture. Merchants with only some silver had to lease space to transport that silver on another merchant's ship. As one British merchant explained of the American arrangement: "a variety of persons will join, and put in a certain sum, perhaps 10,000 or 20,000 dollars each." Only the wealthiest merchants could afford a majority stake in an East Indiaman's cargo, and even they were happy to diversify their funds with lesser merchants' silver taken as freight.[33]

Slowly this freight-based means of pooling wealth began to coalesce into a more formal structure. This was the case with the *Alexander Hodgson,* a Boston venture in which investors divided both ship and cargo into shares. Joint ownership of a vessel was an old practice.[34] But dividing up a ship and its cargo together, as though the two were not to be distinguished, was unusual. Equally unusual were the division of the *Hodgson* into a large number of small shares and the structuring of the venture as a single contract among all the shareholders, rather than as a series of bilateral agreements between small investors and the principle merchants. A single contract was more convenient given the 100 shares on offer, a much more minute division than the eighth- or tenth-part shares into which colonial-era vessels were sometimes divided. Each share cost $800, for a maximum capitalization of $80,000. With so many owners, the contract called for this money to be managed by a ship's husband, who would oversee repairs and the lading of cargo. In 1802, the subscribers signed a formal contract in which they agreed to "a Voyage round the Cape of Good Hope" and "to such part of the world as [the principal owners] shall think best."

Here the merely competent investors deferred to the advice and authority of more affluent merchant-capitalists, just as Fisher Ames had deferred to the judgment of William Gray. Likewise, David Sears and Israel Thorndike, the principle owners, sought out the ships' husband themselves. The *Hodgson* venture was also designed to be temporary, just as in conventional freight renting, in which the freight renters collected their cargoes on the return of the ship (though they were free to invest again with additional specie, if they wished). So the *Hodgson* contract included a provision that "the vessel & Cargo is to be sold & the concern entirely wound up whenever the said Ship & her Cargo or the Proceeds thereof shall arrive in this State."[35]

The complementary relationship between small and large investor was at the heart of the *Hodgson* enterprise. The affluent merchant provided access, expertise, and enough capital to give the venture scale. But he still wanted the diversification of his funds that the capitals of smaller merchants provided. So the contract aggregated smaller, merely competent merchants' capitals with the principal owners' investments. Thorndike and Sears each bought twenty-five shares, representing half the total capital wanted. Other merchants, mostly family, bought in as well: Andrew Thorndike (five shares), Nicholas Thorndike (three), son-in-law Ebenezer Francis (three), his captains William Leech (five) and Tarbox Moulton (two), James Worsley (two), Thomas Stephens (two), and Anna Oliver (one). Taken together, these smaller investors contributed another $18,400, nearly as much as either Thorndike or Sears did on their own.[36] These investors were lesser merchants or captains (often aspiring merchants themselves) involved in fishing, coasting, and Caribbean voyages—cheap and easy ventures that required more elbow grease and barter-credit than specie. Some captained East Indian voyages, but none appear in Salem's customs register as owning a vessel trading to the Indies, only mastering it. Still, they had some silver, and Thorndike gave them a means to enlarge it.[37]

The freight renting of the East Indies trade developed into the venture already described. As seen in Tables 5.1 and 5.2, freight renting endured throughout the French Wars. East Indian voyages

Table 5.1 Average Number of Cargoes per Vessel Entering Salem, Massachusetts, Select Years (total vessels from each region in parentheses)

	Africa	Canada	Caribbean	Europe	East Indies	South America	Average
1790	N.A. (0)	1.00 (1)	1.16 (96)	1.14 (37)	6.88 (8)	N.A. (0)	1.47 (145)
1795	N.A. (0)	1.00 (3)	1.13 (89)	1.38 (52)	3.71 (7)	N.A. (0)	1.34 (151)
1800	N.A. (0)	1.00 (4)	1.75 (103)	1.70 (47)	7.33 (6)	N.A. (0)	1.93 (160)
1805	1.00 (1)	N.A. (0)	1.47 (109)	1.88 (73)	3.09 (32)	N.A. (0)	1.85 (216)
Total	1.00 (1)	1.00 (8)	1.39 (397)	1.59 (209)	4.22 (53)	N.A. (0)	1.67 (672)

Notes: Excludes vessels entering via another U.S. port or originating in the United States. Excludes three vessels of unclear origin in 1790 and one vessel of unclear origin in 1805. Caribbean includes Bahamas, Bermuda, and north coast of South America, among other ports. Europe includes Azores, Canary Islands, Cape Verde Islands, Madeira, Malta, and Smyrna, among other ports. East Indies includes Aden, Batavia, Bombay, Calcutta, Canton, Cape of Good Hope, Isle of Bourbon, Isle of France, Madagascar, Madras, Manila, Mocha, Muscat, Negapatam, Sumatra, and Tranquebar. South America includes La Plata, Montevideo, Pernambuco, Rio de la Plata, and Rio Janeiro. N.A. = not applicable.

Source: NARA (MA), Impost Books of the Collector (Salem, MA), vols. 1–5.

Table 5.2 Average Number of Cargoes per Vessel Entering Philadelphia, Select Years (total vessels from each region in parentheses)

	Africa	Canada	Caribbean	Europe	East Indies	South America	Average
1790	2 (1)	3.67 (9)	3.14 (408)	12.36 (203)	22.2 (5)	N.A. (0)	6.22 (635)
1800	3 (1)	1.82 (17)	3.85 (309)	21.44 (144)	14.5 (26)	3.63 (8)	9.34 (513)
1810	1 (2)	1.8 (5)	8.46 (243)	13.23 (188)	33.29 (17)	5.64 (11)	11 (472)
Total	1.75 (4)	2.32 (31)	4.77 (960)	15.13 (535)	21.31 (48)	4.79 (19)	8.68 (1,620)

Notes: Excludes vessels entering via another U.S. port or originating in the United States. There were two such vessels in 1790, twenty-five in 1800, and eighteen in 1810. Also excludes vessels entering "in ballast" or as a prize. Excludes from the regional listings nine entrants in 1790, eight entrants in 1800, and six entrants in 1810 with unclear regions of origin, but includes them in the overall average. N.A. = not applicable.

Source: NARA (PA), RG36, Customs E1071: Impost Ledgers for the Port of Philadelphia, 1789–1865: Box 1, Vol. 2, January–December 1790, 1800; Box 7, 1807–1810; and Box 8, 1810–1812. For definition of regions, see Table 5.1.

continued to have more complex arrangements than other voyages; there were more separate properties lodged on board East Indiamen than in almost any other line of trade, and voyages to India and China exhibited the most pronounced part of this trend. Because these investments were made in silver, the profits were restricted only to the most well-capitalized men. Perhaps because there were so few well-capitalized men at the start of the early republic, especially in the northern states, investors were more likely to have to band together in a single venture. Their newly cooperative ventures had an enduring appeal that outlasted the initial impetus. The diversification on offer for shipowners—in the midst of a dangerous, global war—played no small part in protecting their wealth.

The tables may understate the number of consignments on larger vessels. Offloading could take months and even run from one year into the next. Since the data in the tables are samplings rather than entire runs, some cargoes unloaded in the months just before or just after the sampled year may have been excluded. This would be more likely to affect voyages with more cargoes to unload, and so the total number of consignments on East India voyages may be understated.

The tables are less useful for showing change over time—one would want a more contiguous run of data to chart such a volatile thing as wartime trade—as they are for showing continuity by averaging the samples.[38] Thus overseas commerce in Salem and Philadelphia remained predominantly Caribbean—more than half the vessels arriving from overseas in every year sampled. At the same time, the comparatively high number of properties-to-vessels in the East Indies trade stands out for its consistency as well.[39]

Making investments in silver gave both competent and affluent investors a common basis for evaluating their investments' success. A merchant who shipped a cargo of timber and flour abroad could hardly compare sales of one commodity to the other. Making East India investments in the same good, silver, rectified this. Since that good was also a form of money, it was also more liquid and fungible. One could then readily compare the price of silver in one Indian port with its price in another (i.e., what cloth it could buy).

One could also compare the supercargo's management across a ship's investments, since the consignees invested with the same thing: money.

In most American vessels, sailing to familiar ports in Europe and the Caribbean where centuries-long contacts kept American merchants apprized of their opposite numbers overseas, the authority to buy and sell cargoes was vested in the captain. East India voyages (as well as voyages to Russia or the cone of South America) separated these duties out into another role, that of supercargo. Because of the outbound cargo of East Indian voyages, and because that cargo was divided into many separately owned properties, the supercargoes assumed greater significance. The silver-denominated cargoes functioned as investment accounts, with the supercargo the shipowner's agent for investing the funds. For both competent and affluent investor alike, the supercargo was the indispensable man.

In his journal, Nathaniel Bowditch recorded his first voyage east and the care, parsimony, and energy required of a good supercargo. In Manila in 1796, he "hired a house at 26 dollars per month which," he took care to note, "was reckoned very cheap." He rented additional storehouses for pepper and sugar at ten and twenty dollars a month, respectively, a "cheap" rate, "it being common to give 100 dols for a house per month." Bowditch sold his ship's goods. It is unclear whether there was much specie on his vessel or not, but he certainly thought it better to carry specie. Though one could make a tramping voyage to India and bring over cloth, "it is certainly well for those who have a stock [i.e., capital] to proceed directly to Manilla, with cash which would greatly shorten the voyage." With silver or without, there was also a need for something to fill the hold, and Bowditch's shipowner filled his with sundries. So Bowditch spent his days selling hats and wine; he found unloading the more unpopular cargoes especially trying. He also kept an eye on the goods. Theft was ever-present: there were break-ins at night, and one of the coolies loading sacks tried to run off with what was in his arms. Supercargoes conducted business in Manila through a broker, who introduced supercargoes to local Chinese sugar merchants for a fee, usually 2 percent of the value of a transaction.

Brokerage introduced the threat of fraud—theft on a larger scale. So a good supercargo kept an eye on the broker, too. One broker was "Infamous," and Bowditch thought there were none who had been in Manila "any considerable time but what has some blur on his character," a common, proto-Conradian aspersion on those who seemed to have been east for too long. Bowditch found one, a Mr. Karr who had come out from Philadelphia, who, despite unkind rumors about him, "in all his conduct" acted "perfectly to our satisfaction."[40]

From such entries his journal turns to describing other merchants, obsessively contrasting their profligacy with his own care. If one had to be satisfied with a merchant "in all his conduct," such things mattered, and Bowditch strongly felt that spendthrift living reflected on a merchant's commercial abilities. "All the English commanders here live in stile rowling about in their Coaches," he noted, while "we Americains make use of what is called here the Coach of Saint Francis"—"shoe leather, which is not quite so expensive." He concluded this observation of how a supercargo should save by quoting a price for shoes. Others lived above what he believed competence, saving, and good business sense (or perhaps station) allowed, spending as though affluent. He noticed the captain of a Swedish ship in port who lived "in stile having coaches ten horses & twenty odd servants & a miss"—scandalized, Bowditch gave the price for the mistress, too.[41]

One American in particular attracted Bowditch's scorn, the first mate of the *Three Sisters*, who had taken over the vessel after the captain's death en route to Manila. "I never saw a man so much above himself," Bowditch wrote. "His replies in general show his haughty disposition." When the mate learned that the vessel's owner had died as well, he seemed oddly unfazed. Bowditch suspected he would take the cargo for himself, so he scrupulously recorded gossip that the mate dressed in the dead captain's clothes, that he pretended to have always been the captain, and that he claimed "he owned a quarter part of the ship." To Bowditch, such violations suggested larger ones, the mate's extravagance convincing Bowditch that a man who assumed authority for himself could assume a cargo as well. Getting used to life beyond one's means could be a strong temptation to that. The mate threw expensive parties, inviting all the Britons and snubbing the Americans. He kept a coach on shore, "more," Bowditch sniffed, "than the Captain of the Spanish company ships do." To this Bowditch watched the mate add "a six oared barge with an awning to it & always a coxwain in the boat." One Englishman in Manila—and this was the clincher—"expressed surprise to find an Americain so polished."[42]

Bowditch did not think it always inappropriate to maintain six-oared barges or to throw parties; he thought these were things an *acting* captain should not do. The mate, for his part, was trying to behave as he thought a captain should. Bowditch had a particularly rigid sense of rank—and parsimony—but most merchants had some idea of what constituted an appropriate expense, and what was fit for a mate was not fit for a captain, just as what was fit for a captain was not fit for a merchant. The boundaries differed, but transgressing them brought the same redress: sensing an unreliable businessman, others became unwilling to trust the violator with their money. To the extent that these boundaries were subjective and in flux, they became even more important for the constancy they seemed to provide.

While returning to Salem, Bowditch reflected on the streetwise thrift that he thought made a good supercargo. He urged "any person trading" to Manila to "be well on his guard, examining the goods he buys and seeing the weight himself." The captain of the Swedish ship foolishly hired someone to "inspect his indigo," but "it was notoriously known that the fellow received bribes from the sellers for to pass their indigo at more than its value." Not surprisingly, the Swedish captain in question was the one with the fifty-dollar mistress. In Bowditch's eyes the transgressions were linked—if he was loose with his own money, he would be careless with other people's money, too. To merchants the tale also explained why a supercargo's job could not be farmed out; the care he was expected to give each property was why he was paid a percentage, not a flat rate, in the first place.[43]

Prosopography

Merchants trading to the Indies, as those trading elsewhere, depended on their reputations as good businessmen. Yet their reputations to fellow investors as good capitalists is easily obscured by their reputations to posterity for their luxury. Luxury and financial success share an uneasy relationship: a lavish home can convey wealth, but rich tastes can signify wealth spent as well as wealth retained, and the boundary between propriety and extravagance is a moving one, particularly among merchants who were becoming increasingly wealthy themselves. Merchants assessed their success through their workplaces and the trappings of their trade—cargoes, wharves, and brigs. Yet other observers did not, and many reserved their choicest comments for a merchant's silverware, not his silver. The dissonance between these two views reveals who invested with whom, and why.

Merchants' account books (the modern tool for examining wealth) shed little light, for with tens of trades outstanding (and at prices to be known only when the vessels returned), merchants eschewed quarterly or annual statements for statements of each transaction as it became known. These were kept as double-entry accounts—so much fish sold for so much wine and the remainder in cash—with the only full accounting coming at death, when the trading stopped and outstanding accounts were settled. Historians are, then, left to guess at the merchants' wealth as much as the merchants themselves were.

Among the wealthiest 1 percent of the wealthiest 1 percent of the population—that incredibly narrow field in which the East India shipowners stood—a few men stood out for their affluence. Two are considered here: Elias Derby of Salem and William Bingham of Philadelphia. Both were much better off than their merchant fathers, and if anyone had been wealthy enough to conduct the East India trade without consignees, it would have been Derby or Bingham. Neither did. Nor, despite being two of the wealthiest men in America, were they as well off as some suggested. To see this requires an imaginative leap: one must look for their cargoes while understanding why others looked for their furnishings.

Elias Hasket Derby led Salem's merchant class. He had taken over his father's business in the 1760s. In the 1780s, he began trading to numerous ports in Asia. Nathaniel Hawthorne, born five years after Derby's death, dubbed him "King Derby," so legendary had the man become. He owned one of the longest wharves in town and a prodigious number of vessels—enough that many town merchants and captains could trace their start in business to a posting as captain or supercargo with Derby. He was also known for his lavish attire: a gold-headed cane and a Sir Roger de Coverley coat. He rode in a famously elegant coach, and his mansion, completed just months before his death, dwarfed the houses of everyone else in town.[44]

His East India trade was wildly profitable. Alexander Baring estimated that on four ships returning from Mauritius at the end of 1795 Derby would reap a total profit of £70,000, roughly $300,000 in 1795 dollars.[45] He thought Derby "very rich"[46] but still "a Chincaneur,"[47]—a quibbler who caviled over sums beneath him, still a cheap Yankee peddler—and so when Derby asked for credit in India, Baring refused. "I would have nothing to do with such business," the Englishman explained.[48]

When Derby died on September 8, 1799, he had just over $1 million.[49] It was perhaps the first time an American had left so much behind. Most of this wealth was derived from shipping his own and others' silver to Asia. By contrast, the richest American in Alice Hanson Jones's study, the South Carolina planter Peter Manigault, had only £32,737 sterling, less than a quarter of Derby's wealth at death.[50] Jones's sample was not broad enough to include the wealthiest Americans to die in 1774, let alone the wealthiest living, and so this comparison cannot be stretched too far. But one might infer that Derby's wealth was of the same order of magnitude as the affluent planters' of the south—itself an accomplishment for a man who rubbed Baring as a peddler made good.

Derby was, in his contemporaries' and successors view, the epitome of Salem wealth—his heirs were all comparative failures, better at fighting over inheritance than turning a successful voyage. So why was it, then, that Baring held him in such disregard? What was is that his fellow Americans saw in Derby that Baring did not?

Other measures of Derby's wealth, such as his mansion, yield a clue. It was, by all accounts, impressive: twelve rooms, plus a kitchen, library, closets and alcoves, with sixteen fireplaces, four chimneys, and a cupola on the roof. Though Mrs. Derby is reputed to have told the architect, "It is not large a-nuf," it was the tallest in Salem. At its back lay extensive gardens. Robert Gilmore, the Baltimore trader, noted enviously that it seemed "more like a palace than the dwelling of an American merchant."[51] Then there was the furnishing. The woodwork in every room was intricately carved: capitals, draperies, cables, beadings, roses, and medallions. Two marble statues flanked the front door, with additional marble busts scattered about for effect.

But the house went almost unlived in. Mrs. Derby passed away only weeks after moving in, and her husband followed her to the grave three months later. Their son Hasket, the only other ever to live there, found the upkeep beyond his means. It was beyond the means of everyone else in town, too; with no buyer, the house was demolished in 1816 and a marketplace built in its location. No trace remains.[52]

Derby also kept a coach and European coachman, hired, supposedly, at Mrs. Derby's insistence. The mansion and the coach, the two most visible signs of luxury, are ascribed to Derby's wife, as if to follow the old trope of blaming luxury on women and, by extension, exonerating otherwise sensible businessmen from such follies. Elias Derby spent $900 for the coach in 1795, ordering it from a coach maker in Philadelphia. His biographer makes much of its elegance.[53] Certainly it was built at the height of Derby's wealth and fame, as its silver-studded design and liveried coachman reflect.

Derby's status as an affluent investor gave him access to business partners, credit, and banking facilities. But his house did not make him affluent: it merely *signified* affluence. And Derby was certainly not the ne plus ultra of wealth. There were others richer still in the English-speaking world, others with whom he had financial dealings; for markets and capital, as class, were international. British Caribbean planters ranked far above Americans (planter or merchant) in the international hierarchy of wealth and class, as Baring's comment suggests. These planters lived on estates in England and in town houses in London—not, to be sure, in the colonies—buying away their origins and hiding their newness to aristocracy. The opulence of these arrivistes far outstripped their American cousins'.

William Beckford's family, for example, made a fortune in Jamaica sugar. Beckford returned to England and the West Country in the mid-eighteenth century to built Fonthill Mansion, four stories tall (no American had a house so high, not even Derby), with wings two stories each,

> connected by corridors, built of fine stone, and adorned with a bold portico, resting on a rustic basement, with two sweeping flights of steps: its apartments were numerous, and splendidly furnished. They displayed the riches and luxury of the east; . . . Its walls were adorned with the most costly works of art, its sideboards and cabinets presented a gorgeous combination of good, silver, precious metals, and precious stones. . . . One apartment was fitted up in the Turkish style, with large mirrors, ottomans, etc., whilst others were enriched with fine sculptured marble chimney-pieces.

The *entrance hall* to Fonthill measured (at the basement level) eighty-five by thirty-six feet, with a vaulted roof supported by stone piers.[54] The house itself was torn down by the 1820s, but the attached abbey survived on the surviving demesne. Beckford had begun putting up the abbey in 1795. It was—and still is—a monument to planter wealth; Derby's mansion might have fit inside it.

So great were the fortunes of Caribbean planters that historians tell the story of George III, on a visit to Weymouth with William Pitt, coming across a Jamaican with such a coach—equipage, livery, out-riders—that he grew jealous. He turned to his minister: "Sugar, sugar, eh? all *that* sugar! How are the duties, eh, Pitt, how are the duties?"[55] Perhaps a planters' coach could inspire a king's envy (if only in legend), but not Derby's.

Derby also fell short when compared with London merchants. Alexander Baring, who had denied Derby credit, personified the

City merchant class. He sailed from Britain in 1795 to purchase land for his father, Sir Francis Baring. As a leading London merchant, Sir Francis maintained a global trading network, was an East India Company director, and advised the British government on financial matters. In the mid-1790s Sir Francis thought his business "more extensive and upon a larger scale than any merchant in this or any other country."[56] By the 1790s, Baring handled various U.S. government transactions on the London markets (and later, with Hope & Co., lent the U.S. government $11.25 million for the Louisiana Purchase; though the United States could not afford so much money at once, Baring and Hope & Co. could).[57]

In 1795, Alexander, only twenty-two, was authorized to draw $100,000 on his father's account. He bought 1.2 million acres of Maine land owned by William Bingham, a Philadelphia merchant and U.S. senator. Alexander stayed in America for six years, impressed by the opportunities for profit. "I should make much more than all my prospects in Amsterdam ever promised in a much shorter period," he wrote his father in 1797.[58] Traveling up and down the coast, he met merchants and members of American "high society." His letters, by a man of capital, reveal much about how some American merchants became so much more successful than others.

The appearance of wealth did not mean one had money to invest. Baring routinely warned his father off this "rather dashing" sort of fellow. "I should not scruple to give them a liberal credit," he wrote. He preferred Bingham, whom he thought "not a dashing man nor inclined to new speculations," but who spent his money in a way a gentleman could understand.[59] Baring noted that to others Bingham seemed overly "aristocratical," but Baring thought him "respectable," a word that showed up often in his correspondence. In the boom time of the 1790s, when new money vied for show, when "dozens of second rate [merchant] houses" trading on credit mushroomed across the country and even "the most hazardous hairbrained adventures"[60] succeeded, Baring preferred to deal with Bingham, a man like him, trading on his considerable private capital, a man who had something to lose.

Bingham impressed Baring. He had married well, to the daughter of Thomas Willing, a Philadelphia merchant and President of the Bank of the United States (1791–1807).[61] Bingham owned several East Indiamen with local merchants, including Gilmore & Co and Mordecai Lewis.[62] He had been interested in the East India trade from its inception and had been an investor in the *Empress of China*.

He also lived well, but Baring made less of this than did people who were less well off. After the American Revolution, the young Bingham couple had taken a grand tour of Europe, bringing back the aspiration of a suitably European "mansion." One English traveler found it fit: "a magnificent house and gardens in the best English style, with elegant and even superb furniture." Neighbor Samuel Breck recalled that "William Bingham, a millionaire . . . lived in the most showy style of any American."[63]

The house was indeed impressive by local standards. Its wide hall had a mosaic marble floor, an American first. Architect Charles Bulfinch wrote a qualified panegyric on its style,

> which would be esteemed splendid even in the most luxurious part of Europe. Elegance of construction, white marble staircase, valuable paintings, the richest furniture and the utmost magnificence of decoration makes it a palace in my opinion far too rich for any man in this country. We are told that his mode of living is fully equal to this appearance of his house. Of this we shall be better able to judge in a few hours as we are to dine there today.[64]

Bulfinch, who had also gone on a grand tour, had seen mansions "in the most luxurious parts of Europe," and knew he was being a bit hyperbolic, but he was one of many who noted Bingham's lavish tastes.

Some thought Bingham aped English aristocracy too much. As one political opponent demurred, he "affects to entertain in a style beyond everything in this place, or perhaps in America." "Mr. usually styled Count Bingham," one Federalist Congressman called him.[65] A local Quaker girl confided in her diary that, with "bow windows back and front [and] with figures of stucco work," Bingham's three-story home looked like a public building, not a humble Pennsylvanian's residence. Brissot de Warville, the French revolutionary, found in the Bingham home "a pomp which ought for ever to have been a stranger to Philadelphia." Even one local Federalist had to confess that, "There is too much sobriety in our American common sense to tolerate such pageantry," despite (or perhaps because of) the Binghams' holding the Federalist "court" of the 1790s at home.[66] Mrs. Bingham used it as a salon—and writers took pains to note that this was unique in the United States. In this vein Bingham's biographer proudly, if tediously, notes that Bingham brought back the "first silver-pronged forks seen in America."[67]

Baring stayed on in America because of his connection to Bingham, with whom he had further business and whose eldest daughter he married. What was it about Bingham that so impressed Baring? Was it his fine living, or was it something less tangible but more valuable—having the president of the Bank of the United States for an in-law, perhaps, or capital itself? Shortly after their marriage the young Barings moved into their own house, appointed with mahogany, chandeliers and, we are told, Chinese wallpaper, as if these were the only marks of success.[68] Bingham moved to England with Baring in 1801. When he died three years later, he left behind a $3 million estate.[69] Perhaps Bingham was, as his biographer bragged, "the country's richest man."[70]

Bingham's real wealth was in silver, not ornament. It was in the ships he had built, in their cargoes, in silver, in land, in London bank accounts, and in the respectability these all gave him. Because he was respectable—a thoroughly subjective judgment made by those around him—he could live well. Yet to many who did not appreciate the finer points of the affluent merchant's world, respect flowed the other way: owning a fine house and living in a high style were sufficient to merit respectability (or suspicion for aristocratic leanings) in and of themselves. Conspicuous consumption could buy the image of affluence for a merely competent man. It was with distinguishing this simulacrum of affluence from the reality of it—distinguishing those who spent their fortunes from those who had capital left over after the house was built—that Baring concerned himself.

The gulf between Baring, a man of affluence, and the *average* American merchant continually shocked him. Such merchants struck him as déclassé and provincial, closer to the farm life around them than the world he knew. "The merchants of this country are generally speaking a low class of men . . . the best at [Philadelphia] and New York are travelling Clerks to English manufacturing houses," he wrote.[71] Unlike Baring, most who were born there had never left their native country. "The Merchants in every part of this continent are extremely ignorant of every thing out of their own Country." How odd, he thought, that Philadelphia, a city that traded with the globe, would have merchants so uninformed. "People send Cargoes to places of which they know nothing but the name."[72]

Baring took sugar traders, importers, and petty shopkeepers, the bulk of the American merchant class, to be "cunning." This he meant unkindly; "intelligence" was a word he reserved for the most affluent few. "Inteligence as well as prudence," he explained, "form *in general* no part of the American commercial character, and their natural substitutes low cunning and diffidence render them disagreable [business] correspondents."[73] "Cunning" meant mechanical know-how: an eye for a trade and the ability to barter and truck, to bargain for the best price, to know a rigged scale (and how to rig one), and to recognize shoddy goods—skills Bowditch exhibited in Manila. Intelligence meant the more expansive knowledge of financial instruments, of how to invest wealth, of how to (and how not to) speak of money in society, of who was who, of what was being read, of liberality—all of which came naturally to Baring. It was the distinction between competence and affluence. In 1799 Sir Francis complained to his son of a competent supercargo Alexander had sent over, "an American Supercargo! Who will chatter like a magpye and think cunning is wisdom." The father also told of Oliver Wolcott, the American Treasury Secretary who wanted help floating treasuries on London. Baring expected Wolcott to possess some financial intelligence but found he did not. Wolcott wanted to leave the subscription for federal debt open: people would sign up for treasuries as word spread, as if they were pledges for charity or subscriptions to a wharf. He had not planned to sound out other City bankers. Sir Francis urged him to do so in order to lock in larger buyers and get a feel for how much the market could raise. He quoted Talleyrand, who, in the midst of the XYZ Affair, was having his own American exasperations. "*Ces sont des ostrogottes qui ne se connaissant pas en affaires.*"[74] Alexander might have smiled. American merchants were wily, but most did not understand affairs as the Barings did. It took Bingham to bridge the divide, a divide an average American merchant, or an average American treasury secretary, could not cross.

Robert Morris

"Excepting among those who speculate beyond their means in real estate," Baring noted, "failures are very rare." This was hyperbole: plenty of merchants failed in other lines of trade, but real estate speculation had particular hazards. Consider Robert Morris. He began well enough, serving as Congress's superintendent of finance during the American Revolution and, as a general merchant, involving himself in numerous lines of trade. He had been concerned in the *Empress of China*. In 1797 Morris called "himself the richest man in America," and Alexander Baring noted "his house is still building in a style fit for Cresus [*sic*] himself." The town house, occupying the Philadelphia block between 7th and 8th, Chestnut and Walnut, was ambitious. He aimed to make it the most lavish home in America, outdoing the Derby mansion then under construction and the Bingham home already built. He slathered the walls with marble as if it were brick. But Morris never got a roof on the building before he was in debtor's prison. Baring thought Morris among the "Mad Speculators and needy Desperadoes" who gambled with money they did not have. Baring frowned not on real estate speculation per se, but speculation on credit. Real estate purchased with *capital,* like Bingham's and Baring's, was respectable enough; an investor could never lose more than he owned if he used his own money. Morris was dismissive of the land agents swarming Philadelphia during the 1790s (he called them mere "hawkers"), but he bought their land anyway. In 1795, he controlled more than 6 million acres in various tracts from Pennsylvania to Georgia. By 1798, he was overextended, unable meet his obligations, and bankrupt. Baring disdained the competent Morris stretching to fill affluent shoes. "The rage for Speculation is so great and the ups and downs in fortunes so sudden," he explained. "Very few [American] houses deserve uncovered credits, the spirit of speculation is so bold, and reverses of fortune consequently so sudden that this must be the case for some time to come." In 1799 Baring elaborated: "The security here is that his business can only be conducted with capital, and that a large one. Every speculation where little of this is required is overdone here for it is in the national disposition of Americans to risk lodging in jail for the chance of a palace."[75]

Morris's house was in fact not *that* extravagant. Though it may well have been one of the largest uncompleted homes in America at the time, even completed it would have paled in comparison to Sir Francis Baring's. By 1803 Sir Francis had spent £150,000 acquiring lands; by 1808 he had spent an additional £15,000 on art, all bought with his own means. Far from dying in debtor's prison, he left his children an inheritance. At his death in 1810 his *private wealth* was valued at £606,000 ($2.6 million in 1810): £400,000 in estates, £30,000 in valuables, and £175,000 distributed among his younger children. In addition, he held £70,000 in the family firm at the time of his death, meaning the £606,000 in private wealth was just that, net of his working business capital (though he had retired earlier in the decade, he held a remaining £70,000 stake in the firm).[76] Derby's wealth at death was almost a third Sir Francis's; only Bingham was of the same scale.

The Barings' Investment in the American East Indies Trade

By the 1790s, the U.S. capital market was international enough for Alexander Baring to invest specie in the U.S. East India trade himself. "The trade is thought a very sure one," he wrote his father[77];

it "has an advantage of steadiness & security above others because as it can only be carried on with real capital it is not subject to the competition of those who have nothing to lose." He knew because he had examined the trade closely. "I am endeavouring to collect some interesting facts on the subject & I think you will be surprised with the growing importance of this business," he explained to his Company-director father.

> The trade is chiefly pursued in vessells from 120 to 5 & 600 tons burthen. The cargoes outwards are generally specie & some times some wines taken up at Madeira & Teneriffe. The returns are made in the general produce of the East which meets a ready sale in every part of the country. The consumption of this country itself is great & increasing but the West Indies have of late been supplied from hence and will continue to take large quantities of piece goods at all times.

If some went to India, others "have lately gone to the Dutch Colonies [present-day Indonesia] & as the regular trade with Holland is at an end will buy up sugar & coffee very cheap."[78]

Baring thought "Europeans could be concerned to great advantage in the Indian voyages, particularly those who have connections in India so as to save the interest of money by giving credits on Calcutta instead of sending specie out as is practised generally."[79] In other words, perhaps Americans could get credit from the Barings in India off an existing account in London. The suggestion was, at first glance, odd. Sir Francis had served two terms as chairman of the East India Company Court of Directors; he was one of the Company's most knowledgeable directors and a staunch representative of the City interest in the Company and of both Company and City interests to the ministry.[80] Few men stood to be as upset by Alexander's comments as his father.

But the Barings were not the first Company men to invest in the American East India trade. David Scott, another Company director, had done so already. The U.S. merchants Philips Gramond & Co. "have constantly drawn on Calcutta & on Canton" through them, noted Alexander. Wistfully, the son pondered the money that Baring capital and U.S. flags might make in the Indies. If his brother in Asia "could attend these to business I could turn all the good connections of this country into his hands & it would be most valuable, but," he admitted, "I suppose it will never be possible." Still, "I have reason to believe there are some large foreign capitals employed in this manner & there is perhaps none where it can be done with so great a proffit & with more perfect security."[81]

By 1799 "never" had come. Willing & Francis, Bingham and Baring (three generations of in-laws), each contributed a third of the cargo for the China trader *Canton*: in all, $200,000 in specie and perhaps $50,000 more in iron and ginseng. Alexander apprised his father on May 9, 1799, informing him that the Baring share was equally Alexander's and Sir Francis's money. He hoped to sell the Baring portion for $100,000 after the ship's return, a roughly 20 percent profit. "I *know*," he told his father, this "can not leave a loss."[82] Here was an English East India Company director's money put into the American East Indies trade; men were accused of treason for less. Certainly it infringed on the Company's monopoly.

Sir Francis heartily approved. Even before learning of the *Canton*, he had already written with another means to facilitate U.S. trade in the Indies. Henry, another of Alexander's brothers, was forming a mercantile house at Canton. Sir Francis urged Alexander to "recommend" Henry to his American friends. Henry's agency was to draw silver from the Company's annual specie shipment to Canton and loan it to private merchants—American, British, or otherwise. This was standard practice, and agency houses were careful to draw on the Company only when it sent "much silver." The Barings were poised to finance and profit from the American East Indies trade on every front. "They will be supported from Bombay, Madras, and China," Sir Francis assured his son, with Alexander supporting them from Philadelphia.[83]

The Company would not be cheated, Sir Francis argued, as the "China trade from America cannot be pushed to a great extent. The chief article will always be tea, and you cannot have a market to take off the surplus quantity. What you import *must* be consumed in America. It is prohibited in Holland and will not sell for ¼ of its first cost anywhere else." Perhaps Sir Francis worried about the political consequences if the tea were re-exported ("must" read as an exhortation), or perhaps he knew there was no market for re-exported American tea—as discussed in Chapter 4, that market emerged later. Either way, as long as he did not have to read about the tea leaving the United States, Sir Francis was happy enough.[84]

The Barings were not alone. Scores of Europeans tried to break into the U.S. East Indies trade. "I find people in general have all some peculiar tye to some house in England," Alexander told his father shortly after his arrival in America. "We may creep into other very respectable connections," he explained, "but it must be gradually." In Boston, "Dickason"—Israel Thorndike's London banker—"has most of the independant business," and "the son resides here."[85] Some historians of the British Empire have argued that the entire U.S. East Indies trade was carried on by private British enterprise under American cover. This is incorrect; the preponderance of the investing capital, signed for as cargoes in American impost books, was American. And the implication that the U.S. East Indies trade lacked an important American component is wrong. The ships were American owned, and the American shipowners took one-third of the profits of any investor—British or American. During the French Wars these earnings were significant. As Cathy Matson has pointed out, U.S. "freight earnings . . . averaged more than $20 million a year between 1793 and 1802, compared to about $6.3 million in 1792. From 1803 to 1812, they rose to an annual average of $31 million, despite the embargo in the middle of that decade."[86] Freight earnings generally were a significant part of shipowners' revenue; valued at roughly 30 percent of all U.S. exports, freight charges were worth more than the sale value of any one commodity.[87]

British investors in London, such as Dickason, directed the peddling of U.S. East India goods in Europe; others, such as Baring, shipped specie from the United States to the Indies. These investments highlight the role of silver. U.S. merchants of competence cobbled their little silver capitals together with those of affluent merchants to make an investment. British investors added theirs, becoming additional consignees. British investors would continue to invest in the United States; after the East Indies trade they tried cotton mills and, later, railroads. Britain had surplus capital, U.S. merchants offered a good return, and British investors could, by looking at the relatively mature industries around them, intuit how the infant American businesses would take shape.

The French "Investment"

One man, whom Baring had met in his first months in America and "with whom I have conversed often," approached the American East India trade differently: Charles Maurice de Talleyrand-Périgord.[88] In America in 1794, the French diplomat Talleyrand proposed his own venture to India.[89] It was not his first Indian scheme. In 1790 and in Paris he had suggested forming an Indian bank. The Constituent Assembly had just resuppressed the French East India Company, and Talleyrand's bank would replace it. "Whoever knows the actual state of the European possessions in India," he explained, "knows that the employees of the English Company there possess immense riches, and that they meet with the greatest difficulties when it comes to the matter of realizing them in Europe."[90] He proposed that the bank accept Company employees' "immense riches" in the form of India goods and sell them in Paris. In return, English Company employees (often called "servants") would receive a bill of exchange drawn on the French bank. Unfortunately for Talleyrand, not too many French capitalists were willing to take their cash out of hiding in the middle of the Revolution. "One of the special characteristics of the revolutions of this century," he later wrote, "is to hold capital captive."[91] One wonders whether Company servants would have been any more forthcoming. Later, as French minister to London, Talleyrand sought out former Company officials and resurrected his bank scheme, only this time it was to be divided between London and the United States, and it would grant American land, rather than French bills, in exchange for Indian goods.[92]

This was what Baring abhorred. Talleyrand's bank would have no capital and would expose investors to a double risk: once in land and once in India goods. It proposed to carry on the East India trade without specie, stability, or basic banking principles. But it was representative of the vast number of ill-conceived schemes—like John Wingrove's proposal for an American East India Company—to use the U.S. trading position to skirt European restrictions.

Talleyrand's partner was to be Thomas Law, who in 1794 was living in New York and beginning, as was Talleyrand, a new life in America. Law had worked for the East India Company in Bengal, where he had reformed local land taxes, rationalizing the jumble of Indian tax farmers into the sort of landlords Englishmen would recognize. The reform proved a British success, and Lord Cornwallis extended it to the rest of Bengal under the rubric of the "Permanent Settlement," an event that earned Law a (somewhat notorious) place in Indian history.[93] Law returned to Britain in 1791, bringing with him £50,000 from his private trading in India. Back in Britain, as Talleyrand would tell it, Law began to feel ill used. He was "received with coldness and listened to with distraction;"[94] he objected to the war with France and resented the Company's attempts to sequester part of his Indian money. Later, Talleyrand described the mortification Company servants felt when they returned to Britain: accustomed to power and flush with wealth, they fit back awkwardly into British society, where less well-off aristocracy would not let them forget their place.[95]

In 1793 Law left for the United States, where, as in British India, money did buy class. There he met President Washington; in 1796, he married the First Lady's granddaughter, Elizabeth Parke Curtis.[96] He stayed in the United States, never quite shaking the stereotype of the "extremely wealthy but eccentric Englishman."[97] Had he brought £50,000 over in 1793, it would have been worth $225,500, enough for a competence at least.[98]

Law and Talleyrand discussed a venture to India at length. Law thought Company employees, hoping to get their wealth home without too many questions or taxes, might sell their wares for American deeds and then resell the deeds when they got back to Britain. In 1795 there was a bubble in U.S. land speculation into which foreign buyers could be drawn, and so for a moment it all seemed reasonable.[99]

The Holland Land Company was interested in Talleyrand's scheme and authorized the purchase of half a million acres in northern Pennsylvania. Talleyrand and his new partner, Beaumetz, paid $25,000 to rig a ship for Bengal, on which they sent no specie, only deeds. Beaumetz arrived in Calcutta in November 1796. But no Briton there wanted to sell his cargo to a French émigré with Dutch deeds for American land that neither of them had ever seen. Somehow, Beaumetz was surprised. Then he died. Talleyrand had already moved on.[100]

The venture illustrated Baring's point: the East Indies trade needed capital, which Talleyrand and Beaumetz lacked. (Talleyrand came to such straits in America that he had to auction off his oddly extensive wardrobe of women's clothing to raise money.[101]) It required reliable, knowledgeable merchants, not Talleyrand, "a proper rogue," as Rudyard Kipling later wrote.[102] Talleyrand's scheme foundered on the division in U.S. merchant society between those who had specie and those who did not—that is, those with affluence and competence on the one hand and the middling sort on the other. It was also a difference that the East Indies trade would reward and deepen as the French Wars continued.

The French Wars opened Continental markets to American businessmen, who exported produce from around the world to meet European demand. As more of Western Europe fell to the French, trading opportunities for U.S. neutrals increased. American merchants supplied French, French-European, and associated Caribbean markets that other countries, having joined the war, could not. At the same time, American capitalists increasingly worked together, enlarging their wealth and allowing for a few affluent, American business leaders to emerge. Eventually, their affluence would rival that of Britain's capitalists. In the meantime, their search for a framework under which they could collaborate would eventually have repercussions in American corporate law and regulation. The growing division of wealth within the top 1 percent of the population and its unique signification—business *capital* rather than genteel consumption—was the first step in that.

CHAPTER SIX

Beyond the British Empire

Seen from the other side of the gun, British expansion in Asia was a time to retrench and hope for survival. Yet the British did not burst forth and conquer all in 1793; the governors-general in India and the cabinets in London took nearly two decades (1793–1811) to conquer all the major French and French-allied ports in the east. Before then, the French, Dutch, and Spanish colonies of Asia limped on, nursed by neutral—and especially American—shipping, remembering their own imperial ambitions, and attempting some common front. Batavia (Dutch), Cape Town (Dutch), the Mascarenes (French), and Manila (Spain), unvisited by British arms, were among them. In these places, in the sometimes decades-long interval between the end of direct communication home and the arrival of British marines (who never did reach Manila this time), the origins of Europe's nineteenth-century imperial history in Asia emerged. American trade nursed these, the non-British empires.[1]

Batavia

Cut from the Netherlands by British ships and from British shipping by colonial authorities, in 1795 Dutch colonists in Batavia (present-day Jakarta) turned to Americans to run their trade home for them. U.S.-carried trade with Batavia and Sumatra grew so extensive that by the 1810s British negotiators worried about Americans establishing a settlement in Aceh or elsewhere in the archipelago.[2] Perhaps British authorities could not imagine trade without empire. In 1807, British officials at Penang imagined the meager U.S. trade at Rangoon to represent an "Ascendancy" of "American Interests" in Burma and believed (entirely false) rumors that the U.S. government was building a "a Ship of War" 400 miles upriver at Ava.[3] All this, of course, met the need of officials staffing a minor outpost to imagine a meaningful role for themselves in the empire. Despite these concerns, U.S. commercial dominance at Batavia was unconnected to any American imperial venture. And because U.S. trade brought no colonial baggage, U.S. merchants were welcome as imperially (if not commercially) disinterested parties in tenuously held ports like Batavia.

Sir Stamford Raffles, governor after the 1811 British conquest, noted in his *History of Java* that

> American trade was carried to the greatest extent during the existence of the anti-commercial system of the late French ruler [Bonaparte], when American traders purchased the Java coffee . . . at Batavia, and by a circuitous route imported it into France. . . . During this period, the purchases of the Americans in the market of Batavia, amounted in some years to nearly a million sterling, for which they obtained principally sugar, coffee, and spices.[4]

Raffles's specificity—he went on in some detail—suggests he wrote this passage with the Dutch shipping lists in front of him.

And well he may have: shipping records from Batavia reveal that between 1796 and 1807 the majority of long-haul arrivals were U.S.-owned vessels: 378 of 586 known vessels (65 percent) in that period (see Figure 6.1).[5] The annual share fluctuated between 50 percent and 80 percent and the vessels came from up and down the American coast: Boston to Baltimore to "Filadelvi" (Philadelphia, in the Dutch spelling).[6] American commercial supremacy at Batavia continued in a diminished form after this as well; the few U.S. vessels reaching Java in 1810 and 1811 were that island's sole commercial link to the outer world.[7]

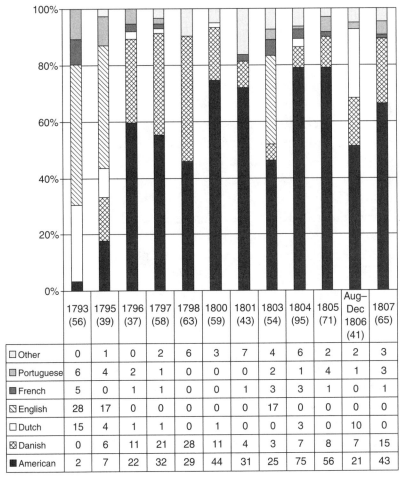

	1793 (56)	1795 (39)	1796 (37)	1797 (58)	1798 (63)	1800 (59)	1801 (43)	1803 (54)	1804 (95)	1805 (71)	Aug–Dec 1806 (41)	1807 (65)
☐ Other	0	1	0	2	6	3	7	4	6	2	2	3
☐ Portuguese	6	4	2	1	0	0	0	2	1	4	1	3
■ French	5	0	1	1	0	0	1	3	3	1	0	1
⊠ English	28	17	0	0	0	0	0	17	0	0	0	0
☐ Dutch	15	4	1	1	0	1	0	0	3	0	10	0
⊠ Danish	0	6	11	21	28	11	4	3	7	8	7	15
■ American	2	7	22	32	29	44	31	25	75	56	21	43

Figure 6.1 Percent Share of Known Vessels Arriving at Batavia by Flag, 1793–1807, for Select Periods (total arrivals in parentheses)

Sources: ANRI HR 2629 (1793); HR 2931 (1795); HR 2632 (1796); HR 2633 (1797); HR 2634 (1798); HR 2635 (1800–1807). Ships marked "private" have been changed to "Dutch," "EIC" to "English," and all military vessels are included in this count. One "Javan" ship has also been made "Dutch," as the ship name and master suggested. "Tosphanhse" had been made Tuscan. "Other" includes Arab, Atchenze, Bremen, Hamburg, Prussian, Ragusan, Spanish, Swedish, Tuscan, and unknown.

U.S. shipping data concur that an American commercial presence continued at Batavia through that period.[8] The scale of American shipping, nearly two-thirds of all long-haul arrivals, is noteworthy for what it reveals of the economic situation of the East Indies and of creole society there.

There was, however, nothing intrinsically American about American merchants' success. No cultural trait, no affinity for business, no Protestant ethic distinguished American businessmen from their Dutch or British cousins. In 1793 and 1795 the U.S. share of shipping was lower because the Anglo-Dutch alliance was known to be in effect. Again in 1803 with the Peace of Amiens, country traders had an important role at Batavia, controlling somewhere between a third and half of vessels arriving at those times.[9] (The country trade, which took place solely within the Indies, was popular with English Company employees trading on their own account.) Throughout the period between 1796 and 1807, neutral Danish traders also maintained a notable place in Batavia Roads.[10] And in 1811, when the British emerged militarily dominant, Britons swept the field of commerce. In the year after the British conquest of Batavia (September 16, 1811 to September 16, 1812), 138 of the 166 long-haul vessels[11] calling on the port (83 percent) were British, representing a massive increase in the share of trade and overall shipping volume.[12] In the same year, only six American vessels called on the island,[13] despite news of the War of 1812 having yet to reach Java (perhaps those vessels that had heard did not go). The U.S. boom at Batavia was due entirely to U.S. neutrality in the French Wars.[14] American merchants brought with that neutrality a shipping capacity few other countries' merchants could match. Desperate Dutch officials even went so far as to hire American, Danish, and Bremen-based ships[15] to carry their trade between Batavia and Japan, with most of the vessels hired being American (ten Americans in all),[16] simply because most of the hirable vessels in port were American. Dutch ships, meanwhile, were busy trying to keep British forces from closing in. As one official of the Vereenigde Oost-Indische Compagnie (VOC, or Dutch East India Company) in Japan explained, "all the Company's own ships which are in the Indies are needed against the enemy."[17] Americans were, metonymically, the empty vessels for others' commerce.

Cape Town

A similar pattern emerged in Cape Town. During the Dutch re-occupation of the Cape (1803–1806), neutral and especially U.S. trade boomed. More merchantmen calling at Cape Town flew the American flag than any other. And that neutral shipping kept the port's commerce alive. Nearly two-thirds of the known vessels arriving at the Cape during the Batavian period were neutral. Less than one-third were French or allied vessels, with a smattering arriving under the British flag as well (see Table 6.1).[18]

The Cape Colony had reverted to Dutch rule on February 21, 1803, as part of the Peace of Amiens. The Napoleonic Wars began just a few months later, leaving the colony cut off from the Netherlands. With much of the Dutch fleet requisitioned for Napoleon's invasion of England, and with British vessels, now enemy craft, shut out of the Cape, neutral and particularly American trade boomed. Indeed, U.S. commerce became the primary link between Dutch Cape Town and the rest of the world.

The neutral and American presence at the Cape was even greater than these raw data suggest, if only because the British and Continental shipping enumerated here was greatest, as on Java, at the beginning and end of Dutch rule. Data for late 1804, a period that would likely give even more neutrals, are unavailable.[19] The American commercial presence at the Cape grew and the trade of the feuding French, Dutch, and British diminished as Batavian rule wore on. So meager was these combatants' trade with the Cape that Cape Town officials recorded more vessels passing their port from the unallied German states (Bremen, Hamburg, Mecklenburg-Schwerin, and Prussia) in 1805 than from Britain, France, and the Netherlands combined.[20] Some may see these flags as mere conveniences for cargoes that were less politically correct—and these vessels probably did carry combatants' cargoes—but the nationalities of the *vessels* and hence of their

Table 6.1 Number of Likely East Indiamen Arriving at Cape Town, Batavian Period

	March 3, 1803–September 19, 1804		January 4, 1805–January 2, 1806		Total	
	Number of vessels	Percentage	Number of vessels	Percentage	Number of vessels	Percentage
French & allies	71	40	15	13	86	29
Total neutral	90	50	97	86	187	64
American	61	34	64	57	125	43
Danish	22	12	22	19	44	15
Other neutral	7	4	11	10	18	6
British	18	10	1	1	19	7
Total	179		113		292	

Source: CTAR BR 536, BR 537. Shipping records for the Batavian period at the Cape exist in two runs, with a three-month gap in the last quarter of 1804. The two periods are listed separately here. The total here thus includes the two periods only, not the entire Batavian period. For definition of "likely East Indiamen," see note 18.

owners were not likely to be ruses: Dutch and French merchants had no reason to hide their identity in a friendly port, and English Company ships, with their distinctive bulk and ornament, would have been hard to disguise.[21]

As on Java, British occupation of the Cape brought a rise in the number of British merchantmen and a falloff in neutral and American shipping. Between September 16, 1795, and July 1800, during the First British Occupation, 694 merchantmen arrived at Cape Town. Nearly two-thirds (440) were British. The last third (248) comprised American and neutral vessels, with a smattering of French and allied vessels calling as well.[22] In the years between 1806 and 1815, during the Second British Occupation, British trade became even more dominant. In that decade, over 1,300 merchantmen arrived at Cape Town; nearly nine-tenths were British, and the remaining share was neutral—largely American trade.[23] The abundance of American shipping during the Batavian period and its relative paucity during the British periods testify both to the lack of any enduring American commercial link with the Cape and Cape Town's particular dependence on neutral shipping during the Batavian period. Neutrality alone commended American bottoms to Dutch merchants.

The Mascarenes

The French Indian Ocean colonies, known collectively as the Mascarenes, followed the same course. On Ile de France (present-day Mauritius), the main French island, Americans bought sugar and coffee as well as some indigo ("much valued," Jacob Crowninshield thought) and cotton (the "best in the world," according to Crowninshield), just as they also bought sugar and coffee on Java. This period in Mauritian history has attracted scholarly attention, most notably from Auguste Toussaint, the island's mid-twentieth-century archivist, whose *La Route des Iles* and *Early American Trade with Mauritius* remain classic studies of Mauritian shipping. In the two decades of the French Wars during which Ile de France remained in French hands (1793–1810), more than three-quarters of long-distance arrivals at Port Louis, the main port on Ile de France, were foreign—748 out of 960 vessels counted by Toussaint in *La Route des Iles*.[24] The few French vessels that did arrive tended to come in 1793, before news of the war had reached Asia, or in 1803, during the Peace of Amiens. Over half (465 of 789) of the foreign vessels arriving at Port Louis were American. Almost a quarter (114 of 789) were Danish; the rest were owned by merchants from a smattering of neutral nations, none with distinguishing frequency.[25] Toussaint's *Early American Trade with Mauritius*, based on additional sourcing, gives larger figures (521 as opposed to 465) for American arrivals at Ile de France. By either count, U.S. trade was the lifeblood of the archipelago. While more than half (268 of 465) of U.S. arrivals came from the United States, U.S. vessels also linked the Mascarenes to France, Europe, and the rest of the Indies.[26]

Arrivals from outside the Mascarenes dropped off after 1808 due to a combination of factors: the increased vigor of the British blockade; the Bayonne proclamation, which ordered seizure of American ships in French ports; and the American embargo. Danish trade fell too, Denmark having shaken off its neutrality the previous year. As at Batavia, British rule eliminated the basis for neutral trade altogether. Thus, between the fall of Mauritius and the end of the war (1810–1815), over 100 long-distance vessels stopped at Mauritius. Only seven were American.[27] Nearly all the rest were British.

Manila

Spain remained France's reluctant ally from 1796 to 1808, leaving Manila—like Batavia, Cape Town, and Mauritius—to keep its links to the Atlantic world in neutral ships. Of the years between 1795 and 1815 from which annual totals survive, only thirty-eight vessels are known to have arrived in Manila from the Atlantic, but thirty of them came from the United States and, of the remaining eight, two came from the United States via India. Esteban Martinez Ballesteros, a Manila customs official, explained that "many

European ships from neutral nations have come in search of sugar and indigo,"[28] commodities which, as U.S. customs records indicate, Americans did carry home. Between 1794 and 1807 the United States imported over 6 million pounds of sugar from the Philippines and over 400,000 pounds each of coffee and indigo.[29] In the context of worldwide sugar trade or even in the context of Manila's trade, this was not a great deal—most ships entering and leaving Manila were sampans shuttling to China; significant numbers of vessels also connected Manila to the Sultinate of Sulu to the south and India to the west, but American traffic provided one of Manila's few links to the Atlantic. In addition to direct trade with the United States, Danish merchants in Tranquebar and Serampore traded with Manila as well, and some were thought vehicles for onward remittance to Copenhagen or London. In all, another fifty vessels were recorded as arriving in Manila from India while flying a distinct national flag (another twenty-eight vessels have no flag listed); most (thirty-one) of this fifty were British country traders, though Danish merchants traded in Manila before 1808 and Spaniards afterward as well.[30] As elsewhere, American traffic at Manila fell off after 1808, not only because of the American embargo but because the Spanish governor, incensed at Napoleon's meddling with the Spanish throne, threw his allegiance to Ferdinand VII and opened his ports to British trade from India in 1809, which then boomed, as happened at Batavia, Cape Town, and Mauritius after their British conquests. American trade did not vanish after the British arrival in these ports, but it was dwarfed by the greater British shipping, and the American and neutral dominance of trade between these East Indian ports and Europe can be considered fairly evanescent.

Economic Legacies

This much might be expected, especially by those familiar with the boom in neutral trade in the Caribbean and Europe. Yet this alteration in Europe's East Indian commerce affected far more than the flags run up masts in colonial ports; it altered the Continent's economic relations with the Indies and the course of European colonialism in Asia.

The ports of Manila, Batavia, Cape Town, and Mauritius were hubs linking to regional economies beyond them.[31] Sugar and coffee flowed to Batavia from the rest of Java and from other islands, carried on Javan, Timorse, Achean, and Balinese vessels. These goods left Batavia for the Atlantic largely in American shipping. There was a significant Chinese trade with Java, but it did not connect Java to other Dutch colonies or to Atlantic markets.[32] The Dutch empire in the Java Sea was linked to the Atlantic largely through American ships. Cape Town also supported a regional, if less substantial, commerce that likewise relied on American shipping for its survival. Ile de France linked to Madagascar, Rodrigues, and Réunion, as well as to more disparate Indian Ocean islands: Agalega, Diego Garcia, the Comoros, and the Seychelles. As with the Java Sea and Cape Colony regions, the Mascarene area linked to the outside world via American ships. Manila took in sugar from Pampanga and Pangasinan; coffee came in from Cavite, just down the bay; and small farmers' produce arrived from further away. Though, as in Batavia, a significant Chinese presence linked Manila to Chinese markets, Chinese merchants did not link Manila to the Atlantic or the European imperial core; that was left largely to American and neutral shipping.[33]

For their part, American merchants were unconcerned with national boundaries; they bought what they could sell anywhere, not just what they could sell in the United States. This heightened their interest in sugar and coffee. Slave insurrection, warfare, privateering, and embargo were destroying sugar and coffee output in the Caribbean, and so U.S. merchants supplemented their supply from Asia.[34] The Caribbean remained the main source of sugar and coffee for Western consumers, but in the East Indian ports themselves, the relative increase in American sugar and coffee purchases, small by international standards, had large local effects. Such was the case in Batavia, where the purchase of approximately $4 million a year of sugar, coffee, and spices seems to have encouraged both Dutch and British governors in their commercial and agricultural reforms. American and neutral purchases kept these colonies producing cash crops and even encouraged the intensification of this sort of agriculture: sugar on Ile de France, coffee on Réunion, sugar and coffee on Java, and sugar again, among other crops, in the Philippines.[35] Later British occupation of many of these places intensified commercial farming further.

Asia and the Indian Ocean had been sources of high-value and finished products—expensive spices and hand-woven cloth—but the Indies were quickly becoming a source of cheaper monoculture, including sugar, coffee, indigo, and cotton. This transition was occurring during the French Wars, but its roots in the period are easily missed because of a number of wrinkles in the local historiography.

Historians of the Mascarenes, for example, have asserted that U.S. merchants were attracted there mainly for Indian cloth, which, we are told, was taken from British merchants by French corsairs in great quantities.[36] Yet this is highly unlikely, for as the French naval and colonial ministry noted before the outbreak of hostilities, Ile de France was simply "not an entrepôt for merchandise."[37] Once the war began, French raiders, few and far between, were incapable of rerouting the vast stream of British Indian commerce to the Mascarenes. Had the French been capable of this, British authorities in India would not have waited until 1810 to take Ile de France. Privateers' interest was more often in food than finery, though indeed finery might buy food. It is not even clear how many British goods French raiders took, or how many reached markets outside the Mascarenes; though people on Ile de France noted Indian cloth on the island during the French Wars, they did not note how much. One good source for clarifying this issue, Mauritian prize auction records, shows Americans buying few auction lots—fewer than two or three per hundred. Many of the lots for sale did not contain any Indian goods at all, but rather Madeira wine or other items destined for sale *to* India; others comprised ship fittings (wood, doors, cabinets, and hinges). French merchants likely resold some of these cargoes on to Americans, but it is unclear how many, and there is no evidence in the auction records themselves of significant amounts of Indian cargo among the prizes or, in lieu of such cargoes, evidence that Americans were sailing halfway around the world for hinges.[38]

U.S. customs records concur. These records list American vessels importing only $966,639 worth of unspecified "goods" (the category under which either Indian cloth or British hinges would have fallen) from Mauritius for the period between 1794 and 1810, while importing more than $37.5 million in "goods" from the British East Indies in the same period. Clearly, India remained their source for cloth.[39] Rather than buy cloth, Americans at Ile de France bought agricultural products: sugar, coffee, indigo, and cotton. Over the same period, Americans brought in 13.3 million pounds of brown sugar from Ile de France, 34.3 million pounds of Réunion coffee, and lesser quantities of indigo and raw cotton. "Leakage" from British India was not the mainstay of the Mauritian economy. Indeed, the large number of American vessels stopping at Ile de France en route *from* India suggests that Americans were probably the ones bringing Indian cloth to Ile de France in the first place.[40] The Mascarenes had been hubs for French trade in Indian cloth in peacetime, but that trade halted during the war years and never revived. Instead, the Mascarenes emerged as commercial entities unto themselves—something the fixation upon Indian cloth obscures. During the French Wars, American commerce nurtured the islands' plantations. Just as elsewhere in the Indies, Americans paid in silver for the fruits of local labor, in the cash-starved Mascarenes, where the local currency had been considerably devalued, this made Americans' demands for sugar and coffee hard to resist.[41]

Java followed a similar trajectory. The High Government at Batavia, previously part of the Dutch East India Company, fended for itself when the Company collapsed in 1795. To do so it maintained the old Company's demands for the forced delivery of sugar, coffee, and other crops from the hinterland to its warehouses—a tax in kind and labor upon its vassals and subjects. Some U.S. merchants, confused at how much like the old system this looked, continued to refer to the "Company" on Java, but in fact the Dutch Company, as a shipping concern, no longer existed. In its place, the High Government at Batavia sold the coffee and sugar in its warehouses to

American and other neutral merchants, who, paying cash, directly financed Dutch operations on Java.[42]

Back in the Netherlands, the various government councils and committees managing the old Company concerns maintained a dirigist approach to the economic links between the Netherlands and the Dutch East Indies: the bureaucratic instincts and private interests of the old Company died hard. But they did die ultimately, in no small part due to American influence. At war with Britain, the Dutch had little means to trade with Java themselves and in 1795 immediately began contracting out to neutrals—Americans among them—to sail from the Netherlands to Batavia, bringing back the sugar and coffee in the High Government's warehouses to the Dutch market. Seven American vessels were chartered in 1795. Another six were hired in 1801 and 1802, and a greater number of Danish vessels were fitted out in the interim. During the Peace of Amiens officials in the Netherlands abandoned foreign carriers and rushed as many Dutch vessels to Java as they could to take off the commodities stored in Batavian warehouses. But the peace did not last, and once war resumed, officials in the Netherlands returned to a policy of hiring neutrals to bring back Javan cargoes: seven American vessels were chartered to carry specie to Batavia, along with orders that the High Government there load them with coffee and sugar. The government in Batavia was reluctant; it got more money from Americans arriving there and buying cargoes on their own account than from those arriving under contract from the Dutch home government, and so Batavian authorities loaded the American ships chartered in the Netherlands with bad goods, and little of them.[43]

For the Americans, letting a vessel out to the Dutch government had become a poor proposition, and so most Americans traded to Java directly instead. Between 1795 and 1805, Dutch authorities hired twenty American merchantmen to run from the Netherlands to Batavia; nearly 300 additional American vessels arrived at Batavia in that same decade. Many brought colonial products back to the United States, often to be sold on to the Netherlands. Others sailed from Java to the Netherlands without Dutch sanction, flaunting the Dutch government's monopoly, in theory at least, on the authorization of direct trade between colony and metropole. Faced with the reality of having neither the ships to trade to Asia directly nor the means to charter a commerce to Asia with which American merchants and the government in Java would cooperate, in 1805 Dutch authorities gave up the pretense of control and permitted a free trade for all merchants between the Netherlands and Asia. The man who permitted this, Grand Pensionary Rutger Jan Schimmelpenninck, was a Dutch revolutionary of long standing (he had been part of the 1787 revolution). It is unclear whether revolutionary ideals influenced his decision to allow free trade.[44] Yet, revolutionary decision or not, the corrosive presence of American free trade, emerging from its own revolutionary tradition, had forced his hand.

Sale of the coffee and sugar delivered to its warehouses was one of the primary sources of revenue for the High Government on Java. Dutch officials there, already precariously positioned, resisted policies from the Netherlands that stood to undermine their revenues and actively encouraged foreign merchants' arrival in Batavia to buy colonial goods outside the contracting done from the Netherlands. Governor Weise went as far as to send a councilor from the Dutch East Indies to the United States to promote further U.S. commercial ventures to Batavia. Once the Netherlands government opened direct trade between the Netherlands and Java in 1805—it permitted foreign trade with the Moluccas that same year as well—it asked James Madison, then secretary of state, to assist that councilor in his endeavor, so crucial had U.S. shipping become for the Javan government's health.[45] Jacob Crowninshield, who had captained a venture to the Indies and remained apprised of trading conditions there from his family's merchant house, reported that American vessels had "exhausted" the Batavian sugar and coffee supplies in 1805, some leaving while still "disappointed of their cargoes."[46]

Manila was the western terminus of the silver galleons crossing the Pacific from Acapulco; those galleons, refilled with silk, porcelain, and chinoiserie, returned to Latin America, having only a passing effect on the Philippine economy as a whole. Manila was simply a place to exchange foreign silver for foreign goods. Chinese merchants returned to China with Latin American silver and came back the next season with more goods to stock the galleons' holds. Commercially, the Philippines was a trans-Pacific appendage of Mexico, subsidized from the Mexican colonial budget. Indeed, so much of Manila's trade was tied up with Mexico that the Manila customs house was under Mexican jurisdiction until 1805. Few galleons sailed in the early nineteenth century: the silver lodes were dwindling, and after 1808 the struggles for Latin American independence interrupted this commerce further; the Mexican War of Independence, which began two years later, soon rendered the galleons impracticable. The galleons did not survive the 1810s.[47] The Philippines no longer faced across the Pacific Ocean to Mexico, but across the Indian Ocean to the Atlantic.

Governor Basco y Vargas (1778–1787), the Philippines' own Bourbon reformer, had already laid the groundwork for an alternate commerce. Vargas was inspired by British administration of the Philippines (1762–1764) during the Seven Years' War, which showed the potential for an export-oriented Philippine economy.[48] One of his most significant reforms was the establishment of the Royal Company of the Philippines in 1785. This Company was meant to encourage the development of a local plantation economy and initiate direct commercial links with Spain. The Royal Company had a monopoly on carrying Philippine colonial produce and Chinese manufactures to Spain (Chinese manufactures going to Mexico still followed the galleon trade). The Company offered bounties, distributed farms tools, and bought land, all to encourage Philippine economic growth, though results were not always successful.[49] In 1785 Manila was opened to European and American merchants trading within Asia so that the Company could acquire from them a stock of goods to ship to Spain. In 1789, Manila was decreed open to European and American merchants trading to the Atlantic as well, in the hopes that the Royal Company might sell Philippine produce to them.[50]

Such economic exploitation of the Philippines was new, some historians even consider it to have amounted to an "agricultural revolution."[51] Spanish rule in the Philippines traditionally had been less concerned with extracting colonial produce for the metropolitan market than had Dutch rule in Java or Spanish rule in the New World. Rather, promotion of the Catholic faith had been the colony's raison d'être. The Spanish economic footprint was so light that through the seventeenth and eighteenth centuries no more than half a dozen lay Spaniards owned *haciendas* (landed estates) at any one time,[52] though a number of Catholic orders possessed *haciendas* producing food crops for the domestic market. Tomas de Comyn, the Royal Company's manager in Manila, thought lay *haciendas* numbered "not more than a dozen" as late as 1810—a marked difference from how Spanish colonization had proceeded in the New World.

Seeing the need to develop Philippine farming, Vargas also pursued agricultural reform, founding a society for the propagation of best practices. The Royal Company continued to invest capital in plantation agriculture, with particular success in sugar, which the Company shipped to Spain. The Company's voyages to Cadiz became a major source of customs revenue for the Manila government, but the French Wars soon interrupted the Royal Company's trade with Spain just as they had the Manila galleons' trade with Mexico.[53]

In stepped the Americans, Danes, and other neutrals on whom the Royal Company had to rely to take its cargoes to Europe. The Company encountered mounting problems in Philippine agriculture as well, in addition to difficulty with Spanish creoles who resisted the idea of becoming planters. As they explained to Governor Vargas's successor,

> the Spanish conquerors of these islands did not leave Spain to take up the plow in Filipinas; much less did they undertake so long and unknown a voyage to set up looms and transplant new fruits. At the first suggestion of this they would have left the islands, and the archipelago would today be in the hands of another power.[54]

And so despite the Royal Company's best efforts, small-scale agriculture remained the rule in the Philippines as largely native or Chinese mestizo upper-class pueblo families—the "real body of farming proprietors," as Comyn called them in 1810—turned some of their lands in Luzon over from rice to other crops. These free native and mestizo farmers, not the Company warehouse (as at Batavia), supplied American trade in the Philippines.

As the Company collapsed, Anglo-American merchant houses were attracted to Manila, providing crucial access to world markets for those upper-class pueblo families involved in export agriculture. Between 1786 and 1800 the Company purchased only 8,044 piculs of sugar (a picul equals 133 pounds). At the same time, foreign merchants purchased more than 29 times that amount. Between 1786 and 1802, foreign purchases of indigo were, by volume, almost four times the Company's. Anglo-Americans were prominent among these foreign buyers, with British merchants from India often working through Danish intermediaries during the war. The Anglo-American presence persisted after 1815, enabling the development of plantation agriculture in the 1820s. British and American trading houses provided crucial services to Groniere's pioneering plantation across the Laguna de Bay in Jalajala.[55]

Despite the differences between these colonies, in the Mascarenes, Dutch East Indies, and Philippines exports to the Atlantic spread cash-crop farming over ever-larger swaths of land, transforming Port Louis, Batavia, and Manila from entrepôts in the French, Dutch, and Spanish trades for exotic, high-value Asian products brought in from India, the Spice Islands, China and Japan, into entrepôts for cash crops produced locally. American and neutral shipping's true significance lay in their support of this trade, which otherwise would have languished throughout the Indo-Pacific. In these ports, Chinese or Indian goods were of little interest to U.S. merchants capable of purchasing those goods from the Asian mainland themselves. Britons carried on in these ports where Americans and other neutrals left off. The conquests of Mauritius and Java and the Spanish realignment toward Britain opened these ports to the country trade of East India Company employees and private British merchants based in India. Their trade was larger than the American trade could ever be; British traders in India had a large supply of India-built ships. These were cheap to construct (compared with ships built in Britain) and, based in the Indian Ocean, able to make shorter trips to Batavia, Port Louis, and Manila than ships based in the United States.

American merchants and private British traders were of a piece, and the transformation of Europe's colonies in Asia was not the product of distinctively British or American styles of commerce, but of Anglo-American enterprise. American and British merchants' individual and competitive efforts—the first in war, the other in peace—to profit from the trade of Europe's colonies in the Indies supported the transformation of European colonialism in Asia into its much-more-recognizable nineteenth-century form. Port Louis, Batavia, and Manila were all occupied by Britain at one time or another; British occupation of the latter in the 1760s spurred the introduction of economic reforms; British occupation of the others in the 1810s encouraged economic transformations already underway. And in the transformation of those colonies in the half century between these dates—what Nicholas Tarling has called an "age of transition" in Asia—American commerce supported them at their most precarious time.[56]

Imperial Links

Links between French Europe and French-aligned colonies in Asia were precarious, because France and its allies could not project sizable naval forces into the Indian Ocean. Nor could they send large numbers of troops on the few vessels that did slip past the British Channel fleet. As Divisional General François-Louis Magallon, then posted at Ile de France, noted, the Mascarenes were "separated from the metropole by an immense interval, lacking in everything, abandoned to themselves"; how they managed "braving and incessantly molesting the enemy and harming her commerce so incredibly" was a "wonder." The Naval Ministry agreed, taking the game suggestion that the inhabitants of the Mascarenes "can defend themselves with their own means," and flipping it on its head: the inhabitants of the Mascarenes would have to defend themselves if there were to be any defense at all. As the French Navy office explained, the French on Ile de France possessed "few means of resistance compared to those their enemies can employ to attack them."[57] Indeed, the Mascarenes dealt such minimal harm to British commerce that the real wonder was how the French could hold out there (and the Dutch and Spanish elsewhere) at all. Likewise, at the Cape the Dutch had barely enough troops to maintain order and deter nearby tribes. The best units had been sent to Java, a colony deemed more crucial, leaving a motley crew of only 2,000: German and Hungarian mercenaries, Javan artillery men, French marines, a "coloured" regiment, Dutch troops, and Mozambique slaves—the flotsam and jetsam of allied empires. The British, by contrast, reinvaded with 6,500 men and considerable battle experience and won handily.[58]

Despite their size, U.S. vessels (smaller than VOC ships) were close to the only link home that Dutch, French, and Spanish colonists had. In 1795, authorities in the Netherlands hired an American vessel to make the Cape and warn the incoming Dutch East India Company fleet of war with Britain.[59] French officials returning home from Ile de France, hoping to avoid stints as prisoners of war, often made the trip on American vessels.[60] Americans and other neutrals carried correspondence around the Indies and between the Indies and Europe for France and its allies. Thus the French foreign minister could tell Napoleon in 1808 that "the American brig *Batavia*" had arrived from New York, carrying a French general's news on Persia. Willem Jacob Van de Graaff, the former governor of Ceylon and president of the High Government at Batavia, took passage from Java to Hamburg on an American neutral. Manila's links with other Asian ports were likewise so dominated by neutrals that when a British ship wrecked off Mindoro and its crew was transported to Manila, the Spanish governor sent the captain on to the British factory in Canton by an American brig.[61] This was not a foolproof system—Van de Graaff's vessel was taken prize—but it was the only method these officials had. Likewise, correspondence from Batavia, the Cape, and Mauritius to Europe was liable to interception by British cruisers, but U.S. shipping was one of the few ways these officials could correspond.[62]

In Ile de France, at least, neutral trade was so dominant that Americans provisioned the island. "Nearly all the supplies of the Isle of France come from us," the American Amasa Delano noted at the onset of the French Revolutionary War.[63] Ile de France planters, like their Caribbean counterparts, found it profitable to devote their land exclusively to sugar and to import food for their slaves from abroad, leaving Ile de France reliant on food from Madagascar, Réunion, the Cape, Batavia, and even Bengal.[64] Ile de France needed neutral-carried supplies to the extent that, as the colonial prefect explained in 1803, "admission of neutrals in these colonies . . . [is] a necessity." Just as Americans re-exported East Indies goods wherever they could find a market, so they ignored national distinctions in the cargoes they brought to East Indian ports, forcing the French in the Mascarenes to hold their noses and buy British, as so many of their compatriots had to do in France. "Since the war," explained the prefect, "only Americans have come here, who are nearly all linked to the English, and there is no other means to provision the colony." Though British patrols tried to stop Americans from running directly to French and allied ports, American captains simply lied, claimed they were heading for some neutral port, and sailed to Ile de France.[65] The American scramble to provision the Mascarenes proceeded at such a pace that, by 1807, the French governor thought further imports could be sold only at a loss.[66]

This was, of course, an imperfect way to run a colony. When U.S. shipping began to disappear in 1807 and 1808, supplies in the East Indian colonies grew short. As French scholar Henri Prentout explains, with the Jeffersonian embargo "all business ceased" at Ile de France, a dire situation for a colonial government that had generated more than half its revenue from customs receipts.[67] Trade collapsed at Batavia as well, and between 1808 and 1811 not a single Dutch ship arrived to make up the loss. Rationing set in, and though basic foodstuffs were not lacking, European foods were. To conserve wine and oil, Governors Herman Willem Daendels and Jan Willem Janssens forbade large parties and the illumination of private homes. Silver became scarce.[68] Because the Batavian economy was connected abroad by American ships, as one dwindled, so did the other.

The lack of national links affected colonial society. Even before the onset of the French Wars, Batavian society "was formed" such that, as historian Jean Gelman Taylor describes, it "was clearly not Dutch any longer" but rather a creole mix, with "locally born wives, Mestizo and Asian kin." Batavian culture was so distinctively mestizo that, Taylor argues, Dutch administrators felt the need to generate a connection in local whites' minds back toward Netherlands society and away from Javan affairs—an attempt that was largely unsuccessful, leaving "Batavia's elite" "more autonomous than before" in the last quarter of the eighteenth century.[69] During the French Wars this local identity strengthened further.

During the French Wars, new colonial administrators could not be sent to Java; increasingly these ranks had to be drawn from the creole population, which strengthened that population's hold on local power. Indeed, by the first decade of the nineteenth century, Governor Daendels began admitting half-Asians into the Javan bureaucracy in order to fully staff its offices. Two Batavian governors in this period even chose to retire to Java rather than go back "home" to the Netherlands. A generation of Batavians grew up cut off from Europe and from Dutch culture. Everything had to be done by locals themselves.[70]

Imperial Legacies

Despite this, none of these colonies sought independence—though historians have long looked for signs otherwise. But the creole "uprisings" of this era—Graaff-Reinet's expulsion of the *landdrost* sent from Cape Town, and Ile de France's expulsion of the commissioners come to enforce the revolutionary ban on slavery—were not national revolts: they were assertions of creole authority over slaves and free blacks, of that white authority that dated from those colonies' first founding and that was crucial, in the creoles' minds, for the maintenance of order. This relative lack of revolt contrasts markedly with Spanish America, nearly all of which had seen revolution by the end of the French Wars. Hardly nationalists, the Africaaners at Graaff-Reinet indicated their *preference* for a British administrator over the Dutch one they so detested.[71] Nor did the Colonial Assembly on Ile de France seek independence, despite fears to the contrary circulating in Paris. "The creole," observed one of the expelled commissioners, "loves the French name and is capable of doing all to sustain and preserve it." Indeed, they knew how to insult those "monsters, greedy-for-French-blood-like-cannibals" Englishmen with the best of them.[72]

Order was the fundamental concern of the few whites in the East Indies. The British naval commander at the Cape feared its loss and reported that the Graaff-Reinetters "are ready at all times to invite the Caffres to assist them in opposition to the Government,"[73] but those very same Graaff-Reinetters were in fact worried that the British would set the 200 or so "hottentots" in town against them.[74] Both concerns were groundless. They reflected British and Dutch desires for stability and the fear of each that the other would be so depraved as to cross race lines to disturb it. Likewise, the creoles on Ile de France who had expelled the French commissioners because they feared abolition willingly submitted to metropolitan authority—French or British—that upheld slavery.[75] In Batavia Daendels' admission of nonwhites to government offices served to maintain the administration, not promote any social or racial goals or a distinctively creole *Indische* culture.[76]

All these colonies supported comparatively small creole populations. Raffles counted 2,028 Europeans and 45,189 Asians on his arrival at Batavia in 1811.[77] In 1797 a French census revealed 59,000 inhabitants on Mauritius: 6,200 whites, 3,700 free nonwhites, and 49,100 African slaves. Cape Town was at least half slave as well.[78] All these colonies required the labor of vast numbers of indentured servants, slaves, and Chinese laborers to survive. None could call upon much coercive power from Europe to protect themselves from slave revolts or the attacks of local rulers; the creole population asserted the coercive power of colonial government—or at least the threat thereof—themselves.[79] Remarkably, and in great contrast to the French Caribbean, there were no major slave uprisings in the Mascarenes.

To a creole population so outnumbered, being part of an empire was likely more attractive than independence. These creoles did not even seem to identify with any one empire in particular. Pro- and anti-revolutionary creoles kept their disagreements from compromising colonial defenses. The Dutch creoles in British-occupied Ceylon were as uninterested in revolt as their brethren in still-Dutch Java. Batavia did not have to side with the Patriot government against Britain—it would, after all, have been protected by British cruisers and nursed by British commerce had it stayed loyal to the House of Orange. But when British troops finally attacked, Orangist creoles did not give up their revolutionary compatriots to the British. Nor, afterward, did creoles who had worked with the French-aligned government resist British rule.[80] And though the British were concerned enough to stamp out pro-Dutch sentiment in the Cape, there was precious little of it to begin with; settlers there had as many Flemish, French, and German ancestors as Dutch. The British took pains to swear their new subjects in Mauritius to "oaths of allegiance," but found they needed to do little more that conduct such a ceremony to assure the quiescence of the French creole population, which remained Francophonic for 150 years of British colonial rule. Even on Ceylon, where many Dutch refused the British oath of allegiance in 1796, Britain gradually accommodated those Dutch residents who remained to British rule.[81]

A similar preference for empire over independence emerged among creoles in the Philippines. When the Penninsular War broke out in 1808, the Philippines was one of the few Spanish colonies that did not declare independence. This was not because the idea failed to occur to anyone—one French merchant in town thought it would nicely settle the issue of which Spanish king to support. Instead, the governor declared for the anti-Napoleonic king and arrested the emissary sent from Ile de France, asking that he "clarify" his position.[82] When the emissary was freed—the governor explaining that it had all been for his protection from anti-French mobs—Manila had fully turned against France and, unlike so many other Spanish colonies, remained Spanish.[83] The separation from Spain between 1796 and 1808 had not tarnished the legitimacy of Spanish rule.

In this sense, Mauritius, Batavia, the Cape, and the Philippines resembled the Anglo-American colonies of an earlier age. Batavia ran itself in the name of Dutch rule in the 1790s just as Virginia had run itself in the name of English rule in the 1640s. The colonists felt so poorly entrenched that they remained attached to the metropole regardless of who ruled there. They remained unreservedly colonial, no matter how long it took to work out who ruled at home, to establish the legal form of the colonial relationship, and to send out new administrators.[84]

The contrast to colonies in the Americas could not be more striking. The revolutions of the 1810s were defining moments in the history of Spanish-speaking America. Yet the lack of revolution in what would become Mauritius, South Africa, Indonesia, and the Philippines in this era is as defining in those countries' histories as the revolutions that did occur in the Americas are for the countries there. In Asia and Africa, unlike in the Americas, European governments could count on the unswerving loyalty of local whites. The Americas—where the French Revolution and the Napoleonic Wars sparked off a great chain of revolutions from Haiti and Mexico on down through South America, and where revolutionary rhetoric and ideology incited revolts among people of every race and mixture—were the exception. Asia, where the vast majority of the world's colonial peoples lived, was the rule. In Asia, Spanish creoles did not revolt, French slaves did not rise up, and there was no Dutch Patriot revolution. Asia was safe for colonialism. It is no small wonder, then, that after 1815 most European governments interested in overseas colonies began their own belated swings to the east. The Culture System in the Netherlands East Indies was the most deliberate example of imperial catch-up.[85] The Europe-wide colonization of Asia after 1815 occurred in tandem with the decline in the economic importance of the Caribbean and British enforcement of the Monroe Doctrine, both further emphasizing the European swing to the east.[86]

CHAPTER SEVEN

The India Trade

In the 1790s, while Americans traded to French, Dutch, and Spanish colonies to the east, the English East India Company dissipated its money on imperial wars that failed to check American trade. Britain took Ceylon and the outlying islands in the Dutch East Indies quickly; among these, Ceylon's cinnamon plantations did prove fairly valuable. But the central enemy ports—Batavia, Manila, and Port Louis—remained untaken for most of the French Wars, closed to Britons but open to neutrals. Meanwhile, U.S. vessels traded heavily in Calcutta, forcing the Company to compete with them there while it absorbed the cost of wars that only marginally advanced its trading position. Both the gambit to make London the emporium of Asia and the Company's own profits rested heavily on the Company's ability to dominate Western trade in India and China.

Alas for the Company, London did not become *the* emporium of Asia because the United States already was one. In part, government policy—permitting U.S. trade to British India and delaying the conquest of enemy colonial possessions—made it so. But the Company suffered from handicaps of its own. U.S. trade with Asia and U.S. re-exports of Asian goods, previously discussed, denied the Company dominance in east-west trade. U.S. trade with Calcutta was one of the most damning parts of this.

The Inefficiency of Monopoly

The scheme to conquer the Indies and make London the "emporium of the world" was an energetic response to the Company's troubles in turning a profit, which had dogged the Company even before the Boston Tea Party. The problem stemmed doubly from the expense of its government responsibilities (maintaining a navy, an army, and administering parts of India) and from its monopoly, which, by guaranteeing a British market for Company purchases in India, made even obvious cost-cutting measures seem unnecessary.

The clearest such measure—aside from starting fewer wars—was constructing cheaper ships. The Company's ships were expensive because the people the Company hired to build its ships had hired themselves: the Company's Committee of Shipping gave Company shipbuilding contracts to the committee members' own shipyards. They built the largest and most ornate merchant fleet in Britain. The workmanship, carpentry, and detail were astounding and unnecessary. British private merchants, trading to the Caribbean or the Baltic, built nothing like them; nor did U.S. East India merchants. The shipyards then leased their ships to the Company for six voyages, which just happened to be the life span of an East Indiaman. The Committee of Shipping provided the Company with a fleet of overpriced, overbuilt rentals that, because of their size and baroque design, were unusable in any other trade.

In reaction to this, free-trade agitators—many of whom would have liked to lease their own ships to the Company or ship their own goods between India and Britain at cheaper rates—opposed the Company's monopoly. They did so from within the Company's Court of Directors and also from Parliament. The Shipping Interest, controlling the Committee of Shipping and allied with some of the City banks, defended the monopoly. This was a political contest between business interests; and by facing business rivals in an exclusively political manner, the Shipping Interest left its opponents' commercial needs dangerously unaddressed. The Company also failed to compete commercially with foreign East India traders, for competitive business practices would cut into the Shipping Interest's profits. This failure to compete made free traders' objections to the Company's monopoly seem principled, as, in part, they were.[1]

During the 1793 renewal of the Company's charter, the ministry, concerned with the war against France, had little time for a protracted legislative battle over the charter. But Henry Dundas was still a reformer and a free trader at heart; and so, rather than abandon his cause completely, he compromised. The Company would lease out 3,000 tons of shipping a year on its own India ships—roughly a third of its total capacity[2]—to private British merchants conducting their own ventures. The Company set the freight rates and still controlled all British ships running between the Atlantic and Asia, yet Dundas hoped private merchants could make some ventures to Asia on Company ships. The Company deterred private merchants from taking up this tonnage by charging exorbitant freight rates (at times 50 percent more than what foreign shippers charged), foisting excessive bureaucracy and red tape on potential shippers, and then, when the private trade did not take off, paying its shills to propagandize the failure. "The studied Plan of the Company ever since the renewal of their Charter has been to crush Private Trade and ruin those concerned in it," complained one private trader to Dundas. In some years, Anglo-Indian merchants did not even take up the full 3,000 tons; so poor were the returns that they invested their funds elsewhere, just as the Shipping Interest wanted.[3]

Yet the Shipping Interest's plan was shortsighted: demand for carrying capacity between Britain and India did not vanish. Other carriers would profit from this demand instead, their growth revealing the Company's inability to make London the hub of Asian commerce. Thus between June 1795 and May 1796—a fairly average trading year during the French Wars—Americans carried 6,500 tons of shipping out of Bengal.[4] This represented more than the total capacity of the Company-carried private trade—though the full 3,000 tons were not always used. Merchants in Britain, such as Thomas Dickason and Sir Francis Baring, invested their own capitals in the American East Indies trade. Perhaps, had private trade on Company ships not been so burdened, Dickason and Baring would not have traded to India in American ships. Such reasoning would have been classically Pittite—the sort of rationalizing Smithian reform the young prime minister was famous for in the 1780s. Because such reform never happened, and because the 1793 act prolonged the Company's and the Shipping Interest's monopoly, U.S. merchants continued to attract and profit from British investment with ease. Anglo-Indian attempts to remit goods and funds to the Atlantic in American ships would stop only, as Dundas acknowledged, when licit trade paid close to what illicit commerce did.[5] Since individual Britons could not send their own ships between India and Britain, and since Company stock did not pay dividends commensurate with the returns of the trade itself, sending their cargoes in American ships from which American shipowners profited made sense. By 1813, when the Company's charter came up for renewal again, the Company had not failed completely—it had conducted *some* trade to India—but it had permitted an embarrassing American success in Calcutta, the very heart of Company India. And it had failed to engross all of Europe's trade with Asia—Robert Dundas's threshold in making London the emporium.

The Jay Treaty

To make matters worse, from the Company's perspective at least, Whitehall put British interests in the North Atlantic ahead of its interests in Asia. The Jay Treaty (1795) was designed to prevent Anglo-American disagreements from turning into open hostilities. For the British it was a means to keep the Americans from reactivating their 1778 alliance with France. British money, troops, and ships were containing the French in Europe and fighting colonial wars overseas, and as the 1794–1795 French counterattacks in the Caribbean showed, those resources were already spread thin. In 1794 British "privateers" operating out of Bermuda had begun hauling U.S. vessels into British prize courts—not just the ones with illicit cargoes or verboten destinations, but every U.S. vessel they could find. This, coupled with the British military occupation of forts within the boundary of the United States, pushed American anti-British sentiment high. Many thought war inevitable.[6] If Whitehall wished not to divert resources and attention to war with the United States and the defense of Canada, confident though it may have been of victory, this was a fight best avoided.

The Jay Treaty was the vehicle for that avoidance. Britain re-affirmed American neutrality in the ongoing French Wars, and the United States gained greater control over its territory. Unsurprisingly, the treaty dealt mainly with the New World. But tucked away in the final version—and perhaps obscured by the treaty's general unpopularity—was another provision. Article XIII dealt with American trade with India and was one of the few concessions John Jay wheedled from the British negotiators beyond the minimum requirements in his instructions.

Before the Jay Treaty the East India Company had, as noted, allowed American ships into its Indian ports. In the 1780s this was in part because of "some floating ideas of the benefits of free Commerce,"[7] as the Company chairmen later grumbled, and, more concretely, because barring American ships from British Indian ports would only drive them to Danish or Dutch Indian ports instead. Article XIII of the Jay Treaty formalized U.S. trade with British India and ensured its continuance at a time when the Company was fast conquering foreign European ports in India and therefore removing its reason to be so forbearing.[8]

The first point in the list of extras Jay was free to pursue was "reciprocity in navigation, particularly to the West Indies and even to the East Indies."[9] Jay's British counterpart seems to have been eager to oblige; lower tariffs in India—paid to the East India Company, not the Crown—were a small price for the prevention of U.S. interference in the war with France.[10] When the Company asked Parliament to clamp down on foreign trade to India in 1797, Dundas made the trade-off explicit. It was paramount to "convince other Nations of the liberality of our commercial Principles." And as "the Americans[,] whose amity with us is at least as desirable as that of any other nation[,] would probably consider themselves hardly dealt with,"[11] "it would be most impolitick indeed to attempt at the request of the East India Co to make the situation of the American trade to India more severe than as settled by a solemn and well considered treaty."[12] In a pinch, Dundas and Pitt had put Atlantic interests ahead of Indian ones.

Rulings from the King's Bench subsequently broadened Article XIII. The Company wanted to permit only a direct U.S.-India trade, but Americans kept slipping out of bounds: going from Calcutta, a British port, to Serampore, the Danish one just up the Hooghly, and then to Europe with a cargo of goods from British Bengal.[13] Some had the audacity to go from London straight to India, and on arrival claim they were coming from the United States—just indirectly.[14] Lord Kenyon, lord chief justice and originally a member of Pitt's government, ruled the stopovers in other Asian ports (which competed with the country trade) and stopovers in Britain and the Continent to be legal. There is no evidence he made this ruling at Pitt's behest, but it would not have been unusual or untoward had he done so. Thus Americans continued to pop in and out of neutral ports like Goa or Tranquebar and reenter British ports at will. They could run between India and Europe in safety and could even try the London market.[15]

To counter this, the Company insisted on a fixed American market for Indian goods sealed off from the rest of the world, demanding that "each Nation should carry on only a direct trade between its' [sic] own territories and the British [Indian] Settlements" "for itself only."[16] This was an unrealistic expectation, since U.S. merchants could not fulfill it. They did not know when their ships would return, what they would bring, or what the market would be like in the future. Nor did U.S. merchants wish to fulfill it: if Indian cloth sold well in Europe, they added Indian cloth from their stores to their next shipments to Europe, as Israel Thorndike had done. What merchant voluntarily gave up a market? The U.S. government was also unwilling to compel its merchants to follow British rules. As long as the merchants paid U.S. tariffs, no one cared. For the customs collector at Calcutta, enforcement was impossible. He did not know whether departing Americans who claimed to be heading home were telling the truth. He could not enforce a British law the violation of which occurred, by definition, abroad. The British ministry did enforce its law on Americans at sea—for example, on the matter of impressment—but only spottily. Impressment did not prevent British sailors from working on American vessels or cause British law to be observed when Navy ships were absent; it merely provided recruits for the captain doing the impressing. The enforcement of commercial law was no more effective, since the issue was U.S. trade departing from British India and leaving British jurisdiction.

The Shipping Interest stuck to a rigid concept of trade. Sir Francis Baring grumbled that the monopoly's defenders maintained "16th. century" "Commercial principles."[17] The Company imagined a stable trade centrally planned in advance: demand, supply, price, and profit each tabulated out years into the future with quill pens. These calculations had little bearing on reality. Edward Parry and Charles Grant, chairmen of the Company's Court of Directors, argued that there was "a certain" and immutable "limit" to Atlantic demand for Indian goods. Despite additional competitors sailing to India, Indian exports could not "go beyond that limit." Yet Atlantic demand depended on the price of Indian goods. Baring did not cite the price elasticity of demand, as economists call this phenomenon, but, ever a merchant, he knew that what he charged buyers affected how much they bought. "I confess it surprizes me to hear such opinions . . . in the Year 1807," he wrote of the Company's assertion. "I have seen them in . . . books published a Century or two ago."[18]

The Chairs could not admit that price affected demand because the Shipping Interest made its fortune inflating India-good prices with its prohibitive freight rates. In 1795–1796 the Company charged £22 a ton on regular Indiaman and £20 on "extra" ships chartered from Calcutta. Meanwhile Danes charged £16 to take cargo to Copenhagen and Americans £15 to Hamburg. In the period between 1796 and 1807, the Committee of Shipping charged the Company between £24 and £36 a ton for freight. This included a nominal "peace freight" to which a war "surplus" was added to make the bill-padding look reasonable. The Company charged even higher rates to the private trade carried on its ships: over £52 a ton in January 1798.[19] U.S. shipping was the ever-cheaper option.

The Direction assumed that British and American re-exporters were engaged in a zero-sum competition for the Atlantic India goods market, an assumption that worked to the Company's detriment. The Company was known for high-quality cloth—Thorndike's Italian correspondents noted as much when they sniffed at his gruff goods. This put Company cottons in a different part of the market than coarser, American-carried weaves. Expensive cloth absorbed shipping costs more easily—its higher purchase price in India meant that freight was a smaller fraction of its end cost in Europe. Americans' lower shipping costs, by contrast, played to their greatest advantage when they also purchased cheaper goods. Since the Company had priced itself out of the low-end market with high freight rates, it made sense to concentrate on finer fabrics. (Additionally, British weavers were able to reproduce the cruder Indian weaves by this time). Yet there is no discussion—in the Direction at least—of ordering even finer, more expensive fabrics, or of attempting to expand not their share of the re-export market but the re-export market itself. But then again, if demand is "limited," the market cannot grow. When the directors did comment about the superiority of Company products, they did so not to devise a way forward for their business, but merely to dwell upon their superiority generally. Meanwhile, Americans expanded the re-export market, selling cheap cloth to low-end buyers who may not have been able to afford the Company's cloth previously.[20]

After the Jay Treaty lapsed, the Company raised its tariff on U.S. exports from India. This was intended to compensate for Americans' advantages as neutrals and to equalize the costs of U.S. shipping and the private trade on Company ships. The tariff increase—to 10 percent—did little. Forbidding U.S. trade with its India possessions might have worked, but the Company could not do this for "political reasons," though the directors noted that if they had had the power to toss the Americans from India without sparking a trade war, they would have done so.[21] And so U.S. trade to India, facing inadequate competition from the Company, continued to grow. The Jay Treaty gave the American merchant confidence that his ship would not be impounded by an overly zealous official, but after 1806 the Company failed to check the growth in U.S. trade all by itself.[22] American trade to and within Asia blossomed with both Crown and Company acquiescence.

The Structure of U.S.-Bengal Trade

U.S. trade at Calcutta proceeded along a variety of lines. Americans brought mostly silver. But it was hard for U.S. merchants to know how much silver would be needed. They did not wish to commit too much—that silver could always be put to another use—but they did not want to short-change their ventures, either, so U.S. merchants supplemented the cash they sent to India with loans, bills of exchange, and by renting out freight space on the return voyage. Yet none of these replaced the fundamental need for, and greater profit in, using silver.

Obtaining a loan in Bengal was often difficult, though cultivating relationships with specific Calcutta houses helped. Borrowers who brought some silver did best, since the silver showed they had something to lose if the venture went sour. Here, as in the Atlantic, the competence and probity conveyed by silver made lending easier. (It had been for lack of silver that Beaumetz, Talleyrand's partner in India, had failed.) The Anglo-Indian house Fairlie, Gilmore & Co. and the *banian* Ramdulal Day both lent to and traded with U.S. supercargoes. Yet because they charged high interest rates, Americans preferred to bring silver.[23] High interest compensated for the difficulties of loan collection. The distance between the United States and India made collection hard, as did the presence of Serampore, where Danish authorities gave debtors asylum. The American trader Amasa Delano fled there to avoid his Anglo-Indian creditors, noting it was "the usual place of resort" for "men in our situation." Delano was not an established merchant with a silver competency but a man on the make. Formerly second officer on the *Massachusetts,* he served in the Bombay marine and acquired a vessel in Mauritius. In Bombay he borrowed funds to buy a cargo for his vessel, only to see the speculation go awry in Calcutta. His creditors took the vessel as payment.[24] With debtor flight an ever-present threat, Calcutta lenders preferred merchants with specie that could be seized in the event of default, and with whom they had other business and, thus, other ways to collect.

U.S. merchants also brought bills of exchange to India, but these were of limited use. *Banians*—Indian traders or brokers—refused them. Britons in India accepted partial payment in bills, as long as the rest was in silver. Thus in 1791 the Danish Asiatic Company purchased one-third of its cloth from Anglo-Indian wholesalers with bills and the rest with specie. But such wholesalers often took bills in order to unload inferior goods. Bills of exchange were also expensive. U.S. merchants sold them in India at a discount to the face value. The discount reflected, in part, the risk of a bad bill. As with a modern bond, the gap between the face value and the discounted price paid the buyer interest. Because these bills functioned like bonds, merchants issuing bills had to compete in the Calcutta money market, offering deeper and deeper discounts, and hence higher rates of interest, to match with the interest the East India Company was paying its bondholders.[25]

Finally, Americans rented space on their vessels to Anglo-Indian merchants wishing to send their own cargoes to the Atlantic. The American shipowner's income from renting out space was less than the profits might be from loading a cargo and selling it on his own account, but leftover space could be rented if a supercargo had no more silver, and there were plenty of Anglo-Indians wanting to ship goods. Take, for example, the freights of Eliza Fay. After a spell in Anglo-Indian high society, Fay supported herself with a shop selling British fashions to Calcutta ladies, accumulating "a little property." In 1794 she took passage with her goods on the American *Henry*, with Captain Jacob Crowninshield, to Ostend. En route, France conquered Ostend, and Crowninshield diverted to the United States, leaving Fay at the Isle of Wight. Crowninshield sold Fay's property on her behalf in the United States, finding "a tolerable market." With the funds he bought Fay a new ship, the *Minerva*, in which his brother would return Fay to India. Fay coppered the *Minerva* in London, from whence Fay and Crowninshield sailed for Bengal.

There she purchased the *Rosalia,* finding an American captain to take her and yet more muslins to the United States. But the *Rosalia* sprang a leak, the muslins were damaged, and Fay hired passage to the United States on the *Hero,* yet another American vessel, with her remaining goods instead.[26]

In Fay's manner Anglo-Indians could send their own cargoes—bought with capital accumulated in India—to the Atlantic on American ships. The Americans sold the goods on commission and remitted the funds to London as bills of exchange. The Company deemed this to be commerce conducted on British capitals, the cargoes being British-owned and thus representing British funds. Inasmuch as American ships carried Anglo-Indian-owned goods, the Company was right.[27] (Yet, since Dundas had intended the private trade on Company ships to bring Anglo-Indian capitals to London; the Company's complaint of Americans trading on British capitals risked damning the Company's own maltreatment of others' funds.[28]) More recent writers have taken the Company's point further, suggesting that there was little that was American about U.S.-Indian trade in this period at all.[29] It is thus vital to understand to what extent Americans carried British cargoes and what that carriage meant.

Parry and Grant used the Company's Calcutta customs ledgers to prove that Americans traded with British funds. Examining the period between 1795 and 1805, they found that the value of goods and specie foreign merchants took from India exceeded what they brought in. The difference, the Chairs believed, was in Anglo-Indian fortunes being remitted to Europe. The Chairs realized their data were imperfect. As they admitted, their analysis excluded Serampore, where Americans traded extensively; Madras, where Americans sold specie for bills on Bengal; and the possibility that foreign merchants used bills of exchange. Additionally, the directors ignored the possibility that foreigners might borrow in Calcutta, or that the difference between what they carried from India and what they carried to it might reflect profits accrued tramping around the Indian Ocean. The Chairs thought they could rule out bills of exchange, since the Americans "would have imported less Bullion" if they could use bills, but Parry and Grant had little way of determining what mix of the remaining options constituted the difference.[30]

Yet after making their best efforts to portray the Americans as conduits for the remittance of Anglo-Indian capital, the Chairs conceded that U.S. silver sales to India—and thus the U.S. purchase of Indian goods without Anglo-Indian funds—remained high. The Chairs calculated that between 1795 and 1800 Americans exported from India 25 percent more than they imported. Yet they also calculated that between 1801 and 1805, Americans exported only 10 percent more from India than they imported—and that U.S. trade in the later period was much greater, "more than doubled," in the Chairs' estimation. (Madras customs data, which noted whether vessels were carrying their owners' or freighted cargoes, roughly confirm the Chairs' estimate. Between 1802 and 1811, less than 10 percent of U.S. tonnage passing through Madras is given as freighted out to Anglo-Indians.[31]) "It is clear from hence that their own capital employed in this Trade rapidly increased and . . . that their profits were large," the Chairs explained. Americans distinguished themselves in this from European neutrals, who in the Chairs' analysis never closed the gap between what they exported from India and what they imported to it. "When the Americans had less Capital of their own," they "carried as much in proportion of British property from the Ganges as foreign Europeans did," but by 1805, Americans were rich enough to trade—even by the Company's estimate—largely by themselves.[32]

This became, in turn, a new Company complaint: the Americans were making too much profit. Sir Francis Baring, debating with the chairmen, noted the about-face. "What becomes of the clamour of America carrying the trade with *British Capitals?*" he asked. "There is far less clamour *now,*" the chairmen replied.[33]

The Company's analysis, though ultimately self-defeating, was also crude: trade at Calcutta cannot be divided by country so simply. Americans traded cloth, loans, and bills of exchange with the same Anglo-Indian houses which asked them to carry British capitals to the Atlantic. These transactions were all of a piece. Trafficking, as Fay did, with British capital on American ships entailed risk. As she discovered, the risks were not only of British law but of damage to a cargo which, for its doubtful legality, was difficult to insure. Thus in 1798, Anglo-Indian merchants, fearing their goods might be seized at sea if sent as freight, sold their cargoes to Portuguese and American supercargoes instead. The Anglo-Indians still profited, though not as much as they might if the goods reached the Atlantic in their own name. In exchange they eliminated their exposure to any risk the cargoes might be lost at sea. The Company did not consider such trade to be conducted with British capitals, but the difference was largely of degree: whether Anglo-Indians rented space for their own property on American vessels or sold that property to American supercargoes, they were part of a supply chain that stretched from Bengali weavers through Anglo-Indian merchants to American shippers and Atlantic consumers. The question was at what point they passed on ownership to the next step in the chain, not whether they and the Americans were in the same chain at all. On Crowninshield's *Henry,* Fay's British-owned goods shared a hold with American-owned cargoes, the balance reflecting the risk-to-reward calculus of the parties: how much shipping risk each could afford for a chance at greater profits.

U.S. East India merchants had an appetite for risk, and as Parry and Grant noted, they were unlikely to rent out space on their ships if they had silver to buy India goods themselves.[34] But transactions paid for in silver did not preclude Anglo-Indian remittance. Anglo-Indians could use Americans' silver to purchase either bills of exchange payable in London or Company bonds wholly or partially payable there. Company bonds issued in Calcutta but payable in London were an innovation of the early 1800s, when Company debt had so saturated the Calcutta money market that only higher interest or payment in London could attract sufficient subscribers.[35] This of course meant that the money market, as neutral shipping, competed with the Company-carried private trade as a vehicle for Anglo-Indian remittances. Anglo-Indians found the Company-carried private trade the worst of the three.

Originally, Anglo-Indians had been forbidden to sell to foreigners; Dundas permitted them to trade with Americans and Europeans during the 1793 charter renewal. The Company objected that Indian cloth would go "directly to the Continents of Europe and

America, without passing through . . . Britain, by which means London will be no longer the Depot for Indian Goods." Instead, the "tribute of India"—Anglo-Indian remittance—would reach London "by Bills of Exchange . . . whilst Private Persons in this Country will become Bankers instead of Merchants." These words were Baring's, dating from a time during his negotiation of the 1793 charter when he saw the Company and the City interests aligned. He had descrived his own subsequent business with U.S. East India traders perfectly. Yet Dundas's reform was sound. Before 1793 Anglo-Indians already sold to foreigners. They had been expected to enforce the ban on themselves, which made it a dead letter. Even if the ban had been somewhat enforced, Anglo-Indians could have evaded it—selling their goods to *banians* who would have then sold them to Americans. Perfect enforcement would have granted the *banians* an exclusive right to trade with foreigners, something no one in London really thought appropriate. Instead, Dundas legalized what he could not stop and what so many others already tolerated, perhaps hoping that Anglo-Indians might remit their funds on the Company-carried private trade instead.[36]

The silver Americans brought was vital to the British Indian economy. The United States was one of British India's most important silver suppliers in the early 1800s. American silver provided liquidity for the Calcutta money market at a time when specie was scarce, enabling private lending as well as the issue of Company bonds. As the Madras reporter of external commerce explained of U.S. trade in 1804, "As a Trade with India it is certainly a very desirable one. They Import for the most part Bullion & Export entirely the Manufacture or Produce of our Territories."[37] Sir Francis Baring recognized this as well. U.S. trade was "the only door of consequence through which silver flows into India," he explained. This trade had to be nurtured, not stifled, lest it hurt India and even perhaps cause a run on the new bank in Bengal. "Whoever will bring *silver* to pay for *the productive industry of a Country* should be received with open arms, and on equal terms whether a Briton or a foreigner," he argued. The Chairs scoffed at the idea that "want of American Silver" would have such effects; the Persian Gulf and

China provided silver as well. But when the War of 1812 prevented
U.S. specie from reaching India, silver grew scarce; interest rates in
the Bengal money market, already stressed by the cost of Minto's
expeditions to Java and Mauritius, soared.[38]

Baring worried that by raising a tariff to stem the Americans'
trade the chairmen risked "destroying the egg in the Hen's belly."[39]
The Chairs, he mocked, were jealous that "America has contributed more than any other Nation toward [India's] success" and had
perversely reasoned it "incumbent on us to institute checks and
throw every impediment in her way." Parry and Grant retorted that
though they were solicitous of India's interests, Britain's interests—
that is, the Company's—were paramount. Yet they would not, the
Chairs noted, tax the silver Americans brought in. It was needed
too much.[40] And so the chairmen, threading the needle, levied their
tariff on Indian exports to the United States instead. This tariff was
designed explicitly to limit Indian exports.[41] Thus while Baring
thought the U.S. sale of silver to India made the United States the
"best Customer to India,"[42] Grant and Parry, seeing Americans as
competitors in the carriage and sale of Indian exports, reasoned
differently: "She is not the *best* but the *worst* Customer."[43] These
were the seeds of two very different interpretations of American
success in India.

The View from Calcutta

Calcutta is 100 miles up the Hooghly River from the sea. The approach to Calcutta—the "garden-reach" of mansions, with lawns
and copses stretching to the river's edge—was the Anglo-Indians'
pride. Fort William and the city stood on one side of the river, an
esplanade between them, and the Company botanical gardens
stood on the other. Company servants lived in the bourgeois boom-
district of Chouringee—a "village of palaces," in Lord Valentia's
phrase—and worked in offices around Tank Square, so named for
the vast sunken pool that "arrests a stranger's attention," as Delano
noted, and that provided water for the populace. From the esplanade to the river and from the streets to the tank, broad steps, or

ghats, reached down. British writers and painters invariably lingered on this scene of European cultural replication.[44]

That scene contrasted with a grittier, if no less colonial, vision in which boatmen offered upriver passage in budgrows (Bengali pinnaces) that often had ties to inns on shore and were sometimes of doubtful safety. Hucksters—"cheats and robbers," one Englishwoman called them—swarmed a Western arrival in Calcutta, offering goods for sale or themselves as servants. Taverns sent men to offer umbrellas against the sun and lodging at gouging prices. Inside, as an 1810 writer explained, "sable beauties" "retail their charms." These servants and porters, street-sellers and whores came from the "Black Town," where most of Calcutta's several hundred thousand lived. The British described it as an expanse of "poor mean buildings," "mud cottages" in "wretched condition," strewn along warrens of "narrow, dirty, and unpaved" streets, "swarming with population," and "abounding with beggars and bad smells." This Calcutta stretched along the river for miles and reached inland as well.[45]

It was a good place to be British. One could find Madeira and claret daily on the tables of even the "middling classes," as one writer noted, and travel about in a palanquin. Such high living could be expensive—an establishment of at least thirty servants was considered necessary for a respectable Anglo-Indian—but it was still cheaper than thirty servants back home. Anglo-Indians thus settled into an affluent rhythm: up before dawn for a stroll or a ride in the still-cool air; work in the morning; tiffin at two o'clock; rest from the heat until five; an excursion, tea, cards, or music in the evening; and supper at ten. Servants tossed the leftover meat out in the night, lest it go rancid by morning, and jackals, dogs, and birds of prey emerged from the forests to dine in the streets. The howls of partiers were echoed from the darkness by the howls of jackals. Both feasted on meat by night while laborers toiled by day.[46]

Neutral Shipping in India

American trade with India can be glimpsed from the customs records these Anglo-Indians kept for the Company. Company records include vessels making direct voyages between Asia and Europe; voyages which do not appear in U.S. customs registers, since such vessels did not touch at the United States en route. And so it is to the Bengal customs records than one must turn.

Among neutrals, the Americans prospered most of all. U.S. shipping in Calcutta easily dwarfed Danish, Hamburg, and Portuguese shipping combined. In the years between 1795 and 1800, the revamped Company customs office in Bengal recorded 161 foreign European and American vessels arriving at Calcutta and 171 departing. These data omit Serampore and thus understate neutral trade generally. Ole Feldbaek's reading of Danish sources suggests this understating of neutral trade could be considerable at times. While Calcutta customs records list two U.S. departures in the 1795—1796 season for London and six for Hamburg, Danish officials at Serampore counted three U.S. departures for London and thirteen for Hamburg. The more conservative British figures, which show a full 107 (66 percent) of arrivals and 117 (68 percent) of departures as American, are used here. British tonnage data similarly show American dominance among the neutrals. Of incoming shipping carried by Western neutrals, 30,727 out of the 57,237 tons (54 percent) were American, as were 32,929 of the 59,639 tons (55 percent) of outgoing neutral shipping (see Table 7.1).[47]

Americans traded at Madras and Bombay as well. Of the 109 U.S.-flagged vessels (31,645 tons) arriving at Fort St. George (the British fort at the heart of Madras) between 1802 and 1811, 70 percent came from or sailed on to Bengal. Over 2,000 other vessels called at Madras in this period, exclusive of Indian ("Asiatic") vessels; U.S. trade at Madras was not a large part of the overall commerce in port.[48] Americans arbitraged between the Calcutta and Madras money markets, selling silver in one port

Table 7.1 Arrivals of Western Neutrals in Calcutta by Tonnage (and Number of Vessels), June 1, 1795–May 31, 1800

	American	Danish	Portuguese	Hamburg	Other	Total
1795/1796	9,182 (29)	4,090 (8)	500 (1)	0	350 (1)	14,122 (39)
1796/1797	6,831 (25)	3,120 (6)	950 (2)	0	250 (1)	11,151 (34)
1797/1798	5,364 (20)	1,600 (3)	900 (2)	1,328 (3)	0	9,192 (28)
1798/1799	4,164 (14)	2,570 (5)	200 (1)	1,419 (4)	0	8,353 (24)
1799/1800	5,186 (19)	4,425 (8)	3,550 (6)	600 (2)	658 (1)	14,419 (36)
Total	30,727 (107)	15,805 (30)	6,100 (12)	3,347 (9)	1,258 (3)	57,237 (161)

Note: "Other" includes Venice, Genoa, and Prussia.
Source: "An Account of All Foreign Ships and Their Tonnage, Imported & Exported at the Several Settlements in India, for 5 Years Last Past, 1795 to 1800," OIOC L/MAR/C/547 9-19.

(usually Madras) for bills of exchange paid in the other at a favorable rate of interest. Americans trading to Madras for its own sake sold specie and European goods—principally alcohol—to Anglo-Indians in exchange for Madras fabrics, a trade the Madras reporter thought had "fallen off" since the 1790s, "the Manufactures of Bengal being purchased with much more facility and at a cheaper rate."[49]

From Bombay, British traders exported large quantities of cotton to China. American merchants, unable to source this cotton as advantageously as British merchants, scarcely traded in Bombay.[50] What trade they did conduct involved importing specie and European goods for the Anglo-Indian population in exchange for Gujarati goods. In the periods from 1802 to 1806 and from 1807 to 1811, only thirteen U.S.-flagged vessels, carrying 3,797 tons, arrived at Bombay. Roughly 900 British vessels, carrying over 400,000 tons, called at Bombay in the same period.[51] In both Bombay and Madras—as at Calcutta—Anglo-Indians dominated the country trade. This was instructive: where British free traders could traffic, they used their large and and inexpensive India-built fleets to keep American shippers out. Bombay merchants would not sell to American carriers cargoes that they could carry to China so profitably themselves. The Company, by contrast, had no such success keeping Americans at bay in the commerce between India and Europe.

Crucially, Americans were the only neutrals at Calcutta to combine a large shipping capacity with small vessels. Americans constituted two-thirds of the neutral ships in the Ganges but only half the neutral shipping capacity. The average European neutral at Calcutta had a carrying capacity of over 500 tons; the average American vessel carried just over 280 tons.[52] The English Company's vessels, even larger, had a 600- to 1,200-ton carrying capacity. (The capacity of Company vessels was growing. Ships built for the Company in the 1770s and 1780s averaged just over 800 tons. A new class of 1,200-ton vessels launched in the late 1780s pulled the average tonnage of Company vessels upward, such that between 1790 and 1812, ships built for the Company averaged just over 1,000 tons. In 1812, the Company claimed these larger vessels helped them overawe Indians and rule the Subcontinent, but the vessels were really just boondoggles for the Shipping Interest.[53]) Hamburg vessels were similar to American vessels in size, but fewer than ten Hamburg ships called at Calcutta in this period, leaving the niche to the Americans. The smaller vessels were more efficient; any economy of scale in the larger ships was obliterated by the cost of cargo and vessel waiting in port. This cost, called demurrage, was one of the most expensive for early modern merchants. Merchants loading their cargoes on a ship to send abroad had to wait until all the other cargoes were loaded before the ship would depart, a process that could take days, weeks, even months. Smaller vessels could be loaded quickly, while the supercargo of a vessel might have to decide whether to wait for cargoes or to go home half full. If he waited, the prices in the Atlantic were liable to change as swifter competitors brought their merchandise to market.[54] Longer stays in port also drove up port fees and other secondary costs.

American captains met the demurrage problem by keeping port stays short. Both their primage (their percent share of the profits) and their privilege (their allotment of shipping for personal trade) encouraged this, requiring quick departure for the best profit. Britons in Calcutta noted how brief the American stay in Calcutta was. And indeed, there appears to have been a decrease in turnaround time for U.S. ships in port during the French Wars. As Wellesley noted, U.S. ships "disposed of their imports, purchased their cargo for exportation, and left the port" within twenty or twenty-five days, taking less time in port than equivalently sized and rigged British ships, despite the Americans' smaller crews. Company customs officials in Bengal likewise noticed that Americans put "homeward cargoes on Board" their 300-ton vessels within "20 or 25 days." Thomas Twining, of the British tea merchant family, noted on his departure from Calcutta in 1795 how few crew manned the American vessel on which he sailed—roughly a third of what he though an equivalent British vessel would have needed—and how, despite the labor shortage, the captain made startlingly rapid (and self-interested) work of his stay in Calcutta.[55] Likewise, U.S. vessels calling at Madras between 1802 and 1810 had relatively smaller crews. U.S. vessels carried one crewman for every fifteen tons of carrying capacity. East India Company vessels had one man for every eight tons; British private traders hired one man for every six tons. Despite having larger crews, Company vessels still took longer than the Americans in port.[56] Company vessels were noted for superior discipline at sea—and certainly, their larger crews gave them an advantage in battle— but Americans kept their crews smaller and drove their men harder in port, where it counted most. Nor does the sailing speed of American vessels appear to have suffered from their relatively skeletal crews.

East India Company ships had to wait for a convoy. Though the Company captains earned primage and privilege, their inability to leave earlier than other ships in the convoy deprived them of any incentive to hurry; convoys load and sail at the speed of the slowest vessel. British private traders in India, like the Americans, routinely avoided convoys, even when French privateers were known to be about. As Rear Admiral Rainier explained, the country traders refused convoy because of "the nature of the trade they carry on, which principally consists in bold speculations, requiring caution and secrecy in the execution."[57] Speed was not an American trait per se; it was common to any private trader rushing to reach a market.

This is especially apparent in the shipping records from St. Helena, the South Atlantic island where the Company watered its ships. Neutral East Indiamen and British slavers and whalers watered there, too. There was little commerce at the island beyond taking on water and supplies (though Company vessels did supply the island with rice and other foodstuffs from time to time). Shipping records at St. Helena reveal captains' abilities not as traders but as sailors, and provide a means of comparing how swiftly vessels calling at St. Helena got under way. East India Company captains were sluggish. In the period from 1793 to 1796, American East Indiamen stayed at St. Helena an average of eight days; other neutrals also stayed for eight days on average. British whalers returning to the North Atlantic stayed in port an average of twenty days—some vessels sailing quickly while others waited for a convoy, if one were set to sail soon. Company captains were not free to make this decision, however, and their vessels waited an average of twenty-six days in port before their convoys departed. All else aside, a stop at St. Helena meant that Company vessels reached North Atlantic markets three weeks later than American ones.[58]

The Company's position was further worsened by its warehouse and auction system back in London. Rather than auction off lots as they arrived, which—had the convoys not been in place—would have encouraged captains to catch the start of the season or the latest trend in the European market, the Company warehoused incoming goods and rotated them out to auctions at preset intervals. Newly arrived cargo could take months or even years to reach auction. Whether a ship came into London a month early or a month late, its cargo went up for sale at a predetermined date along with the cargoes of tens of other Company ships. To be sure, the warehouses stabilized the supply of goods for the London market. And London warehouses, like American merchants with their own warehouses, could put stock back on the market to meet demand. But since one warehouse and auction system covered the entire Company, no one within the Company had the incentive to skip the convoys and rush to market goods which the warehouses lacked. For company employees to strive to preempt one another hardly makes sense. In different circumstances one would expect the Company's competitors to try to sell at earlier dates or store different quantities of different goods, but there were no such competitors in Britain.

Such planning was necessary, however, from the perspective of the Company's directors. Scheduling sailing times, cargoes, and auctions years in advance were the only way they could operate the Company and provide for future costs. And one cannot object to planning as such—all businesses draw budgets. But the East India Company engrossed an entire sector of the British market, which gave it a monopoly on planning. Whatever budget the directors cooked up excluded other or better British budgets and product mixes. Perhaps a rival British Company might have allocated more or less funds to the war in India, or altered vessel size, or had vessels carrying goods for re-export to Europe skip the convoy. Since there were no rival British firms to do this, the Company tautologically claimed that its way of managing things was the only way possible.

The Company's management of the Indian trade did have its benefits. Calcutta employees organized cloth supplies well ahead of Indiamen's arrival. Contracts to supply woven cloth—type, quantity, and price all carefully specified—were farmed out up to a year in advance.[59] When the Company's vessels arrived in Calcutta, cloth destined for London was ready to be loaded and there was little need to buy on the open market. An American ship captain who had to compete on the open market for cloth would often find his own cloth purchases, even for a small vessel, large enough to drive up the price. (Some U.S. merchants tried to set up agencies in Calcutta to contract ahead, but this was not usually the case.) A 1,200-ton Company ship would have pushed up prices on the open market all the more. By planning in advance, Company directors protected themselves from gluts, dearths, and price fluctuations. Yet though American buyers were more exposed to shifts in the Indian cloth market, they could—and did—turn these variations into opportunities. By trading in the spot market and sailing when they pleased, Americans arbitraged gluts, dearths, and price fluctuations between India and the Atlantic, racing cargoes to Europe that were not in their or the Company's warehouses before the Company could react.[60]

Thus in so many ways the American East India trade was the reverse of the British one. While the Company auctioned off goods in London at fixed intervals, Americans sailed and wholesaled haphazardly. While Company ships lingered in port, American vessels rushed. While Company servants in India contracted ahead for cloth, Americans were exposed to the open market. Americans also made direct voyages from a variety of Atlantic ports to India, while all Company cargoes passed through London, where they were offloaded, warehoused, and reloaded on different ships before reaching buyers. Smaller ships were better suited to all these facets of the Americans' position.[61]

The Americans enjoyed one final advantage: neutrality. The English Company tried mightily to overcome this advantage;

smuggling to and from France and French Europe became common and was an implicit part of Dundas's commercial plan. Nonetheless, before 1807 Americans could sail to France directly, if not always without some trouble, while British smugglers had to bear the costs of transshipping through London. Even when not shipping directly to France—which never occurred as often as apocalyptic Company customs collectors feared—Americans could re-export to France with less need to bribe their way through port.

The Company still had the largest part of the Atlantic India goods market. Thus, even though it was faced with considerable structural disadvantages to its absorption of Europe's trade with India, the Company made no effort to change, even when faced with a declining share of the carriage of Indian goods to Atlantic markets. The decisive question was how far the Company's decline and the concomitant American increase would go. The Shipping Interest, representing those who procured the Company's shipping, was quick to blame American neutrality for the American boom. It was a valid point, but not thought through. For if the Company could not compete with the Americans on the basis of neutrality, would this not be all the more reason to innovate elsewhere? The directors' alternative—the status quo—either assumed the Americans would never become grave rivals or tacitly admitted defeat.

The Shipping Interest ruthlessly quashed reformist sentiment. David Scott was one anti-Shipping Interest member of the Company. A close ally and confidant of Dundas, Scott had risen to wealth through private trade in Bombay. He was an avid free trader and abhorred monopolies. In 1796–1797 he found himself chairman of the Company's Court of Directors and a Trojan horse for Dundas, who also secured Scott a seat in Parliament from Angus. Scott was Dundas's agent and mouthpiece in the Court, Scott and Dundas together seating others within the Company and in the Direction. In 1798 Scott suggested that the Company allow Anglo-Indian shipbuilders (connected with the Company's employees in India) to provide the Company with ships constructed in India in order to lower shipping and freight costs. It would redound to the Company's profit. Scott also saw it as a way to build up British commerce in India. Dundas agreed. Unsurprisingly, the Shipping Interest, which saw the matter as a threat to their profits, did not. Instead, it attempted to oust Scott. They subsequently accused him of illicit trade with foreign (Danish) merchants in Manila on the eve of the British invasion attempt there and, implicitly, of treason. "My character has been assassinated," Scott lamented. But it was only with considerable effort that he proved the charges unfounded. Yet something of the spirit of the charges stuck, on the not wholly unfounded principle that exporting British capital to finance foreign nations' East India trade violated the Company monopoly. Throughout Scott's ordeal, Sir Francis Baring remained silent about his own links to U.S. East India firms and about his knowledge of Scott's. Yet Scott's experience may have colored Baring's own tangle with the Shipping Interest in 1807. If they were willing to spend such time and energy attacking Scott, would they not do the same if they knew what Baring had done? (Fortunately for Baring, they did not.)[62]

In summary, U.S. merchants had three interacting advantages over the Company in their trade to the East: they operated with less bureaucratic encumbrance; they enjoyed a neutrality that gave them readier access to the markets of Europe; and they faced a Company that, by dint of its monopoly, sought to perpetuate the status quo by blaming the Americans' success on their neutrality rather than face their superior organization. As managers of a Parliament-granted monopoly (not even an earned one), it was easy for the directors to brand the Americans as scofflaws and have done with it. They were doing better for themselves than they would in open competition (for surely an end of the Company's monopoly would end the Shipping Interest's stranglehold on company shipping), and there was the legitimate fear that, given a fair fight against other British merchants, the Company might fail. The Shipping Interest attacked and complained, but in the security of its monopoly had no plan to adapt. Competition was too much trouble.

The Emporium and the Shipping Interest, 1793–1807

The Shipping Interest stood in fundamental conflict with the goal of making London an Asian emporium. It preferred that Company ships be expensive and few, but to make London an emporium, the ships had to be many and cheap. In 1795–1796 Bengal Governor-General Sir John Shore hired Anglo-Indian-built shipping to carry cargo to London. He explained that "the produce of Bengal should be carried to Europe on the Company's ships in preference to those of a neutral power." Scott likewise explained to Mornington that to bring "into the Thames almost the whole of the Eastern Commerce" the "superabundant produce" of India would have to come to London as well.[63] By "superabundant produce" Scott meant cloth left on the Calcutta market after the Company's purchases and after other Westerners had purchased for their own consumption. It referred to a surplus in excess of the Company's budgeted cloth purchases, but not a surplus in excess of market demand, since if the Company left this cloth in Calcutta, neutrals bought it and sold it in French Europe. (Similarly, "extra" ships referred to vessels exceeding the Company's original plan, but not exceeding market demand for carrying capacity. This stilted language tried to fill the gap between Company dirigisme and market reality.)[64]

The straightforward solution was to buy all the cloth in Calcutta and sell it in London. But the Company could not afford to buy that much cloth, freight it at the Shipping Interest's rates, and also pay for its Indian wars. As Wellesley explained to the Court of Directors in 1800, the supply of Indian goods reached "an extent far exceeding the amount which the capital applicable to the purchase of the Company's investment can embrace." Shore and Wellesley thus loaded the surplus cargo on "extra" ships built by Anglo-Indians in India, paying for the cloth and the wars rather than paying the Shipping Interests' freight rates for additional vessels. Wellesley argued that this was for the greater good, since less-expensive India-built ships were needed to "render London the universal mart for the manufactures and produce of India." Foreign ships had "low freight," "strict economy in the management of the concern," and made "voyages and returns of extraordinary expedition and celerity." They would outcompete regular Company ships. "It is impossible," he warned the directors in 1800, "that [British] goods can reach the markets of the continent of Europe through the channel of the public sales in England, at so low a price as the goods conveyed directly from India to the same markets in foreign bottoms." Lord Minto, who also waged expensive wars, similarly hoped a freer trade in Calcutta would leave more Company funds for the Bengal government. The Shipping Interest was furious at this, thinking the Anglo-Indians' ships should have been its own, and saw further India-built ships barred from London in 1803.[65]

That same year, the Bengal reporter of external commerce estimated that there was £1 million of cloth for sale in Calcutta. The Company could not afford to buy this cloth and carry it to London on Shipping Interest ships, so it left the cloth on the market. Thus cargoes it failed to purchase traveled on vessels it failed to hire to markets it failed to service. The Company could not stop American capitals from buying the cloth the Company had left in Calcutta. The Company treated the re-export market as a right—as the Company's Crown-given market in Britain was—but the re-export market could not be granted by fiat; it had to be won by competition. Without lowering the Shipping Interest's freight rates the Company could not hope to dominate that re-export market.[66] The Anglo-American transactions in Bengal provided, in their aggregate, evidence of a free-trade alternative to the East India Company in bringing Indian goods to Atlantic markets.

The promotion of an Asian emporium and the development of east-west shipping were separate issues. The Danish experience reveals this. While English Company officials were asking the ministry to clamp down on American trade, Danish officials opened up Danish commerce in order to maintain Copenhagen as an emporium of Indian goods and to keep Danish shipping competitive in east-west trade. Copenhagen welcomed a U.S. vessel entering from the Indies in 1796, and that year Denmark removed all requirements that vessels arriving in Denmark from India be even nominally Danish. Opening up shipping at Copenhagen maintained the city's position as an Indian emporium, benefiting local merchants who handled such business on commission, while doing little to help Danish carriers enlarge their share of east-west traffic. By contrast, the English Company objected to foreigners' voyages between India and London—voyages which, though bad for the Company, would have enhanced London's position as an emporium. In 1796 Denmark also ended the requirement that Danish vessels in India call at Copenhagen. This cut in the opposite direction, benefiting Danish shippers at the expense of Copenhagen commission merchants. Danish carriers could subsequently sail from India directly to Hamburg or Genoa, competing with Americans in these routes. The English Company, by contrast, insisted that return voyages come to London rather than ports like Glasgow or Dublin. Danish officials simultaneously attracted U.S. shippers to Copenhagen and allowed Danish shippers to rival U.S. merchants in other ports.[67] The Company's policy did the opposite: it tried to keep Americans out of London and also failed to serve other ports directly, making London less of an emporium while also conceding large portions of east-west traffic.

Emporium Redux, 1807–1811

The goal of making London an emporium for East Indian goods found new proponents after Henry Dundas's departure from government. In 1807, Robert Dundas took over his father's post at the Board of Control and intensified the free-trade push. He oversaw a re-examination of Company finances, which were a guesswork jumble at the best of times and which, after Wellesley's tenure in India, came into focus as a jumble of debts.[68] Faced with a budgetary crisis, the Company scaled back its India trade, which had become its least profitable business. Specie shipments to Asia came to a halt. The Company still traded to China, and it still collected tax revenue from the Indian interior, but for the rest of the war it rarely sent silver to India to purchase textiles.[69]

By this time Sir Francis Baring had shifted from his 1793 position, when, as a City banker, he had supported the Company's monopoly and the Shipping Interest (and ergo a limited Indian establishment). He and other City bankers were now increasingly willing to back Britain's commercial links with the United States at Company expense. Baring did not always make this trade-off explicit, but it was always in the background. Grant, who had been more solicitous of Dundas's ideas in the 1790s, became a hard-line supporter of the Shipping Interest. The two men had traded sides.[70]

Making London an Asian emporium had not originally required that British conquests in Asia be permanent. It was a common British strategy to use the enemy's overseas possessions as bargaining chips in peace negotiations. In the 1790s, Britain expected to keep only some of these conquests. Meanwhile, trade would develop new routes, away from Bordeaux and Amsterdam and toward London, that might be more lasting. But in the 1800s, this policy accommodated a spirit of permanent imperial expansion, particularly after 1807 as both sides sought the complete defeat of the other rather than negotiated peace. The emporium issue became even more contentious as the war extended into the economic realm.

As long as the war continued, Britain would not have to return its conquered possessions, and in 1807 there was no end to the war in sight. Britain had to be able to finance its side of the war indefinitely. Tightening the economic links between Britain and its colonies fit this objective, and in this context the idea of London as an East Indian emporium took on new resonance. Re-exports might help undermine the Continental System, now that London was one of the few places where Continentals could buy tea, cloth, and spices from Asia, in addition to sugar from the West Indies and British manufactured goods. East India imports were hardly a panacea, but they were a component of a grander economic vision.

The emporium idea had originally been a free-trade argument; but by 1807 Charles Grant and the Shipping Interest had adopted the idea as well. All sides accepted that Britain should become a re-export hub for Asian goods. In 1800 advocates saw the emporium as means to ensure competition in Continental markets after the war ended. In 1807 emporium advocates did not imagine open, legal competition in Continental markets in a time of peace, but rather the coercion of Europe to buy from the Company's London auctions (through smugglers) in perpetual war since there would be no other venders of Asian goods.[71] With the prospect of neutral trade being swept from the sea, the Company, to the delight of the Shipping Interest, might profit without having to change at all. New Orders in Council clamped down on neutral commerce, and President Jefferson's embargo kept U.S. shipping at home. Edward Parry and Charles Grant hoped "rising demand ... for Piece Goods & Pepper for exportation from London" would lead to "a favorable change" in British re-exports.[72] In 1808 London was Europe's only source of East Indian produce. With the Dundases' insistence on the matter, the directors had little alternative—short of competitive business practices—but to hope it worked.

It did not. By the end of 1808 the Shipping Interest had already cried foul. The nature of "this long War" had changed. Previously they had "always" maintained, despite French regulations, "our trade to the Ports under the dominion of France."[73] But the French had tightened their trading restrictions. The Company might "be permanently shut out from the Continent."[74] Rumors ran through London that only Americans could "convey our Trade" to Europe, which was somewhat odd, given the U.S. embargo, but at least acknowledged the last-ditch possibility that Americans—if somehow shut of of Bengal—might smuggle Company goods to Europe.[75] The Company had made its purchases for the European market sluggishly. In 1810 and 1811 it placed large orders of Indian goods to take advantage of the American embargo, despite the embargo having already ended in 1809. Fortuitously, if not quite to the Company's credit, the purchases reached London a few months before the War of 1812, providing cloth for potential European buyers just as the American competition fell away for a completely different reason.[76]

The Justification of the Shipping Interest

The American free traders were different rivals than the European monopolies the Company had faced previously, and the Shipping Interest was not only financially but also intellectually unfit for their competition. Thus the Chairs unwisely complained that *any* American re-export of Indian goods robbed the Company's commerce; this tacitly accepted that American re-exports could be held against them. By this standard, even if the Company increased its re-exports to Europe, as long as Americans maintained a significant minority of Canada's, the Caribbean's, or French-occupied Europe's India goods market, the Company had failed. Thus American re-exports were, as Parry and Grant lamented, a "dangerous rivalship set up against the Company's Commerce."[77]

The Shipping Interest's self-justification was a foolish thing to put on paper. Perhaps the Chairs thought such internal memoranda would remain out of the public view. Perhaps Parry and Grant, seeing the Company's monopoly as a justly granted prebend, failed to grasp that their complaints about American commercial rapacity might also prove Company ineptitude, particularly to those who did not accept the Company's monopoly as an a priori good. Grant understood many of the Americans' advantages already discussed. Americans "navigate in vessels not calculated for defence, of little cost, very sparingly manned and equipped, sailing singly out and home at the moment it suited them, without waiting for convoy, or being subjected to . . . War Freight, War duties, [or] War demurrage." This gave neutrals "great and decisive superiority over the Company" "in the Indian Commerce." This was "eminently the case with respect to the Americans," who now "interfere with us" "in the Southern parts of Europe in the West Indies and North America." These points did not, for Grant, prove why the Company should change, but only why a direct comparison between American and Company trade was inappropriate.[78]

Parry and Grant lamented that Americans "abundantly supplied" "Europe generally and France in particular" with "Indian

Commodities" "at very reasonable prices."[79] They admitted that even before Napoleon's blockade made re-exporting more difficult, "the Americans . . . supplanted us at the foreign Markets of Europe with Indian Commodities sometimes even immediately imported from the East."[80] Americans earned "far greater gains than are derived from the same trade by British subjects" on Company ships.[81] But that was too bad, because "throwing open the Trade to give a fair chance to British subjects" would be "the annihilation of the Company."[82] There was no thought to the logic running the other way—that the Company might be annihilated to give Britons a fair chance. Americans, Parry and Grant added, prospered because they lacked "the labour, expense, or risk of rearing and maintaining any settlements of their own" in Asia.[83] By this they meant to suggest that American and Company trade should not be compared, not the free traders' conclusion that Indian trade and Indian government should be separated. Baring counseled quiet: "Are we not near the end of our Charter? Is it wise or prudent for us to discuss the subject of *Competition?*"[84] But Parry and Grant could not help themselves. How dare Baring imply "the incompetency of the Company to carry on the National Trade with India."[85] They showed no realization that they had already implied as much. And then Parry and Grant returned to their ur-complaint: the Americans were succeeding, and it was not "fair."[86]

U.S. trade continued to flourish between 1809 and 1811; though Congress's Non-Intercourse Act barred U.S. trade to Britain and Canada, commerce to India continued apace. Even with the Royal Navy's best efforts to stop the carrying trade, and even after the Company increased tariffs on Americans trade with India, that trade boomed. With the Shipping Interest's acceptance of the idea that Britain should be, for the indefinite future, the emporium of the trade of Asia, the terms of the debate now changed. It was no longer whether Britain should compete with the Americans. It was whether the Company was the best means to do it.

CHAPTER EIGHT

America's China and Pacific Trade

On the south China coast, a few days' piloting up the Pearl River, lay the provincial capital and commercial hub of Canton (present-day Guangzhou). Western merchants, Americans among them, traded silver for tea there, the final destination for much of the silver dug out of the mines of Potosí. In this period U.S. trade—as part of the general trade of Atlantic states with China—remarkably foreshadowed the future of Western imperialism in the Pacific.

Free trade was, despite Adam Smith's sentiments, amoral. It made for better commerce: private merchants got goods more cheaply, shipped them faster, and met consumer tastes better than monopolied companies did. But this did not make them more moral than other men. If anything, freed from the Company's minimal regulation and oversight, private merchants were more pernicious than the Company was. In this, as in so much else, they were effective. American and British free traders were notoriously unscrupulous in trading with Natives in the South Seas and on the Pacific Northwest Coast. And without always admitting its evils, they sold opium in China. Their tremendous success would lead in 1833 to the end of the East India Company's China-trade monopoly.

As American trade with China grew, so did Americans' urge to find a substitute for the silver they were obliged to bring. American merchants scoured the Pacific Rim, harvesting everything from fur to sandalwood, but they could find nothing to sell to China that matched their own purchases other than silver. Western purchases in silver—a "pocketable" commodity for the porters and officials in the river delta—had profound political consequences in China that became readily apparent once Britons and Americans found something that sold there better than tea did in the West: opium.

The China Trade

Good statistics for Sino-Western trade are difficult to come by. Chinese records do not survive. The fullest count of Western trade at Canton aggregates U.S. and European shipping records, a labor that Rhys Richards has completed by compiling English and Dutch East India Company data with individual American ships' logs.[1] Richards's data tables consider U.S. arrivals in the Pearl River

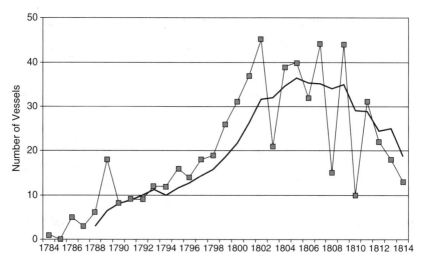

Figure 8.1 American Vessels Arriving at Canton, with Five-Year Moving Average, 1784–1814

Source: Rhys Richards, "United States Trade with China, 1784–1814," *The American Neptune* 54, Special Supplement (1994): 9.

Delta between 1784 and 1814. His is not a comprehensive list, but it thoroughly portrays extant Dutch, British, and American sources. The comparison underestimates U.S. trade to China, since the sources for U.S. vessels are piecemeal—compiled from various ships' logs and Company accounts—but the British and Dutch sources comprehensively represent their own countries' trade to China. Since the loss of some U.S. records appears to be random, it is still possible to compare U.S. trade from earlier and later years; the data here might be considered a representative sample and a minimum count of U.S trade to China.[2]

The number of American arrivals at Canton closely resembles the general arc of U.S. foreign trade between 1784 and 1814: a low baseline in the 1780s, followed first by a surge after 1794 and the outbreak of the French Wars, then by a decline as American neutral shipping became more difficult after 1810 (see Figure 8.1). Within this trend there is notable variance, some due to the arbitrary, if necessary, division of the data into yearly increments. A five-year moving average smoothes this variance and shows the general trend more clearly. Other elements of the variance are attributable to politics (here the annual divisions come in handy), the dip in 1803 reflecting the Peace of Amiens; the rise in 1804, the onset of the Napoleonic Wars; the dip in 1808, the Jeffersonian embargo; and the falloff in 1812, the War of 1812.

U.S. trade boomed in China, as in the rest of the Indies, in part because it replaced Continental European shipping, which averaged fewer than three arrivals a year at Canton by 1804 and dropped to zero by 1809.[3] One French visitor noticed that Americans had taken over the French trading house at Canton. Yankees had taken down the tricolor, raised "their stars" in its place, and in a speech for the occasion cried (in a passage the Frenchman underlined), *"We raise the fortunes of the United States on the wreckage of France."* "Not too friendly," he grumbled.[4]

Dutch shipping suffered similarly, with the Dutch government chartering neutral Swedish East India Company and American vessels to carry its trade to China. In the end, as with Dutch trade to Java, the dirigiste idea of coordinating trade to Asia from half a world away failed, and the Netherlands supplemented its chartered voyages to China with tea purchases on the American open market. Additional tea was likely smuggled into the Netherlands. This was a complete reversal from the 1760s, when the Dutch had smuggled tea to America.[5]

Richards's data also give tonnage figures, though this information is much less reliable since there were various ways to measure tonnage and Dutch and British tonnage figures for American vessels were probably estimates (Americans did not permit Company officials on board to measure their ships). Despite the guesswork, the tonnage data reveal a general division among American ships between larger and smaller vessels. Large vessels rounded the Cape of Good Hope in the southern summer, sailing east across the Indian Ocean, perhaps with a stop at Mauritius or Batavia before making Canton. They carried mostly specie, along with trade goods picked up en route. Small vessels rounded Cape Horn during the southern summer, and crossed the Pacific, usually with stops in the South Seas or Hawaii for sandalwood, or the American Pacific Northwest for fur. Fur purchases finished in September—a year after their voyage began—with the vessels reaching Canton for the winter trading season. They brought silver as well as fur, sandalwood, and sea slugs.[6] U.S. vessels arriving at Canton from fur- and sandalwood-producing areas averaged only 185 tons, while the other U.S. vessels—arriving from America, Europe, or the rest of the Indies—averaged 340 tons, nearly twice that.[7]

The Pacific vessels' size reflected their cargo and its procurement. Sandalwood, sea otter pelts, and seals were collected by hand from the wild, either by American sailors or by Native Americans and Pacific Islanders who traded them to U.S. vessels. Filling even a small vessel with furs could take an entire season. To fill up a larger ship would have taken years or required a small tender. Indeed, some fur traders already took years to fill up their ships, wintering in Hawaii between seasons or, as time wore on, on the Northwest Coast.[8]

But no Pacific cargo could replace silver. A shipload of pelts or sandalwood was not as valuable as the same space filled with tea, and silver—money—was the only means to make up the difference in value of the two equal volumes. One estimate of American imports at Canton for the years 1804–1808 states that $3.3 million of the $4.3 million worth of imports on U.S. vessels was specie, 78 percent of the total value of U.S. sales there.[9]

Sending a ship to China for tea entailed a particularly high opportunity cost—that is, it entailed missing opportunities to send that ship to other destinations. A China voyage lasted a year or more. During that period, the same vessel plying a route to the Caribbean or Europe might make three or more voyages. To be worth the trouble, the profit on a single China voyage had to be worth the profits of several Atlantic ones. In addition, tea was a light and bulky commodity—meaning that one ship filled with tea carried fewer salable pounds than the same ship filled with, say, Caribbean sugar.[10] Wholesale merchants often priced tea in chests: because it was a bulky good, what mattered most was the value by volume—and the lost opportunity to carry other goods in the extra space the tea required. Thus suggesting tea's expense to the merchant by comparing its per-*pound* price to sugar, as at least one historian has done,[11] is pointless. Per-pound prices mattered to the consumer. For the merchant, what mattered was the opportunity cost of sailing time and shipping space. To make up for the lost time and lost space, the merchant needed his tea to have a higher value by volume.

Tea's lightness affected the China trade in other ways as well. While sugar was dense enough to serve as ballast itself, fully laden tea ships still needed ballast. For this, tea ships often carried porcelain, which was wrapped in dunnage and lined the holds. Since each tea ship required a bottom cargo of china plate, China supercargoes bought porcelain, whether it could be sold profitably or not. Westerners' thirst for Chinese tea thus subsidized the price of their Chinaware. Chinese potters adapted to this role: eighteenth-century Chinese export porcelain is known for being thick, bulky, and cheap, valued not for workmanship or artistry—for which contemporaries and later critics deprecated it—but for mass. Back in the United States, the porcelain often sold at a loss anyway, leaving the key sale in tea.[12]

The silver that purchased all that tea was, on the other hand, extremely compact. It took up so little space as to be virtually volumeless, the kegs or boxes slipped under the captain's berth. Therefore China-bound ships needed trade goods as ballast for their silver, which was the real cargo. Those crossing the Indian Ocean traded at Isle de France or India or Batavia; those crossing the Pacific took on cargoes in Polynesia or the Pacific Northwest. Since silver constituted, as a rule of thumb, three-quarters of the value of U.S. sales at Canton, fur, sandalwood, sea slugs, bird nests, Indian Ocean goods, and any ginseng brought from the United States *together* comprised the last quarter. Thus, across all the various imports Americans sold in China, a ship's hold of such goods was worth one-fourth of the same volume of tea, porcelain, and nankeen. Moreover, the value of goods Americans bought at Canton often exceeded the value of what they sold there, since some merchants took advantage of the small but growing credit and debt markets on the China coast to buy more tea. Thomas Willing, for example, was able to sell his own bills of exchange in Canton by the 1790s (this market, as noted, was facilitated by the East India Company and the Bank of England).[13] The statement that in China a given volume of tea was worth triple the value of the goods Americans brought may thus be taken as a conservative estimate.

Furs were probably some of the least valuable cargoes Americans brought to China, since they entailed less processing than other goods. Fur was bulky and appears to have had a relatively low value for volume compared with tea. A precise value-by-volume is difficult to determine, yet it is clear a given volume of furs was unable to buy the same volume in tea, in part because Chinese demand for fur was less than U.S. demand for tea (rising U.S. fur sales in China ruined the price of fur there, since U.S. supply swamped Chinese demand, but rising supplies of tea in the United States did not equally overwhelm U.S. demand). Furs were also light and bulky enough that vessels leaving the Pacific Northwest carried sand and rock ballast. Nevertheless, fur added another leg to the voyage and another chance to profit.[14]

Sandalwood was not terribly valuable, either; one of the earliest attempts by an American statistician to measure the sandalwood trade put the value of sandalwood sold by Americans at Canton over a four-year period (1818–1821) at an average of $100,000 a year.[15] This was enough to buy only one vessel-load of tea during a time when at least ten to twenty American vessels a year cleared Macau. Sandalwood and furs defrayed only a small portion of the silver that would need to be imported or that the letters of credit bought.

According to contemporary American estimates, the returns on an investment in the fur-and-China trade, over a two-year voyage to the Northwest Coast and China, varied between 200 and 500 percent.[16] These estimates may be fantastic—certainly they exceed Fisher Ames's returns—yet this trade, "systematically and perseveringly" pursued, was certainly lucrative.[17] Despite the several turnovers of cargo, it was the sale of tea in the United States or Europe that determined the profitability of a venture. The fur and sandalwood trades let in merchants who might otherwise have found the specie requirements of the Canton trade beyond their means. The two trades were also quite damaging, both in terms of the social effects on Native peoples and the physical effects on the environment in the Pacific islands and the Pacific Northwest, and the rapacity of American merchants in these areas testifies to how fiercely American traders worked to achieve even marginal relief from their dependence on silver.[18]

The Voyage to the Pacific

Rounding Cape Horn was nasty business. Richard Henry Dana, the Harvard student whose maritime autobiography became a best-seller, recounted the frigid conditions with such vividness that Herman Melville thought the passage must have been "written with an icicle." John Child, another Massachusetts man, wrote a similarly chilling account. Child kept a journal of his voyage around Cape Horn on the *Hunter* in 1810. Though early summer, the weather was already "quit[e] cool" if not "very cold" for days on end. As they proceeded further south, "stiff gales of wind" and "hard squalls" of rain and hail greeted the crew on deck and up in the rigging. "Calm with snow" was a break from the windy weather.[19]

For it was the wind, not the cold, that bedeviled men rounding Cape Horn. At Tierra del Fuego, just north of Cape Horn, summertime temperatures averaged 52 degrees Fahrenheit; winter temperatures averaged 31 degrees. This was warm enough for the mountains to bear forests of wind-stunted trees and for Natives to grow hardy grains. But at its southernmost point, unguarded by the Andes, Antarctic storms ripped through the air and cut to men's bones. The sea "was running higher and higher," Dana recalled.

> It became almost as dark as night. The hail and sleet were harder than I had yet felt them; seeming almost to pin us down to the rigging . . . we ourselves cold and nearly blinded by the force of the storm. . . . The little brig was plunging madly into a tremendous head sea, which at every drive rushed in through the bow-ports and over the bows, and buried all the forward part of the vessel.

"Throughout the night," on another watch, "it stormed violently—rain, hail, snow, and sleet beating upon the vessel—the wind continuing ahead, and the sea running high. At day-break the deck was covered with snow." Men found the chill wind difficult to forget off-shift, lying below in an unheated room. "Our clothes were all wet through," Dana remembered, "and the only change was from wet to more wet. It was in vain to think of reading or working below, for we were too tired, the hatchways were closed down, and everything was wet and uncomfortable, black and dirty, heaving and pitching."[20] The only relief was north.

In these southern latitudes some American China traders hunted seals. South Georgia Island, a volcanic blip in an otherwise featureless sea, was one stop. Others hunted seals near the Falklands, on Kerguelen in the Indian Ocean and, slightly further north, the at Juan Fernandez islands in the Pacific. Sealers stationed parts of their crews on these islands for months at a time in squat, smelly huts braced against the cold and the wind as the men went about, quite literally, clubbing baby seals.[21]

More commonly, American fur traders went to the North Pacific, to the arc from Alaska to California where James Cook and John Ledyard had first fallen upon the idea of selling fur for tea.

Sea otter pelts from this region sold better than sealskins at Canton.[22] American trade in the Pacific Northwest was extensive and not always salutary. On their arrival at the mouth of the Columbia in 1805, the American explorers Meriwether Lewis and William Clark found all its trappings: Natives at the mouth of the Columbia spoke some English and were tolerably informed of the language of trade, including "musquit, powder, shot, [k]nife, file, damned rascal" and "son of a bitch." (Other Americans noticed "go to hell" had entered Native lexicons.) From local information Clark listed twelve fur-trading ships belonging to men "who speake the English language." Though neither Lewis nor Clark saw any fur trading ships in their stay on the coast—the explorers wintered there after most traders had gone—there were other, physical remnants of the traders' presence. Native men sported old sailors' clothes and "red blue or Spotted Cloth" and held American and British trade goods. Clark noticed that American or British sailors had left their marks on the women, too; one wore the name "J. Bowman" tattooed on her left arm—it is unclear what she or Mr. Bowman supposed it meant. Clark noticed that "many of the Chinnooks appear to have Venerious and pustelus disorders" as well.[23]

Monopolies and Corporations

Between 1793 and 1815, Americans dominated the Northwest Coast fur trade. Of the 292 known fur-trading vessels to arrive on the coast during that period, 201—more than two-thirds—were American, the product of free trade. The war assisted this boom, but monopoly restrictions on British traders helped more. Even after 1815, when an average of nine U.S. vessels a year reached the Pacific Northwest, an average of only two British vessels reached the Pacific Northwest annually. In 1833, with the fall of the East India Company's China-trade monopoly, private British merchants were finally free to sell their furs in Canton, at which time the number of British trading vessels on the Pacific Northwest Coast surpassed the Americans.[24]

European countries continued to erect corporations to manage their trade to the Pacific Northwest during the French Wars, for state-granted monopolies afforded a pleasing illusion of control over a trade, and over imperial ambitions, so far from Europe. Thus the Russians, as noted, organized the Russian-American Company in 1799 as a monopoly to oversee fur trading and to develop Russian colonies in Alaska and down the North American coast. The Russian-American Company took over from several previously competing Russian firms and was modeled on the English East India Company and the Hudson Bay Company (HBC).[25] The biggest monopolies, however, were British. The East India Company monopolized British sales at Canton, and its employees allowed other Britons to import furs there only if they got the commission to sell them. The Company forbade British merchants from reaching the Northwest Coast by circling Africa.[26] Meanwhile, the South Sea Company held the monopoly on British trade in the South Pacific. It had been inoperative since the 1720s, but it still held licensing rights for British trade on the South American Pacific Coast, and so Britons had to buy a license or risk being taken prize if caught without one. Some British merchants paid both firms, some paid neither, some flew fictitious flags (the Austrian flag was especially popular), and some chose not to bother. But Britons sailed to the Northwest Coast with costs or risks that Americans did not have to bear.[27]

Enterprising Britons tried to work around this. From India, James Strange (Henry Dundas's future son-in-law),[28] decided to try to outfit a voyage to the Columbia River, influenced, as many, by "an attentive perusal of Captain Cook's last Voyage." With David Scott's patronage he organized two vessels that left Bombay in December 1785 and arrived on the Northwest Coast in June the next year. Accustomed to India, Strange found American Indians quite odd. He deplored "the Beastly filth in which the Natives . . . pass their lives." "It was impossible to move a Single step," he wrote, "without being up to the ancles in Mud, Fish, Guts & Maggots . . . alike felt within and without doors." They ate lice, he claimed, and practiced cannibalism. Strange recalled meeting one man with "three hands and a Head" in a basket. "He informed me *they were good to eat.*" The man "very composedly put one of the hands in his mouth, & stripping it through his teeth, tore off a considerable piece of the flesh, which he immediately devoured, with much apparent relish."[29] Perhaps because he was busy exploring, Strange's trading did not go well. He encountered two more British vessels outfitted by rival Company employees and managed to get only a few skins.[30] Despite his commercial failure, the East India Company approved of the voyages and feigned interest in his suggestion that they look into "the propriety or possibility of forming a Settlement or Settlements, in the North West Coast of America, with a view to establishing a trade in Furs between thence and China." But the Company dallied. Two years later the directors still explained they would "peruse at our leisure . . . his proposal for making a settlement there"—and that they did not wish to be rushed.[31] It is hard to escape the suspicion that monopoly bred indolence.

Many failed to grasp the key to Americans' success. John Meares, whose ill-starred expedition to the Northwest Coast had sparked Spanish ire in 1970, shared the British taste for monopoly. He thought the trade "must be carried on by one Firm or Company." Competition would "so lower the price of them as to make the Trade no longer profitable."[32] Alexander Mackenzie, who was involved with both the HBC and the North West Company (NWC)—he was the first Westerner to walk across North America, beating Lewis and Clark by a decade—also thought that a single, exclusive company should control the Pacific fur trade and urged the East India Company, HBC, and NWC to cooperate accordingly.[33]

In the Canadian interior, the Hudson Bay and North West Companies vied for control of the fur in Rupert's Land—the expanse north of the Great Lakes and the St. Lawrence Basin and east of the Continental Divide, centering on Hudson Bay. But while these monopolies waged political fights for trading privileges, American fur traders were *actually trading.* Even the NWC found it could halve its expenses by sending its furs from Canada to a port on the American Atlantic and then reshipping them to China in U.S. vessels, rather then hiring a British vessel to go from Eastern Canada around Cape Horn to China.[34] While Britons continued to stew in their own alphabet soup, Americans merchants profited from British trade. Such was the case with John Jacob Astor.

The Multimillionaire

John Jacob Astor was affluent. The son of a German butcher, Astor sailed to London in his teens and then to New York. He arrived in early 1784 and, after returning to London to open accounts and sell furs, settled in New York. By 1794, New York business directories gave fur as Astor's only business.[35] Europeans demanded beaver and Chinese consumers demanded sea otter; Astor supplied both.[36]

In his first decades in New York, Astor developed the American merchants' usual web of business relationships. Sometimes acting as an agent for another, sometimes a full partner in an enterprise, occasionally retailing furs in New York, often buying them inland and shipping them in bulk to Europe, he did everything. His activities depended on whether he was upstate in town, the season, and how much capital he had. In these early years he was mobile, making trips to Albany, Montreal, and Lake Superior.[37] But he soon settled down, mirroring his fellow merchants in Philadelphia and Massachusetts, many of whom had graduated from the captain's cabin to the merchant's chair themselves.

As for so many other American merchants, the French Wars changed everything. Europe had once bought three-eighths of the North American fur supply, but after 1793 Canadian fur merchants were cut off from French and European customers, and the overlapping monopolies of the NWC and the East India Company prevented significant Canadian sales at Canton. U.S. fur merchants suddenly began raiding Canadian fur supplies on both coasts of North America for markets in China and Europe.[38]

Searching for a way to avoid the British restrictions on exports to France and the East India Company's monopoly at Canton, the NWC hit upon using Astor, its former rival. It formed partnerships with Astor and several other merchants to ship furs to

China. The furs traveled from Montreal to New York, where a judicious application of shipping law made them "American," before traveling on to China. Tea and silks made up the return cargo. The American partners, including Astor, were free to sell the tea and silks on the U.S. market—the most valuable leg of the trade. Meanwhile, the NWC could not share in the tea without violating the East India Company's monopoly. The partnership continued for three voyages, though the NWC's part of the trade was the least profitable and, financially, one of the least significant. Even with a shipload of fur, their American partners still had to bring specie to be able to afford to refill the ship with tea. While Astor profited handsomely from the tea, the NWC *lost* £13,484 on the first venture in 1792, £16,260 on the second in 1793, and £22,824 on the third in 1794.[39] In the 1810s the NWC reached a similar arrangement with the Perkins merchant house of Boston, which agreed to supply the NWC's Pacific coast settlements and carry the Company's furs to Canton as American property. The Perkinses received a fourth of the gross profits and a 5 percent commission on the sales of fur in China and tea in the United States.[40] By hiring Americans, the Company allowed U.S. merchants to profit from British commerce. As with the Sir Francis Baring's and Thomas Dickason's investments in the American East India trade, the NWC diverted capital and profits to U.S merchants that, if Britain's corporate monopolies and trading restrictions had not been in place, might have gone to British traders instead. Its British furs had become packing material for Americans' silver.

Astor was no anti-monopolist. He and other Americans aspired to monopolize the fur trade just as the NWC and HBC hoped to do, but this was beyond Astor's reach. Astor ultimately aped the British model so completely that he linked his monopolied pretensions to the establishment of an American imperial presence on the Northwest Coast. He failed miserably. (His settlement at Astoria was an example of the American failure to link monopoly and empire and will be discussed in Chapter 10.) But initially, Astor and other Americans were unable to form such a ruinously ambitious company. Rather than trying to dominate an area's fur trade with a permanent outpost there, Astor's operations and those of most other China traders on the Northwest Coast were peripatetic. This suited the reality of the Northwest Coast, where imperial control and the lines of supply to imperial posts were both precarious. In later years, some Russian outposts were forced to trade their furs for food and supplies from American vessels, giving up their principal commercial resource simply to survive. Before 1815 few U.S. firms maintained a full-time agent even at Canton—though Russell & Co. and Perkins & Co., both of Boston, were notable exceptions. Most U.S. tea merchants, including Astor, relied on the judgment of their roving and perpetually competing captains and supercargoes, rather than incurring the sunk costs of local offices or imperial ambitions in Canton or the Pacific Northwest.[41]

Sandalwood

Hawaii was the only major mid-Pacific stopover in the northern hemisphere. Fur traders found it the perfect waypoint between America and China, and by the 1820s whalers increasingly stopped there too. The island was full of fat pigs raised, deliciously, on sugar cane, enough to feed tens of men for days. Hawaiian yams could last for months at sea, much longer than other starches such as plantains, bananas, sweet potatoes, and breadfruit. Coconuts were cheap and plentiful, yielding food and a refreshing change of drink from the maritime routine of coffee, water, grog, and tea. And of course there was taro. Produce, as at the Cape, was plentiful. One American visitor noted purchases of hogs, fowls, sweet potatoes, bananas, "Plantain, Sugar Cane, Cabages, Water Mellons, Bread fruit and allmost all kinds of Vegetables."[42] Hawaiian women also had a certain appeal—rest stops at Hawaii presenting the opportunity to "mate the copper coulered lasses," as boatswain John Walters recalled. This made the Hawaiian islands a welcome respite from Walters's standard fare of "stormes and ship wrecks and cannon balls and hu[n]gary belly and cold biter night."[43]

The other appeal of Hawaii was its sandalwood. American merchants swarmed the Pacific in search of it like locusts, trading fiercely for it on each island until the supply was depleted. Sandalwood grew wild in Hawaii, but it was not harvested heavily until after 1810, after American merchants had depleted the supply on Fiji.[44] Several American traders tried to secure a monopoly on Hawaiian sandalwood but, as with so many other monopolies, the concession was difficult to enforce. King Kamehameha abrogated the contract. Attempts to secure a similar concession from Kaumualii, Kamehameha's erstwhile rival and subsequent vassal on Kauai, came to naught when British merchants intervened.[45] Kamehameha and Kaumualii were eager to sell as trade in sandalwood became a means to acquire the weapons and trappings of power. But this meant other political aspirants was eager to trade, too. Kamehameha had set a royal monopoly on the sale of sandalwood, but it extended only as far as his writ. The king's conquests and his monopoly helped preserve Hawaii's supply for a time, but the trees fell more swiftly after his passing, when political rivals vied for influence through sandalwood-bought guns and ships, much as on other Pacific islands.

A Hawaiian sandalwood monopoly was impractical because there were other supplies of the wood, just as the NWC's monopoly was impractical as long as there were other suppliers of fur, and just as the East India Company's monopoly on tea in Canada made little sense in the face of American competition. These were national monopolies, existing only within the domains of one nation's laws, representing no practical control over any one good (unlike, for a time, the Dutch East India Company's monopoly of nutmeg). But Kamehameha was a shrewd leader and businessman, and no fool. He sent a vessel, the *Kaahumanu*, with sandalwood to China rather than satisfying himself merely with supplying American merchants.[46] His successors sent three Hawaiian vessels to the Pacific Northwest to acquire furs as well.[47]

Pacific Islanders harvested sandalwood to trade with passing crews; Americans crews also harvested it themselves. As they rounded Tierra del Fuego and approached the South Seas, seamen began to hone their tools for collecting the wood. "Finished grinding 800 Axes and commenced grinding hatchets," John Richards Child, the American seaman, wearily noted one day in his journal.[48]

American and Native leaders both acted with appalling brutality for profit. Child noted at one Marquesan island that sandalwood was "very rar[e] in this place and very ha[r]d to be got for the Natives are most constantly at war." One Native chief, given only as "Sow," suggested to the captain of another American vessel that he "would fill his Brigg with S[andal]wood" if the captain would help him fight a rival village.[49] The captain agreed and sent the first officer and "fore stout men and with muskits pistoles cutlases &c" to fight (Child spelled this with a Boston accent), but they were "defated on acont of the weather being wet so that thare muskets ware of no use." The rival villagers "beat and speard" them to death, roasting and eating three of them. Unchastened, Childs's own captain threw his crew into another local war in exchange for sandalwood, sending men and a cannon on shore. They were defeated and, frightened of being eaten, left the field piece behind as they ran. "Thus our grait warourers had to flee in danger shaim and disapintment," Child reflected.[50] Despite the disappointment, it is hard to imagine the crewmen had joined the sandalwood ship seeking a fight—there was always the navy for that—though some may have sought Marquesan adventure. Yet, such were the profits of the tea trade, and such was the disregard for the safety of their crews, that American captains traded their men's lives for pieces of wood.[51]

Americans brought other Pacific goods to the Chinese market, including trepang and birds' nests. Trepang, also known as sea slug, is endemic to the Celebes, Fiji, and the South Seas. Local divers harvested it from the sea floor, American crews joining in the labor of washing, draining, gutting, boiling, scraping its exterior with coral, then drying and sometimes pickling it. Trepang was gelatinous and thus provided a sought-after texture in Chinese cuisine. Flavorless, it showcased the stocks and sauces in which it was served.[52]

Birds' nests were a similarly extravagant addition to wealthy Chinese kitchens. The nests were from the golden shrike, native to eastern Borneo. The shrikes bound their nest together and to cave walls with saliva. This preserved the nest from predators, until men thought the spit itself worth eating. Local climbers harvested the dried nests; American captains shipped them to China. There the nests were boiled and the saliva consumed in the ensuing broth.[53]

A "tragedy of the commons" bedeviled the American (and private British) trade around the Pacific: a spiral of brutality in which Native Americans, Pacific Islanders, and Anglo-American captains increasingly distrusted each other, expected the worst, and visited their earlier rough treatment on the next comer. (A similar dynamic emerged in the pepper-trading ports of Sumatra.) Oft-repeated stories of Indian massacres on the Pacific coast led to American reprisals against uninvolved Native groups, who were inclined to retaliate against uninvolved Americans, and so the cycle went.[54] American captains, not expecting to stay on the coast permanently, unlike the Russians or traders at HBC posts, felt especially unconstrained by any need to develop good long-term relations. Some even engaged in slave trading along the coast. One captain, William Sturgis, was careful to explain that "in each and every case where a vessel was attacked or a crew killed" by Natives in the Pacific Northwest "it was in direct retaliation for some life taken or some gross outrage committed against that tribe." In 1810, Samuel Fergurson worried that Natives would "revenge themselves on us for pas injuries received from others," if they could.[55] But few Americans were so discerning, and few Natives retaliated against just the offending vessel.

In Hawaii, unified rule helped, and King Kamehameha saw to it that Westerners were able to visit the islands safely. But as much as Kamehameha tried to avoid a repetition of Cook's apotheosis, he was not always successful. In 1790 the captain of the U.S. merchantman *Eleanora*, on the coast of the Big Island—where Kamehameha's rule was already established—ordered the massacre of scores (some accounts suggest hundreds) of islanders in retaliation for the theft of a small boat. In reply, islanders killed all but one of the crew on the *Fair American*, the *Eleanora*'s sister vessel. The *Eleanora*'s captain may have feared the canoes that came around his vessel had ill intent, but the result was another ship's crew dead. Unsurprisingly, American fur and sandalwood traders carried more armament than other U.S. merchantmen did.[56]

Unified rule helped in the Sultinate of Sulu as well. The sultanate stretched from just north of Manado, the principal Dutch outpost in the Celebes, to just south of the Spanish outpost at Zamboanga. The sultan signed a trade accord with Manila that saw a steady stream of Sulu *prahus* and Chinese sampans sail between Manila and Jolo at the end of the eighteenth century. Jolo prospered as Western merchants supplied it with staples like rice and sugar in exchange for trepang, birds' nests, and mother of pearl. By 1804 Robert Farquhar estimated that the "Dutch, the Portuguese, the Spaniards and the Americans" had taken half this trade.[57]

In Sulu, as on the Northwest Coast and in Polynesia, U.S. merchants also traded guns for natural products. These firearms flamed competition for control of the commodities that purchased them. Sales of firearms to local rivals, and their subsequent competition for resources to buy more arms, often exhausted supplies of fur, sandalwood, and birds' nests because the demand in China for these goods outstripped Pacific supply. As Sir Stamford Raffles complained in 1811, Americans, "as they have no object but commercial adventure, are by no means scrupulous how they acquire their profits, and as firearms are in the highest request especially among the more easterly isles these would be considered as the most profitable articles. They have already filled the different clusters of islands in the South Seas with firearms, and they would not fail to do the same" in the Dutch East Indies if they could. This was dangerous to anyone, such as Raffles or Kamehameha, seeking unified control. "If such active and enterprising traders . . . are permitted the free range of the eastern Archipelago, perhaps it would be difficult to devise a measure more injurious to our political influence as well as our commercial interests." A decade later the American consul at Manila complained, similarly, that U.S. merchants calling at the port were "very unwilling to give me a list of their cargoes"—the implication being that the cargoes were guns. Spanish customs records confirm that U.S. gun shipments passed through Manila.[58]

The View from Canton

American traders also played a rather nasty role in China. Along with British private traders, they helped corrode Chinese government authority at Canton. Fur traders often smuggled goods ashore to avoid customs duties, undermining imperial authority at the port and forcing customs officials to "squeeze" the remaining licit traders even harder. Private British and American merchants were proud to evade Chinese customs, seeing the evasion as a mark of distinction as well as good fun. One British seaman described staging a fight between sailors on deck in order to scare off Chinese customs officials, bragging "we paid not one farthing of duty for our skins which we sold in China—the [customshouse] officers dared not come on board."[59] Western traders did not fully understand the Chinese customs establishment: the business of the various checkpoints along the river and the full amount of duties to be paid were unclear to them, and they sometimes mistook legal taxes for shakedowns. That actual shakedowns were common did not help; nor did many merchants' perfect willingness to evade the law. The fur trade, and Anglo-American private trade at Canton generally, served as the tip of a wedge, facilitating conditions conducive to the sale of opium: both fur and opium were shipped by private merchants, both were smuggled into the bays and rivulets and up the sea coast from the Pearl River Delta, and both evaded the established arbiters of Sino-Western contact at Canton, making them impossible to police.

One might expect there to have been considerable imperial oversight at Canton. It was an important city in the Qing Empire, the seat of the Liangguang Governor-General[60] and a military command center. The governor-general, provincial governor, provincial treasurer, provincial judge, and the local military commander were authorized to inform the Throne on provincial matters, marking a strong administrative interest in the city. A posting in Canton was considered as a "troublesome, difficult and wearisome thoroughfare,"[61] making it a post for the emperor's most trusted and reliable men, on a level with Beijing, Chengdu, Xi'an, and Suzhou.

The Pearl River and its tributaries made Canton a major commercial center, certainly *the* most important Chinese hub so far south. Yet Western commerce faced more restrictions than proper oversight. Western traders came through the Portuguese enclave of Macau, the coastal station downriver from Canton. Though Macau remained Chinese territory, the Portuguese were suffered to govern the territory as they saw fit. Macau served as a base for British, French, Dutch, and American merchants, since it was the only port in China where Western merchants could live year round, merchants removing to Canton only for the trading season. This constricted Western trade. Macanese affairs were left to Portuguese authorities, keeping the odious business of supervising a foreign community at one remove from Qing officials. This was an ordinary devolution for an early modern state, but one which left Qing officialdom unfamiliar with the idiom and practice of Western trade.

Officials hoped to collect revenue from Western trade without the trouble of interacting with foreign merchants—they were no more interested in understanding the Western merchants than those Westerners were interested in understanding Qing officialdom. Better simply to collect the tariffs—or, if a merchant, to evade them—than attempt to make sense of troublesome foreigners. Thirteen merchant firms—co-*hong*—were authorized to trade with Western merchants. They supplied tea and served as intermediaries between Western merchants and the Qing officials. The *hong* were also responsible for paying tariffs on Western trade to the Superintendent of Maritime Customs. The Superintendent—the *hoppo* so scorned by Western merchants—was the central official in this arrangement. He occupied a lucrative role and, like the governor and governor-general, could communicate directly with the Throne. Yet despite the wealth and power his role might be expected to yield, the superintendent was increasingly unable to control his underlings or effectively oversee Western trade, for the government's writ in Canton was corroding.[62]

The superintendent's position made for "corruption," in our contemporary parlance. The superintendent, the governor, and the governor-general used their positions for personal gain at the expense of both the emperor and the people. Yet the word "corruption," with its moral bent, hardly does justice to the deed. China in the Qing was a prebendal system: offices were expected to support officials in their work. "Salaries formed but a small, indeed an insignificant part of their income. The official could neither have lived on his salary, nor have covered the administrative costs which it was his official obligation to cover," explained Max Weber in his study of Chinese religion. Instead, "he financed most of his administrative expenditures from fees and tax-income and retained a surplus."[63] There was no division between a private and public purse; levied funds paid for officials' private needs as a matter of course. This could be quite expensive for officials who needed to recoup the cost of purchasing an office—especially such a plum post as a customs superintendency—for which donatives were expected by his various superiors.[64] Such gifts greased the wheels of "patrimonial officialdom," as Weber termed it, in which "office-holding . . . rests on the ruler's personal discretion and favor."[65] This was especially true for the customs office, which was not part of the regular Chinese bureaucracy. It was not staffed by the usual scholar-literati elite, as the governors' offices were. As part of the Imperial Household Department, it was staffed in part by imperial bondservants (baoyi), both Manchus and Manjurified Chinese; and filled wholly at the emperor's pleasure. The superintendent directly served the imperial house.

In this context "corruption" did not mean that officials had profited from their posts—as we might understand the term today—but that they had lost the emperor's trust. Imperial morality set the emperor's righteousness as a font of the government's good functioning and so, solipsistically, an official's poor performance was a sign of his immorality, and the loss of the emperor's trust meant one was inherently corrupt. This was especially true for the Imperial Household. And yet corruption maintained its more prosaic definition as well. Since officials had to live off the fruits of office, if the emperor scrutinized an official, he could always find corruption, but only if he looked. Corruption became political—a tool for the emperor to police his officials. These tensions were magnified for the superintendent, whose access to millions of taels of silver each year made his risks and rewards all the greater (a tael is equivalent to one and one-third ounces and exchanged at three taels to £1 in this period).

The emperor knew that his superintendent in Canton was taking a cut, and the superintendent himself was in the same position with regard to his inferiors. Clerks and *junminfu* officers milked foreign captains and supercargoes in the channel from the Boca Tigris to the Canton embankment. Some superintendents were successful at limiting this, but the short tenure of their office made change seem unwise. It could risk the emperor's cut—a certain cause for dismissal—and it would also risk the superintendent's, which had to be taken as quickly as possible before he was ordered to move on. There was no guarantee that reforms would be continued after he left. Furthermore, enforcement was impossible. The channels and islands of the Pearl River Delta made it easy for guards and clerks to shake down foreign captains for a few taels in exchange for looking the other way while they traded with nonlicensed merchants:[66] a small bribe to a guard avoided a much larger tax to the government. And so American and British captains made sport of evading Chinese tariffs.

Of the money that came in as a proper tariff, a share went into the provincial fisc, another into the emperor's privy purse, and a third into the superintendent's own. The governor's share *alone* surpassed 1,000,000 taels of silver annually in the 1790s.[67] As a result of such funds, the superintendent's office was the constant object of political contest and ambition.

Thus the political and economic structure of China's system of trade with the West made it particularly vulnerable to bribery. Smuggling into the delta escalated; the gradual increase in bribe taking by customs-house guards and magistrates' *yamen* along the coast ate away at the superintendent's and governor's authority, and these officials' peculation ate away at the Throne's rule. The balance between evasion and enforcement held as long as high and lowly officials perceived a self-interest in partial compliance.

If the balance tipped to evasion, the Chinese state would lose its ability to gather information and enforce its rule along the coast. The balance ultimately did tip toward evasion, and in doing so it prepared the way for, and was exacerbated by, opium, a commodity that was both profitable and illegal and that thus *had* to be smuggled.

Opium

Silver was the wedge; opium followed. By the 1790s it was common knowledge among Chinese officials that the drug was entering the country by foreign ships, that drug runners were bribing their way past customs, and that opium abuse was spreading. In 1799 the Jiaqing emperor, recently installed on the throne, lamented the addiction; his words sound eerily prescient to readers familiar with drugs today. It was at first, he thought, "persons without homes or professions" who bought the drug. They were vagabonds, wanderers, and itinerant peddlers whom the government had problems tracking. They settled down for a while, "prepared an Extract from" the drug, and opened up shops to sell it.[68]

Had the drug stayed among the hoi polloi and "vagrants and disreputable persons," perhaps the government would have been unconcerned. The emperor knew that the down-and-outs of his empire huddled together in their dens to smoke. "Their inducement on this occasion," he wrote, "appears to be the power which this substance communicates to those who partake of it, of not closing their Eyes for entire Nights, and spending them in the gratification of impure and Sensual desires." But when the habit "extended itself"—a helpful euphemism—to "members and descendants of Reputable families" or, worse, to students in the imperial examination system and even to "Officers of Government" (i.e., people who mattered), then the government took notice. For when society's betters "make an habitual use of it," "their respective duties and occupations are neglected." In time the addicts, by now "sufferers," grew ill but could not quit. Doctors were useless. Addicts craved food, and within a few years a user could easily smoke away his last penny until he had to choose which hunger to feed. Some starved. Others became "thieves and robbers" to support their habit. Still others mixed the opium with liquor, making one of the most readily obtainable poisons, and took their own lives.[69]

This vision reflected Qing moral tropes: unsavory vagabonds led perfectly good students (and hence future officials) astray, never the other way around. And a benevolent emperor was now intervening. Commissioner Lin, whose 1839 crackdown sparked the Opium War, did moralize against examination candidates and degree holders smoking opium. He did not want the empire administered by scofflaws and addicts. But his exhortations fell flat. No one reached the metropolitan examinations (the highest level) without a patron, and degree holders passing the exam together drew upon one another for support. Degree holders—addicts or not—were too well connected to oust easily. Hence, one tended to blame "vagrants."[70]

Opium's penetration into lower but useful classes soon became a concern in itself. Soldiers were stoned, "utterly worthless with their spirits and muscular powers." Clerks and runners were often addicts as well. Along the coast, many took bribes from the smugglers to keep the opium coming, others seized drug stashes and dealt it themselves.[71]

Opium traffic encouraged the violation of imperial authority. Foreigners and local officials were both to blame, the emperor thought: "We discover [that] Opium is imported by Foreigners, . . . by the means of small Craft it is landed by degrees at Macao and thence conveyed privately to [Canton], while the Custom house Officers and Guards at the different stations . . . suffer it to pass without examination or inquiry, being doubtlessly bribed to a large amount for that purpose."[72] But all the emperor could do was tell his bureaucrats to try harder and threaten then with his vigilance.[73] And so on down the bureaucracy the scolding went. The governor investigated. He found the emperor's suspicions correct—it was probably a short investigation—and ordered the customs superintendent to order the *hong* merchants to order the Western merchants to stop dealing drugs. They did not.

American merchants bought their opium largely in Smyrna, though they also obtained quantities from India and Java. Americans bought the drug through the good offices of the English Levant Company, since the United States had no official treaty relations with the Ottoman Empire until 1830, meaning that, as Samuel Eliot Morison pointed out, "an English trading corporation," and a monopoly at that, "fostered an important branch of American commerce."[74] Opium was such an Anglo-American business that American merchants flew the Union Jack at Smyrna. The U.S. consul there—in reality just another merchant, as he was unrecognized by the Ottoman court—noted in 1810 that "all the American vessels that arrive hoist English colours."[75] Americans took to themselves almost the entire Levant opium trade to China, since the East India Company's trade restrictions prevented private British merchants from shipping Turkish opium to China, and the merchant marine of nearly every other state in Europe was destroyed or bottled up by the Royal Navy. Between 1806 and 1812, U.S. imports from the eastern Mediterranean—largely opium—quadrupled in value. Americans financed these purchases by selling sugar, rum, and, interestingly enough, East Indian goods. American merchants sold Indian cloth, pepper, spices, tea, and even coffee from Mocha, in modern-day Yemen, which they shipped around Africa. The Yemen-Smyrna coffee trade was lucrative. The Derbys entered the Yemen-Turkey route as early as 1788, and others followed.[76] The expense and red tape placed on shipments crossing Suez made circumnavigating Africa to bring Red Sea coffee to the Eastern Mediterranean a profitable proposition. And to buy Yemeni coffee, most Americans of course brought specie.[77]

The trade was brisk: six opium traders arrived in 1805, and the numbers only increased.[78] Thirteen arrived in the second half of 1809, and those were only the ones coming from America direct.[79] Another eleven came from Malta and Britain between March 15, 1809 and March 7, 1810.[80] In the year before the outbreak of the War of 1812, Americans imported just shy of $1,000,000 worth of goods at Smyrna,[81] and scholars have estimated that during the whole of the Napoleonic Wars, an average of a dozen U.S. vessels called at Smyrna annually, importing $1 million of goods each year.[82] With their millions, they bought opium.

Opium was the only substitute for specie that Britons or Americans could sell in bulk to China. It was compact, unlike furs or sandalwood, making it easier to replace a shipful of opium with a shipful of tea. As a result, most China traders carried opium. For its part, the East India Company held a monopoly on cultivating the drug in Bengal. But the Company did not want to sell opium to China directly; getting caught would jeopardize the tea trade, the Company's most lucrative business. The Company's tea reserve was intended to protect against such temporary shortages of tea, a sign of the importance the Company placed on stable tea sales (the reserve also meant Company tea was several years old by the time it reached someone's cup, since old tea had to be rotated out of the warehouses and sold to prevent its becoming a loss). Instead, the Company auctioned its opium in Bengal to private merchants, usually its own employees, who shipped the drug to China themselves. The co-*hong* maintained a similar stance toward opium: they were supposed to prevent traffic in the drug, but some dealt in it anyway, and those that did not often lost business to unlicensed merchants who would deal in opium. In both cases free traders, not the monopolies, trafficked and peddled. As long as the Company maintained its office in Canton, the British free traders were held in check—their demands for greater access to Chinese ports and the legalization of opium were balanced against the Company's need to maintain an open tea supply and a decent working relationship with Chinese authorities.

U.S. merchants came in a strong second to the British merchants who dominated the Canton opium trade and the tea trade. Significantly, the Americans were the only traders fully free to explore alternatives to importing silver to Canton. Because sandalwood and furs—both difficult for British traders to bring to Canton— did not well enough, they resorted to opium. Had private British traders been free of the East India Company and HBC restrictions, they would likely have followed their American cousins to the Pacific Northwest, but they would not have been able to pay for their purchases of tea at Canton with furs either. Only opium had enough value for volume for do that. But British merchants did not need to follow their American cousins to learn this; they knew, by seeing the heaps of fur U.S. merchants brought in and the kegs of silver those merchants were still obliged to pay, that the only commodity worth selling in China, besides silver, was opium.[83]

Death of the India Monopoly

In 1806 Americans bought more goods from British India than the English East India Company did. How could this have been? British India was the East India Company's sovereign possession; the Company had justified India's conquest on the logic that possession would regularize and secure the Company's trade, and the Company justified its monopoly on the trade between Britain and India by the same reason. But by 1806 Americans shipped more from the Company's Indian territories than did the Company itself. In 1809 Americans shipped more *into* India than the Company did, too. The runaway success of U.S. trade with India had far-reaching implications: it was one of the primary reasons that in 1813 Parliament revoked the Company's monopoly on Indian trade.

Historians often attribute the collapse of the East India Company's monopoly to the lobbying efforts of British industrialists. The standard argument is that textile manufacturers sought an Indian market for their goods and believed the Company was inadequately vending their cloth in India. By destroying the Company's monopoly, British industrialists could sell to India themselves. Recent scholarship has begun to question this *post hoc ergo propter hoc* reasoning, suggesting a different source for the government's choice to revoke the Company's monopoly—the French Revolutionary and Napoleonic Wars.[1] As P. J. Cain and A. G. Hopkins point out, "Abolition in 1813 of the Company's formal monopoly of trade with India was essentially a wartime measure which was implemented principally to improve the flow of Indian commodities to Britain. The decision was not taken at the behest of a lobby representing Britain's new manufactures."[2] Indeed, far from confident in their abilities to export abroad, as late as 1794, some Manchester "Muslin + Callico Manufacturers" still found it difficult to compete with Indian cloth in the British home market.[3]

Yet even those historians who regard the decision as a wartime measure overlook how U.S. trade, enabled by the French Wars, abetted the loss of the Company's monopoly. Parliament allowed private British trade to India in order to concentrate India's trade with the West in British hands and reduce the American commercial presence in India, something the Company had proved powerless to effect.[4] The 1813 charter question sat at an intersection of economic thought, politics, and raw economic data rare in early modern history.

Free Trade as a Provincial Idea

The Company had always argued, in the best Orientalist tradition, that its experts on the ground in Asia made it uniquely qualified to manage trade there. By 1800 the Company had a 200-year record of managing trade to Asia,[5] during which time the trade had benefited countless British businesses, from London shipbuilders to provincial tea sellers; the Company's stock and bond issues were some of the most basic instruments underpinning the British financial system; and the customs revenues from its imports were a crucial source of income for the government. Though the Company enjoyed its record of success in the City, the free traders' proposals were unproven and risky, if not downright dangerous—the airy domain of "Scotch" professors and self-interested country merchants. How could any reasonable Briton object to the Company's work? The Company's supporters merely asked that their trade, "a Trade of such certain and substantial benefit, may not be sacrificed for arguments of doubtful speculation." Such a request seemed all the more reasonable in 1813 with Britain at war. It was not the time "to adopt any measure of experiment" that, come failure, would only bring down "disastrous consequences," especially when the Company had already established "a commercial system in which we have hitherto so greatly prospered."[6]

Such arguments had served the Company well in the past, but in 1813 British economic liberals found a counterargument in the United States. American merchants, they reminded Parliament, had been trading to the Indies for decades. And the Americans were prospering. Even Leeds's manufacturers failed to make the strictly industrial argument against the Company that one might have expected; instead, they included an American component to it, suggesting "that the trade to *China* and the *East Indies* may, with perfect safety and great national advantages, be thrown open to the Country at large, is fully exemplified in the instance of the United States of *America*." There, they continued, "merchants, unprotected by Charter, exclusive privileges, or corporate capacity, have carried on an extensive and flourishing commerce with . . . all the Countries within the limits of the *British East India* Charter."[7] Residents from the manufacturing county of Lancaster reminded Parliament that "the *East India* Company cannot deny, [that] other foreigners, particularly *Americans,* have for many years carried on an extensive and successful commercial intercourse" to the east.[8] The merchants of Lynn concurred: "The extensive and flourishing commerce which the citizens of America have carried on for several years with India, and particularly with the Chinese empire, without any sort of restraint, is a proof that these expectations of the advantages to be obtained from the exertions of private individuals are not unfounded."[9] The merchants of Bridlington echoed Lynn precisely—so precisely, in fact—that the argument about American trade appears to have been included in the campaign boilerplate. In the effort against the Company's monopoly, the American argument was central.[10]

U.S.-India trade made two things clear. First, it fed the argument that it was possible to trade to the east without a monopoly, showing that free trade to the east was not just an abstract theory but a present reality that Britain could adopt, if she so chose. Second, that reality made the theory itself (i.e., that open trades were better than monopolized ones) seem less abstract. In *The Wealth of Nations,* long a liberal bible, Adam Smith had piled abuse on the Company and its monopoly to establish just this idea.[11] With the debate on the Company's charter, Smith's free-trade friends could prove and enact their ideas by pointing to the standing success of U.S. free trade to India. The Glasgow merchants did so with glee. The principle that free trade was more efficient than monopoly, "a fundamental one in political economy," was "strikingly exemplified in . . . the trade from the United States of America to the East Indies and China." The American trade, "carried on by individual citizens of those states," was an unparalleled success in its "rapidity of progress"—that is, its growth—while "the trade of the British empire with those countries had been progressively [if oxymoronically] on the decline."[12] The Company's trade dwindled not out of ill luck, but, as the shipowners from Liverpool put it, "from a deficiency either in the capital or in the energy and enterprize of the Company."[13] And that, argued the merchants of Dublin, was understandable, since "all monopoly in trade has ultimately proved injurious."[14]

The Company's critics did more than harp on the "baneful effect of monopolies"[15]—they stressed their *right* to free trade in language that has, for American readers (then and now), a familiar tone.[16] Welsh merchants bluntly claimed, "It is the inherent and unalienable right of the people of this Empire to trade. . . . The exclusive privilege enjoyed by the *East India* Company is an infringement of, and altogether incompatible with, that right."[17] Bristol's merchants asserted their "inherent right" "to the full and free enjoyment of trade and commerce."[18] Scottish petitioners had never seen "a monopoly so truly inconsistent with commercial liberty"[19] as the East India Company's. As another Scottish letter claimed, they were "entitled to an equality of privileges in trade and the commercial pursuits of its [Britain's] subjects."[20] "Inherent and unalienable right," "entitled": these were British terms born of a long line, the same line from which the rhetoric Bostonians had hurled at the East India Company forty years earlier emerged.[21] These terms pointed to an old question: did a monopoly given to one infringe on the property rights of all?[22] Some petitioners declaiming the injustice of the Company framed their argument in this way, claiming "an infringement of general rights."[23] That is, the Company's monopoly infringed on the right of British subjects to use their property however they saw fit—even if that meant sending it to India.

Others, adept at playing British heartstrings, used a more patriotic voice: "the full and free right to trade" within the empire "is the undoubted birthright and inheritance of the people of this empire," Bristol's merchants wrote.[24] The Company's privileges, claimed a Glasgow petition, deprived all else "of privileges which they are proud to prize as their birth-right," and which "no temptation could induce them willingly to relinquish," which "no payment is sufficient to purchase."[25] Britons asserted that the freedom to trade was their "birth-right, unalienable by any charter."[26] Here, the merchants from British outports organizing the free-trade lobby captured the patriotic high ground. They argued that free trade to the Indies was better for the British nation and the British Empire as a whole, as opposed to the Company's call for deference and tradition, which seemed in 1813 to benefit a narrow few at national expense. Thus, having established the viability of free trade by pointing to the Americans, and having asserted its inherent superiority to corporate monopoly, free traders now demanded that British "principles of justice and liberal policy" apply.[27]

The Politics of Free Trade

There was more than art and rhetoric in the free traders' attacks—there was politics, too. Much of Georgian Britain's politics can be reduced, as Sir Lewis Namier showed, to a competition for sinecures and contracts which benefited but a few. Indeed, most of the petitions sent in to Parliament were written by country merchants as deeply invested in snatching up the Company's business for themselves as the Company was in defending it. Few writers on either side of the debate were disinterested. Free-trade writers, however, unlike the Company, lacked a following in government to see to their interest. And since they could not count on buying votes extensively—again, unlike the Company—they had to find a sympathetic politician willing to fight the Company on his own account, allowing themselves to be co-opted to his cause. Thus the 1813 debate combined a recognizably modern organized lobbying and propaganda campaign with a decidedly old-fashioned game of politics. The free traders would provide the pamphlets; a politician would provide the votes. That politician was Robert Banks Jenkinson, second Earl of Liverpool.

To some readers, this may seem odd. The Liverpool administration (1810–1827) is often recalled as a conservative force, not a liberal one. His government has been elided with Arthur Wellesley's (1828–1830) as the grand archetype of Tory conservatism by later generations of writers for whom "liberal" signified either the Liberal Party or a fondness for social upheaval, neither of which describes Liverpool. This is the influence of scholars from the Victorian period onward who dated the era of liberal enlightenment from the Reform Act of 1832, passed after Liverpool's tenure, and from the revocation of the Company's China-trade monopoly in 1833. In contrast, Liverpool is remembered for implementing the infamous Corn Laws in 1815 (which barred the import of foreign wheat until the domestic price reached a predetermined ceiling), the repeal of which became a major reformist issue after his departure from government.

Yet Liverpool was also a Pittite liberal. He rose to prominence as a minister and acolyte to William Pitt the Younger. He, along with Perceval, Portland, Canning, and Castlereagh, united after Pitt's death in 1806 as "Mr. Pitt's friends," a loose grouping that moved between government and opposition, forged to protect Pitt's legacy and the principles for which he—and they—had stood. It is these men, not the elderly Duke of Wellington, with whom the early Liverpool should be linked. The Pittites were law-and-order liberals who favored equality before the law (and, hence, equal property rights), economic reform, and domestic peace. Perceval, whose administration immediately preceded Liverpool's, was even more hostile to the East India Company than Liverpool; Canning, who immediately succeeded Liverpool, was active in mitigating the Corn Laws. Liverpool was in the mainstream of Pittite opinion. He studied Adam Smith in his youth, was a proponent of free trade, and, if not a doctrinaire proponent of laissez-faire, generally eschewed government intervention in the economy. "Government or Parliament never meddle with these matters at all," he noted in 1819, "but they do harm."[28] He favored the Corn Laws only because he was not powerful enough to resist the agriculture lobby in Parliament, and then only as a temporary measure. Privately he favored an easier version in 1815 (set on a sliding scale), and he sought to soften the laws later as well. Liverpool formed his economic opinions in the midst of war with France, related domestic unrest in Britain, and as a member of Pitt's cabinet. He was a Tory, a liberal, and a Pittite at once.[29]

In March 1812, Perceval appointed Robert Hobart, the Earl of Buckinghamshire, to head the Board of Control, the government body charged with oversight of the Company. Buckinghamshire, formerly Governor of Madras (1794–1798) and more commonly remembered as Lord Hobart, his title before succeeding to his father's earldom, brought considerable familiarity with Anglo-Indian free traders to the job. Indeed, he was inveterately hostile to renewing the Company's Indian monopoly, and may well have been given the India portfolio for this reason. Buckinghamshire was a minor figure in the Perceval cabinet and a cipher to Robert Dundas, who had led the Board of Control previously. Dundas controlled the family political machine that dominated Scotland, making him, with Scotland's votes in his pocket, a valuable addition to the Portland, Perceval, and Liverpool governments. It was Dundas who, over the course of 1807 and 1808, decided that it was finally time to do away with the Company's Indian monopoly, taking up his father's and Pitt's free-trade legacy at the Board of Control.[30]

Dundas's decision ignited the free-trade debate in Company and government circles. Replacing Dundas just a year before the bidecennial vote on the Company's monopoly, Buckinghamshire would probably not have been chosen for the post had his opposition to the Indian monopoly been in doubt. From then on Dundas could count on an amanuensis to complete his work, which Buckinghamshire did, reaffirming his commitment to the Dundas line a month after assuming his post when the Company requested a £2.5 million loan from the government. Buckinghamshire demanded the

India trade be opened in return, and the Company—forgetting that beggars cannot be choosers—rebuffed him. This was before the War of 1812 and Napoleon's invasion of Russia, both of which began in June of that year. The Buckinghamshire/Dundas policy appears to have been initially calculated on the assumption of continued American competition in India and a permanently entrenched French Empire in Europe, where Americans might re-export Indian cloth.[31] For Dundas and Buckinghamshire, a free trade to India was the best way of returning Indian trade to British hands. Liverpool, who took office in May 1812, retained Buckinghamshire in the post and similarly opposed the Company's Indian monopoly, though he suggested he might be willing to leave the Company with its monopoly on the China trade and its authority to govern India.

Parliamentary opposition, much more free trade–minded than the government, was less generous. Some elements sought to destroy the Company entirely. And so the Company tried to convince Liverpool and Buckinghamshire to alter their views. Despite a series of letters and meetings, Liverpool and Buckinghamshire were unmoved.[32]

After the general election of November 1812, both sides prepared for the inevitable fight in Parliament. The Company retained eighty-two "East-India" Members of Parliament (MPs)—that is, Company stockholders as well as men who represented London and the City interests (themselves major Company shareholders) and in the past could be expected to vote with the Company as a matter of course. These men were for the most part within Liverpool's government; thus the Prime Minister, less than a year in office, had to vie with the Company for the support of his own backbenchers. It is a strong testament to his Smithian convictions that Liverpool would risk dividing his government over the matter while still fighting Napoleon.

The timing of the vote, May 1813, is key. In May, Napoleon was weakened but not defeated; he was still emperor of much of Western Europe, and the idea of a Europe without him was still hard for cabinet officials to imagine—let alone expect any time soon.[33] The allies did not defeat him decisively in central Europe until November of that year. Meanwhile, though American merchants were chased from British India during the War of 1812, free traders continued to refer to the history of American trade there and acted as though its renewal were imminent, perhaps playing on an idea that the war in America would not likely last as long as the war to overthrow Napoleon.[34] Indeed, in June 1813 Napoleon had signed an armistice with Britain's erstwhile allies in Central Europe, which, though short-lived, showed that even as late as mid-1813, consolidation of Central and Western Europe remained within the emperor's grasp. With such unreliable allies on the Continent, British victory in Europe did not appear imminent.[35]

In the May 1813 vote, the opposition, chagrined to support either the Company or Liverpool, walked out of the Commons. This put the full weight of the decision on the East India MPs within Liverpool's government. There remained 131 members to vote on the final bill. If the Company's eighty-two "East India" MPs voted as a bloc, they could easily defeat it. But they did not, and Liverpool carried the vote, 88–43. The Prime Minister had needed at least seventeen "East India" MPs to vote his way; he had gotten thirty-nine. Perhaps, before his passing, Baring had persuaded some City merchants of the merits of a more liberal line. In addition, between November 1812 and the vote on the India-trade monopoly in May 1813, the free traders' propaganda campaign—along with the ministry's political muscle—concentrated on turning those wavering "East India" MPs against the Company.[36]

To swing these thirty-nine MPs to their side in the winter of 1812 and 1813, the liberals delivered their coup de grace: the Company's own records. The Company had kept customs records at the Indian ports under its control, and the records from Bombay, Madras, and Calcutta (1802–1811) revealed a boom in American trade just when the East India Company's trade collapsed. Those records were brought before Parliament. Thus Lord Buckinghamshire, defending Liverpool's East India Bill in the House of Lords, resorted to the economic liberals' formulation: to be sure, "practical advantages ought not to be sacrificed to theoretical speculations; but," he went on, "here actual experience was brought in aid of speculative policy." He "only called upon their lordships to grant to British subjects, the same advantage as were enjoyed by the Americans." The mountains of data—statistics, combined with oral testimony from witnesses familiar with the Company's business— backed the arguments of Buckinghamshire and the free traders perfectly.[37]

The Economics of Free Trade

Buckinghamshire drove the point home with just that data. He recalled, as previously mentioned, that in 1806–1807 the United States and European nations bought "nearly 1,600,000£" worth of goods from India, "whereas the imports of the Company for that year had been only 1,200,000£." Would not the £1.6 million "carried on as it was by Americans . . . have been a considerable object to British subjects?"[38] It was a good question, and a damning one at that, the data for which ironically came from the Company's own accounts of imports and exports in India between 1802 and 1811 (see Figures 9.1a and 9.1b). They showed an India-wide decline in the Company's trade.

These data were aggregated from the customs records of Bombay, Madras, and Calcutta. In the latter, the main port in British India, the Company had been keeping detailed customs records since 1795. Before that, a "sea customer" had maintained the Company customhouse, but he did not keep comprehensive or well-organized accounts of the port's business. In 1795 modernization saw the position of sea customer replaced with that of a more diligent customs reporter who recorded all ships entering and leaving the port, along with (among other things) their captains, owners, tonnage, nationality, origin, and destination. Guards were posted and the customs warehouses were locked to keep goods secure from theft and smuggling, allowing the reporter a reasonably accurate count of commerce. In addition to a shipping list, the reporter began taking account of the value and quantity of all goods imported and exported at Calcutta and the presidency (a multiprovince administrative unit) at large. These data were then tabulated to show the value of the

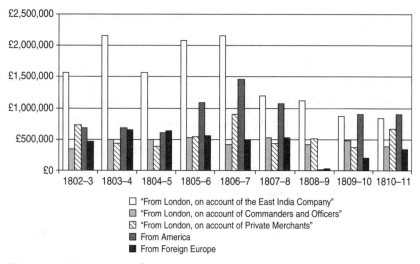

Figure 9.1a Imports to India, 1802–1811

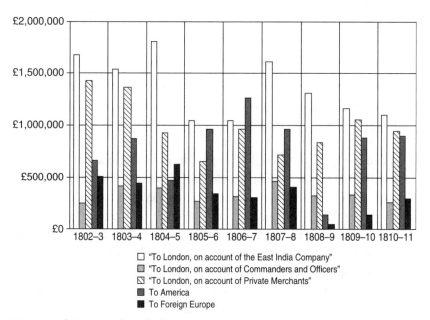

Figure 9.1b Exports from India, 1802–1811

Source: House of Commons, "Statement of the Commerce of British India with London, America and Foreign Europe; from 1802–3 to 1810–11, both inclusive," in item no. 136, "Accounts and Papers relating to the East India Company's Shipping," *Sessional Papers, 1812–1813, East India Company,* vol. 8, 264–267.

port's various imports and exports by good, origin or destination, and carrier's nationality. A copy was sent on to London annually. In 1802, this system was expanded to include Madras, Bombay, and their respective presidencies—the customs system thereby embracing all of British India. These data are remarkable; they are the first recognizably modern customs and trade statistics for India.[39]

In addition to the Company's own trade with India, two other lines of legitimate British-Indian trade existed. The first was the "privilege" allowed to captains and officers on Company ships. These men were allotted a share of the ship's carrying capacity for their own trade. This was a means of paying officers but also an acceptance of a trade that otherwise would have been smuggled. As the number of officers sent out on each Company ship remained fairly constant, the value of this commerce did not alter much. The second was the licensed private trade on Company ships. Though the private trade did pick up somewhat, neither it—encumbered by the Company's excessive freight charges—nor the Company's own trade stanched the rising tide of American imports into India. From 1802 to 1807, with the United States neutral but most other Western states consumed by the Napoleonic Wars, U.S. imports into India grew rapidly. The near-total collapse of the American import trade in 1808 and 1809, due to President Thomas Jefferson's embargo, did little to stop it. As soon as the embargo ended, U.S. trade recovered, even surpassing Company sales in India.

The Company accounted for its annual investment for the period between 1802 and 1811 by dividing it into merchandise, including woolen long ells and other textiles, and specie. In the first five years (1802–1803 to 1806–1807) the Company's average shipment of specie to India ran to just over £1 million per year, or 56 percent of the total investment; the rest was comprised of British manufactures and Madeira. But in three of the last four years (1807–1808 to 1810–1811), the Company's investment included no specie at all; in the fourth year, specie constituted barely 20 percent of the investment (£230,000). The specie was not replaced by merchandise, and so the overall value of the investment declined. A smaller investment sent out meant fewer funds to buy goods for home.[40]

Was it that the Company did not or could not compensate for the lost specie by increasing its investment in British merchandise?[41] Certainly those historians who emphasize the British manufacturing lobby's influence think the former. But the latter is closer to the truth. Specie and merchandise, especially textiles, were not interchangeable. They served opposite purposes in the transitional economy of early nineteenth-century British India. Specie fed directly into the old trade with the old economy of Company India: cash for cloth, and weaving work farmed out by the Company in a complex putting-out scheme that historians have labeled proto-industrialization. Imports of British textiles to India ran directly against this; British textiles were the new trade with the new Indian economy, whereby India was not a producer but a consumer, a colonial market that bought the manufactures of the metropole and exported cash crops (hence the directors' suggestion that as British manufacturers pushed Indian cotton cloth from the British and European markets, India "must endeavour to compensate her loss by the farther improvement of her other various and valuable productions particularly Indigo, Raw Silk, Cotton and Hemp.")[42] The new trade overcame the old only gradually, and two distinct Indian trades ran parallel for some time. But if the Company were to begin selling British cotton weaves—as opposed to woolens—to India, it could hardly be expected to purchase like cotton weaves in return.

Rather, it made sense to bring British cloth to India only if some other commodity could be purchased with it, like indigo, sugar, or raw cotton. (Buying Indian specie was not an option; the Company's Indian government was notoriously cash poor at this time. Total specie exported from India, by foreigners and the Company alike, amounted to only £31,000 for the entire 1802–1811 period.) Thus the nature of the Company's investment affected what it could buy. If it planned to buy cotton cloth in India, it had to bring specie or woolens; if it planned to buy agricultural goods, it could bring specie, wool, or cottons. To compensate for the decline of specie in the Indian investment, the Company would have to sell more cloth to India—wool and cotton—and to the extent that it sold cottons, buy more cash crops. But cash crops were bulky and cheap, too cheap to ship on the overpriced, baroque monstrosities the Company called ships. So the Company treated cash crops either as ballast or as supplement to its main purchase in India, cloth, as the specie-rich investments of the early 1800s suggest. Moreover, were the Company to hazard its way fully into the indigo, raw cotton, or sugar markets, it would be entering the core business of one of the most powerful lobbies in Britain: the West India sugar lobby. To suppose the sale of British cotton cloth to India is also to suppose the sale of Indian sugar, raw cotton, and indigo in Britain, which the high cost of Company shipping and the power of the Caribbean sugar lobbies prevented.[43]

This brings us to India's exports to the West and the data Buckinghamshire quoted. The Company's share of India's exports—the Company's original raison d'être—fell between 1802 and 1811, though less precipitously than its imports to India. Trade on privilege remained relatively constant. British private merchants exporting from India to the West did lose some ground initially, but seemed to be making something of a recovery after 1807–1808. The American trade, however, grew. By 1806–1807 U.S. exports from the Company's own territories in India exceeded the Company's, as noted. It was the only year that happened, but American trade remained significant subsequently; its recovery from the Jeffersonian embargo was rapid, and in 1810–1811 the values of American, Company, and British private trade came close to converging.[44] In both imports to and exports from India, the American trade was a strong rival to the Company, increasing its overall share of both the import and export markets over the period when the Company's share declined. This evidence, presented before Parliament, was devastating.

Americans absorbed much of the Indian export trade by importing specie to India. While the Company curtailed its specie investment in 1807–1808, Americans did not, importing over £1 million of specie into India in a year when the Company imported none. Baring thought Company orders declined for "want of funds." Funds were not sent because, as Parry and Grant explained, the "Market here was overstocked with piece goods."[45] And so orders for piece goods fell from £1.3 million in 1805 to less than half that in 1809. Yet the Americans found no glut. Though U.S. sales to India also fell—reaching near zero in 1808–1809 because of President Jefferson's embargo—they rose to more than £800,000 in 1809–1810 and 1810–1811, years when the Company imported no specie at all. In these years Indian specie imports from the United States comprised more than two-thirds of all specie brought there, U.S. silver's rarity making it easier to exchange for large return cargoes. Between 1802 and 1811, 89 percent of the cargo shipped to India by the United States was in specie, as opposed to only 41 percent of India's imports from the English East India Company and 32 percent of Indian imports from Great Britain as a whole. The dearth of specie available to merchants in the United States, considered severe in the immediately post-Revolutionary period, had clearly evaporated by 1800.

In many ways the American economy complemented the old Indian economy better than the British one did. Before 1760, the East India Company had sold British specie for Indian cloth, which is what the American traders now did. In this sense, the American economy of the early 1800s—especially of the northern states conducting much of the trade to Asia—resembled the British economy of the 1750s: on the brink of industrialization, demanding cloth, having little capacity to make such cloth on its own, yet possessing enough silver to buy it abroad. U.S. commerce provided relief—albeit temporary—for India weavers, U.S. purchases pushing against the trend of deindustrialization caused by the Company's declining orders. When the Company did not continue Britain's old silver-for-cloth trade, Americans replaced it.[46]

Just as bad as the trade figures was the written record of the Company's own customs officers, especially the Reporter of External Commerce in Bengal, who was responsible for tabulating annual trade figures and sending them on to London. Every year he attached a short essay to those figures. His comments on the American trade were cutting. Already in the 1790s the Bengal reporter noticed the American boom, commenting that the American exports from India "will be reshipped *from* America *to France*," to supply the market shut to Britain.[47] In 1804 his successor noted again that the Americans "have obtained permission to dispose of India produce in France," and that if the Company tried to shut them out of British Indian ports, they would simply go to non-British ones (such as Serampore). He concluded acerbically, "Even the natural monopolizing spirit of the Dutch and Portuguese have given way to the sound policy of encouraging commerce; while Great Britain alone wishes to continue the same system, under their present extended empire, as when the Honourable Company possessed solely a few acres of ground round their respective factories."[48]

It was indeed a bad sign that the Company's own customs officials found its "monopolizing spirit" stifling. Another reporter continued the assault, writing of the "rapid . . . strides by which the enterprising merchants of the United States have advanced . . . [in] British India"—in contrast with the Company's decline. U.S. trade, perhaps hyperbolically, far surpassed "every thing of the kind heretofore recorded in the commercial history of British India."[49] While the reporter duly noted the decline in Indo-American trade that Jefferson's embargo occasioned, the impression of American commercial success remained and was reaffirmed in the postembargo rebound.

The Company sought a way to excuse the Americans' success. In its own internal memorandum, which was brought before Parliament as evidence in March 1813, the Company found a reply to the free traders' cries. "The great progress and profit made by the Americans in the India trade," wrote the Committee of Correspondence, "proceed essentially, not from their activity, or the advantage of individual enterprise, but from their neutral character." No British merchant, Company or private, was going to be able to sell Indian goods to Napoleonic Europe—only a neutral party, like the Americans, could do that. Americans dominated the neutral trade not just in India but in Europe and Latin America as well, the Company pointed out, where private British traders had abounded but then foundered because of the war. The Americans' ability to be cheaper and faster than the British was, argued the Company, a function of their neutrality. After all, the Americans were cheaper than British private traders, too. And in 1813, with American ships stripped of their neutrality and the Royal Navy chasing them down, U.S. trade was withering. The free traders' dream of a cheaper, easier, and more open commerce to India was, the Company said, an illusion.[50]

Free traders laughed. Neutrality was not the only cause of Americans' success; their willingness to innovate for the market, rather than forcing the market to fit them, was just as crucial. It was a defect "in the energy and enterprize of the Company," as Liverpool's petitioners had put it.[51] There was nothing particularly American about Americans' innovations, nothing that private British traders—or the Company, had it wished—could not adopt on their own. The Company paid too much for its ships; Americans built vessels at a fraction of the cost. The Company's ships sailed together in seasonal fleets; the Americans sailed singly and came and went as they pleased. Company ships took months to load cargo; American captains worked their crews harder to cut down turnaround time in port. Private British traders shipping with the Company, and thus bound by Company shipping times, were at a disadvantage to Americans. "The celerity with which they conduct their commercial operations is surprising," wrote one correspondent, rather surprised at Americans, in 1800; "Instances occurred last season of several of their ships disposing of their imports, purchasing their export cargoes, and leaving the port in twenty and twenty-five days from the date of their arrival."[52] The contrast with the lethargy of Company captains was clear. Indeed, in the Company directors' own correspondence even the most staunch defenders of the monopoly admitted that "when various Neutral Ports were open to us . . . the Americans in particular . . . supplanted us at the foreign Markets of Europe with Indian Commodities sometimes even immediately imported from the East, and supplanted us also in our own Colonies."[53]

This was not for Britons having difficulty in port. Private British merchants, despite the Continental System, exported to Copenhagen and the Hanse towns routinely, even with the latter under French rule by 1810. French commanders there, as noted, were happy to look the other way when a British shipment came in, provided the right bribe.[54] Despite the Continental System, Britain re-exported an average of over £2.5 million goods per year across the North Sea to France, the Low Countries, and Germany between 1803 and 1812, turning places like Helgoland into multimillion-pound smugglers' dens. British merchants exported on average more than £1.5 million of Indian cloth per year in this period.[55] By 1812, even Company officials—trying to show that they had made an effort to capture European demand—bragged that "three-fourths" of the Company's "imports from India have hitherto been for the supply of the continental markets."[56] But if India goods could be exported across the Channel so easily, why were the Americans still so successful? The excuse of American neutrality was a Company canard.

From the Exchequer's point of view, the most salient part of the trade data was the section on India's exports to the West. As the Company's Indian exports fell, private British exports from India (on Company ships) rose. And the sales on those exports, which went to London, paid customs duties that made up a significant fraction of the government's budget. Unleashing private British merchants to take back market share from the Americans was a way to put the government's revenue on a sounder footing—better that London's coffers be filled rather than Washington's with the duties from British Indian goods.

Ironically, the whole case against the Company had come from the Company's own records. With such clear proof, continuing the Company's monopoly seemed absurd. The merchants of Bristol simply had to

> refer to the information before the House, to show that the trade carried on by the E.I. Company has decreased at the very time when, by British exertions, its field has been extended . . . and that foreigners, by the advantages of free and unfettered exertions, have been at the same time successfully competing with the E.I. Company . . . in the trade of the Company's own settlements, . . . whilst such trades have been long and obstinately denied to the subjects of the United Kingdom.[57]

The Company, the liberals gloated, had made their case for them.

Consequences

The 1813 debate was a step in the British Empire's transformation from mercantilism to liberalism. When the liberals of the 1830s passed the Reform Bill (1832), ended the company's remaining monopoly on trade to China (1833), abolished slavery (1833), and debated the Corn Laws, they were finishing the work of 1813 and building on a political momentum accumulated over twenty years. William Wilberforce's 1807 ban on the slave trade presaged the outright abolition of slavery in 1833. So, too, the demise of the India-trade monopoly presaged the end of the Company's China-trade monopoly. None of this is to suggest that the 1813 free traders, let alone Liverpool, were Cobdenites. But, as D. J. Moss has explained in his study of Birmingham's role in the charter debate, "for some twenty years" the 1813 assaults on the Company were "used as examples of the power of organized public opinion and subsequent assaults upon Westminster sought to duplicate the methods used then." "It is from the experiences of 1812–1813," he concluded, that this agitation "can be traced."[58]

The year 1813 was a defining moment not just for Britain, but for the empire. It provided for the liberals' free-trade notions to be tested. If they were right, if free trade indeed was the better way to run the empire in the east, then the success of private merchants would prove that. It did. The Company's India trade limped along for years after 1813, trying in vain to compete with private British traders, gradually vanishing in a whimper as private merchants shipped more goods more quickly and more cheaply than the Company. Meanwhile, these private traders ensured that Britain's trade with India boomed. In the nine years after 1813, average British imports from Asia stood at £7.3 million per year, whereas they had stood at £4.5 million for the nine years before.[59] Similarly, British exports to Asia grew from an average of £1.8 million in 1804–1812 to £2.9 million in 1814–1822—both post-1813 figures being nearly two-thirds again as large as their pre-1813 counterparts. The Company remained saddled with the cost of its ships; even as late as 1827, free traders chided it for charging £20 per ton in the

India trade while other traders charged £5 per ton.[60] Thus, by the time of the 1833 debate on the Company's China-trade monopoly, economic liberals could point to the records of *British* private merchants successfully trading between Britain and Asia.

The British transition from a Company empire to an empire of free trade would leave much of Asia ravaged in the course of the nineteenth century: the free-trade empire proved much more rapacious than the Company had ever been, particularly in China. American traders, who believed in free trade both with their heads and with their purses, had highlighted the possibilities of a free trade with China to the British. The downfall of the East India Company's China-trade monopoly in 1833 was in some part due to a need to compete with the U.S. trading presence in China, but it owed more to the British free traders' own success against the East India Company in India, where British free trade had been permitted in no small part due to the American free-trade example in the years before 1813. The 1813 debate proved an opening wedge for British advocates of free trade to argue in 1833 that the monopoly on trade to China should also fall—setting the stage for the British free-trade empire in China and the Opium Wars. With the fall of the Company's China-trade monopoly, liberalism animated the entire British Empire.

CHAPTER TEN

American Capital and Corporations

By 1810 growing hostilities between the United States and Britain made war between them hard to avoid. In Macon's Bill No. 2, Congress made an offer to Britain and France: whichever of them loosened its commercial restrictions first would win congressional embargo upon the other. Anti-British sentiment in America—exercised by neutral trading rights, impressed sailors, and the prospect of taking Canada—combined with Napoleon's claimed compliance with Macon's Bill to turn the embargo against Britain. War between Britain and the United States followed thereafter. U.S. neutrality had made the French Wars quite profitable for American merchants; U.S. belligerency was a disaster for them. The U.S. East Indies trade subsided for the duration of the war, which lasted from June 1812 to December 1814. News of the end of hostilities did not reach the United States or the Indies until 1815.

American action in the east was limited. Three American privateers headed for the Indian Ocean shortly after the war began, the prospect of fat East India Company prizes doubtlessly on their owners' minds. Two reached the Indies; one, the *Hyder Ali,* named for the founder of the Mysore dynasty that so exercised the British, was captured off the Nicobar Islands in 1814. (Officials at Penang, still convinced of their importance, fretted over an American attack for another year.) The U.S. naval frigate *Essex* reached the Pacific via South America, making the Marquesas and taking a dozen British whalers before being seized by British forces at Valparaiso in

1814. In 1815 the U.S. Navy sent another force eastward: the frigate *President*, to be joined by the sloops *Hornet* and *Peacock*. Though the British took the *President* outside New York, the *Hornet* and *Peacock* made the South Atlantic island Tristan da Cunha, where the *Hornet* found and defeated the British sloop-of-war *Penguin*. The two American ships were eventually chased out of the South Atlantic. The *Peacock* reached the Indies and the Sunda Strait in June 1815 and attacked the much smaller East India Company sloop *Nautilus*—a vessel so small that the British naval historian William James thought the Americans could "almost hoist [it] aboard." The captains of the *Peacock* and *Hornet* were unaware of the peace, and after taking the *Nautilus*, the *Peacock* gave it up the next day after definitive news of the war's end. This was the extent of American naval action in and near the Indies. The U.S. Navy was more concerned with the Atlantic and the Great Lakes, though the eastern seas had booty to offer vessels that made it so far. (One of the *Essex* navigators brought British charts of the Indies, ideal for locating British merchantmen.) Still, Britain, not the United States, maintained an imperial interest in the Indies, and so British force predominated there.[1]

Even before the war, U.S. trade was precarious, though merchants had confronted similar difficulties before. In 1801, with peace looming, Israel Thorndike and William Bingham sought investments outside maritime trade. The 1808 trade embargo spurred a turn to manufacturing in the United States. And so in 1811 and 1812 U.S. merchants anticipating war knew they would have to pull their capitals from the sea and invest it elsewhere.

During the war, the British blockade confined American shipping to port, so U.S. merchants invested their capital in domestic banking, manufacturing, and real estate. This transfer of capital left landed businesses more prominent in the post-1815 northern U.S. economy. (Southern cotton, deeply connected to the northern manufacturing, emerged more prominently as well.) This transfer of capital reveals the progress of capital accumulation, which took two forms. As discussed, affluent Americans amassed capital sufficient to become investors in their own right. In addition, U.S. businesses accumulated large capitals themselves, using the corporation as a vehicle to organize and invest their funds. Affluent East India and carrying-trade merchant-investors crucially (but hardly exclusively) shaped and used the new corporate form.[2] For finance to play a significant role in American economic life, capital first had to be accumulated and organized in meaningful amounts. Because East India wealth was denominated in silver, it was especially important in this process. Opportunities to finance American businesses attracted overseas capital, such as that of the Barings,[3] as well as domestic capital, such as Fisher Ames's; these funds were invested broadly not only in the East Indies trade, but also in banking and real estate, all sectors in which large stocks of specie held particular advantage. On the eve of the War of 1812, as specie-capital exited the East India trade, the vehicle for its accumulation was, as often as not, the corporation.

Creating Corporate Capital

American Revolutionary sentiment had left "company" a dirty word. Yet, ironically, because the Revolution had carved the automatic grant of monopoly out of corporate charters, corporations were used more widely for business after the Revolution than before. This combination of British heritage and American Revolution gave the American corporation a distinct pedigree. In Britain it was partnerships, not corporations, that led the way. But in the United States, as the newly competitive corporate form spread across the business landscape it acquired a legitimacy that monopolied corporations, such as the East India Company in colonial America or the Bank of the United States (BUS) in the early republic, lacked. American corporations were not universally successful—their mutual competition ensured that some would fail—but their facility for building capital meant that those corporations that withstood normal business competition did so with more money than earlier enterprises, a process occurring in association with the attainment of affluence by early republic merchants. And just as the Americanization of the corporation helped the accumulation of capital in business, so it brought the merchant's competitive ethos to corporate law.

In accumulating capital, merchants sought to attract investors with specie and discourage speculators trading on credit. When these merchants referred to their corporations' "stock," they signified its assets: a fund of wealth for investment or perhaps a store of goods. The *Universal Dictionary of Trade and Commerce,* a widely circulated eighteenth-century merchant's manual, evoked this sense when defining corporate banks as a "company of monied men, who . . . agree to deposit a considerable fund or joint stock": such as "the bank of England."[4] By contrast, the related but distinct sense of "stock" as shares, as the fractional ownership of a corporation and thus of its underlying assets, could seem speculative. Hence, "the pernicious practice of stockjobbing" was disparaged in the 1790s, as were those who made a living trading stocks.[5] Requiring payment for initial shares in silver gave a firm a solid capital base; it also separated such firms from the jobbers and speculators who spoke of buying shares with loans rather than capital and who would contribute little to a company's financial foundation. Additionally, firms issuing stock for specie also sought buyers interested in a share of the company's profit—its returns—rather than those seeking a theoretical and inherently prospective resale of the stock.[6] Issuing shares for hard money allowed conservative and affluent businessmen to limit corporate ownership to the sufficiently wealthy; banks in particular found this technique useful. Such share prices were set high enough to exclude middling buyers; and investors were limited to the network of friends, family, and business associates whom the principal investors had already cultivated. Corporations thus served as a means to magnify wealth by attracting certain kinds of investors—just as the specie-freight-renting system of the East India trade. Unsurprisingly, East India merchants, affluent and competent alike, founded some of the most significant early American corporations. Corporations held other attractions: compared to partnerships, they provided a more liquid flow of assets in and out of the business, and though admitting new investors might have seemed risky, if the above caveats were pursued, well-vetted and well-capitalized investors could join without having to dissolve and re-form the corporation at every change of ownership, as partnerships were required to do. Corporate hierarchies also created new space for leadership as the affluent, American investor commanded more of other people's capital.

In practice, corporate capital functioned similarly to private business funds. The Manhattan Company's charter, one of the most liberally interpreted, was an early attempt to maintain flexibility in the uses to which corporate capital could be put. The Manhattan Company was chartered as a water company, but it became a bank (it is now part of J. P. Morgan Chase). No one less than Aaron Burr secured its charter from the New York legislature in 1799 with a maximum capitalization of $2 million and a clause permitting the use of its "surplus capital" in "any other [legal] monied transactions." Alexander Hamilton, who approved of the water company, missed the "surplus capital" clause and felt duped by Burr, as many Federalists did. Burr wanted the bank to assist his political campaigns; the bank would compete with existing, pro-Federalist banking establishments in New York City.[7] Since they were in separate states, the first chartered banks in the new republic enjoyed de facto monopoly. These were, as Bray Hammond has suggested, "public banks," and some Federalists flattered themselves that their self-interest was in the public interest, ginning up opprobrium at Burr's cheek for disrupting a public good.[8] Burr's actions were self-interested too—he was also a company director—but it is hard to fault his surplus capital clause, which sought to put his investors' money to the most profitable use. According to one of his more sympathetic biographers, Burr explained in Albany that "the directors should use the surplus capital in any way they thought expedient and proper. That they might have a bank, an East India Company, or anything else."[9] After the bill's passage, Rufus King's correspondent Robert Troup wrote similarly that "we are to have a new bank established by the [Manhattan] Company and that they will also embark deeply in the East India Trade and perhaps turn their attention to marine insurance."[10] At a meeting of Manhattan Company directors that same year, Burr proposed investing in marine insurance or overseas trade—both, as banking, being specie-intensive businesses.[11] Burr had obtained a bank by the back door; the state legislature still voted on individual acts of incorporation and the political culture still expected corporate charters to limit the businesses in which corporations engaged. The Manhattan Company's charter was an opening wedge, beginning the gradual transformation toward acts of general incorporation and the assumption that corporations were free to engage in whatever business their managers saw fit.[12] The state's interest in what a corporation did vanished along with the expectation that a chartered company was, in any meaningful sense, a devolved tool of state. Instead, the corporation became a convenient means of organizing several persons' capitals. The assignment of corporate capitals to distinct enterprises—one had to be either a bank *or* a water company—bore little resemblance to the diverse enterprises in which businessmen allocated their funds. The Company did not "embark deeply" in the East India trade, for that trade was still thought best pursued through separate voyages, and the Manhattan Company's shareholders likely included a number of men with East India ventures in progress who would not relish the competition.[13] But the "monied" transactions in which specie might be engaged were just as likely to include insurance and banking as Asian trade, and it was a small leap for merchants to move among these.

Stephen Girard, Israel Thorndike, and John Jacob Astor all transferred East Indian affluence and expertise to the financing and organization of other businesses. They were far from the only affluent investors in America, and as some of the wealthiest Americans they were exceptional investors. But by virtue of their extreme affluence and their attention to specie they financed, organized, and led other, merely competent, investors, continuing to transform how American business capital was organized. The story of each reveals different alternatives, powers, and limitations to the business corporations arising throughout the economy of the early republic.

Stephen Girard and Banking

Stephen Girard was yet another prominent Philadelphia merchant who spanned, as William Bingham and Alexander Baring had, the East Indies and banking. All three were general merchants with

East India portfolios, as most American East India merchants were. One gets the sense, from how late in the Napoleonic Wars Girard continued trading, that banking was actually his last choice.[14] This was understandable; in Pennsylvania, banking was particularly difficult, and banks themselves remained politically suspect.[15] And yet in the end Girard became a banker, just as the Barings had, even serving as a de facto Bank of the United States during the War of 1812—palpably demonstrating the ends to which large funds, once acquired, could be put.

The BUS, an invaluable part of Hamilton's financial program, could not secure a new federal charter in 1811. This was due partly to enduring anti-monopoly sentiment and partly to the vagueness of the Constitution's commerce clause. The legal basis for a federal charter was shaky enough to deter most other businesses from seeking a federal grant—the boom in corporate charters in the early 1800s was entirely at the hands of the states. In Pennsylvania, the Bank faced ideological opponents, who rejected it as a monopoly, as well as interested adversaries who had either an agrarian displeasure for its tight money policies or a fellow banker's distaste for competition. When the Bank applied for a Pennsylvania state charter in 1811, Harrisburg rejected it, though its authority to charter banks was not in doubt. Thus with war imminent, republican legislators in Washington and Harrisburg had shut down the main lender to the U.S. Treasury and the primary means for controlling the U.S. money supply. (The U.S. government kept an account with the Bank, into which it deposited tariff receipts. These were largely denominated in private banknotes. The Bank could present the notes to the issuing banks and ask for redemption in specie, reducing the paper money in circulation.[16]) The war and the Bank's fall inflated the banknote supply, placing a premium on specie and causing a suspension of many banks' activities. The U.S. government had to secure war loans without the Bank—and without the Barings, however adept they were at befuddling Parliament with their financial wizardry. Congress can hardly be considered inconsistent, however; while axing the BUS, it cut military spending, too. A last-minute appeal by the Bank for a charter from New York was rejected.[17]

Stephen Girard had been buying shares in the BUS with shipping funds from Britain, initially on the advice that the Bank charter would pass in Harrisburg. This left him the largest shareholder in the largest, nonexistent bank in the United States, the Bank's assets allowing his shares to retain some value. His growing association with the old Bank was politically dangerous, however. He bought its main property on Philadelphia's Third Street and kept on its cashier to work in the new bank he now planned to open behind BUS doors with BUS capital. Meanwhile, competing financial interests began to worry about Girard, as his prospective bank, massive in scale and with the incalculable sense of solidity that the old, be-columned offices would provide, could be difficult competition.[18] Local bankers lobbied the state legislature against incorporating Girard's bank.

If he could not incorporate, he could also not form a partnership. Pennsylvania law forbade unincorporated groups from performing bank functions.[19] Girard thus opened his bank at his own risk, with only his capital, using the offices and much of the staff of the old BUS to do so.[20] Chartered banks could issue banknotes as legal tender (accepted as payment for U.S. taxes), another privilege Girard's bank lacked. Though businesses might accept private notes, they did so at discount and at their discretion, depending on the "bank" in question. The public perceived note issuing as the main function of banks, and indeed this was the principal business of most banks. Banknotes circulated *as* money; they could be redeemed at any time for specie from the bank vaults. These notes were thirty- or sixty-day loans off that specie base. The short tenor was thought to prevent depreciation.[21] Notes, easier to transport and store, served as an easy alternative to metal coin, as long as the issuing bank was believed to be able to back the notes. Since banks stood and fell on their own, for banks specie had, as one historian notes, "overriding" importance.[22] Banks acquired specie at their stock offerings (bank deposits, earmarked as depositors' property, were not considered an appropriate base for issuing loans). But Girard could not raise capital by issuing stock.[23] To overcome these deficiencies Girard needed more capital and a better reputation than the average chartered bank had. Specie made for good capital and a reputation.

Girard had plenty, from the East Indian and carrying trades and other ventures. His bank was enormous, and it was a testament to his wealth and reputation that he could, in his own person, be a bank. Girard brought over $1 million of his own money from Britain. Another $2 million in BUS deposits added to the aura of stability around his enterprise.

The U.S. Treasury turned to Girard to help fund the war with Britain. The Treasury issued an initial $10 million in debt, of which Girard bought $1 million. The federal government issued another $16 million the following year, but could find buyers only for the first six million. Desperate, Secretary Albert Gallatin—the man who had, decades earlier, asked after Thomas Twining's Indian neckcloth—begin advertising in newspapers for advice. Perhaps he would have been better off consulting more closely with bankers, as his predecessor Oliver Wolcott might have been in London: Girard ultimately bought $5.3 million in debt, and John Jacob Astor another $2 million.[24]

Girard did not incorporate his bank, but he was not opposed to corporations on principle. In fact, he had taken a lead role in the Philadelphia Society for the Encouragement of Manufactures (1806), a corporation formed to trade wool, cotton, and linen textiles. The Society was, like many corporations of its day, pitifully small. It had a total authorized stock of $10,000, to be achieved through the sale of $50 shares "payable in installments" of $10 each, geared, clearly, toward men who did not have as much as Girard. It is unclear how many shares were ever sold. Other corporations went down a different path from the Society's. The Manhattan Company had an authorized capitalization more than 200 times the Society's. Many early national banks issued stock at $500 a share; few set shares at $50. One needed competence or affluence to afford a share of such a company. The Society, for its part, lamented that the "many advantages congenial to the manufacturing of Woolen, Cotton, and Flaxen Wares . . . have not hitherto arisen to any degree of perfection," but, without much capital, did little about it. The Society was, in the end, just a warehouse that could buy and sell cloth. The state legislature had granted the Society's charter precisely because it was so innocuous. Here was no leviathan monopoly but just another semi-civic, semi-profitable charter, like the poorhouses, wharf companies, libraries, and water companies (as the Manhattan Company pretended to be) that supplied the necessities of start-of-the-nineteenth-century living. Those who did buy shares in the Philadelphia Society may well have been artisans or mechanics; certainly they were by and large the sort of Philadelphians whose names were not passed down in history books. None is mentioned in any biographical dictionaries or registers for Philadelphia, though one appears to have chaired the Philadelphia Democratic Party's 1808 general ward meeting and another appears to have been a Freemason.[25]

Some economic historians have condemned as "prohibitive" the high prices of shares in these corporations. At a time when the average Philadelphian possessed roughly $600 in total wealth, such shares were certainly out of reach for most,[26] even more so if stock purchases were made in specie. Corporations requiring this excluded anyone without a competence:[27] Such policies gave banks real capital and ensured the soundness of the financial system—a system that survived the end of the BUS in part because banks had silver in their vaults. A durable financial system benefited even those Americans who, for their lack of specie, were excluded from banking or the East India trade. Banks and their shareholders benefited too: amassing several hundred dollars in specie usually required some business sense, keeping out all the rogues and "needy desperadoes," the Talleyrands of the world, who did not have specie but dabbled in business. American capitalism in the early republic was meritocratic, not democratic, and banks' policies for issuing stock reflected that sensibility; directors aimed not to exclude the working poor (whom one doubts the directors ever imagined would have contemplated bank shares) so much as those who were poor at business. Affluent American merchants set share prices so as to keep out those who did not have, at the very least, a competency. They excluded those who, by a definition of merit as earned wealth, did not deserve to join.

Despite their capital accumulation, corporations in the early republic were still small, and this made exclusion important. One $500 share of the Manhattan Company, out of a total authorized stock of $2 million, represented 0.025 percent of the whole. Should enough less capable investors acquire shares, they might control a decisive block of votes. As a fraction of total market capitalization, one $500 share of the Manhattan Company is the equivalent of tens of millions of dollars in J. P. Morgan Chase, the Manhattan Company's descendant, today. Yet $500 in 1800 was much easier to obtain than tens of millions of dollars are today. It was within the reach of the above-average but hardly wealthy Philadelphian with a couple of thousand dollars at his disposal, someone approaching a competence. Tens of millions today is a more than a competence. Though more small investors own shares of American companies today, a small investor in 1800 could control a much larger share of a company's stock. Silver provided the means to vet those who could afford a $500 share.

Girard's move from shipping to banking, as opposed to industry, was common; the term "merchant banking" endures as a vestige of the links between banking and trade. As "educated merchants," Thomas Willing explained to a correspondent from the Massachusetts Bank in 1784, "we established our book on a strict mercantile plan." This was, he thought, the "only safe method to avoid confusion."[28] Pelatiah Webster, a Philadelphia merchant and a prolific writer on political economy, also emphasized the link between banking and trade, explaining that a bank was a "mercantile institution" that "will more naturally and properly fall under the direction of merchants than any other sort of men."[29] Merchants founded many banks to fund the purchase and wholesale of the commodities they imported. Short-term notes could fund a wholesaler's purchase of pepper, repaid from the proceeds of his sales to retail merchants. The short-tenor notes of mercantile banks were useful only in transactions such as this, in which the borrower could repay quickly. Land banks, which issued mortgages for a longer term, were a different business altogether. The links between "money banks," as banking historian Bray Hammond has called these financial institutions, and the overseas and East Indies trades run deep.[30]

Mercantile banks often lent to their own shareholders, a practice the economic historian Naomi Lamoreaux has evocatively termed "insider lending." This was, as Lamoreaux points out, hardly as deleterious as the modern sense of the terms suggests. In contrast to European banks, American banks originated in a capital-poor environment and served to help transform the U.S. economy, particularly in the northern states, into a capital-rich one. As in the East Indies trade, this was an exclusionary process that favored those who already possessed capital. Thus many East India traders also owned bank shares, and many bankers also invested funds in the Indies. Banks lent to the same clubby group of family members, business associates, and old partners whom they trusted and with whom they had long done business as merchants. These men were, as the Massachusetts Bank reported in 1792, "opulent Merchants of extensive business and credit, but a small part of whose property is in the funds of the Bank." "Insider lending" provided a means for merchants to monitor each other. At the Massachusetts Bank, a single nay vote from one of the directors could reject a loan—in this case, it was literally a black ball—and though Lamoreaux has stressed this as a sign of how much merchants lent to themselves, it is equally instructive to read this practice in reverse: bankers were so conservative with their money that it was difficult to find a loan to which there would not be some objection. The only loans that passed were those in which the applicant was a friend or family member of a director, or a bank director himself, in which case it was wise for the other directors to vote yes lest their own loans be shot down. According to some estimates, conservative U.S. bank lending kept the value of banknotes in circulation below the value of the silver backing them throughout the 1790s and kept the note-to-specie ratio relatively stable until the War of 1812.[31]

Since bankers lent to themselves, merchants who did not own bank stock often clamored for another bank to help finance their own businesses, while shareholders in existing banks fought to prevent such competition. This interested clamor broke down the pretense of monopoly and spread banks and other corporations across the business landscape. Just as many of the petitioners to Parliament for or against the East India Company's monopoly made only a narrow case for their economic interest—as London shipbuilders, Exeter weavers, and Glasgow merchants did—so the clamor for and against the chartering of new banks reduced to a competition of interests, with the difference being that American lawmakers, finding an easy combination of expediency and Revolutionary sentiment, took less prodding than Parliament did to permit competition. Thus, while there was only one bank in New England in 1784, by 1810 there were fifty-two, and by 1830 there were 172.[32] High share prices excluded those without a competence from banking, but they did not prevent others with capital from forming rival banks. Though the Pennsylvania bank lobby was able to prevent Girard from receiving a charter, it was unable to stop the massive wave of bank charters granted in 1814 or prevent Girard from banking without a charter. Nor did Girard's inability to secure a charter last. When the Second Bank of the United States finally passed Congress after the war, his bank was a major initial investor, so much so that it links the First and Second Banks of the United States. Girard remained a major shareholder in the second bank for a couple years, getting out, fortuitously, just before the crash of 1819. Thus banking, as the East India trade, expanded among the competent and affluent but excluded those with no sum of capital, no stock of specie, in the first place. American banking and the American East Indies trade developed in tandem, were interrelated, and exhibited similar traits.[33]

Israel Thorndike and the Boston Manufacturing Company

Thorndike's career followed the trend among East India merchants toward larger accumulations of wealth. His capital, like others', attracted and commanded smaller sums, and like Girard he made the transition from accepting silver shipped as rented freight to selling shares in corporations. Thorndike, along with a number of other investors, many of whom were also East India merchants, founded the Boston Manufacturing Company (BMC), a firm more commonly known by its later name, the Lowell Mills. It was the first U.S. business to consolidate the full textile manufacturing process, from raw cotton to woven cloth, under one roof. And though the BMC is usually recalled for its significance in industrialization—before the BMC, all weaving in New England was done as outwork—it is the company's financial significance that pertains here.[34] The Lowell Mills of the 1820s were, in terms of wealth invested, far larger than any other U.S. mill had been. What is more, the BMC's founders and early managers, Thorndike among them, derived much of their wealth and experience from trading Indian cottons. The careers of Thorndike and other BMC figures reveal much about the links between East Indian and corporate finance.[35]

On October 18, 1813, the principal shareholders of the BMC met for the first time. They were in the counting room of a fellow shareholder's store on Broad Street in Boston. Then and in the weeks that followed they sketched out the Company's business. Cotton was an expensive proposition: physical plant, wages, and supplies were not cheap; the shareholders subscribed $100,000 toward the start-up cost. The BMC held an additional $300,000 in authorized stock, for which they could raise the money by forcing existing shareholders to make a second payment up to the value of their original purchase, on penalty of relinquishing their shares. Since BMC shares—like a modern partnership in this respect— carried such a financial burden, their purchase was not to be taken lightly. This obligation, combined with the $1,000 share price, kept out more middling merchants (though, since even well-capitalized merchants did not always have kegs of cash on hand, they could be paid for in $100 installments). By restricting ownership to the competent and leadership to the affluent, the BMC's directors cultivated an image of wealth and prudence. Among the principal shareholders, several had previously invested in Indian textiles: Patrick Tracy Jackson (who bought twenty shares of the BMC), James Jackson (five shares), James Lloyd (five shares), and Israel Thorndike (ten shares). Their names, save for Patrick Tracy Jackson's, all appear in the Salem, Massachusetts customs records as importers of Indian cloth. There may well have been other India-goods investors among the initial shareholders. Many were from Boston, and Boston customs records did not survive. Still, even via Salem, Nathan Appleton (five shares) and Francis C. Lowell (fifteen shares) had invested in the China trade, which required the same level of managerial experience and capital reserves as an Indian investment.[36]

James Lloyd had previously invested $15,000 in an Indian-piece-goods venture aboard the *Argo,* which returned to Salem in 1805. Since U.S. money sent to India tended to be denominated in specie, this was not an easy investment. It was considerably more difficult for Lloyd to ship $15,000 to India than, say, to Cuba, where the welcome given to U.S. credit and U.S. goods meant his cargo would not have to be in silver.[37] Lloyd's investment was a step toward amassing a capital of some competence.

Patrick Tracy Jackson was closer to affluence. Jackson was born in Newburyport, Massachusetts, son to a local merchant, and apprenticed to another merchant in town at age fifteen. By 1802, then in his early twenties, he had risen to become supercargo for the ship *Hannah* on its voyage to India. He served as an India supercargo for the next four years, managing shipments between India, Cape Town, Penang, and the United States, making much of his money in sales commissions. Specie was of course all-important, and after inquiring into fitting out an Indian venture of his own in 1803, Jackson estimated that he would need to borrow $100,000 in silver for a voyage. Apparently, no one was interested in lending him the money—at least, no one who would not rather invest in an India voyage himself. Still, by 1806, Jackson had amassed enough capital to become a merchant in his own right. He settled down in Boston, where he continued in the East Indies trade, importing, distributing, and re-exporting Indian cottons.[38]

Israel Thorndike, for his part, never sailed to Asia, but was a sedentary merchant who sent large amounts of specie there. He also raised large sums from other investors, handing their specie to his supercargoes to invest. Thorndike's role was primarily as financier.[39] As the East Indies trade was led, though not dominated, by a few men, Thorndike's previous experience was instructive. East Indian demand for specie limited the field of investors; among those, some like Thorndike had more specie and more experience than others. So he led, recruiting additional investors and organizing their investments to India on his ships. Thorndike brought this ability to reach out to smaller investors, an ability that enlarged the capital at his disposal and made an otherwise prohibitively expensive trade available to men like Lloyd and to the BMC.[40]

Jackson and Thorndike developed managerial skills in the India trade as well. As business historian Kenneth Wiggins Porter noted, "the knowledge of textiles acquired, and the capital accumulated" in the trade with India enabled Jackson "to become one of the pioneers in American textile manufacturing." Kishichi Watanabe, in his study of the BMC, agreed, noting that because Jackson "engaged in the Far East trade . . . his career prepared him for the top managerial position" at the BMC. Indeed, between 1802 and 1806, Jackson's voyages to Calcutta put him in contact with one of the most prolific textile manufacturing centers in the world. In port, Jackson oversaw the purchase of Indian weaves: silks, chintz, bandannas, seersuckers, and various muslins, financed by his banian, Ramdulal Day. The muslins in particular suggest a connection to later manufacturing efforts, since plain white ones were, as noted, the cloth of choice for American and English printers to stamp or to paint with their own knockoffs of Indian designs.[41] In Calcutta, Jackson managed accounts for numerous others—his first voyage as supercargo had him superintend the consignments of thirty-three different investors—daily checking prices, deciding when to buy or sell, and borrowing additional money or arranging additional ventures as circumstances dictated. He had a broad license; the owners were half a year and half a world away. They had given money, not goods, and money was a very salable thing.[42]

Trading in Indian textiles also put Jackson at the heart of the English East India Company's operation—and the Company was still the principal Western buyer for Indian textiles in 1800. Jackson likely encountered the Company's purchasing system, whereby the Company contracted for the future delivery of cotton goods at fixed dates.[43] The prospect it offered—if not always the reality—was of a much more regular and reliable trade than Jackson's. His trade was tied to the fluctuations of the textile market, which was affected by the season and his competitors. Leaving Boston for India, he had no way of knowing when he would arrive or how much cotton goods would cost. Sometimes he could not even know when he would leave Bengal; Calcutta authorities barred ships from leaving port when they heard that French privateers were operating in the area. Though such uncertainties may have made free trade, as a system, superior to the monopoly, from the individual trader's viewpoint they were nothing but anxiety inducing. Although planning (i.e., management), when combined with the Company's monopoly, provided its managers with no incentive for improvement, planning was not in itself bad. In Calcutta Jackson could observe and learn management, and at the BMC he could compete.

The most remarkable thing about the BMC was that it was incorporated at all. In 1813, most American businesses were partnerships. The Slater Mill, which pioneered the U.S. manufacture of cotton yarn in 1790, was one. Samuel Slater had been the first American industrialist to use Richard Arkwright's carding engine; by the time of the BMC, there were tens—probably hundreds—of U.S. mills carding and spinning cotton along Arkwright's system. The Slater Mill and the putting out system were small-scale endeavors common in early American business: decentralized and labor intensive but not capital intensive.[44] Industrial development often occurred on an even smaller scale than Slater-style mills.[45] Slater-style mills were initially capitalized at $20,000 to $30,000; the BMC was more capitalized and more complex, and this seems to have encouraged its founders to favor the corporate form. Its high level of capitalization and the extent of its organization made the BMC stand out among U.S. manufacturers. Its founders appointed one of their own, Jackson, as treasurer; in effect, he was the chief operating officer. But Jackson had other responsibilities, too; like the other shareholders, he ran several businesses at once, and he could give only limited attention to the BMC. That soon proved insufficient. In 1815, the shareholders appointed Jackson factory superintendent as well, gave him a house on the factory site, and asked that he oversee the daily goings on there. They required that he give "his whole time & attention to the concerns of the Boston Manufacturing Company" and "enter into no commercial speculation or other business, that may take from the just & necessary attention to the duties of his office." In exchange, they offered him a $3,000 salary; he was granted a raise to $5,000 in 1819. Jackson was one of the first factory managers in American history. One wonders whether the East India Company's cotton delivery system in India influenced Jackson's management of the BMC.[46]

As an East Indies merchant, Thorndike worked with investors in Massachusetts, raising capital for more voyages. He gave his name and his silver to the enterprise; this encouraged other investors. This formative experience in what was, in effect, an executive role groomed him for his next: President of the BMC. The presidency was a somewhat honorific position; Jackson, as treasurer, maintained the accounts and managed day-to-day affairs, but the president still presided over shareholder meetings and chaired the board of directors. He was as likely to be a moderator, smoothing over disputes, as to lead out in front. Some presidents were more powerful than others. James Lloyd served until 1815, with limited effect on company policy. Thorndike was more successful; he sometimes used his authority as a director and a major shareholder to take the lead in formulating business strategy. Thorndike assumed the presidency of the BMC in 1817 and held it until 1831, shortly before his death. During this time, he oversaw significant expansion. The company sold additional shares to its first investors and brought in new investors as further capital was needed. When the BMC had consumed the available waterpower on the Charles River, Thorndike, along with Jackson, served on the shareholder committee that looked into and suggested the purchase of the Merrimack Manufacturing Company. That expansion led to the wholesale damming of the Merrimack River and the founding of the factory town of Lowell. By 1820 Jackson and Thorndike were the BMC's first and second largest shareholders, respectively. Throughout, Thorndike worked among shareholders or directors behind the scenes while serving in public as the face of the company. Just as he had given his name and his capital to his Indian enterprises, now he gave them to the BMC to build investor confidence.[47]

Capitalists such as Thomas Willing, William Bingham, and the Barings took pains to distinguish themselves from the grocer-merchants and petty-industrialists around them. Girard and most other major mid-Atlantic capitalists eschewed manufacturing for banking and real estate, which they considered—not a little self-flatteringly—more dignified. The BMC's distinctive capital requirements preserved the firm's reputation as a sounder business than the mills around it. Thorndike's concern for capital and probity extended to other businesses, such as the Suffolk Bank, which was linked to BMC owners' industrial concerns and which was also specie oriented.[48]

Such links between banking and manufacturing was not new. In 1812, the New York Manufacturing Company had sought a corporate charter in Albany, proposing "manufacturing of iron and brass wire and of cotton and wool cards." The proprietors, not well-moneyed men and unable to attract any bank loans, worried about the "difficulty of inducing persons to invest their money in untried enterprises." Approaching the link between banking and industry from the standpoint of a lack of capital rather than a surplus, the Company's petitioners asked for and received "the privilege of annexing a banking institution."[49] Such schemes urged affluent investors such as Thorndike to keep unmoneyed men out of the BMC.

American merchants' capital accumulation progressed from small-scale shipping to renting freight for silver, to partnerships in a single voyage, to business corporations. Each stage included more investors and raised larger amounts of capital while containing vestiges from the previous stage. The BMC resembled, in terms of structure, a modified partnership rather than a corporation. To be sure, its corporate charter allowed investors to come and go with greater ease than in a partnership, but the BMC's ability to force shareholders to redouble their investments was more common among partnerships than corporations. Limited liability applied neither to partnerships nor corporations at this time (Massachusetts even imposed *unlimited* liability for a corporation's debts on its shareholders, singling out manufacturing corporations in particular). With no legal division between the collective wealth of the group and the individual wealth of each owner, one owner's insolvency could endanger the entire enterprise. The Bankruptcy Act of 1800, which gave the formerly wealthy a means to escape their debts, only underscored the importance of selling shares for specie, to be paid upfront. This weeded out the insolvent and provided ready funds upon which the business could draw.[50]

Here was a corporation adapted from existing business practice, its origins in partnerships and shipping ventures instead of the monopolied and often very unbusinesslike corporations of which there was so much predecence by 1813. Rather than a government-devolved interest, the BMC was a business venture first and last, with a corporate form merely wrapped around it. Corporate law eventually caught up to business practice, though state-granted corporate charters in the early nineteenth century continued to contain private and public elements. In their public nature they were conceived as tools of the state and their grants were said to imply monopoly, but as politicians doled out charters to different lobbies, there were soon rival banks in the same city (witness the Manhattan Company), multiple turnpikes and railroads on the same route, and competing ferries and bridges on the same crossings; these monopolies existed in theory, not in practice. Many states received income or stock from corporations they chartered, and it was difficult to charter only one when politicians might charter a rival and take revenue from two. Over time corporate charters thus became vehicles for private, competitive commerce. The Supreme Court finally resolved this conflict between established law and current practice by ruling against implied monopoly in *Charles River Bridge v. Warren Bridge* (1837).[51] The BMC was one of the newer sorts of companies, designed from the start as competitive business (Jackson was a pioneer in marketing at the BMC). This distinguished it from the East India Company or, to some degree, the BUS. If the BMC faltered, other mills would move in (as the BMC had moved in and bought the Merrimack Manufacturing Company). If the East India Company faltered, as it did in the 1770s, it was bailed out by the government since it fulfilled important state aims. Thus the American corporation had roots in the crown charters and monopolies taxonomized by Blackstone, and equally significant roots in the relationships American businessmen formed around them.

John Jacob Astor and Astoria

John Jacob Astor's name eventually became synonymous with old money, but he was a parvenu in the new republic. He was, like Girard, an immigrant for whom English was a second language (even after decades in America, he sustained a thick German accent),[52] and who made his own money with his own work. He was no Horatio Alger; *that* sort of story, as Astor's biographer John Haeger notes, is useless for understanding Astor. Astor arrived in the United States when it was easiest for merchants to pass from competence to affluence, when new levels of wealth became available but before they were filled, as they would be in later years when the gap between local grocers and national tycoons became so great that it could be bridged only in fiction.

Astor's early ventures in fur and his expansion into the China trade continued. Between 1806 and 1810, his business in that line was so extensive that he tried to maintain a ship coming from and going to China at all times. As late as 1804, he still did not send ships to Europe, instead purchasing space on other merchants' vessels for his furs and teas bound there, but he eventually re-exported his teas to Europe himself, and by 1810 the profits from this leg of the trade grew so much that he had to buy two brigs to shuttle tea to Europe.[53]

Astor had other interests as well. Like Girard and other contemporaries, he invested wealth from the China trade in local real estate.[54] Between 1803 and 1806, $300,000 of his returns from the China trade went into Manhattan properties.[55] The sale of furs and of the returning tea were still his core interests in 1807, however, when his most recent critical biographer estimates that his net wealth exceeded $1 million. Within a few years he would have that much invested in real estate alone. This real estate business was diverse—and unlike Morris's, bought with capital. Astor traded city lots, realizing quite early on that the city's expansion north would transform Manhattan farmland into tenements. In the 1780s, lots just a thousand yards from Pearl Street and Wall Street stood unoccupied; by 1860 the settled area of Manhattan reached as far north as Forty-second Street. Astor's investments reached from the city's pre-Revolutionary commercial heart north to what would become the upper fifties. Not only did he purchase and develop lots for resale, he offered mortgages, financed hotel construction, maintained a significant portfolio of rental properties, and invested in railroads and banks serving his lands. And as with Girard, Astor was interested in banking, becoming a prime mover in establishing the Second Bank of the United States, whose New York office he directed.[56] The transition from trading in specie to banking was a natural one; Astor, like Girard, was both a merchant-banker and a financier.

Astor also speculated in Western lands in upstate New York and, most remotely, at Astoria, in present-day Oregon. Astoria was intended as the seat of a fur trading operation which, Astor hoped, might dominate the Pacific Northwest. It failed: an object lesson in the overreach to which egos primed with monopoly and imperial ambition were prone. Astor's project in Astoria failed not because Astorians (or Americans in general) were uninterested in empire but because the U.S. government and Astor were incapable of projecting force abroad. As his authorized biographer, Washington Irving, explained, had Astoria been "properly protected by government," it might have had a chance at political success.[57] Geopolitics aside, commercial success was unlikely, for Astor was poor at compelling his employees at Astoria to conform to his instructions. Nevertheless, with his new American Fur Company, Astor attempted to monopolize the American fur trade in the Pacific Northwest, just as the Hudson Bay Company tried to monopolize the British fur trade. He met with a similar lack of success.

It is difficult to imagine Jefferson's administration granting Astor such a monopoly, though developing trade on the Pacific Coast did interest the president. Meriwether Lewis had proposed to Jefferson a trans-Western fur trade whereby furs would be caught on the Missouri River and in the Rockies, sent down the Columbia River, and then shipped across the Pacific to China. Astor appears to have read Lewis's proposal.[58] He formed the American Fur Company in 1808 and expected to raise $1 million in stock, with each $500 share carrying with it (as with the BMC) the obligation to pay another $500 should the Company's managers demand it. He intended to lead the firm as its major stockholder, while drawing smaller investors as Thorndike had done. Astor cloaked the company in claims of its "great public utility" in order to get it past the New York state legislature. Once passed, he began suggesting to his Canadian rivals that he held a monopoly charter from the federal government.

The British companies continued to undermine each other politically. The North West Company, which monopolized the fur trade from Fort William to the Atlantic, lobbied to take over the Hudson Bay Company's Pacific-Coast fur monopoly. It also sought to horn in on the East India Company's grant and obtain the right to sell furs at Canton.[59] Rather than compete commercially, the monopolies simply had their lobbyists compete in Whitehall—a sign of just how ridiculous and ineffective monopolies granted by the state were. While shills for the Canadian fur trade turned out such tracts as *American Encroachments on British Rights* (1808) and pressured Lord Wellesley, then foreign secretary, the Companies themselves failed to compete with Americans in global fur markets.[60]

By 1809 the American Fur Company had nonofficial federal support, but little more, and its stock was yet to be sold off. Astor contacted the Russian outpost at Sitka, hoping to form a condominium against the British. "Long experience . . . has proved . . . that, when two companies come in contact, they must join and come to a friendly understanding or both be ruined," he explained. (Astor was a free trader by necessity, not inclination.) Astor formed a separate partnership in New York in 1810, confusingly called the Pacific Fur Company, which he planned to nest in the American Fur Company's wings. The Pacific Fur Company sent overland and sea parties to the Pacific Northwest Coast to form a trading settlement there and to draw Native American fur traders away from British settlements and rival American ships. The settlers were to stock furs for the supply of Astor's subsequent vessels. The expedition was considered militarily and politically significant enough for Astor's *Tonquin*—sent round South America to the Northwest Coast—to receive a U.S. naval escort for the initial part of its voyage, in order to protect its men from impressment.[61] Continental hegemony, a Jeffersonian goal this project seemed to represent, demanded as much. But Astor, like the East India Company's directors, had little control over his employee's actions. They founded a trading settlement at Astoria but made little other headway, as different factions began pursing their own course at their employer's expense, just as the East India Company's servants in India had done, and soon even Astor's pretense of a monopoly on the coast was lost.

The U.S. government hoped Astor's trading plans would help secure a more favorable North Pacific border for their territorial claims against Britain. And Astor acted with the intention of furthering American political goals in the Pacific Northwest. Yet when Astor pressured President Madison as to "whether the government . . . have or will assert any claim to that, or any part of that country," he received no answer. The U.S. Navy did not consider defense of Astoria a priority, a problem after 1812, but a perfectly reasonable decision from the navy's standpoint, for the heart of the war lay in Atlantic waters. The one ship contemplated for dispatch to the Pacific was reassigned to the Great Lakes. British forces amassing around Astoria forced its sale in 1813, and though Monroe later hoped to claim the region in peace talks, Britain already occupied it.[62]

Astoria's failure encouraged the American merchants who remained in the East Indies trade to stick to what they knew they could do: opportunistic tramp voyages around the Pacific Rim. Even as merchant houses sent agents out to reside in Asian ports, Americans had no armed bases to lose. Astor himself returned to the China trade after the War of 1812, and without the encumbrance of a Northwest Coast factory he profited handsomely. His efforts to assert American territorial ambitions in the Pacific Northwest had rivaled the British companies' efforts to assert British claims; in trade, his companies matched the British Companies in failure.

American corporate success was predicated on competition. This competitive environment was not the product of ideologically consistent free traders. None of the merchants discussed here was an avatar of Revolutionary, anti-corporate ideology. Thorndike, a member of the Essex Junto, was connected to those New

Englanders so upset by the War of 1812 that they threatened secession from the Union. Girard tried to run his own personal BUS while the Bank and its monopoly remained highly contentious. Astor openly sought to monopolize the fur trade. They were not Revolutionary purists (Astor, after all, did not ever arrive in America until 1784); they were capitalists unleashed by the liberalizing, anti-monopoly spirit of the Revolution and the simple fact of American independence to accumulate wealth, to enter new trades, and to finance their business in ways and to degrees impossible before. These men were not always the sort of free traders whom revelers at the Boston Tea Party might have liked. Nor did they have to be, for free trade was amoral. Their commercial environment was the product of American Revolutionary and British free-trade ideology; U.S. politicians, abhorring chartered monopolies as much as they loved collecting revenues from newly chartered corporations, forced U.S. merchants to compete.

In the early republic, affluent merchants eschewed Joseph Barrell's idea of a public economy—specifically, his attempt to use private business for public good—and contented themselves with the fulfillment of their personal economic interests.[63] Banks and other corporations lost their semipublic role. Despite Girard's public-spirited efforts in the War of 1812, by Jackson's presidency the merger of public and private interests behind the Second Bank of the United States was more attacked than praised. Few merchants trading to the Northwest Coast pretended to advance American territorial interest with their private trade. Gone with the expectation that business corporations should serve as tools of state, the assumption that such corporations had to fulfill any public good vanished as well. The idea of running Astoria through a corporation was an anachronism, the failure of which validated those entrepreneurs drawn to the corporate form solely to further their private ends. The corporation was no longer primarily an arm of the state, but primarily a means for aggregating private capital.[64]

As affluent U.S. merchants amassed capital, they honed a business culture that emphasized specie and respectability, though not always caution. They were investors, as the bankers and financiers of the City. Affluent men such as William Bingham, Israel Thorndike, John

Jacob Astor, and Stephen Girard, looking to the merchants and bankers of London as their models, built a meritocratic, American merchant-capitalist ideal. This ideal focused on capital and the "intelligence," in Baring's word, to invest it, and on the aura of probity that was both conveyed by and that itself conveyed this. This process was not limited to their personal worlds or their private accounts and proceeded similarly, and with many of the same people, among American corporations, which became additional vehicles for aggregating wealth and for excluding those deemed insufficiently respectable. These corporations were, as Andrew Schocket has recently argued, a means for "a new, more-secure, and . . . more far-reaching economic elite" to function "on a scale unheard of before the American Revolution" with the specie ethic that had been at the core of the American trade to Asia.[65]

Conclusion

Before 1815 the American East Indies trade made the United States and Britain more like one another—ironically, given how fundamental the Boston Tea Party had been in driving the two apart. In the most basic sense, this meant that both countries now traded to Asia. But more than that, the American East Indies trade helped economic liberals and lesser merchants upend the East India Company's monopoly and expanded the role of free trade in the British Empire, opening Britain's trade to Asia. The trade also made the United States more like Britain by abetting capital accumulation among the American moneyed elite, allowing them to amass enough capital to become financiers and thereby make more substantial investments in the banks, factories, roads, canals, and real estate that were such an important part of the nineteenth-century American economy.

These developments amounted to the rise of some of London's economic provinces: outport England, Scotland, the mid-Atlantic states, and New England. Before 1776 the Company had been the sole legal vessel for British and British-American trade to Asia; after 1813, and as a consequence of the American Revolution and the American East Indies trade, the link between the English-speaking Atlantic and India was open to Briton and American alike. The dual transformations the American East Indies trade brought during the French Wars gave private traders parity with the Company both in access to Asian trade and in the capital needed to conduct it. These merchant-financiers broadened the global North just as the British Empire swung east, and they made the East Indies trade increasingly central to the economy of the nineteenth-century empire.[1]

No longer preoccupied with the right to sell minor luxuries from peripheral regions, the nineteenth-century British free trade to Asia harnessed the whole of Britain's economic might to capitalize on the new heart of the imperial interest: the east. Asian agricultural commodities would be the core of this trade, and as Britain's cloth came to rival India's after 1813 British merchants' hard-won freedom to trade translated into an opportunity for British industrialists to export British manufactures to Asia as well. Liberalization of the British East Indies trade broadened the financial basis of and ownership in the trade with Britain's Asian empire. Meanwhile, the American trade to the East Indies helped lift American merchants to affluence for the first time. With their British cousins, American capitalists took part in the transatlantic financial system that would govern so much of the nineteenth-century world economy. The East Indies trade, and neutral trade during the French Wars generally, helped make these dual transformations possible.

Two Transformations

The East Indies trade was concomitant with the financial—rather than the industrial—transformation of the Anglo-American world, as capital accumulation became more meritocratic and less prebendal on both sides of the Atlantic. Indeed, from the perspective of nineteenth-century economic, colonial, and world history, the collapse of the East India Company's monopoly and the rise of new East India traders would be one of the most significant recombinations of wealth and one of the most seminal moments of, as Schumpeter would later term it, "creative destruction."

In the United States, wealth generated in the carrying trade and the trade to Asia contributed to the creation of the affluent investor, with Thorndike, Girard, Bingham, and Astor as prime examples, though hardly the only ones. Despite their investments in real estate, these men remained outside landed society. Unlike plantation owners, these merchants had no pretense of aristocratic obligation to the lesser sorts around them, and this has made them easy to mischaracterize: the Quaker girl who disapproved of Bingham's town house, and the apocryphal tales of Astor in the 1840s, old and tossed in a blanket, laughing greedily about his wealth, reveal this middling sensibility about wealth and spending and the social obligations the rich owe the rest. The sense that these men were too wealthy reflects a middle-class sumptuary observation, not an aristocratic sense of obligation. In the new American Republic there were no aristocrats and there was no particularly gentlemanly capitalism, at least not in the northern states. With no natural aristocracy, northern merchants created an elite of hard-money wealth.

This degree of wealth was new, and this elite required deliberate fashioning, since there had been no affluent merchants in the colonial era. The emerging capital that was amassed, measured, and valued for its own sake, as well as the specie within it, became a merchant's most significant measure of status, driving the solipsistic logic of accumulation. Northern business culture had, to be sure, plenty of trappings: an affluent merchant had to be properly attired. Yet the trappings of refinement were not the essence of wealth but the signifiers of it, and the wealth those trappings signified was specie itself, not inheritances, patronage, rent rolls, or slaves. Money in the early Republic did not, in the northern states, buy class—because money *was* class. This differentiated early American merchants from the Barings, whose services to the Crown (financial and otherwise) earned their family a baronetcy and a peerage. American accumulation could not culminate in rank and peerages, and so capital itself remained the marker of status. Such money was also an ideal credential with which to win the confidence of competent men with capital to invest.

U.S. merchants thus conveyed their financial stature through urban, not rural, properties and through business, not leisure. These men were not merchant-aristocrats or country gentlemen but businessmen. The suggestion that Bingham "held court" was thus a slur from his contemporaries and an exaggeration of later writers.

Northerners, merchants included (and merchants of nearly any wealth), were inheritors of the ideals of the colonial American "middling sort." Consequently the expression of wealth among their elite retained a strong sense of middling rather than aristocratic values, more suited to overgrown shopkeepers than grandees. Merchants kept their fortunes comparatively hidden, or at least invested, until they retired, when, as with Elias Derby, it was considered appropriate to spend them. While working, they advertised their worthiness to those who mattered—other investors—rather than to the broader population. There was an unspoken, ever-shifting, but quite real barrier between appropriate and inappropriate displays of wealth, and it was this groping, perhaps only half-consciously, toward that moving line that compelled so many middling Americans to condemn Bingham for crossing it.

It was this foreign line that Baring was constantly trying to work out in his American acquaintances as he drummed up business for his father. Manses and landholdings did not signify a merchant's wealth as much as ships in the harbor, wharves, capital goods, and a glimpse of those kegs of silver as they were heaved onto the ship and whisked under the captain's bed. This was what distinguished Bingham from Baring's "chicaneurs" and "needy desperadoes" or a man like Talleyrand, who sought to sell in Bengal land no party to the transaction had ever seen. Thorndike likewise defined himself as a businessman, not a man of leisure. In 1810 he left Salem for Boston to be nearer his business, where he maintained an understated garb; seeking not to offend Bostonian tastes by ostentation, he pursued inconspicuous consumption.[2] A China-trade merchant's chinaware was never his mark or store of wealth, only mere accoutrement. Instead, the mark and store of wealth became—in a way that would have seemed crass in the southern states—money itself: silver its own proof, not nearly as exciting as great country estates or extravagant East India Company ships built to impress and employ as much as to function, but all the much more enriching for it.[3]

In this way a shipping merchant could seem more solid than someone who vended stock certificates and bonds or held large amounts of paper money, for the more specie in a transaction the more reliable the merchant. In bad times when paper was worthless silver kept value, and so a discernment for capital and hard money entered the American business world to an extent that merchants of earlier eras could not have afforded—hence the transition of so many well-capitalized merchants to banking. In the silver-driven capital markets of the northern states, the affluent merchant was the patron of his competent client, whom he financed and led. These increasingly monetized relationships eventually took the form of shareholding in the affluent merchants' corporations. This logic grew slowly, but the benefits of larger capital stocks (which could extract rent, or interest, from the smaller stocks on freight) impelled American and British merchants and bankers to combine, just as the largest, most uncompetitive corporation in the world was collapsing.[4]

The East India trade continued to demand silver after 1815, the U.S. Treasury Secretary reporting in 1820 that "the only drain to which the metallic currency was subjected to was the demand for it for the prosecution of trade to the East Indies and China." Silver from Latin America balanced out this "drain," allowing U.S. merchants to share in global silver flows without inciting too many save-our-specie arguments against the Indies trade. After 1815 China continued to take $4 million to $5 million in Spanish silver annually, with demand for silver peaking in 1826. In the 1820s silver became the dominant metal in the U.S. economy, largely eclipsing gold. For U.S. merchants, the defining question about their capital continued to be how much of it was in silver and how much of it was in paper.[5]

Britain, too, made its own sort of transition from an aristocracy of wealth to a meritocracy of one, with private traders asserting parity with the chartered East India Company at the same time U.S. merchants did. The Company's fall in 1813 was in part due to its directors' inability to meet this transition. The many petitions to Parliament in 1813 in support of the Company did not—as the merchants attacking the Company did—claim to benefit all Britain. They claimed a benefit for themselves; London shipwrights argued that the Company's patronage and baroque ship-work kept them in employ; woolen manufacturers, Cornwall miners, and numerous other workers articulated their case for the Company: it patronized them; it should be patronized. Such was the sociopolitical role of the Company as its directors imagined it (it was the "Honourable" Company after all, a telling pretense). Yet characterizing the Company's contracts not as mutually profitable patronage, but solely as the patron's expense, implied that a more money-conscious firm would not buy as much tin or wool or ship-work fripperies as the Company had, which damned the Company as a business. Private merchants similarly argued that a grant to them of the right to trade to Asia supported and patronized "ailing" businesses. Their claims tended to cancel out those of the Company's supporters, reducing to a zero-sum conflict of interested groups, to be resolved by whichever held the greatest sway in Parliament. This was how the Company's directors saw politics in 1813.[6] Free traders succeeded in part by going above this zero-sum game, making the liberal argument that through their access to and competition in the East Indian trade all Britain would benefit, not only their narrow selves.

The economic apparatus of the British Empire, which P. J. Cain and A. G. Hopkins have characterized as an extension of British property rights abroad,[7] relied on an increasingly free-trade property regime (as well as some settlers and much violence).[8] The post-1813 opening of the India trade thus entailed a significant increase in the number of merchants, bankers, and financiers who could directly involve themselves in the business of Britain's eastern possessions. The revocation of the Company's Indian trade monopoly was also a crucial step in the gradual withdrawal of the nineteenth-century British state from choosing among competing business interests—a reform that conceived of the East Indian trade not as a favor to be bought but a business to be won, and a reform already in place in Britain's Atlantic empire.[9] This was the logical consummation of the Dundas-Pitt vision. Just as Dundas had sought to create London as the emporium of the Indies during the French Wars, so, after 1815, as Cain and Hopkins point out, freer trade and a return to hard money "were designed to turn Britain into the warehouse of the world rather than its workshop."[10]

The U.S. East Indies Trade after 1815

The American East Indies trade continued after 1815. But with general peace in Europe, Americans could no longer profit from their role as neutrals in wartime. European vessels plied the routes to their respective colonies in Asia, leaving Americans with a smaller share of east-west trade. "We have lost our carrying trade which once was so profitable," Henry Lee exclaimed in 1816. The abolition of the Company's India-trade monopoly (effective April 10, 1814) allowed Anglo-Indian and British merchants to enter the field, lessening the U.S. advantage further. Private British ships plying the Britain-India route charged £6 to £8 a ton—an extremely competitive rate—and preferential duties gave these British shippers further advantage over American carriers. U.S. consumption of Indian goods continued, but the re-export market was lost. Britain had finally become India's emporium. The remaining U.S. trade to Asia flourished most notably in China, where the Company's monopoly still held.[11]

After 1815 the U.S. East Indies trade evolved toward a more permanent, more highly organized structure. It was not carried on with the corporate form, but more merchant houses did send junior partners—younger brothers and sons—to man branch offices in Asia. The business model that had worked so well during the unpredictable times of the French Wars—discrete ventures dissolving at voyage-end—gave way to one in which large firms maintained more-lasting presences. A few permanent American agency houses or branch offices had been set up in China already. These included those of Samuel Snow of Rhode Island, who built the American factory at Canton; the Blight family of Philadelphia, which kept an agent in Canton from the late 1790s onward; and Edward Carrington, also of Rhode Island, who established himself in Canton in the early 1800s and left in 1811. Among the most prominent were the Boston firm of Perkins & Co. and the concerns of Timothy Pitman and J. P. Sturgis. This process, begun during the French Wars, continued after, as more firms sent out permanent residents to handle their commerce and to assume business on commission from merchants without a house in Canton. Though some merchants rented freight according to the consignee model well into the 1830s, the trend toward larger partnerships with greater capitalization made renting out freight space, either to make up the capital for an outward voyage or to free up specie to be spread across more vessels, less central to the trade.[12] The older model had been well suited to East India merchants who were still building their affluence and to the instability of the war years. But with peace, already-affluent merchants found a permanent presence in Asia more valuable.[13]

American merchants returned to importing Indian cloth, Chinese porcelain, and Chinese nankeens after 1815. In some years Indian cloth imports reached values equal to those during the height of the French Wars, though this cloth seems to have been consumed in the United States rather than extensively re-exported (the U.S. population grew considerably in the first decades of the nineteenth century, providing a larger U.S. consumer base). A shift from re-export toward domestic consumption is more clearly seen in tea. Though the English East India Company retained its monopoly on tea, giving American tea merchants only lumbering competition in Britain, Canada, and the British Caribbean, European merchants were free to return to China after the war. The return of French and Dutch merchants to China meant a decline in the European re-export market for American merchants. While U.S. tea imports between 1815 and 1819 surpassed 3.2 million pounds a year (the average import level between 1795 and 1812), U.S. tea re-exports struggled to reach 1.6 million pounds a year (the average level of re-exports for the period between 1799 and 1812, when tea re-exports peaked). A greater share of U.S. tea imports was consumed domestically after 1815 than before. The tea that was still re-exported likely went to those regions where the Company's monopoly still held sway.[14]

The U.S. pepper trade declined in overall terms after 1815, with imports failing to exceed 4 million pounds in the immediate postwar period, though they regularly exceeded that figure during the Napoleonic Wars. Pepper re-exports, which in the Napoleonic period fell below 2 million pounds only during the embargo and the

War of 1812, never exceeded that threshold in the aftermath of the French Wars. This was likely due to the loss of the European re-export market. Chinese "goods" was the only category of Asian import to show an appreciable increase in the immediate postwar years, likely reflecting, as the tea trade, an increase in domestic demand, perhaps for nankeens.[15]

"Indies" and Empires

The American commercial presence in the Indies was, unlike Britain's, unimperial. During the French Wars, American intermediaries carried goods and silver between French-aligned colonies in Asia and French Europe. The Americans often demanded cash crops but made no reciprocal attempt to foist their manufactures on the Indies. Americans lacked both long-term colonial ambition in the Indies and the manufacturing capacity to do this. This contrasts with private British merchants who, after 1813, lobbied for opening up capital flows to India to permit the expansion of cash-crop agriculture there.[16] It is no great leap to connect this with British manufacturers' attempts to sell to the Indian Subcontinent after 1813, as many scholars of the British Empire and nineteenth-century India have done.

The U.S. government lacked imperial ambitions in the Indies, even after 1815. Though various Americans settled in Hawaii in the 1820s, the U.S. government eschewed formal conquest or annexation, and there remained an equivalent British presence in those islands and an independent Hawaiian Kingdom. The USS *Essex* had demonstrated the limits of U.S. imperial efforts in the Pacific when, as American merchantmen previously, it was dragged into the internecine wars of the Marquesas. In the midst of the War of 1812 its captain attempted to annex the island of Nuka Hiva for the United States, going so far as to rename Nuka Hiva as Madison's Island, after the American president. But the U.S. government ignored his claim. The complete inability of U.S. forces to protect Astoria similarly shows the impotence of the United States in this region.[17] U.S. efforts to "show the flag" in the Pacific, such as the Wilkes exploring expedition and Commodore Perry's black ships, remained decades in the future.

Even in the mid-nineteenth century, the United States provided little counterweight to British imperial expansion in Asia. Chinese authorities discovered this to their chagrin when they unsuccessfully tried to set American merchants against their British cousins on the eve of the Opium War. Yet being an unimperial channel of commerce had its advantages for U.S. merchants. When Houqua, one of the *hong* in Canton, sought refuge for his millions as the Opium War began, he entrusted the funds to an American correspondent. He urged that the money be invested in railroad stock— the request of a man well informed of financial and industrial developments abroad. Here Americans combined neutrality among the imperial powers with a participation in the flow of east-west capital usually associated with empire.

France and the Netherlands returned to the Indies after 1815. As post-1815 European imperial efforts in Asia intensified, they also diverged. This divergence can be seen even in the dwindling use of the term "Indies," in place of which narrower language denoting increasingly exclusive national empires emerged. As opposed to a vague Indies, Britons increasingly spoke of an "India" over which most, if not quite all, of the competing European claims no longer held sway. Likewise Britons preferred "Australia" over the less-British-sounding alternative, "New Holland." The French later had their "Indo-China," which, unlike the more-capacious "East Indies," linguistically severed the Mascarenes from French Asia. The Netherlands controlled a "Dutch East Indies" from which British influence was expelled, in place of a larger unit—such as what Britons called the Indian Archipelago, which included Malaya.[18] Americans continued to trade with these regions, but the United States pursued no formal empire in Asia until the 1890s. In the meantime, affluent Americans' newly acquired capital was largely directed inland.[19]

In the end, free trade was neither inherently good nor evil. It is associated with the abolition of slavery as well as the distribution of opium, with peace as well as war. When merchant-capitalists in Britain and the United States eradicated the East India Company's

India monopoly, one of the most significant vestiges of early modern statism and political economy in the Anglo-American world, they enabled both the good and bad of free trade to reach Asia. Such an act heralded the economic dynamism of the British imperial and American economies at a time when Anglo-American capitals were larger and freer than ever before to remake the nineteenth-century world.[20] Just how capital shaped the nineteenth century is, however, another story.

Archival Sources

Archives

Archivo General de Indias, Seville
  Filipinas Series
Arsip Nasional Republik Indonesia, Jakarta
  Hoge Regering Series
  Marine Series
Baker Business Library, Harvard University
  Boston Manufacturing Company Papers
  Thorndike Papers
The Baring Archive, London
  "Correspondence in regard to Maine Lands, 1792–1836"
Bibliothèque Nationale de France
  Nouvelles Acquisitions Françaises, Department of Western Manuscripts
British Library
  Additional Manuscripts Collection
  Oriental and India Office Collection
British National Archives, Kew (formerly Public Record Office)
  Board of Trade Series
  Colonial Office Series
  Foreign Office Series
  Records of the Boards of Customs, Excise, and Customs and Excise
  Treasury Series
  War Office Series
Cape Town Archives Repository, South Africa
  Archives of the Port Captain
  Batavian Republic Series
  Colonial Office Series
  First British Occupation Series

Henry Dundas Papers
Politieke Raad (Council of Policy)
Centre d'accueil et de recherche des Archives nationales, Paris, various series
Centre des Archives d'Outre Mer, Aix-en-Provence
    Correspondance a l'arrivée
      Extrême-Orient
      Compagnies des Indes et Inde française
      Ile de France
    Correspondance au depart
Historical Society of Pennsylvania
    William Birch, "Autobiography"
Massachusetts Historical Society
    Columbia Papers
    Log of the Ship *Hunter*
    Papers of Maj. Samuel Shaw
    Winslow Family Papers
Nationaal Archief, Den Haag, Netherlands
    VOC Archives
National Archives and Records Administration, Philadelphia, PA
    Impost Ledgers for the Port of Philadelphia
National Archives and Records Administration, Waltham, MA
    Impost Books of the Collector (Salem, MA)
National Archives of Mauritius
    Great Britain Series
Philips Library, Peabody-Essex Museum, Salem, MA
    Salem East India Marine Society Journals
St. Helena Archives, The Castle, Jamestown
    List of Ships Arriving at St. Helena, 1793–1803

Newspapers

Boston Evening Post
Boston Gazette (1790)
Columbian Centinel
Herald of Freedom (1790)
Massachusetts Gazette and the Boston Post-Boy and Advertiser (1773)
The Massachusetts Gazette: And the Boston Weekly News-Letter (1773)
New York Packet (1788)
Oriental Herald (1827–1829)
Pennsylvania Gazette (1773)

Abbreviations

Add. Mss.	Additional Manuscripts Collection, British Library
AGI	Archivo General de Indias, Seville
AHR	*American Historical Review*
ANB	*American National Biography,* John A. Garraty and Mark C. Carnes, eds. (New York: Oxford University Press, 1999)
ANRI	Arsip Nasional Republik Indonesia, Jakarta
ASP	*American State Papers: Commerce and Navigation,* vols. 1 and 2 (Washington, DC: Gales and Seaton, 1832)
CAOM	Centre des Archives d'Outre Mer, Aix-en-Provence
CARAN	Centre d'accueil et de recherche des Archives nationales, Paris
CTAR	Cape Town Archives Repository, South Africa
DNB	*Dictionary of National Biography* (Oxford: Oxford University Press, 2004), www.oxforddnb.com
Hansard	*Hansard Parliamentary Debates,* 1st series (London: T. C. Hansard, 1803–1820)
HER	*Economic History Review*
HSP	Historical Society of Pennsylvania
ING Baring	The Baring Archive, London, "Correspondence in Regard to Maine Lands, 1792–1836"
JEH	*Journal of Economic History*
LCP	Library Company of Philadelphia
Maur	National Archives of Mauritius
MHS	Massachusetts Historical Society
NAF	Nouvelles Acquisitions Françaises, Department of Western Manuscripts, Bibliothèque Nationale de France
NARA (MA)	National Archives and Records Administration, Waltham, MA
NARA (PA)	National Archives and Records Administration, Philadelphia, PA
Neth	VOC Archives, Nationaal Archief, Den Haag, Netherlands
OED	*Oxford English Dictionary* (Oxford: Oxford University Press, 2009), dictionary.oed.com

OIOC	Oriental and India Office Collection, British Library
PEM	Philips Library, Peabody-Essex Museum, Salem, MA
PMHB	*Pennsylvania Magazine of History and Biography*
PRO	British National Archives, Kew (formerly the Public Record Office)
WMQ	*William and Mary Quarterly*

Notes

Introduction

1. Kenneth Pomeranz's *The Great Divergence: China, Europe, and the Making of the Modern World Economy* (Princeton: Princeton University Press, 2000) uses New World colonialism to explain the great divergence.
2. P. J. Cain and A. G. Hopkins, *British Imperialism, 1688–2000*, 2nd ed. (New York: Longman, 2001), 7–8, 36. Richard Sylla and Robert E. Wright, eds., *The History of Corporate Finance: Development of Anglo-American Securities Markets, Financial Practices, Theories and Laws* (London: Pickering & Chatto, 2003), among others, emphasize capital, though this is new. François Crouzet examined the link between the French Revolutionary Wars and British industry, and Douglass North connected re-exports and economic growth with subsequent U.S. industrialization. The tendency "to equate development with industrialization" is, as Cain and Hopkins note, simplistic. Some scholars have ignored capital altogether. See, for example, Immanuel Wallerstein, *The Second Era of Great Expansion of the Capitalist World-Economy, 1730s–1840s* (San Diego: Academic Press, 1989).
3. Pomeranz, *Great Divergence*, 42–43. Just as economists have various definitions of "money supply," economic historians might profitably employ various measures of world capital stock—gold and specie being one of the more limited. The wealth in the U.S. South and British Caribbean tended to be "locked in" to labor, land, and crops or paid out as rent, and was thus less fungible. David L. Carlton and Peter A. Coclanis, *The South, the Nation, and the World: Perspectives on Southern Economic Development* (London: University of Virginia Press, 2003), 19.

1. Revolution

1. Benjamin Fanueil to ?, Boston, November 15, 1773, PRO CO.5.133, f 9–10.

2. [Elisha Hutchinson?], Boston to [blanked out], London, November 1773, Copy, PRO CO.5.133, f 9–10, 15. Minor spelling and punctuation variations exist among the letters.

3. Blank, Boston to London, November 1773, PRO CO.5.133, f 15.

4. Blank, Boston to London, November 1773, PRO CO.5.133, f 15–16; Richard Clarke & Sons, Boston to Abraham Dupuis, London, November 1773.

5. Blank, Boston to London, November 1773, PRO CO.5.133, f 16–17; *Boston Evening Post,* November 8, 1773, 2.

6. Blank, Boston to London, November 1773, PRO CO.5.133, f 17.

7. Blank, Boston to London, November 1773, PRO CO.5.133, f 17; Benjamin Woods Labaree, *The Boston Tea Party* (Boston: Northeastern University Press, 1964), 110; Arlene Phillips Kleeb, "The Boston Tea Party: Catalyst for Revolution. An Exhibition Commemorating the 200th Anniversary" (William L. Clements Library, University of Michigan, December 1973).

8. Blank, Boston to London, November 1773, PRO CO.5.133, f 17–18.

9. Benjamin Fanueil to ?, Boston, November 15, 1773, PRO CO.5.133, f 11–12.

10. Benjamin Fanueil to ?, Boston, November 15, 1773, PRO CO.5.133, f 12.

11. *Massachusetts Gazette and the Boston Post-Boy and Advertiser,* November 15–22, 1773, 3; *The Massachusetts Gazette: And the Boston Weekly News-Letter,* November 26, 1773, 2.

12. *The Massachusetts Gazette: And the Boston Weekly News-Letter,* November 26, 1773, 2.

13. Labaree, *Boston Tea Party,* 113.

14. Labaree, *Boston Tea Party,* 113, 122, 151. Not all consignees fled to Fort William: Elisha Hutchinson was in Middleborough, Richard Clarke was in Salem, and Joshua Winslow stayed in Marshfield (Labaree, *Boston Tea Party,* 122).

15. *Boston Evening Post,* December 27, 1773, 2.

16. Henry Hutton, Charles Pastor, and Jonathan Burch, Customs House, Boston, to The Right Honorable The Lord Commissioners of His Majesty's Treasury, January 4, 1774, PRO T 1.505, f 2; *The Massachusetts Gazette: And the Boston Weekly News-Letter,* December 23, 1773, 1. Alfred Young examines the memory of the Tea Party in *The Shoemaker and the Tea Party: Memory and the American Revolution* (Boston: Beacon Press, 1999).

17. L. H. Butterfield, ed., *Diary and Autobiography of John Adams,* vol. 2 (Cambridge, MA: Belknap Press, 1961) (December 17, 1773), 85–86.

18. John Tyler, *Smugglers and Patriots: Boston Merchants and the Advent of the American Revolution* (Boston: Northeastern University Press, 1986), 198–205.

19. Butterfield, *Diary of John Adams,* vol. 2 (December 17, 1773), 86.

20. PRO CUST 16/1 f 8, 41, 71, 127, 129, 185, 231.

21. Labaree, *Boston Tea Party,* 104.

22. Francis S. Drake, *Tea Leaves: Being a Collection of Letters and Documents Relating to the Shipment of Tea to the American Colonies in the Year 1773,*

by the East India Tea Company (Detroit: Singing Tree Press, 1970), 210, 223, 294–295, 324. Winslow's lack of prominence may be for lack of surviving papers. Other members of the Winslow family maintained Tory sympathies. John Sparhawk to [Issac?] Winslow, Portsmouth, Massachusetts, July 22, 1775, MHS, Winslow Family Papers, Box 1 of 2, Ms. N-486.

23. Bernard Bailyn, *The Ordeal of Thomas Hutchinson* (Cambridge, MA: Belknap Press, 1974), 264–265.

24. The elder Clarke retained assets. At death he held stock in the Bank of England and, recovering pragmatism from loyalty, U.S. Treasury bonds.

25. Drake, *Tea Leaves*, 210, 223, 294–295, 324; Bailyn, *Thomas Hutchinson*, 372.

26. George Otto Trevelyan, *The American Revolution, Part 2* (London: Longmans, Green, 1903), 239, quoting George Selwyn; Bailyn, *Thomas Hutchinson*, 386; See also Mary Beth Norton, *The British-Americans: The Loyalist Exiles in England, 1774–1789* (Boston: Little, Brown, 1972).

27. *Boston Evening Post*, December 20, 1773, 3.

28. Of the 100 dealers present, seventy agreed to ban tea outright. Just nine wanted to ban Company tea only. Labaree, *Boston Tea Party*, 162.

29. *Boston Evening Post*, December 27, 1773, 3.

30. Ellen D. Larned, *History of Windham County, Connecticut*, vol. 2: *1760–1880* (Worcester, MA: Charles Hamilton, 1880), 116–119; "Virginia Non-Importation Agreement," August 1, 1774, in Commager, ed., *Documents of American History* 80, as cited in T. H. Breen, "'Baubles of Britain': The American and Consumer Revolutions of the Eighteenth Century," *Past & Present* 119 (May 1988): 92–93, 98.

31. *Massachusetts Spy*, December 23, 1773, as cited in Breen, "'Baubles of Britain,'" 99. For the Covenant, see Arthur Schlesinger, *The Colonial Merchants and the American Revolution, 1763–1776* (New York: Longmans, 1918); Ann Withington, *Toward a More Perfect Union: Virtue and the Formation of American Republics* (Oxford: Oxford University Press, 1991).

32. Labaree, *Boston Tea Party*, 161, 164; Pauline Maier, *From Resistance to Revolution: Colonial Radicals and the Development of American Opposition to Britain, 1765–1776* (New York: Knopf, 1972), 282; John C. Miller, *Origins of the American Revolution* (Boston: Little, Brown, 1943), 345, 350–351.

33. Breen, "'Baubles of Britain,'" 72–104, quotation at 98. Miller, *Origins of the American Revolution*, 345.

34. Butterfield, *Diary of John Adams*, vol. 2 (August 27, 1774), 113. For the correction see John Adams to Abigail Adams, July 6, 1774, in *Adams Family Correspondence*, vol. 1, ed. L. H. Butterfield (Cambridge, MA: Belknap Press, 1963), 129–130, as cited in T. H. Breen, *Marketplace of Revolution: How Consumer Politics Shaped Independence* (New York: Oxford University Press, 2004), 317. Viable figures for coffee consumption during the Revolutionary period itself do not exist.

35. Butterfield, *Diary of John Adams*, vol. 2 (June 21, 1779), 386; Claude C. Robin, *New Travels through North America: In a Series of Letters . . . in the Year 1781* (Boston: 1784), 23, as cited in Rodris Roth, "Tea Drinking in 18th-Century America: Its Etiquette and Equipage," Contributions from the Museum of History and Technology, Paper 14, 63.

36. N.Y. Col. Doc., vol. VIII, 400, as cited in Arthur M. Schlesinger, "The Uprising against the East India Company," *Political Science Quarterly* 32 (March 1917): 73–74; Huw Bowen, "Perceptions from the Periphery: Colonial American Views of Britain's Asiatic Empire, 1756–1783," in Christine Daniels and Michael V. Kennedy, eds., *Negotiated Empires: Centers and Peripheries in the Americas, 1500–1820* (New York: Routledge, 2002), 283–300.

37. Thomas Hutchinson to Lord Hillsborough, Boston, August 25, 1771, Massachusetts Archives, Hutchinson Correspondence, vol. 27, 219, as cited in Tyler, *Smugglers and Patriots*, 189; Schlesinger, "Uprising against the East India Company," 63.

38. Butterfield, *Diary of John Adams,* vol. 2 (February 14, 1771), 5.

39. *Boston Evening Post*, October 18, 1773, as cited in Schlesinger, "Uprising against the East India Company," 71.

40. Pauline Maier, "The Revolutionary Origins of the American Corporation," *WMQ*, 3rd series, 50, no. 1 (January 1993): 81–82. Thomas Paine, back in England defending the French Revolution, likewise attacked chartered English corporations in the *Rights of Man*. To Paine a charter meant "taking rights away . . . charters . . . leave the right, by exclusion, in the hands of a few." Thomas Paine, *The Great Works of Thomas Paine: Complete. Political and Theological* (New York: 1878), 164.

41. *New York Journal*, November 4, 1773, as cited in Schlesinger, "Uprising against the East India Company," 74; *Massachusetts Spy*, October 14, 1773, cited in Tyler, *Smugglers and Patriots*, 194; *Journals of the Continental Congress*, vol. 1 (Washington, DC: Government Printing Office, 1904), 98, as cited in Schlesinger, "Uprising against the East India Company," 76. For New York's tea trade, see Cathy Matson, *Merchants & Empire: Trading in Colonial New York* (Baltimore: Johns Hopkins University Press, 1998), 303–311.

42. John Dickinson, "A Letter from the Country," Fairview, November 27, 1773, in *Memoirs of the Historical Society of Pennsylvania*, vol. 14 (Philadelphia: HSP, 1895), 459–560; Amartya Sen, *Poverty and Famines: An Essay on Entitlement and Deprivation* (Oxford: Clarendon Press, 1981); Adam Smith, *The Wealth of Nations* (London: ElecBook, 2001), 691, http://www.ebrary.com, accessed November 20, 2009; Emma Rothschild, "The East India Company and the American Revolution," unpublished paper, Centre for History and Economics, King's College, Cambridge University, April 2002.

43. Miller, *Origins of the American Revolution*, 345.

44. *Pennsylvania Gazette*, December 8, 1773, 2–3. Emphasis added.

45. *Massachusetts Spy*, July 7, 1774, in Schlesinger, "Uprising against the East India Company," 77; John R. Galvin, *Three Men of Boston* (New York:

Thomas Y. Crowell, 1976), 264. For Spain as British foil see P. J. Marshall, "'A Free though Conquering People': Britain and Asia in the Eighteenth Century," in *"A Free though Conquering People": Eighteenth-Century Britain and Its Empire* (Burlington, VT: Variorum, 2003), 8.

46. Paine, *Great Works,* 38.

47. Larned, *History of Windham County,* vol. 2, 123–124.

48. Sir William Blackstone, *Commentaries on the Laws of England,* vol. 1, ed. George Sharswood (Philadelphia, 1860), 468–471.

49. As late as the 1790s the Massachusetts state legislature chartered over 200 corporations without one being for trade. Maier, "Revolutionary Origins," 54; William Robert Scott, *The Constitution and Finance of English, Scottish and Irish Joint-Stock Companies to 1720,* vols. 1–3, passim, and vol. 2 (Bristol, UK: Thoemmes Press, 1993), 3–237; John Brewer, *The Sinews of Power: War, Money and the English State, 1688–1783* (New York: Knopf, 1988).

50. C. A. Bayly, *Indian Society and the Making of the British Empire* (New York: Cambridge University Press, 1988).

51. Louis Hartz, *Economic Policy and Democratic Thought: Pennsylvania, 1776–1860* (Cambridge, MA: Harvard University Press, 1948); Maier, "Revolutionary Origins," 54.

52. Maier, "Revolutionary Origins," 64–73, 82.

53. Maier, "Revolutionary Origins," 68. See also Susan Pace Hamill, "From Special Privilege to General Utility: A Continuation of Willard Hurst's Study of Corporations," *American University Law Review* 49 (October 1999): 81.

54. Andrew Jackson, "Bank Veto," July 10, 1832, in *Messages of Gen. Andrew Jackson: With a Short Sketch of His Life* (Boston: Otis Broaders, 1837), 148–149.

55. Emma Rothschild, "Global Commerce and the Question of Sovereignty in the Eighteenth-Century Provinces," *Modern Intellectual History* 1, no. 1 (2004): 6. Smith drew upon other economists, some of whose ideas resonated in Britain and the American colonies. Emma Rothschild, *Economic Sentiments: Adam Smith, Condorcet, and the Enlightenment* (Cambridge, MA: Harvard University Press, 2001); Forrest McDonald, *Novus Ordo Seculorum: The Intellectual Origins of the Constitution* (Lawrence: University Press of Kansas, 1985).

56. Smith, *Wealth of Nations,* 837.

57. Smith, *Wealth of Nations,* vol. 2, 758, as quoted in Maier, "Revolutionary Origins," 59.

58. On Smith's readership: Joyce Oldham Appleby, *Liberalism and Republicanism in the Historical Imagination* (Cambridge, MA: Harvard University Press, 1992), 4. Though Samuel Fleischacker notes Smith's influence in the United States on noneconomic matters from 1776 to 1790, it seems Americans had been informed by and were practicing British free-trade ideas well before 1776, as the Boston Tea Party indicates. Samuel Fleischacker, "Adam Smith's Reception among the American Founders, 1776–1790," *WMQ,* 3rd

series, 59, no. 4 (October 2002): 897–924; Joyce Oldham Appleby, *Economic Thought and Ideology in Seventeenth-Century England* (Princeton: Princeton University Press, 1978).

59. Rothschild, *Economic Sentiments,* 52–71.

60. Hansard, vol. 17, cols. 456–457 as cited in Rothschild, "Global Commerce," 8.

61. Rothschild, *Economic Sentiments,* 27. Smith's solutions were liberal, modern, and radical: destroy the Companies; free mankind. Napoleon Bonaparte read *The Wealth of Nations* while imprisoned on St. Helena and concurred with Smith that free trade "agitated all imaginations, shook an entire people; it was entirely identical with equality, led naturally to independence, and, in this respect, had much more to do with our modern system" than the "old system" of protected monopolies. This was, in part, hyperbole: in office he did as much to blockade trade as to end the Company system. Though his pronouncements must be taken with a grain of salt, they likely to reflect the genuine sentiments of a man who was, in his own way, a violently radical modernizer. Comte de Las Cases, *La Mémorial de Sainte-Hélène,* vol. 2, ed. Joël Schmidt (Paris: Éditions du Seuil, 1968), 1441, as cited in Rothschild, *Economic Sentiments,* 30.

62. "Two Letters by Christopher Gadsden, Feb., 1766," ed. Robert M. Weir, *South Carolina Historical Magazine* 75 (1974): 175, as cited in Appleby, *Liberalism and Republicanism,* 184; William Wirt Henry, *Patrick Henry: Life, Correspondence and Speeches,* vol. 2 (New York, 1891), 192, as cited in Appleby, *Liberalism and Republicanism,* 185.

63. *Pennsylvania Gazette,* February 8, 1773, as cited in Miller, *Origins of the American Revolution,* 341–342. Perhaps because of their common provincialism, Smith and the colonists were more able to question established authority than home-county businessmen. Rothschild, "Global Commerce," 6. Cf. Bernard Bailyn and John Clive, "England's Cultural Provinces: Scotland and America," *WMQ,* 3rd series, 11 (April 1954): 200–213.

64. Oscar Handlin, *Commonwealth: A Study of the Role of Government in the American Economy: Massachusetts, 1774–1861* (New York: New York University Press, 1947); Hartz, *Economic Policy and Democratic Thought.*

65. José Engrácia Antunes and Nuno Pinheiro Torres, "The Portuguese East India Company," in Ella Gepken-Jager, Gerard van Solinge, and Levinus Timmerman, eds., *VOC 1602–2002: 400 Years of Company Law* (Deventer: Kluwer Legal Publishers, 2005), 161; Huw Bowen, *East India Company: Trade and Domestic Financial Statistics, 1755–1838* [computer file] (Colchester, Essex: UK Data Archive [distributor], September 2007), SN: 5690.

66. Class as discussed in this book is not meant to imply class consciousness.

67. On business organization see Joseph Stancliffe Davis, *Essays in the Earlier History of American Corporations,* 2 vols. (Cambridge: Harvard University Press, 1917); Maier, "Revolutionary Origins," 51–84; Robert B. Ekelund Jr. and Robert Tollison, "Mercantilist Origins of the Corporation," *Bell Journal of Economics* 11, no. 2 (Autumn 1980): 715–720; Paul J. McNulty and Giulio Pontecorvo, "Mercantilist Origins of the Corporation: Comment," *Bell Jour-*

nal of Economics 14, no. 1 (Spring 1983): 294–297; Oscar Handlin and Mary Handlin, "Origins of the American Business Corporation," *JEH* 5, no. 1 (May 1945): 1–23; Oliver E. Williamson, "The Modern Corporation: Origins, Evolution, Attributes," *JEH* 19, no. 4 (December 1981): 1537–1568; Shaw Livermore, "Advent of Corporations in New York," *New York History* 16, no. 3 (July 1935): 286–298.

68. R. R. Palmer, *The Age of the Democratic Revolution* (Princeton: Princeton University Press, 1959). In *The Crisis* (1776), Thomas Paine reflected back on the Tea Party, finding it "remarkable that the produce of" the Indies, "transported to America, should there kindle up a war to punish" England. Paine, *Great Works*, 91. One need not accept his interpretation to admire his global view of these events. P. J. Cain and A. G. Hopkins, *British Imperialism, 1688–2000*, 2nd ed. (New York: Longman, 2001), 101; Holden Furber, "The Beginnings of American Trade with India, 1784–1812," *New England Quarterly* 11, no. 2 (June 1938): 235–265; Susan S. Bean, *Yankee India: American Commercial and Cultural Encounters with India in the Age of Sail, 1784–1860* (Salem, MA: Peabody Essex Museum, 2001); Amales Tripathi, *Trade and Finance in the Bengal Presidency, 1793–1813* (Calcutta: Oxford University Press, 1979), 1–119.

69. P. J. Marshall, "The Eighteenth Century Empire: British Politics and Society from Walpole to Pitt 1742–1789," in *"A Free though Conquering People": Eighteenth-Century Britain and Its Empire* (Burlington, VT: Ashgate, 2003), 195; C. A. Bayly, *Imperial Meridian: The British Empire and the World, 1780–1830* (London: Longman, 1989); V. T. Harlow, *The Founding of the Second British Empire, 1763–1793*, 2 vols. (New York: Longmans, Green, 1953–1964).

70. Marshall, "Eighteenth-Century Empire," 195; Michael Fry, *The Dundas Despotism* (Edinburgh: Edinburgh University Press, 1992); Holden Furber, *Henry Dundas, First Viscount Melville, 1742–1811* (Oxford: Oxford University Press, 1931); Cyril Matheson, *The Life of Henry Dundas, First Viscount Melville, 1742–1811* (London: Constable, 1933). In defining "free trade" narrowly as freedom to trade, and not necessarily low tariffs, this book diverges from Robinson and Gallagher. See John Gallagher and Ronald Robinson, "The Imperialism of Free Trade," in William Roger Louis, ed., *The Robinson and Gallagher Controversy* (New York: New Viewpoints, 1976), 62–63.

2. America Sails East

1. Richard L. Garner, "Long-Term Silver Mining Trends in Spanish America: A Comparative Analysis of Peru and Mexico," *AHR* 93, no. 4 (October 1988): 898. This is a conservative figure. Other conservative estimates put colonial Latin American silver production at 150,000 tons. Dennis P. Flynn and Arturo Giraldez, "China and the Manila Galleons," in A. J. H. Latham and Heita

302 · Notes to Pages 32–33

Kawakatsu, eds., *Japanese Industrialization and the Asian Economy* (New York: Routledge, 1994), 71.

2. Kenneth Pomeranz, *The Great Divergence: China, Europe, and the Making of the Modern World Economy* (Princeton: Princeton University Press 2000), 159.

3. The transfer of silver from Europe to Asia in the early modern period was sometimes criticized for its effects on the balance of trade. Joyce Oldham Appleby, *Economic Thought and Ideology in Seventeenth-Century England* (Princeton: Princeton University Press, 1978). By the French Revolution such critiques were commonplace. Marcel Dorigny, "La place de l'Ocean Indien dans l'économie coloniale "girondine": Une réorientation industrialiste de la colonisation?" in Claude Wanquet and Benoît Jullien, eds., *Révolution française et océan indién* (Paris: L'Harmattan, 1995), 95–103.

4. K. N. Chaudhuri, "Foreign Trade," in Tapan Raychaudhuri and Irfan Habib, eds., *The Cambridge Economic History of India,* vol. 1 (New York: Cambridge University Press, 1982), 398.

5. Pomeranz, *Great Divergence,* 271.

6. For conservative estimate: Kent Deng, "Miracle or Mirage? Foreign Silver, China's Economy and Globalization from the Sixteenth to the Nineteenth Centuries," *Pacific Economic Review* 13, no. 3 (2008): 327. Broader estimate based on yuan data (300 million–350 million silver yuan in 1680 to 1.14 billion–1.33 billion yuan in 1830) from Yeh-chien Wang, "Secular Trends of Rice Prices in the Yangzi Delta, 1638–1935," in Thomas G. Rawski and Lillian M. Li, eds., *Chinese History in Economic Perspective* (Berkeley: University of California Press, 1992), 57. Yuan converted to metric tons at rate of 23.85 grams of silver per yuan. For conversion rate see Deng, "Miracle or Mirage?" 322n23. For Company data: Huw Bowen, *East India Company: Trade and Domestic Financial Statistics, 1755–1838* [computer file] (Colchester, Essex: UK Data Archive [distributor], September 2007), SN: 5690.

7. Flynn and Giraldez ("China and the Manila Galleons," 71–86) estimate the Franco-Anglo-Portuguese silver trade at 50 metric tons of silver a year in the seventeenth century and come to a similar number for the Mexico-Manila trade, though data for the latter are sparser. No information on the eighteenth century is available. Flynn and Giraldez's main documentary support for their hypothesis comes from Ch'üan Han-sheng (全漢昇), "The Inflow of American Silver into China from the Late Ming to the Mid-Ch'ing Period" (明清間美州白銀的輸入中國), *The Journal of the Institute of Chinese Studies of the Chinese University of Hong Kong* (香港中文大學中國文化研究所學報) 11, no. 1 (September 1969): 59–79. Ch'üan Han-sheng (全漢昇) estimates one-third of the American silver that reached China came via the Pacific, the rest through Europe and India. "Estimate of Silver Imports into China from the Americas in the Ming and Ch'ing Dynasties" (明清門美洲白銀輸入中國的估計), *Academia Sinica: Publications of the Institute of History and Philology* (中央研究院歷史語言研究所集刊) 66, no. 3 (September 1995): 679–693.

8. John K. Fairbank, *Trade and Diplomacy on the China Coast: The Opening of the Treaty Ports, 1842–1854,* vol. 1 (Cambridge, MA: Harvard University Press, 1953), 76; Frederic Wakeman, "The Canton Trade and the Opium War," in Denis Twitchett and John K. Fairbank, eds., *Cambridge History of China,* vol. 10, part 1 (Cambridge: Cambridge University Press, 1978), 173. The opium trade was an important cause of China's net outflow of silver, but not the only one. Economic pressures within China intensified the effect of the opium trade on the silver supply.

9. Adam Smith, *The Wealth of Nations,* vol. 1 (London: ElecBook, 2001), 283, 287, 292, http://www.ebrary.com, accessed November 20, 2009).

10. *Connecticut Gazette,* May 20, 1774.

11. W. T. Baxter, *The House of Hancock: Business in Boston, 1724–1775* (Cambridge, MA: Harvard University Press, 1945), 16–21; Robert Wright, *Origin of Commercial Banking in America, 1750–1800* (Lanham, MD: Rowman & Littlefield, 2001), 8–9.

12. Edwin J. Perkins, *The Economy of Colonial America,* 2nd ed. (New York: Columbia University Press, 1988), 163.

13. Gordon C. Bjork, *Stagnation and Growth in the American Economy, 1784–1792* (New York: Garland, 1985), 15.

14. John J. McCusker, *How Much Is That in Real Money?* (Worcester, MA: American Antiquarian Society, 2001), 53, 110. Bjork argues for an immediate postwar boom in 1784, followed by severe depression between 1786 and 1787 and a recovery by 1789 (Bjork, *Stagnation and Growth,* 62). Robert A. East, *Business Enterprise in the American Revolutionary Era* (New York: Columbia University Press, 1928), 252–257.

15. Bjork, citing *American Museum,* gives four as the number of ships, which is too low (Bjork, *Stagnation and Growth,* 33–36). Gary M. Walton and James F. Shepherd, *The Economic Rise of Early America* (Cambridge: Cambridge University Press, 1979), 184.

16. Walton and Shepherd, *Economic Rise,* 189, 198.

17. The military asked the Hospitals Office to investigate and compile a list of brothels so that some attempt might be made to improve soldiers' health. The Hospitals Office detailed "according to the most accurate Information I can obtain, a specific List of such Houses as are suspected, or known to admit of that loose and disorderly description of Women, thro' an intercourse with whom the Health of the Private Soldiers of this Garrison becomes most materially affected, and themselves rendered for a time incapable of military Duty!" and [enclosure to above] "Houses of Resort for Loose Women." Inspector of Hospitals Office, June 21, 1815, to Major Rogers, Military Secretary, Cape Town, CTAR CO 68 (1815), 421, 423, No. 45 and enclosure.

18. Nigel Worden, Elizabeth van Heyningen, and Vivian Bickford-Smith, *Cape Town: The Making of a City: An Illustrated Social History* (Claremont, South Africa: David Philip, 1998), 35–83. Paving came with the British occupation.

19. Jose Burman, *In the Footsteps of Lady Anne Barnard* (Cape Town, South Africa: Human & Rousseau, 1990), 22–23; James Zug, *American Traveler: The Life and Adventures of John Ledyard, the Man Who Dreamed of Walking the World* (New York: Basic Books, 2005), 39.

20. Zug, *American Traveler,* 39.

21. "Cape Town and Mauritius, 1802. Moses H. White. Journal kept on board the Ship *Herald* from Boston to the Cape of Good Hope &c. Richard Derby, Esqr., Commander," in Norman R. Bennett and George E. Brooks Jr., *New England Merchants in Africa: A History through Documents, 1802 to 1865* (Boston: Boston University Press, 1965), 4.

22. The impressively named *Empress of China* reached Asia first. But the *Harriet* reached the Cape—and hence the gateway to the Indies—before the *Empress* did. Samuel Eliot Morison, *Maritime History of Massachusetts* (Boston: Houghton-Mifflin, 1961), 44. Philip Chadwick Foster Smith, in *The Empress of China* (Philadelphia: Philadelphia Maritime Museum, 1984), casts doubt on the *Harriet's* primacy. Yet Cape Town records confirm that the *Harriet* reached South Africa in April 1784. No papers of Captain Malet or the *Harriet* are known to survive. Morison claims that Captain Malet purchased a cargo of tea from an English East India Company captain for double its value—so alarmed was the captain at the idea of Americans sailing to China themselves. Cape Town records indicate East India Company ships at the Cape in the 1783–1784 and 1784–1785 seasons were the *Spy, Swallow, Winterton, Raymond, Northumberland, Norfolk, Ponsborne, Middlesex, Tocoles, Busbridge, Valentine, Hillsborough, Earl Cornwallis, Tortoise, Ganges, Resolution, Royal Bishop, Fox, Bessborough, Calcutta,* and *Britannia.* Ship logs from all but the *Spy, Swallow, Tocoles,* and *Tortoise* survive; none indicates encountering or trading with the *Harriet,* but not every captain would have found the event worth noting. The *Spy and Swallow* were not at the Cape at the time, the *Tortoise* has no surviving log, and the *Tocoles* is an irretrievable Dutch corruption of the original English name. Neth VOC 4307 522. Anthony Farrington, *Catalogue of East India Company Ships' Journals and Logs, 1600–1834* (London: British Library, 1999). Louis Dermigny, using French archival sources, claims Malet bought a cargo "from various European vessels" in port, and in a second voyage bought 70 boxes worth 7,000 piasters. Louis Dermigny, *La China et l'occident: Le Commerce à Canton au XXIIIe Siècle,* vol. 3 (Paris: S.E.V.P.E.N., 1964), 1137. For smuggling at the Cape see Johannes De Hullu, "On the Rise of the Indies Trade of the United States of America as Competitor of the East India Company in the period 1786–1790," in Margot E. van Opstall, Marie Antoinette Petronella Meilink-Roelofsz, and G. J. Schutte, eds., *Dutch Authors on Asian History: A Selection of Dutch Historiography on the Verenigde Oostindische Compagnie* (Providence: Foris, 1988), 139–153.

23. "Ships List," July 1, 1783, to May 5, 1784, Neth VOC 4307, Reel 1395-2, No. 538. Cape records are spottier, the best being the "Journal of Cape Governors"

(CTAR VC 34), which mentions vessels less systematically, though sometimes with more information on a particular vessel. Index in guide G22. 1791 Census returns for the entire Cape colony, not just Cape Town, count 3,613 male burghers, with 2,460 women and 6,955 children. Nonmilitary employees of the Dutch East India Company at the Cape, and their dependents, numbered approximately 1,500 more. C. W. de Kiewiet gives the population in the western districts as 13,500 at this time. C. W. de Kiewiet, *A History of South Africa Social and Economic* (Oxford: Oxford University Press, 1957), 30. Europeans at the Cape owned over 17,000 slaves. George McCall Theal, *History of South Africa, 1691–1795*, vol. 2 (London: Swan Sonnenschein, 1888), 289–290.

24. Though provisions were available for all, the Cape was not a free port as far as trade was concerned. "Sketches of the Political and Commercial History of the Cape of Good Hope," CTAR BO 223, 293. Cape sources understate English East India Company trade, since Company ships often stopped at Anjouan (Johanna) rather than the Cape prior to 1800. However, Cape sources do provide a good basis for comparing American East India traffic with European East India traffic generally.

25. The term "likely East Indiamen" excludes naval, whaling, and slaving vessels. Naval vessels include vessels labeled fire ships, Company troop transports, royal ships, war ships, frigates, and corvettes. Whaling vessels include those listed as departing on whale hunts. Some slave ships were clearly noted—the Dutch sometimes recorded how many slaves were on board—but other ships, such as those passing from Mozambique to Santo Domingo, probably carried slaves as well, though they were not noted as such in the records. Slave vessels here include those passing between Guinea, Mauritius, Bourbon, Madagascar, or the East African coast on the one hand and Angola, the Caribbean, or the United States on the other. It is possible that not all these vessels were in fact on slaving voyages. Since most of the slavers were French or Portuguese, it would mean that the annual East India trade totals for France or Portugal might be too conservative by one or two ships.

26. Depression years here are 1784–1785 to 1787–1788; recovery is 1788–1789 to 1791–1792. Outlying years, which would emphasize this division further, have been dropped.

27. The Congressional committee interviewing him included John Kean, John Bubenheim Bayard, and Charles Pettit. The latter two were merchants. Pettit, a major Philadelphia merchant, may have had East India investments. "John Kean," in John Howard Brown, ed., *Lamb's Biographical Dictionary of the United States*, vol. 4 (Boston: James H. Lamb, 1901), 477; "John Bayard," in Brown, *Lamb's Biographical Dictionary*, vol. 1, 228–229; "Charles Pettit," in Brown, *Lamb's Biographical Dictionary*, vol. 6, 231. See also "Charles Pettit," in Dumas Malone, ed., *Dictionary of American Biography*, vol. 14 (New York: Charles Scribner, 1943), 517–518; Edmund C. Burnett, ed., *Letters of Members of Continental Congress*, vol. 8, *1785–1789* (Washington, DC: Carnegie

Institute of Washington, 1936), 298n2; and John C. Fitzpatrick, ed., *Journals of the Continental Congress 1774–1789*, vol. 29: *July 1 to December 30, 1785* (Washington, DC: U.S. Government Printing Office, 1933), 904n25.

28. Rufus King to John Adams, New York, February 3, 1786, in Rufus King, *Life and Correspondence of Rufus King*, vol. 1 (New York: 1894), 155. Congress did not mention "unfettered" and free trade as the reason for declining Wingrove, noting instead that Wingrove's citizenship barred them from any further action. Joseph Stancliffe Davis, *Essays in the Earlier History of American Corporations*, vol. 2 (Cambridge, MA: Harvard University Press, 1917), 287–288.

29. Tyler Dennett, *Americans in Eastern Asia: A Critical Study of the Policy of the United States with Reference to China, Japan and Korea in the 19th Century* (New York: Macmillan, 1922), 28. It is unclear whether this is the same O'Donnell noted in J. Thomas Scharf, *Chronicles of Baltimore: Being a complete history of "Baltimore town" and Baltimore city from the earliest period to the present time* (Baltimore, MD: Turnbull Bros., 1874), 238.

30. Fort William to Court of Directors, December 14, 1787, para. 57, Foreign Dept.; C. H. Philips and B. B. Misra, eds., *Fort William–India House Correspondence and other contemporary papers relating thereto*, vol. 15, *Foreign and Secret 1782–1786* (Delhi: Controller of Publications, Government of India, for the National Archive of India, 1963), 169. Others in the Company, including counsel in Bengal, discouraged prosecution. See OIOC H/605, 59–60, December 14, 1787. On the issue of nationality, see Caitlin Anderson, "Aliens at Home, Subjects Abroad: British Nationality Law and Policy, 1815–1870" (PhD diss., Cambridge University). For O'Donnell's return to the United States, see Phineas Bond, Philadelphia June 2, 1789, to His Grace the Duke of Leeds, PRO FO/4/7 205.

31. John Adams to Richard Henry Lee, London, September 6, 1785, in Richard H. Lee, ed., *Memoir of the life of Richard Henry Lee and His Correspondence*, vol. 1 (Philadelphia: H. C. Corey and I. Lea, 1825), 143–144.

32. John Jay, "Report of Secretary for Foreign Affairs on Mr. Adams' letter of January 27, 1787," July 31, 1787, in *Journals of Congress*, vol. 33 (1787), 445.

33. The commerce clause is no longer a "constitutional battleground," and thus its previous contentiousness is partly obscured. Alpheus Mason and Donald Stephenson Jr., *American Constitutional Law* (Upper Saddle River, NJ: Prentice Hall, 2002), 248.

34. Max Farrand, ed., *The Records of the Federal Convention of 1787*, vol. 2 (New Haven: Yale University Press, 1911), 143, 157; Merrill Jensen, ed., *Documentary History of the Ratification of the Constitution*, vol. 1: *Constitutional Documents and Records, 1776–1787* (Madison: State Historical Society of Wisconsin, 1976), 246, 285.

35. George Mason objected as well. Farrand, *Federal Convention*, vol. 2, 635, 640.

36. Jensen, *Documentary History of the Ratification of the Constitution,* vol. 4: *Ratification of the Constitution by the States: Massachusetts* (Madison: State Historical Society of Wisconsin, 1998), 289.

37. Gerard Carl Henderson, *The Position of Foreign Corporations in American Constitutional Law: A Contribution to the History and Theory of Juristic Persons in Anglo-American Law* (Cambridge, MA: Harvard University Press, 1918), 20.

38. Farrand, *Federal Convention,* vol. 2, 181.

39. Henderson, *Foreign Corporations,* 19.

40. Jensen, *Documentary History of the Ratification of the Constitution,* vol. 5: *Ratification of the Constitution by the States: Massachusetts* (Madison: State Historical Society of Wisconsin, 1998), 654.

41. Thomas Jefferson to Alexander Donald, February 7, 1788, in Jensen, *Documentary History of the Ratification of the Constitution,* vol. 8: *Ratification of the Constitution by the States: Virginia* (Madison: State Historical Society of Wisconsin, 1998), 354.

42. Jensen, *Documentary History of the Ratification of the Constitution,* vol. 4: *Massachusetts,* 428.

43. Samuel Bryan as "Centinel," *Independent Gazetteer* (Philadelphia), January 2, 1788, as cited in Bernard Bailyn, ed., *The Debate on the Constitution: Federalist and Antifederalist Speeches, Articles, and Letters During the Struggle over Ratification* (Part 1) (New York: Library of America, 1993), 689.

44. Jensen, *Documentary History of the Ratification of the Constitution,* vol. 5: *Massachusetts,* 798, 867.

45. *Massachusetts State Convention,* 24–26 and quotation at 84. See also Simeon E. Baldwin, *American Business Corporations before 1789,* vol. 1 ([New York?]: Annual Report of American Historical Association, 1902), 272–273.

46. Henderson, *Foreign Corporations,* 20. Toward the end of his life Madison explained that he had intended the commerce clause not to grant the federal government a new power so much as to deny states the imposition of tariffs on trade with one another, a problem endemic to the 1780s. Yet, written decades later and with a strong eye to history, this may be a mere justification. Farrand, *Federal Convention,* vol. 3, 478, citing Madison to J. C. Cabell Montpelier, February 13, 1829. James Madison, *Letters and Other Writings of James Madison,* vol. 4 (Philadelphia: J. B. Lippincott, 1865), 14–15.

47. N. St. Clair Clarke and D. A. Hall, eds., *Legislative and Documentary History of the Bank of the United States including the original Bank of North America* (Washington, DC: Gales and Seaton, 1832), 91, 595.

48. William Gouge, *Short History of Paper Money and Banking in the United States* (1833), as cited in James Willard Hurst, *The Legitimacy of the Business Corporation in the Law of the United States, 1780–1970* (Charlottesville: University Press of Virginia, 1970), 30.

49. Thomas Randall to Alexander Hamilton, in Arthur Harrison Cole, *Industrial and Commercial Correspondence of Alexander Hamilton Anticipating His*

Report on Manufactures, vol. 1 (Chicago: A. W. Shaw, 1928), 145; Jacob E. Cooke, *Tench Coxe and the Early Republic* (Chapel Hill: University of North Carolina Press, 1978), 170. Coxe traded to China through his Philadelphia partnership, Coxe & Frazier, in the 1780s. Robert E. Wright and David J. Cowen, *Financial Founding Fathers: The Men Who Made America Rich* (Chicago: University of Chicago Press, 2006), 42–43.

50. East, *Business Enterprise,* 241.

51. Harold C. Syrett, ed., *Papers of Alexander Hamilton,* vol. 5 (New York: Columbia University Press, 1961), 532n1, and vol. 11 (1965), 242n2.

52. Eleanor Roosevelt Seagraves, ed., *Delano's Voyages of Commerce and Discovery: Amasa Delano in China, the Pacific Islands, Australia, and South America, 1789–1807* (Stockbridge, MA: Berkshire House, 1994), 5.

53. Morison gives 800 tons, others 900, though this may be due to a difference between tons and tons burthen or between differing methods of calculating tonnage (Morison, *Maritime History of Massachusetts,* 52). Shaw gives 820 (Samuel Shaw to The Honorable Mr. Englehard, Shabander, Batavia, September 4, 1790, MHS, *Papers of Maj. Samuel Shaw,* "Samuel Shaw Letterbook").

54. Seagraves, *Delano's Voyages,* 5.

55. Josiah Quincy, *The Journals of Major Samuel Shaw, the First American Consul at Canton. With a Life of the Author* (Boston: Wm. Crosby and H. P. Nichols, 1847), 117.

56. Seagraves, *Delano's Voyages,* 4, 6.

57. On chronometer use see Rupert T. Gould, *The Marine Chronometer, Its History and Development* (Woodbridge, UK: Antique Collector's Club, 1989), 213–214. Gould, quoting Samuel E. Morison, *Maritime History of Massachusetts* (n.p.), recalls that as late as 1823 when the Boston fur-and-China-trade firm Bryant and Sturgis learned that one of its captains had spent $250 on a chronometer, the partners excoriated the captain: "Could we have anticipated that our instructions respecting economy would have been so totally disregarded, we would have sett fire to the Ship rather than have sent her to sea." Delano makes no mention of star charts. Amasa Delano, *A narrative of voyages and travels, in the northern and southern hemispheres: Comprising three voyages round the world, together with a voyage of survey and discovery, in the Pacific Ocean and oriental islands* (Boston, 1817), 35–36.

58. The ship missed Java Head, the traditional navigational reference point for ships crossing the Indian Ocean, by three weeks.

59. Seagraves, *Delano's Voyages,* 16.

60. Randall remained in China, handling the *Columbia'*s furs. Shaw left Canton on January 25, 1789, reaching Newport, Rhode Island on July 5, 1789. The ship was launched in September 1789, too late for Shaw to insist on changes in the hull construction or wood type. Quincy, *Journals of Major Samuel Shaw,* 117, 115. In his *Narrative,* Delano was careful not to impugn any reputations. He notes only that untreated wood was fine for vessels on northerly

routes. Yet this implies knowledge that such wood was unsuitable for vessels sailing in the tropics—indeed, rot was the reason the wood was treated in the first place.

61. On January 2, 1790, Shaw wrote President Washington requesting a renewal of his commission as consul to China. This may have occasioned the delay. (MHS, *Papers of Maj. Samuel Shaw,* "Samuel Shaw Letterbook," Samuel Shaw to George Washington, Boston, January 2, 1790.) The offer was renewed.

62. Philip Freneau, "On the First American Ship That Explored the Rout to China and the East-Indies after the Revolution," as cited in Smith, *Empress of China,* xiii.

63. "Samuel Shaw," in John A. Garraty and Mark C. Carnes, eds., *ANB,* vol. 19, 1999, 752–753. Josiah Quincy, Shaw's only biographer, suggests he may have drafted the Society's constitution. Quincy, *Journals of Major Samuel Shaw,* 111.

64. Samuel Shaw to John Jay, New York, May 19, 1785, and John Jay to Samuel Shaw, June 20, 1785, MHS, *Papers of Maj. Samuel Shaw,* "Samuel Shaw Letterbook,"

65. Samuel Shaw to John Jay, New York, January 30, 1786, MHS, *Papers of Maj. Samuel Shaw,* "Samuel Shaw Letterbook." Shaw's primary responsibility was to relay as much commercial intelligence as he could back to Jay.

66. Chinese consumers preferred Korean or Manchurian ginseng to the American variety, which Chinese apothecaries relegated to low-grade use. American ginseng never constituted a large proportion (by value) of the goods U.S. merchants sold in China.

67. Joseph Fletcher, "Sino-Russian Relations, 1800–62," in Denis Twitchett and John K. Fairbank, eds., *The Cambridge History of China,* vol. 10, part 1 (Cambridge: Cambridge University Press, 1978), 318, 321–323. Joseph Fletcher, "Ch'ing Inner Asia *c.* 1800," in Twitchett and Fairbank, eds., *The Cambridge History of China,* vol. 10, part 1, 39–41. The first permanent Russian establishment was at Kodiak Island in 1784, east of Unalaska, where Cook and Ledyard had encountered the Russians. Aleksandr Baranov, whom Cook met, was manager there. As Kodiak's supply dwindled, the Russians relocated to Sitka, which became the main Russian foothold in Alaska. The Russian-American Company, created in 1799, aimed to sell Alaskan furs to China. It combined Kamchatkan and Alaskan trading ventures and used forced Aleutian labor. Though it took two years for Alaskan fur to reach the Sino-Russian land crossing at Kiakhta, American ships could reach Canton from Alaska in five months and at a fraction of the cost. (Russian authorities falsely believed that the Amur River—which reached deep into Manchuria from the Pacific—was not navigable by oceangoing vessels and never developed a proper sea link between their Siberian and Alaskan holdings.) Thus, American merchants sold supplies to the Russian outposts in Alaska and marketed Russian furs in Canton.

68. The fur trade was halted at Canton in November 1791. Fredrick W. Howay, ed., *Voyages of the "Columbia" to the Northwest Coast 1787–1790 and 1790–1793* (Boston: MHS, 1941), 134.
69. "Some Account of a Voyage to the South Sea's in 1776–1777–1778 Written by David Samwell Surgeon of the Discovery," in J. C. Beaglehole, ed., *The Voyage of the* Resolution *and* Discovery, part 2, Monday October 26, 1778 (On Unalaska) (Cambridge: Cambridge University Press, 1967), 1141–1142.
70. "???" in Beaglehole, *Voyage of the* Resolution *and* Discovery, 1404.
71. Nor was Ledyard first. While writing, he had an unauthorized and anonymous account in front of him, which had been published in London in 1781. Fredric W. Howay has attributed it to Lt. John Rickman, though Ledyard himself was once considered the author of the 1781 edition. James Kenneth Munford, ed., *John Ledyard's Journal of Captain Cook's Last Voyage* (Corvallis: Oregon State University Press, 1963), x.
72. Zug, *American Traveler*, 85–88; J. C. Beaglehole, *The Life of Captain James Cook* (London: Hakluyt Society, 1974), 631; Edward G. Gray, *The Making of John Ledyard: Empire and Ambition in the Life of an Early American Traveler* (New Haven: Yale University Press, 2007), 48–50.
73. Munford, *Ledyard's Journal*, 70.
74. Mss. Sparks 112, 99–100, as cited in Munford, *Ledyard's Journal*, xlvi.
75. Howay, *Voyages of the "Columbia,"* vi.
76. *Columbia, Papers Relating to the Second Voyage*, August–November 1790, Folder 1 (n.d.), MHS, Reel P 210, frames 28–31.
77. Wadsorth Correspondence, January 12, 1785, as cited in East, *Business Enterprise*, 253.
78. Joseph Barrell to Samuel Blachley Webb, Boston, October 11, 1787, in Worthington Chauncey Ford, ed., *Family Letters of Samuel Blachley Webb, 1764–1807* (New York: Cambridge University Press, 1912), 350, as cited in Anne E. Bentley, "The Columbia-Washington Medal," *Massachusetts Historical Society Proceedings*, vol. 101 (1989), 124.
79. Bentley, "The Columbia-Washington Medal," 123.
80. Joseph Barrell to John Adams, Boston, November 14, 1787, Adams Papers, MHS, as cited in Bentley, "The Columbia-Washington Medal," 120.
81. *Pennsylvania Packet and Daily Advertiser*, October 8, 1787, as cited in Bentley, "The Columbia-Washington Medal," 121.
82. Bentley, "The Columbia-Washington Medal," 123–126; Letter to Nathaniel Barrell, in Jensen, *Documentary History of the Ratification of the Constitution*, vol. 5: *Massachusetts*, 492.
83. Nellie B. Pipes, ed., *The Memorial of John Mears to the House of Commons Respecting the Capture of Vessels in Nootka Sound* (Portland, OR: Metropolitan Press, 1933), ii. See also F. W. Howay, ed., *The Dixon-Meares Controversy* (Toronto: Ryerson Press, 1929), and William R. Manning, *Nootka Sound Controversy* (Washington, DC: Government Printing Office, 1905).

84. "Robert Haswell's Log of the First Voyage of the 'Columbia,'" in Howay, *Voyages of the "Columbia,"* 84–85; Robert Gray to Joseph Barrell, Nootka Sound, July 13, 1789, in Howay, *Voyages of the "Columbia,"* 123.

85. *Columbian Centinel,* August 11, 1790. Emphasis in original. Both Gray and Kendrick implicitly acknowledged a British claim to the region as well by referring to Northern California—and perhaps also land further north—as "New Albion." The phrase was Francis Drake's, who had coined it in his raids on the Spanish Pacific in the sixteenth century. "John Kendrick's Instructions to Robert Gray on Board Ship Columbia Lying in Britts harbour in falklands Islans," February 1788, in Howay, *Voyages of the "Columbia,"* 114. Also, Robert Gray to Joseph Barrell, Nootka Sound, July 13, 1789, in Howay, *Voyages of the "Columbia,"* 122. See also Warren L. Cook, *Flood Tide of Empire: Spain and the Pacific Northwest, 1543–1819* (New Haven: Yale University Press, 1973), 146–199, 250–270.

86. The Nootka Sound Convention eventually permitted settlement of territories in northern California and above it by declaring the area open to all nations. In 1792 Spain held fortifications as far north as Vancouver Island in Canada (Santa Cruz de Nutka [1789–1795]). The Russians also claimed Nootka but had yet to venture so far south. It is unclear whether Gray was aware of the Convention when he sighted the Columbia River in 1792.

87. Edward G. Porter reported that Gray, on formally naming the Columbia River, planted coins under a pine tree there on May 19, 1792, though he gave no evidence for this. Porter's account is not supported by John Boit's log, nor in the fragment of the official *Columbia* log covering the river's discovery. Boit did remark that the river mouth "would be a fine place to sett up a *Factory.*" Gray's log did not mention claiming or settling on the river, though it did mention that on the afternoon of May 15, "Captain Gray and Mr. Hoskins, in the jolly-boat, went on shore to take a short view of the country." That same day, Boit claims he "landed abrest the Ship with Capt. Gray to view the Country and take possession." The words "and take possession" were inserted later into the manuscript with a different pen. The several claims that a possession-taking ceremony took place were made years after the fact and are unsubstantiated by any evidence from 1792. *Massachusetts Historical Society Proceedings,* 2nd series, vol. 7 (1891), 420; "Remarks in the Ship Columbia's voyage from Boston, (on a Voyage, round the Globe) by John Boit," in Howay, *Voyages of the "Columbia,"* 399; "Remnant of the Official Log of the 'Columbia,'" in Howay, *Voyages of the "Columbia,"* 437; "Remarks in the Ship Columbia's voyage from Boston," in Howay, *Voyages of the "Columbia,"* 398, 398nn3–4.

88. *Columbian Centinel,* August 11, 1790, as cited in Howay, *Voyages of the "Columbia,"* 145–146. Cf. *Boston Gazette,* August 16, 1790.

89. *Massachusetts Historical Society Proceedings,* 2nd series, vol. 7 (1891), 418.

90. *Boston Gazette,* August 16, 1790. Cf. *Herald of Freedom,* August 10, 1790.

91. Robert Gray to John Kendrick, Canton, February 4, 1790, in Howay, *Voyages of the "Columbia,"* 135.
92. Robert Gray to John Kendrick, Canton, January 29, 1790, in Howay, *Voyages of the "Columbia,"* 133.
93. Thomas Randall to Joseph Barrell, New York, August 24, 1787. MHS Columbia Papers, 1787–1817, Ms. N-1017.
94. "Sham sale" was Kendrick's phrase. John Kendrick to Joseph Barrell, Macau, March 28, 1792, in Howay, *Voyages of the "Columbia,"* 471, xii–xiii.

3. Commerce in a World at War

1. Michael Fry, *The Dundas Despotism* (Edinburgh: Edinburgh University Press, 1992), 209.
2. Hansard, vol. 33, col. 582 as cited in Fry, *Dundas Despotism,* 211,
3. The Danes had previously occupied Hamburg, removing that city-state from the roster of neutrals as well.
4. U.S. overseas trade quickly bounced back from the two setbacks in this period: the Quasi War, 1798–1800, and the embargo of 1808.
5. Austria and the United States, respectively.
6. Maurice Dupont and Etienne Taillemite, *Les guerres navales françaises du Moyen Age à la guerre du Golfe* (Paris: S.P.M., 1995), 131–226.
7. Michael Broers, *Europe under Napoleon, 1799–1815* (London: Arnold, 1996), 38. For Bordeaux, see Paul Butel, "Le port de Bordeaux . . . ," *Révue de l'Histoire Moderne et Contemporaine* 19 (1972): 128–148, esp. 129.
8. Ernest Labrousse and Fernand Braudel, *Histoire économique et sociale de la France,* vol. 3 (Paris: Presses universitaires de France, 1970–1982), 102.
9. F. E. Melvin, *Napoleon's Navigation System: A Study of Trade Control during the Continental Blockade* (New York: Appleton, 1919), 48.
10. Nicole Charbonnel, *Commerce et course sous la Révolution et le Consulat à La Rochelle* (Paris: Presses Universitaires de France, 1977), 36–40, 45–46.
11. Broers, *Europe under Napoleon,* 39, 145–146.
12. N. A. M. Rodger, *The Command of the Ocean: A Naval History of Britain, 1649–1815* (London: Allen Lane, 2004), 549. The incident remains a point of ire for Danes.
13. The army grew before and during the Peninsular War (1808–1812) into a force capable of opposing the French directly. Less conservative numbers give the British army at 36,000 men and French army at 850,000 men. Fry, *Dundas Despotism,* 231.
14. Fry, *Dundas Despotism,* 199, 219 passim; E. A. Benians, J. Holland Rose, and A. P. Newton, eds., *Cambridge History of the British Empire,* vol. 2: *The New Empire* (Cambridge: Cambridge University Press, 1940), 128. Piers Mackesy argued that trade was "the dominant factor in Britain's East and West Indian strategy." Piers Mackesy, *The War in the Mediterranean, 1803–1810* (New York: Longmans, Green, 1957), 8. Contrast Michael Duffy, "World-

Wide War and British Expansion, 1793–1815," in Peter J. Marshall, ed., *The Oxford History of the British Empire: The Eighteenth Century* (New York: Oxford University Press, 1998), 184–207. See also John Ehrman, *The Younger Pitt: The Consuming Struggle* (London: Constable, 1996); V. T. Harlow, *Founding of the Second British Empire, 1763–1793*, vol. 2 (New York: Longmans, Green, 1964); C. A. Bayly, *Imperial Meridian: The British Empire and the World, 1780–1830* (London: Longman, 1989); Christopher D. Hall, *British Strategy in the Napoleonic War, 1803–1815* (Manchester: Manchester University Press, 1992); Cyril Northcote Parkinson, *War in the Eastern Seas, 1793–1815* (London: Allen & Unwin, 1954); M. E. Yapp, *Strategies of British India, Britain, Iran, and Afghanistan, 1798–1850* (Oxford: Clarendon Press, 1980).

15. Fry, *Dundas Despotism,* 190.

16. Duffy, "World-Wide War," 189n11. The Caribbean figure may include landed property and slaves; the East India figure does not appear to.

17. P. J. Marshall, "The Eighteenth-Century Empire," in *"A Free though Conquering People": Eighteenth-Century Britain and Its Empire* (Burlington, VT; Variorum, 2003), 189.

18. Duffy, "World-Wide War," 187.

19. A modest British force also took Gorée in West Africa in 1799. Duffy, "World-Wide War," 190–191; Fry, *Dundas Despotism,* 227.

20. Alfred Thayer Mahan, *The Influence of Sea Power upon the French Revolution and Empire, 1793–1812* (London: Sampson, Low, Marston, 1892), 121. Cape forces attacked Buenos Aires on June 27, 1806. The British withdrew on August 12. London reinforcements, originally intended for Buenos Aires, invested Montevideo on February 3, 1807. The British expected to be greeted as liberators; creoles saw them as invaders. After a second attempt on Buenos Aires on July 5, 1807, the British gave up the Rio de la Plata, agreeing to evacuate within ten days of July 7. Alan Frost, *The Global Reach of Empire: Britain's Maritime Expansion in the Indian and Pacific Oceans, 1764–1815* (Victoria, Australia: Miegunyah Press, 2003), 260–265. Various plans to attack the Spanish American colonies were considered. See, for example, Curtis to Spencer, Cape of Good Hope, December 19, 1800, in Herbert W. Richmond, ed., *Private Papers of George, Second Earl Spencer,* vol. 4 (London: Navy Records Society, 1924), 243; John Lynch, "British Policy and Spanish America, 1783–1808," *Journal of Latin American History* 1 (1969): 1–30; William W. Kaufmann, *British Policy and the Independence of Latin America, 1804–1828* (New Haven: Yale University Press, 1951), chapters 1–3; Charles Esdaile, "Contradictions in the Implementation of British Grand Strategy, 1808–1814," in *Consortium on Revolutionary Europe 1750–1850: Proceedings,* vol. 19, part 1 (1989), 544–559; C. K. Webster, ed., *Britain and the Independence of Latin America, 1812–1830,* vol. 2 (London: Oxford University Press, 1938), 309–316.

21. "Mémoires généraux," CAOM C^2, 1 17, 326.

22. A second Mahé, the French capital of the Seychelles, capitulated in 1794 and 1804. Guy Lionnet, "Les effets de la Révolution française aux Seychelles," in

Claude Wanquet and Benoît Jullien, eds., *Révolution française et océan indién* (Paris: L'Harmattan, 1996), 192.

23. "Extract from a Proclamation of General Dumoriez to the Batavians," February 1793, in George McCall Theal, *Records of the Cape Colony from February 1793 to December 1796. Copied for the Cape Government from the Manuscript Documents in the Public Record Office, London* (London: William Clowes, 1897), 3.

24. Pitt to Spencer, Park Place, October 1801, in *Spencer Papers*, vol. 4, 304; Fry, *Dundas Despotism*, 192, 212; J. P. W. Ehrman and Anthony Smith, "Pitt, William (1749–1806)," *DNB*, accessed May 10, 2005; Cyril Matheson, *The Life of Henry Dundas, First Viscount Melville, 1742–1811* (London: Constable, 1933), 228. Dundas was particularly interested in the Cape, in part because of an erstwhile romantic connection to Lady Anne Barnard, the de facto first lady of the Cape. A. B. Grosart, "Barnard, Lady Anne (1750–1825)," rev. Stanley Trapido, *DNB*, accessed May 8, 2006; *The letters of Lady Anne Barnard written to Henry Dundas from the Cape and elsewhere, 1793–1803, together with her journal of a tour into the interior and certain other letters*, ed. A. M. Lewin Robinson (Cape Town, 1973); Robert Simple, *Walks and Sketches at the Cape of Good Hope: To which is subjoined a journey from Cape Town to Blettenberg's Bay* (London: 1803), iii. Not all thought the Cape worthwhile. Curtis, commanding naval forces in the First British Occupation, declaimed it "physically impossible[;] it can ever be fruitful or produce articles of any consideration," such as sugar or coffee, and it was thought less than ideal for the navy. Curtis to Spencer, January 13, 1800, Cape of Good Hope, in *Spencer Papers*, vol. 4, 207.

25. George McCall Theal, *History of South Africa under the Administration of the Dutch East India Company, 1652 to 1795* (London: Swan Sonnenschein, 1897), map 6, 352.

26. Roland Thorne, "Hobart, Robert, Fourth Earl of Buckinghamshire (1760–1816)," *DNB*, accessed April 20, 2006.

27. Sir John Dalrymple to Earl Spencer, August 23, 1799, in Herbert W. Richmond, ed., *Private Papers of George, Second Earl Spencer*, vol. 3 (London: Navy Records Society, 1923), 20. Britain took Padang, on the west coast of Sumatra, and Ambon, the principle entrepôt in the Molucca spice group. The British also besieged Ternate, in the northern Moluccas, which fell in 1799. Britain took Amboyna in February 1796 and Banda a month later. A few cities on the Java Sea remained Dutch: Banjarmasin on Borneo, Palembang on the Sumatran east coast, western Timor, Makassar (present-day Ujungpandang, on Sulawesi), and Java itself. Britain occupied the Minahasa Peninsula, northern Sulawesi, in 1801. Minahasa remained under British control until 1816. Attacks on Amboyna and Banda were from Company forces; it is unclear which other attacks were by Company or Crown forces.

28. Wellesley gave up the conquest of Java "with considerable reluctance." Marquess Wellesley to his Excellency Vice-Admiral Rainier, Fort William, Octo-

ber 22, 1800, in Montgomery Martin, ed., *The Despatches, Minutes, and Correspondence of the Marquis Wellesley, K.G. during his Administration in India,* vol. 2 (London: John Murray, 1836–1837), 401. Dundas ordered the Company to attack the Mascarenes on October 15, 1793, with 5,000 men and a naval squadron, but this decision was put off when Lord Conwallis returned to Britain in February 1794 and advised against it. C. H. Philips, *The East India Company, 1784–1834* (Manchester: Manchester University Press, 1940), 88–89. Wellesley later considered a second attack around 1801 but was dissuaded by the refusal of Admiral Rainier, who was commanding the East Indies Squadron, to participate without specific orders from home. Curtis thought no partisan force could be expected to support the British side, necessitating more British troops, and he was also chagrined to relinquish forces at the Cape to the mission. *Spencer Papers,* vol. 4, 159–160, and Spencer to Christian, December 23, 1798, in *Spencer Papers,* vol. 4, 189. Rainier may have been something of a ditherer; he certainly did not understand the need for action and sacrificed activity to the concentration of his forces and a defensive posture at most turns, when in fact there was very little to defend against between 1796 at 1805. The privateering would have been best dealt with not through enforced convoys, but by destroying the privateers' base, Ile de France.

29. Chinese forces repulsed the latter. Hosea Ballou Morse, *The Chronicles of the East India Company Trading to China, 1635–1834,* vol. 2 (Oxford: Clarendon Press, 1926–1929), 370; "Extract of Letter from the Supra cargoes at Canton to the Secret Committee, 29 March 1802. Received per Duke of Buccleugh [a ship name] the 29th August 1802," OIOC G/12/195, f210. See also Herbert J. Wood, "England, China, and the Napoleonic Wars," *Pacific Historical Review* (1940): 139–156.

30. Some claimed the Cape Colony was too costly to keep in 1802. This is debatable. L. F. C. Turner, "The Cape of Good Hope and the Anglo-French Conflict, 1797–1806," *Historical Studies Australia and New Zealand* 9 (1961): 368–78, as cited in Duffy, "World-Wide War," 200n37.

31. Britain had guaranteed Portugal's neutrality at Amiens, but had been eyeing its colonies at least since 1804. Broers, *Europe under Napoleon,* 38. For the fall of the Mascarenes, more storied in French than in English, see Roger Lepelley, *La fin d'un empire: Les derniers jours de l'Isle de France et de l'Isle Bonaparte 1809–1810* (Paris: Economica, 2000); Parkinson, *War in the Eastern Seas,* 297, 306.

32. French proposals for the Philippines, made around the time of the retrocession of Louisiana, may have been inspired by the retrocession or bruited about as an alternative. Frost, *Global Reach of Empire;* Captain J. Colnett to Spencer, November 1800, in *Spencer Papers,* vol. 4, 293–294. Colnett had been involved in trading in the Pacific Northwest, Hawaii, and China, and so his imagination tended to drift in this direction. Andrew C. F. David, "Colnett, James (*bap.* 1753, *d.* 1806)," *DNB,* accessed September 2007.

33. Naval and Colonial Minister to Citoyen Robert, Paris, Le 6 Brumaire An 6 [October 27, 1797], CAOM B 236 180.

34. Benians, Rose, and Newton, eds., *Cambridge History of the British Empire,* vol. 2, 167.

35. Fry, *Dundas Despotism,* 158, citing National Library of Ireland, "Dundas Papers," 55, 182.

36. Matheson, *Life of Henry Dundas,* 201.

37. Fry, *Dundas Despotism,* 188.

38. Before Fry's revisions, J. W. Fortescue, in *History of the British Army* (London: Macmillan, 1899–1930), set much of the tone, advocating Grenville's preference for fighting France in Europe and criticizing Dundas's interest in overseas colonies (later defended by Mahan), which he saw not as affording the war in Europe but at the expense of it.

39. Ehrman, *The Younger Pitt,* vol. 2, 269; Fry, *Dundas Despotism,* 191. The proposed operation, in 1793, was to support Royalists on St. Malo. The Duke of Richmond backed it and the concentration of British forces in France. He did not want to "fritter away" troops "in french Flanders, and the West Indies, in the Mauritius and the Mediterranean and in Brittany" but instead "terminate this War." (Richmond to Dundas, July 1, 1793, B.L. Loan Ms 57 (Bathurst), vol. 107, as cited in Ehrman, *The Younger Pitt,* vol. 2, 268. Opportunities to support Royalists remained thin. Sir Sidney Smith was pleased to discover "evidence of the existence" of Royalists in March 1796, which meant that prior to that the Admiralty was unsure there was a coherent Royalist force in Normandy. Sidney Smith to Spencer, *Diamond,* off Jersey, March 15, 1796, in Julian S. Corbett, ed., *Private Papers of George, Second Earl Spencer,* vol. 1 (London: Navy Records Society, 1913), 238.

40. Dundas to Spencer, Somerset Place, March 24, 1796, in *Spencer Papers,* vol. 1, 240. George John Spencer served as First Lord of the Admiralty from 1794 to 1801, adding the Admiralty's views to those of the foreign and war offices.

41. James Falkner, "D'Auvergne, Philippe (*bap.* 1754, *d.* 1816)," *DNB,* accessed September 2, 2007. The Dundas-d'Auvergne correspondence may be found at PRO WO/1/921–926.

42. Edward Ingram, ed., *Two Views of British India* (Bath: Adams & Dart, 1970), 206. Dundas's defense is in Hansard, vol. 35, cols. 1072–1073.

43. Dundas to Pitt, July 9. 1794 PRO 30/8/157 f 176, as cited in Duffy, "World-Wide War," 190n13.

44. Ehrman, *The Younger Pitt,* vol. 1, 465; Fry, *Dundas Despotism,* 220. Mornington also maintained links to Grenville. C. A. Bayly, "Wellesley, Richard, Marquess Wellesley (1760–1842)," *DNB,* accessed May 8, 2005. Dundas previously reached out to Hobart during Sir John Shore's tenure in Calcutta. Fry, *Dundas Despotism,* 220. Hobart's resentment of Mornington's succession to the governor-generalship may have informed their debate on the East India bill in 1813. On Mornington and trade in the 1790s, Amales Tripathi,

Trade and Finance in the Bengal Presidency, 1793–1833 (Calcutta: Oxford University Press, 1979), 38, 50. The Mornington-Dundas relationship was complex. See Iris Butler, *The Eldest Brother: The Marquess Welelsley 1760–1842* (London: Hodder and Stoughton, 1973); Ingram, *Two Views*; Fry, *Dundas Despotism*.

45. Fry, *Dundas Despotism*, 198.

46. Henry Dundas to the Chairman, April 2, 1800, in *Papers respecting the Trade between India and Europe* (London: E. Cox & Son, April 1802), 7.

47. George Smith to Henry Dundas, November 26, 1786; Ehrman, *The Younger Pitt*, vol. 1, 413, citing Harlow, *Second British Empire*, vol. 2, 556.

48. P. J. Cain and A. G. Hopkins, *British Imperialism, 1688–2000* (New York: Longman, 2001), 90.

49. "Notices sur l'Inde," Anonymous, 1800 or 1801, NAF 9374 5.

50. Tripathi, *Trade and Finance*, 75.

51. Board of Control's Secret Drafts, October 2 and October 31, 1799, cited in Philips, *The East India Company*, 101.

52. Rayford Logan, *Diplomatic Relations between the United States and Haiti, 1776–1891* (Chapel Hill: University of North Carolina Press, 1941); David Geggus, *Slavery, War, Trade, and Revolution: The British Occupation of St. Domingue, 1793–1798* (New York: Oxford University Press, 1982); Laurent Dubois, *Avengers of the New World: The Story of the Haitian Revolution* (Cambridge, MA: Belknap Press, 2004). L'Ouverture got production up to two-thirds of prewar levels with forced labor.

53. By 1805, the recaptured Dutch Guianas were producing more cotton for British mills than the whole of the British West Indies. Duffy, "World-Wide War," 192.

54. John Wolffe, "Wilberforce, William (1759–1833)," *DNB*, accessed May 10, 2005; Brian A. Smith, *A Guide to the Manuscript Sources for the Study of St. Helena* (Todmorden, UK: Altair Publishing, 1995); Barbara George, *St. Helena: The Chinese Connection: The History of Chinese Indentured Labourers on St. Helena, 1810–1836 and Beyond* (Bristol, UK: privately printed, 2002).

55. Parkinson, *War in the Eastern Seas*, 22. Amboyna's stock of splces, while not large enough to alter the Company's fortunes, were enough to enrich Rear Admiral Rainier, who commanded the expedition to the Moluccas in 1796. Personal gain seems to have been one of Rainier's motives. Parkinson, *War in the Eastern Seas*, 94–95. For cinnamon see Alicia Schrikker, *Dutch and British Colonial Intervention in Sri Lanka, 1780–1815: Expansion and Reform* (Leiden: Brill, 2007).

56. Fry, *Dundas Despotism*, 221; Parkinson, *War in the Eastern Seas*, 80.

57. "Notices sur l'Inde," Anonymous, 1800 or 1801, NAF 9374, 15; C. Northcote Parkinson, *Edward Pellew, Viscount Exmouth* (London: Methuen & Co., 1934), 328, as cited in Duffy, "World-Wide War," 200. Indian debt rose from £11 million to £28 million. Tripathi, *Trade and Finance*, 88.

58. Some private traders did bring Javan goods to Calcutta.

59. Duffy, "World-Wide War," 202, table 9.2.
60. Michael Fry, "Dundas, Robert Saunders, second Viscount Melville (1771–1851)," *DNB,* accessed March 30, 2006.
61. Robert Dundas to Liverpool, July 13, 1810, Melville Castle Add. Mss. 38245 f131, 133. Indeed, he complained again the same month of Minto's letter being "a great deal *longer* than necessary" (f143, emphasis in original). Minto's prolixity preceded him. Michael Duffy, "Kynynmound, Gilbert Elliot Murray, first earl of Minto (1751–1814)," *DNB,* accessed September 3, 2007.
62. Sam A. Mustafa, *Merchants and Migrations: Germans and Americans in Connection, 1776–1835* (Burlington, VT: Ashgate, 2001), 206–207; Spencer C. Tucker and Frank T. Reuter, *Injured Honor: The Chesapeake-Leopard Affair, June 22, 1807* (Annapolis, MD: Naval Institute Press, 1996).
63. Edward Parry and Charles Grant, Chairs, to Directors, East India House, October 14, 1807, OIOC H/494, 51.
64. Parry and Grant to Baring, East India House, October 1808, OIOC H/494, 313.
65. Baring represented the City Interest's gradual defection from the Shipping Interest at this time. Tripathi, *Trade and Finance,* 95.
66. OIOC H/494, 5–333.
67. Edward Parry and Charles Grant, Chairs, to Directors, East India House, October 14, 1807, OIOC H/494, 37.
68. Edward Parry and Charles Grant, Chairs, to Directors, East India House. October 14, 1807, OIOC H/494, 59–61. Emphasis in original.
69. Parry and Grant to Baring, East India House, October 1808, OIOC H/494, 227, 229, 233, 237.
70. Edward Parry and Charles Grant to the Directors, on private trade, East India House, London, October 14, 1807, OIOC H/494, 15, 83.
71. Hansard, vol. 25, col. 703; Fry, *Dundas Despotism,* 291.
72. Alan Schom, *Napoleon Bonaparte* (New York: HarperCollins, 1997).
73. Jean Mistler, "Hambourg sous l'occupation française: Observations au sujet du Blocus continental," *Francia* 1 (1973): 453, 455.
74. It is unclear whether this increase was related to the Walcheren campaign. British customs data discussed here and below are from François Crouzet, *L'économie britannique et le blocus continental (1806–1813),* vol. 2 (Paris: Presses Universitaires de France, 1958), 890–891. B. R. Mitchell, *British Historical Statistics* (New York: Cambridge University Press, 1988), gives data for tea but not for Indian cloth.
75. Broers, *Europe under Napoleon,* 218. See also M. Senkowska-Gluck, "Pouvoire et société en Illyrie napoleonienne," *Révue de l'Institut Napoleon* 136 (1980): 57–78, esp. 61; P. Pisani, *La Dalmatie de 1797 a 1815* (Paris, 1893), 359–360, 234, 373, 385; M. Senkowska-Gluck, "Íllyrie sous la domination napoléonienne, 1809–1813," *Acta Politica Historica* 41 (1980): 99–121, 116; and Frank J. Bundy, *The Administration of the Illyrian Provinces of the French Empire, 1809–1813* (New York: Garland, 1987), 333–380. Quotes from Bundy on 380, 356, 355. Smuggling continued in

Italy as well. John A. Davis, *Naples and Napoleon: Southern Italy and the European Revolutions, 1780–1860* (New York: Oxford University Press, 2006), 145–149.

76. Mistler, "Hambourg sous l'occupation française," 455. The uptick in re-exports in 1809 includes an increase in traffic with Sweden as well.

77. Crouzet's data do not allow re-exports to be cross-referenced by good and destination.

78. Such a division, performed for coffee and sugar, does produce figures that are substantially less volatile, the standard deviations being 42 percent and 30 percent for sugar and 28 percent and 55 percent for coffee, with the same yearly division.

4. America's Re-export Boom

1. Robert E. Lipsey, "U.S. Foreign Trade and the Balance of Payments, 1800–1913," in Stanley L. Engerman and Robert E. Gallman, eds., *The Cambridge Economic History of the United States,* vol. 2 (Cambridge: Cambridge University Press, 2000), 687; Timothy Pitkin, *A Statistical View of the Commerce of the United States of America . . .* (New Haven: Durrie & Peck, 1835), 145.

2. P. J. Marshall, writing that "by the 1790s Britain had to a very large extent achieved her long-standing objective of becoming the principal emporium for American and Asian goods for Europe as a whole," disagrees but gives no quantitative evidence. P. J. Marshall, "The Eighteenth-Century Empire," in *"A Free though Conquering People": Eighteenth-Century Britain and Its Empire* (Burlington, VT: Variorum, 2003), 191.

3. Cathy Matson, "The Revolution, Constitution, and New Nation," in Stanley L. Engerman and Robert E. Gallman, eds., *Cambridge Economic History of the United States,* vol. 1 (Cambridge: Cambridge University Press, 2000), 395.

4. Douglass North, *Economic Growth of the United States, 1790 to 1860* (Englewood Cliffs, NJ: Prentice Hall, 1961), 221, 228.

5. *Putnam,* Nathaniel Bowditch, Master, "Remarks on the N.W. Coast of Sumatra," November 1802–December 1803, PEM, Salem East India Marine Society Journals No. 20, 608–610. On rigged scales: Charles Oscar Paullin, *Diplomatic Negotiations of American Naval Officers* (Baltimore: Johns Hopkins University Press, 1912), 347.

6. The modern names of these places are not always evident, even with longitudinal and latitudinal coordinates, but Bowditch's "Sooso" is probably Susoh, his "Tangar-Tangar" may be Tanjongbunga, and his "Mingin" is probably Manggeng, all in present-day Aceh, Indonesia. Bowditch noted that gold dust bought silver dollars at a ratio of 1 to 13.5, comparing unfavorably with the U.S. bimetallic peg of 1 to 15. *Putnam,* Nathaniel Bowditch, Master, November 1802–December 1803, "Remarks on the N.W. Coast of Sumatra," PEM, Salem East India Marine Society Journals, No. 20, 608–610.

7. *ASP,* passim. Compiled from import and export data from annual totals for years indicated. Import data for the years 1791–1792, 1792–1793, and 1793–1794 are lacking.

8. Closer parsing would be nearly impossible, since consignments might be "signed for" at the customs house by another merchant.

9. *ASP,* passim.

10. Sam A. Mustafa, *Merchants and Migrations: Germans and Americans in Connection, 1776–1835* (Burlington, VT: Ashgate, 2001) 183.

11. *ASP,* passim.

12. Stuart Weems Bruchey, *Robert Oliver, Merchant of Baltimore, 1783–1819* (Baltimore: Johns Hopkins University Press, 1956), 237.

13. Ewer to Dundas, May 31, 1801, in John Bastin, ed., *The British in West Sumatra (1695–1825)* (Kuala Lumpur: University of Malaya Press, 1965), 115; John Bastin, *The Changing Balance of the Early Southeast Asian Pepper Trade* (Kuala Lumpur: University of Malaya in Kuala Lumpur, Department of History, Papers on Southeast Asian Subjects, 1960), 45.

14. John Bastin, *Essays on Indonesian History* (Singapore: Eastern Universities Press, 1961), 42.

15. Fort Marlborough to Court. September 29, 1806, in Bastin, *British in West Sumatra,* 133.

16. Bastin, *Essays on Indonesian History,* 41, 47–79.

17. Court to Fort Marlborough, February 24, 1806, in Bastin, *British in West Sumatra,* 130.

18. Court to Bengal, July 30, 1806, in Bastin, *British in West Sumatra,* 131–132.

19. This could have been due to high Company freight rates or to the "Concern," which monopolized trade at Bencoolen. The Concern may have seen the shipment of pepper to London as a way to overbill the Company for its members' profit. More research on this is needed. See Ewer to Mornington, April 8, 1800, Bencoolen, in Bastin, *British in West Sumatra,* 104.

20. Court to Bengal, July 30, 1806, in Bastin, *British in West Sumatra,* 131–132.

21. Bastin, *Changing Balance,* 48. See also Lee Kam Hing, *The Sultanate of Aceh: Relations with the British, 1760–1824* (Kuala Lumpur: Oxford University Press, 1995); James Duncan Phillips, *Pepper and Pirates: Adventures in the Sumatra Pepper Trade of Salem* (Boston: Houghton Mifflin, 1949); George Granville Putnam, *Salem Vessels and Their Voyages: A History of the Pepper Trade with the Island of Sumatra* (Salem, MA: Essex Institute, 1922).

22. For the tea trade, see Robert Gardella, *Harvesting Mountains: Fujian and the China Tea Trade, 1757–1937* (Berkeley: University of California Press, 1994), and Robert Gardella, "The Antebellum Canton Tea Trade: Recent Perspectives," *American Neptune* 48, no. 4 (Fall 1988): 261–270.

23. *ASP,* passim.

24. *ASP,* passim; Simon Schama, *A History of Britain,* vol. 3: *The Fate of Empire, 1776–2000* (New York, Hyperion, 2002), 108. For the resurgence in tea drinking see Robert C. Alberts, *Golden Voyage: The Life and Times of*

William Bingham, 1752–1804 (Boston: Houghton-Mifflin, 1969), 161, 313; Thomas Twining, *Travels in America 100 Years Ago* (New York: Harper & Brothers, 1894), 30, 34–35; and T. A. B. Corley, "Twining, Richard (1749–1824)," *DNB*, accessed January 11, 2006]. Dermigny claims U.S. re-exports began with the fall of the Orangist government in the Netherlands in 1795, though he does not base this claim on U.S. customs data. Louis Dermigny, *La China et l'occident: Le Commerce à Canton au XXIIIe Siècle*, vol. 3 (Paris: S.E.V.P.E.N., 1964), 1163. This claim appears to have become widespread. Elias Derby does seem to have re-exported tea to the Netherlands in 1799. Richard H. McKey Jr., "Elias Hasket Derby, Merchant of Salem, Massachusetts, 1739–1799" (unpublished PhD diss., Clark University, 1961). By 1801, Thorndike noted Holland as a good market for tea re-exports (I. Thorndike to Winslow, Beverly, November 8, 1801, Thorndike Papers, vol. 6, Baker Business Library, Harvard Business School). But large-scale tea re-exports first appear in U.S. customs records for the year ending September 30, 1800.

25. *ASP*, passim; Galabert, Mémoire sur l'Inde An 11., CARAN AF/IV/1211.
26. Francois Crouzet, *L'économie britannique et le blocus continental (1806–1813)*, vol. 2 (Paris: Presses Universitaires de France, 1958), 890; *ASP,* passim. The year's supply of tea that the Company kept in London contributed to this stability, though U.S. merchants maintained back stock as well. Comparison of U.S. and U.K. wholesale tea prices would shed light on the abilities of U.S. and U.K. merchants to re-export tea. This requires further research.
27. Papers respecting the supply of Tea and other Indian and China Goods, to the British Colonies on the Continent of North America, May 1824, John Richardson, Esqr., a Member of the Legislative Assembly, of Lower Canada, to John Inglis, Esqr., Member of the Court, of Directors of the India Company, Montreal, September 2, 1822, OIOC H/706, 1.
28. Captain Weltden, late Commander of a Ship in the East India Company's Service to the Chairman and Deputy Chairman of the East India Company, Kensington, December 23, 1823, OIOC H/706, 14–15.
29. Extract of a communication from the Montreal Committee of Trade to James Stuart, Esquire, March 8, 1823, OIOC H/706, 84.
30. Quebec, January 13, 1824, Remarks upon the Tea Trade of Canada, John Richardson, Esqr., OIOC H/706, 30–31.
31. Papers respecting the supply of Tea and other Indian and China Goods, to the British Colonies on the Continent of North America, May 1824, "Schedule of the importation of Tea and Coffee at the Port of Quebec for 9 years from 1814 to 1822," OIOC H/706, 89; Julian Gwyn, "Comparative Economic Advantage: Nova Scotia and New England, 1720s–1860s," in Stephen Hornsby and John G. Reid, eds., *New England and the Maritime Provinces: Connections and Comparisons* (Montreal: McGill–Queen's University Press, 2005), 116–121.

32. Hoh-cheung Mui and Lorna H. Mui, *The Management of Monopoly: A Study of the East India Company's Conduct of Its Tea Trade, 1784–1833* (Vancouver: University of British Columbia Press, 1984), 5–9.

33. *ASP,* passim. U.S. merchants brought home crafts from Oceania as well; these remain some of the best-preserved Pacific Island artifacts from the period before and during intensive Western contact. All dollar values here represent purchase prices in Asia, not sale prices in the United States or abroad.

34. Alexander Baring to Sir Francis Baring, Philadelphia, May 12, 1801, ING Baring, 1.

35. Israel Thorndike's instructions to William Leech, *Cyrus,* Master, July 9, 1800, Thorndike Papers, vol. 4. British and American manufacturers pirated Indian designs extensively; fabric after the Salempore style may have been made in Manchester. Customs valuations thus seem the most reliable metric of these cloths. Florence Montgomery, *Printed Textiles: English and American Cottons and Linens, 1700–1850* (Bristol and Tokyo: Thoemmes Press and Kyokuto Shoten, 1970), 16–17, 102, and passim.

36. Re-exports of merchandise taxed by their original purchase price abroad are difficult to compare with re-exports of commodities such as tea, pepper, and coffee, which were taxed and recorded by weight. Price lists might allow the conversion of pounds of tea to a U.S. *wholesale* price, but this should not be compared with the *purchase* price of porcelain in China.

37. Alexander Baring to Francis Baring, Philadelphia, February 12, 1797, ING Baring, 1.

38. Phineas Bond, Philadelphia, July 3, 1789, to His Grace the Duke of Leeds, PRO FO 4/7, 255 (see also PRO EXT 1/3); Amales Tripathi, *Trade and Finance in the Bengal Presidency, 1793–1813* (Calcutta: Oxford University Press, 1979), 30.

39. Minutes of the Committee of Trade, January 1786 to August 1786, PRO BT/5/3, 148.

40. Minutes of the Committee of Trade from January 1, 1805, to February 28, 1806 (January 1, 1805, 2–3, and December 7, 1805), PRO BT/5/15, 359–364. There were two Barbados reports from Mr. Alderman Rowcroft and Simon Cock, Esquire. Additional regulations would have had little effect when the existing ones were already being ignored.

41. Edward Parry and Charles Grant, Chairs, to Court of Directors, East India House, October 1808, OIOC H/494, 213.

42. Dorothy Burne Goebel, "British Trade to the Spanish Colonies, 1796–1823," *American Historical Review* 43, no. 2 (January 1938): 299.

43. The pattern of Thorndike's East Indian trade and of his sales of East Indian goods in Europe resonates with the experience of Robert Oliver. Bruchey, *Robert Oliver,* 53–253.

44. On his death in 1832 Thorndike was worth $1.5 million. Presumably, he was worth something less than that in the 1790s. J. D. Forbes, *Israel Thorndike, Federalist Financier* (New York: Exposition Press, 1953), 48; David Hackett

Fischer, "The Myth of the Essex Junto," *WMQ,* 3rd series, 21, no. 2 (April 1964): 198. Thorndike and his papers at Baker Library await a modern biographer.

45. "Sales of Sundry Merchandise Received of the Ship *Mary* Nicholas Thorndike Master from Calcutta by Order and for Account and Risque of Mr. Israel Thorndike, Merchant, Beverly," Thorndike Papers, vol. 1.

46. Thorndike, Instructions to William Leech, July 9, 1800, Thorndike Papers, vol. 4, 1, 9.

47. Thorndike Papers, vol. 5.

48. Thorndike to Stephen Jones Jr., Boston, July 28, 1801, Thorndike Papers, vol. 5.

49. Israel Thorndike to Thomas Dickason Jr., Beverley, October 25, 1801, Thorndike Papers, vol. 6.

50. Invoice of 31 Bales of India Cottons, Enclosed with Bill of Lading for Acct. of Israel Thorndike in Brig Sally & Betsey, Samuel Allen, Master, Boston to Nantes & Bordeaux, July 29, 1801, Thorndike Papers, vol. 5.

51. Thorndike to Thomas Dickason Jr., Beverly, December 3, 1801, Thorndike Papers, vol. 6.

52. Webb, Holmes & Co., Leghorn, to Capt. John Thissel of Ship *Mary* in Genoa, Dated January 13, 1802, received in Genoa January 16, 1802, Thorndike Papers, vol. 7.

53. De Larrard & Co., Barcelona, to Captain Thissel of Ship *Mary,* Genoa, January 30, 1802, received February 15, 1802, Thorndike Papers, vol. 7.

54. Heath & Co., Genoa, to Israel Thorndike, Beverly, February 10, 1802, Thorndike Papers, vol. 7.

55. Account, Sales of *Mary,* John Thissel, Master, for I. Thorndike, March 1, 1802, Genoa, Thorndike Papers, vol. 7.

56. "Invoice of Sundry Merchandise shipped on board Schooner *Two Friends,*" December 1801, Thorndike Papers, vol. 6.

57. Israel Thorndike to Tarbox Moulton, Instructions, December 12, 1801, Beverly, MA, Thorndike Papers, vol. 6.

58. "Sales of the Cargo of the Schooner *Two Friends* of Beverly Sold by Tarbox Moulton commenced in Mary Golant January 13 1802," Thorndike Papers, vol. 7.

59. Rayford W. Logan, *The Diplomatic Relations of the United States with Haiti, 1776–1891* (1941; reprint, New York: Kraus Reprint, 1961), 130; Laurent DuBois, *Avengers of the New World: The Story of the Haitian Revolution* (Cambridge, MA: Harvard University Press, 2004).

60. Tarbox Moulton, Cape Francois, February 15, 1802, to Israel Thorndike, Thorndike Papers, vol. 7.

61. Tarbox Moulton to Israel Thorndike, March 9, 1802, from Trinidad, Thorndike Papers, vol. 7.

62. Tarbox Moulton to Israel Thorndike, April 1, 1802, "at sea," Thorndike Papers, vol. 7.

63. Tarbox Moulton to Israel Thorndike, April 28, 1802, St. Domingo, Thorndike Papers, vol. 7.

64. Tarbox Moulton to Israel Thorndike, St. Domingo, April 30, 1802, Thorndike Papers, vol. 7.

65. The Caribbean–New England run trained captains (in seamanship and business) for the New England–Europe, New England–Pacific Northwest Coast, and New England–India routes. Promotion was quick; one or two profitable Caribbean voyages would be enough to promote a captain to the China trade. Logan, *Diplomatic Relations*, 137.

66. "Invoice of 32 logs of Mahogany & 51,339 lbs of 'Oirn' [iron?] shipped on Board the Schooner *Two Friends*, by Tarbox Moulton, Mater, on Acct. & Rect. of Israel Thorndike Esqr. of Beverly," and "Venta y Caroamento dela Goleia Americana nombrada los Dos Amigos su Capn. Terbor Moultan," Santo Domingo, June 3, 1802, by Pedro Catell, Thorndike Papers, vol. 8.

67. Cap Français, July 8, 1802, Account of Sales & Neat proceeds of Sundries received pr the Schooner *Two Friends*, Tarbox Moulton Master of Beverly, Last of St. Domingo, Thorndike Papers, vol. 8, 36.

68. "List of articles in demand at Cape Francois," March 28, 1802, Likely compiled by Tarbox Moulton for I. Thorndike, Thorndike Papers, vol. 7.

69. Cf. "Sales of the Cargo of the Schooner *Two Friends*," July 10, 1802, which put the total proceeds at $38,022.59, and "The Returns of the Schooner *Two Friends* Cargo from the West Indies by Tarbox Moulton, Master. July 10, 1802," which put it at $33,792.95. For the impounding (and subsequent release of his cargo?), see St. Domingo, April 30, 1802, Tarbox Moulton to Israel Thorndike, Thorndike Papers, vol. 7.

70. North American merchants may have bought East Indian goods in Europe and sold them in the Caribbean before 1783 as well.

71. *ASP*, passim.

72. "Sir F. Baring's Paper," September 3, 1800, OIOC L/MAR/C/50 No. 8, 363.

73. *ASP*, passim; Michelle Craig McDonald, "The Chance of the Moment: Coffee and the New West Indies Commodity Trade," *WMQ*, 3rd series, 62, no. 3 (July 2005): 441–472.

74. Indigo, 37.25 percent (1789–1801); raw cotton, 15.43 percent (1789–1801). *ASP*, passim.

75. Robert and Gale McClung, "Jacob Crowninshield Brings Home an Elephant," *American Neptune* 18, no. 2 (April 1958): 138.

76. McClung, "Jacob Crowninshield," 140.

77. *The Diary of William Bentley, D.D.*, vol. 2 (January 1793–December 1802) (Gloucester, MA: Peter Smith, 1962), 235, August 30, 1797.

78. John Kuo Wei Tchen, *New York before Chinatown: Orientalism and the Shaping of American Culture, 1776–1882* (Baltimore: Johns Hopkins University Press, 1999); Sirajul Islam, "American Maritime Activities in Calcutta: Cases of Elephant and Ice, 1785–1880," *Journal of the Asiatic Society of Bangladesh (Humanities)* 49, no. 1 (June 2004): 41–60.

79. *Diary of William Bentley*, vol. 2, 235, August 28, 1797.

80. Edward R. Barnsley, "History of China's Retreat," paper presented to Bucks County Historical Society (Doyleston, PA: printed by Bristol Printing Company, 1933), 6–9; Harold Donaldson Eberlein and Cortlandt Van Dyke Hubbard, "China Hall," in *Portrait of a Colonial City, Philadelphia, 1670–1838* (Philadelphia: J. B. Lippincott, 1939), 472–481.

81. Twining, *Travels in America,* 36, 55, 128.

82. Twining, *Travels in America,* 54, 85–86. On the status and fashion that Indian goods conveyed, see Jonathan Philllips Eacott, "Owning Empire: The Matter of India in the English-Speaking World, 1730–1850" (Ph.D. diss., University of Michigan, 2008).

83. Richard Henry Dana, *Two Years before the Mast* (New York: Airmont, 1965) 442–443.

84. Thorndike Papers, passim. Thus British merchant John Bainbridge recalled receiving remittances from Antwerp on account of American sales there. *Minutes of Evidence taken before the Right Honourable the House of Lords in the Lords Committees, appointed to take into consideration so much of the speech of his royal highness the Prince Regent as relates to the Charter of the East-India Company* (London, 1813), OIOC A/2/15, 959–960; Bruchey, *Robert Oliver,* 160, 254.

85. Tripathi, *Trade and Finance,* 58.

86. ING Baring, vols. 1 and 2.

87. Donald R. Adams Jr., *Finance and Enterprise in Early America: A Study of Stephen Girard's Bank, 1812–1831* (Philadelphia: University of Pennsylvania Press, 1978), 11–12.

88. Ole Feldbaek, *India Trade under the Danish Flag, 1772–1808* (Lund: Studentlitteratur, 1969), 189.

89. Edward Parry and Charles Grant, Chairs, to the Court of Directors, East India House, October 14, 1807, OIOC H/494, 83.

90. *Minutes of Evidence,* A/2/15, 961; Adams, *Stephen Girard's Bank,* 11–12.

5. Merchant Millionaires

1. Claudia D. Goldin and Frank D. Lewis, "The Role of Exports in American Economic Growth during the Napoleonic Wars, 1793 to 1807," *Explorations in Economic History* 17 (1980): 6–25. Douglass North emphasized the buoyant effect of re-exports on the early republican economy, though he did not have a chance to reply to Goldin's analysis, which remains definitive. Douglass North, *Growth and Welfare in the American Past* (Englewood Cliffs, NJ: Prentice-Hall, 1974), 72. Also Douglass North, *The Economic Growth of the United States, 1790–1860* (Englewood Cliffs, NJ: Prentice-Hall, 1961). Growth of 1.08 percent would not be considered low by most economic historians when compared to early modern growth generally, but it is low for "boom" times. Donald R. Adams Jr., "American Neutrality and Prosperity, 1793–1808: A Reconsideration," *JEH* 40, no. 4 (December 1980): 713–737.

2. Robert C. Alberts, *Golden Voyage: The Life and Times of William Bingham, 1752–1804* (Boston: Houghton-Mifflin, 1969); J. D. Forbes, *Israel Thorndike, Federalist Financier* (New York: Exposition Press, 1953); John Haeger, *John Jacob Astor: Business and Finance in the Early Republic* (Detroit: Wayne State University Press, 1991); Richard H. McKey Jr., "Elias Hasket Derby, Merchant of Salem, Massachusetts, 1739–1799" (PhD diss., Clark University, 1961).

3. This was intentional: the Mint wanted the few coins it did issue to remain in the United States, with Spanish coins to supplement them. As the director of the U.S. Mint explained, "national coins" were "protected by foreign coins, which were preferred for export." David A. Martin, "Bimetallism in the United States before 1850," *Journal of Political Economy* 76, no. 3 (May–June 1968): 430–433. The quotation is from Mint Director S. Moore to C. P. White, chairman, House Select Committee on the Coinage, May 25, 1832, House of Representatives, House Report 278, 23rd Congress, 1st session, vol 2, no. 261, 84, as cited in Martin, "Bimetallism in the United States before 1850," 430. Arthur J. Rolnick and Warren E. Weber, "Gresham's Law or Gresham's Fallacy," *Journal of Political Economy* 94, no. 1 (February 1986): 185–199.

4. Jacques M. Downs, *The Golden Ghetto: The American Commercial Community at Canton and the Shaping of American China Policy, 1784–1844* (Bethlehem, PA: Lehigh University Press, 1997), 415n56, citing Earl C. Tanner, "The Early Trade of Providence with Latin America" (PhD diss., Harvard University, 1950); M. G. Buist, *At spes non fracta: Hope & Co., 1770–1815* (The Hague: Nijhoff, 1974), 295–333; John Coatsworth, "American Trade with European Colonies in the Caribbean and South America, 1790-1812," *WMQ*, 3rd series, 24, no. 2 (April 1967): 255; John H. Reinoehl, "Some Remarks on the American Trade: Jacob Crowninshield to James Madison 1806," *WMQ*, 3rd series, 16, no. 1 (January 1959): 103. Stuart Weems Bruchey, *Robert Oliver Merchant of Baltimore, 1783–1819* (Baltimore: Johns Hopkins University Press, 1956), 263–333.

5. Kenneth A. Lockridge, "Literacy in Early America 1650–1800," in Harvey J. Graff, ed., *Literacy and Social Development in the West: A Reader* (New York: Cambridge University Press, 1981), 184; Kenneth A. Lockridge, *Literacy in Colonial New England: An Enquiry into the Social Context of Literacy in the Early Modern West* (New York: W. W. Norton, 1974).

6. Lockridge, "Literacy in Early America 1650-1800," 183–200. Lockridge counts signatures on wills to estimate literacy. E. Jennifer Monaghan, *Learning to Read and Write in Colonial America* (Boston: University of Massachusetts Press, 2005); Edward E. Gordon and Elaine H. Gordon, *Literacy in America: Historical Journey and Contemporary Solutions* (Westport, CT: Praeger, 2003); Deborah Keller-Cohen, "Rethinking Literacy: Comparing Colonial and Contemporary America," *Anthropology & Education Quarterly* 24, no. 4, Alternative Literacies: In School and Beyond (December 1993): 288–307.

7. Lockridge, "Literacy in Early America 1650–1800," 186. Alice Hanson Jones's *Wealth of a Nation to Be: The American Colonies on the Eve of the Revolution* (New York: Columbia University Press, 1980) emphasizes wealth inequality in New England.

8. John J. McCusker and Russel R. Menard, *Economy of British America, 1607–1789* (Chapel Hill: University of North Carolina Press, 1991), 226, 229. The taking of frontier land was, however, abetted by the at times still brutal disease environment for American Indians.

9. On farming in American capitalism, see Allan Kulikoff, *The Agrarian Origins of American Capitalism* (Charlottesville: University of Virginia Press, 1992).

10. Jeffrey G. Williamson and Peter H. Lindert, *American Inequality: A Macroeconomic History* (New York: Academic Press, 1980), 21–25.

11. United States Historical Census online, University of Virginia Library, http://fisher.lib.virginia.edu/collections/stats/histcensus/php/county.php. "Mid-Atlantic" here means Delaware, New Jersey, New York, and Pennsylvania; it does not include Ohio, which became a state in 1803 and is not counted for 1810.

12. Martin, "Bimetallism in the United States before 1850," 440.

13. A pound sterling was worth $4.44 in 1774.

14. The mid-atlantic provided a slightly more equalitarian model, with the top decile in New Jersey, Pennsylvania, and Delaware controlling only 35 percent of physical wealth.

15. The merchant was Samuel Neave of Philadelphia. "Physical wealth" excludes paper assets and liabilities.

16. Jones, *Wealth of a Nation to Be,* 51, 37, 164 165, 177.

17. Daniel Vickers, "Competency and Competition: Economic Culture in Early America, *WMQ,* 3rd series, 47, no. 1 (January 1990): 3, 12. Vickers uses "competency" to describe the "human needs of individual families" and "sufficient property to absorb the labors of a given family" in describing small farmers rather than small merchants. In both his sense and the sense used here, "competency" means the producer owns the means of production and negotiates the sale of his labor or goods freely. The word, Vickers notes, is "necessarily imprecise" and suggested different degrees of wealth and property in different contexts.

18. *OED,* "competency," accessed July 8, 2006.

19. Jane Austen, *Emma* (1815), I, ii; as cited in *OED,* "competence," accessed July 8, 2006; Richard Lord Wellesley, *Disp.* 1803, 365, as cited in *OED,* "competency.", accessed July 8, 2006.

20. Charles F. Briggs, *The Adventures of Henry Franco,* vol. 2 (1839), 237; James Fenimore Cooper, *Red Rover,* vol. 2 (1827–1828), 215; Charles F. Briggs, *Bankrupt Stories, Edited by Henry Franco* (1843); Nathaniel Parker Willis, *The Legendary, Consisting of Original Pieces Principally Illustrative of American History, Scenery and Manners,* vol. 1 (1832), 76; Charles Brockden

Brown, *Arthur Mervyn; or, Memoirs of the Year 1793*, vol. 2 (1799–1800), 169; Steven Epley, "Rowson, Susanna (*bap.* 1762, *d.* 1824)," *DNB*, accessed June 20, 2006; Susanna Rowson, *The Inquisitor; or, Invisible Rambler*, vol. 1 (1793), 46.

21. Nathaniel Hawthorne, *Mosses from an Old Manse*, vol. 2 (Boston: Ticknor and Fields, 1865), 90; Alexander Baring (AB) to Francis Baring (FB), Boston, December 11, 1795, #7, ING Baring. On Baring's correspondence see François Crouzet, "A Banker's View of America: Letters of Alexander Baring, 1795–1801," in *Britain, France and International Commerce: From Louis XIV to Victoria* (Brookfield, VT: Variorum, 1996), 264–279; Downs, *Golden Ghetto*, 236.

22. Theodore S. Fay, *Hoboken: A Romance* (New York, 1843), 93.

23. Susanna Rowson, *Reuben and Rachel; Or, Tales of Old Times*, vol. 2 (1798), 178.

24. Lydia Maria Francis Child, *The Coronal: A Collection of Miscellaneous Pieces* (1832), 201. Notably, the character being described was "the young West Indian."

25. Willis, *The Legendary*, 62. For "affluence and independence" see William Hill Brown, *The Power of Sympathy; or The Triumph of Nature*, vol. 2 (1789), 31, and Charles Brockden Brown, *Arthur Mervyn*, 223. For "affluence and leisure" see Catharine Maria Sedgwick, *Clarence; or A Tale of Our Own Times*, vol. 2 (1830), 173.

26. Bernard Bailyn and Lotte Bailyn, *Massachusetts Shipping, 1697–1714: A Statistical Study* (Cambridge, MA: Belknap Press, 1959).

27. Bills of lading: Thomas L. Winthrop on *Cyrus* to Calcutta, June 30, 1800; John Lowell, July 1, 1800; Daniel Gilman & Co., July 1, 1800; I. Thorndike to Winslow, Beverly, November 8, 1801, Thorndike Papers, vol. 4, Baker Business Library, Harvard University. Emphasis added.

28. Thomas M. Doerflinger, *A Vigorous Spirit of Enterprise: Merchants and Economic Development in Revolutionary Philadelphia* (Chapel Hill: University of North Carolina Press, 1986), 293; Carl Seaburg and Stanley Patterson, *Merchant Prince of Boston, Colonel T. H. Perkins, 1764–1854* (Cambridge, MA: Harvard University Press, 1971), 156.

29. Samuel Eliot Morison, "The India Ventures of Fisher Ames 1794–1804," *American Antiquarian Society* 37 (April 1927): 15; Fisher Ames to William Gray, Dedham, December 16, 1797, and Ames to Gray, Dedham, March 19, 1799, as cited in Morison, "India Ventures," 21.

30. Ames to Gray, Dedham, December 16, 1797, and Ames to Gray, Dedham, March 19, 1799, as cited in Morison, "India Ventures," 19, 21.

31. See Table 5.2. This discussion draws from the *Impost Book of the Collector* (Salem, MA), vol. 1, NARA (MA) and the RG36 Customs E1071: Impost Ledgers for the Port of Philadelphia, 1789–1865, box 1, vol. 2: January–December 1790 NARA (PA). For ports categorized as Caribbean, Europe, and Indies, see the note for Table 5.1. A merchant might sign bond for a

cargo at the customs house on behalf of a correspondent overseas or out of town, and so the question of which names (and how many and in what weight) attach to which properties is by no means clear. Yet the customs registers indicate a minimum number of properties, whoever owned them. All goods signed for by any one merchant were lumped together under his name. If he also signed for goods bought by a partnership, a separate entry was made for property signed for on behalf of that firm. Impost books show property imported, but, read backward, suggest how many discrete properties were originally exported as well.

32. *Astrea* manifest remains at MHS. The cobbling together of funds in the East India trade without the use of incorporation may be paralleled in the whaling industry. Eric Hilt, "Incentives in Corporations: Evidence from the American Whaling Industry," *Journal of Law & Economics* vol., 49 no. 1 (April 2006): 197–227.

33. *Minutes of Evidence taken before the Right Honourable the House of Lords in the Lords Committees, appointed to take into consideration so much of the speech of his royal highness the Prince Regent as relates to the Charter of the East-India Company* (London, 1813), A/2/15 952.

34. Indeed when Boston merchants advertised a subscription for the contruction of an East Indiaman in 1785, they offered to sell $300 shares in the ship to "any citizen" who could afford them. Charles Oscar Paullin, *American Voyages to the Orient, 1690–1865* (Annapolis, MD: United States Naval Institute, 1971), 11. The merchants in question—among them Walter Heyer—appear to have lacked even a competency. It is unclear whether the vessel was built.

35. Contract, Subscribers of the *Alexander Hodgson,* Beverly, August 6, 1802, Thorndike Papers, vol. 8, 53.

36. Contract, Subscribers of the *Alexander Hodgson* Beverly, August 6, 1802, Thorndike Papers, vol. 8, 53.

37. *Impost Books of the Collector* (Salem, MA). NARA (MA).

38. Thus in the Philadelphia data, the upward drift in the average number of consignees reflects an uptick in the European average for 1800 (not sustained in 1810) and a separate increase in the Caribbean average for 1810.

39. A vessel's previous port of entry is not always an accurate reflection of its entire voyage, though it is more likely to suggest what cargoes the vessel would carry. Thus the low numbers for Africa do not indicate a boycott of the slave trade. Americans sailed to Africa and returned via the Caribbean; most African departures thus appear as Caribbean arrivals. Likewise, some Atlantic arrivals represent tramp voyages originating anywhere.

40. Thomas R. McHale and Mary C. McHale, eds., *Early American-Philippine Trade: The Journal of Nathaniel Bowditch in Manila, 1796* (New Haven: Yale University Southeast Asia Studies, 1962), 38, 43, 54–55, 62.

41. McHale and McHale, *Early American-Philippine Trade,* 45.

42. McHale and McHale, *Early American-Philippine Trade,* 50–51, 54–55.

43. McHale and McHale, *Early American-Philippine Trade*, 62.

44. McKey, "Elias Hasket Derby," 9.

45. AB to FB, Boston, December 11, 1795, ING Baring, 6. In 1795, £ = $4.53. Lawrence H. Officer, "Exchange Rates between the United States Dollar and Forty-one Currencies," MeasuringWorth, 2009. http://www.measuringworth .org/exchangeglobal/, accessed November 22, 2009.

46. AB to FB, Philadelphia, February 26, 1796, ING Baring, 1.

47. AB to Caspar Voght, Esqr., Philadelphia, January 9, 1797, ING Baring, 3.

48. AB to FB, Boston, December 11, 1795, ING Baring, 7.

49. The actual total was $1,063,799. McKey, "Elias Hasket Derby," 490.

50. Based on the Consumer Price Index, Manigault left $3,297,689.21 in 1774. Jones, *Wealth of a Nation to Be*, 171, 177; McCusker, "Comparing the Purchasing Power of Money." Lee Soltow, *Distribution of Wealth and Income in the United States in 1798* (Pittsburgh: University of Pittsburgh Press, 1989), also charts the rise of northern, urban merchant wealth.

51. McKey, "Elias Hasket Derby," 451, citing Fisk Kimball, "The Elias Hasket Derby Mansion in Salem," *Essex Institute Historical Collections* 60, no. 4 (October 1924): 273–292. The Derbys declined Charles Bulfinch's offer to design and build the mansion.

52. McKey, "Elias Hasket Derby," 455.

53. McKey, "Elias Hasket Derby," 459.

54. J. Britton, *Graphical and Literary Illustrations of Fonthill Abbey, Wiltshire, with Heraldrical and Genealogical Notices of the Beckford Family* (London, 1823), 25–26, as cited in Eric Williams, *Capitalism and Slavery* (Chapel Hill: University of North Carolina Press, 1944), 87–88. The building did not last long; all but one wing was torn down by 1823. Britton, *Fonthill*, 26.

55. Ragatz, *The Fall of the Planter Class in the British Caribbean, 1763–1833: A Study in Social and Economic History* (1928; reprint, New York: Octgaon Books, 1963), 50, cited in Williams, *Capitalism and Slavery*, 91.

56. John Orbell, "Baring, Sir Francis, First Baronet (1740–1810)," *DNB*, accessed May 10, 2005.

57. Buist, *Hope & Co*, 188–190.

58. John Orbell, "Baring, Alexander," *DNB*, accessed May 10, 2005.

59. AB to FB, May 5, 1796, ING Baring, 2, 6–7. Baring preferred Northern merchants, arguing that "the Northern States are always some degrees above their neighbours in every thing and the Scale sinks lower as you go South. There are comparatively more good houses at Boston than either here or New York, they have better ideas of regularity and principle, and to the South of Baltimore . . . there is nobody worth trusting." AB to Caspar Voght, Esqr., Philadelphia, January 9, 1797, ING Baring, 2.

60. AB to FB, Boston, December 11, 1795, ING Baring, 5, 6–7.

61. In this in particular, the Baring/Bingham/Willing family connections are striking, given the Barings' future lending to the U.S. government.

62. Alberts, *Golden Voyage*, 160. For more on Bingham, see Wendy A. Nicholson, "Making the Private Public: Anne Willing Bingham's Role as a Leader of Philadelphia's Social Elite in the Late Eighteenth Century" (MA thesis, University of Delaware, 1988), and Ethel E. Rasmussen, "Democratic Environment— Aristocratical Aspiration," *PMHB* 90, no. 2 (April 1966): 155–182.

63. Alberts, *Golden Voyage*, 163.

64. Alberts, *Golden Voyage*, 162–163.

65. Congressman Theodore Sedgwick. Alberts, *Golden Voyage*, 218.

66. Alberts, *Golden Voyage*, 158–159, 213; Robert J. Gough, "Bingham, William," *American National Biography Online*, http://anb.org, accessed December 12, 2005. It was called a "Republican Court;" here "Republican" means non-monarchical, not Jeffersonian.

67. One suspects this impressed Bingham's biographer more than it did Baring. Alberts, *Golden Voyage*, 158. U.S. silversmiths could make forks with steel handles but not steel tines.

68. This is now the Powel House in Philadelphia; the rooms can be seen in the Metropolitan Museum of Art in New York and the Philadelphia Museum of Art. Alberts, *Golden Voyage*, 346.

69. Orbell, "Baring, Alexander," *DNB*. This should not be taken to mean that Baring and Bingham were equally wealthy; Bingham was in his fifties when he died, Baring was more than twenty years his junior.

70. Alberts, *Golden Voyage*, ix. Many business biographers fixate on whose subject was richer. George Wilson, *Stephen Girard: America's First Tycoon* (Conshohocken, PA: Combined Books, 1995), and Axel Madsen, *John Jacob Astor: America's First Multimillionaire* (New York: John Wiley, 2001), put the claim in the title. Donald Adams deemed Girard "the wealthiest merchant in Philadelphia, and, with the possible exception of his friend John Jacob Astor, in the entire nation." Donald R. Adams Jr., *Finance and Enterprise in Early America: A Study of Stephen Girard's Bank, 1812–1831* (Philadelphia: University of Pennsylvania Press, 1978), 6. Yet these merchants calculated profit and loss on a venture-by-venture basis; with so many ongoing ventures, the question of who was richer becomes unknowable and absurd. Haeger, *John Jacob Astor*, 91–92. It is enough to know they were affluent, among the first American millionaires, and part of the first American investing class.

71. AB to Caspar Voght, Philadelphia, January 1, 1797, ING Baring, 1–2.

72. AB to Caspar Voght, Philadelphia, January 9, 1797, ING Baring, 1–2.

73. AB to Caspar Voght, Philadelphia, October 29, 1797, ING Baring, 2. Emphasis added.

74. FB to AB, London, March 9, 1799, ING Baring, 1.

75. AB to Hope & Co., Philadelphia, January 9, 1797, ING Baring, 14; Ellis Paxson Oberholtzer, *Robert Morris, Patriot and Financier* (New York: Macmillan, 1903), 297, 299, 301, 312; Clarence L. Ver Steeg, "Morris, Robert," *American National Biography Online*, http://anb.org, accessed December

13, 2005; AB to Caspar Voght, Philadelphia, January 9, 1797, ING Baring, 1–4; AB to Caspar Voght, Philadelphia, October 29, 1797, ING Baring, 2; AB to C. Wall, Philadelphia, January 20–February 5, 1799, ING Baring, 6. A modern study of the early American Russia trade would make an excellent doctoral thesis.

76. Pounds converted to 1810 U.S. dollars on the rate of £4.3 = $1. I have taken £606,000 in preference to Orbell's earlier assessment of £625,207, with £68,507 in the Baring Brothers firm. John Orbell, *Baring Brothers & Co., Limited: A History to 1939* (London: Baring Brothers, 1985), 20; Orbell, "Baring, Sir Francis," *DNB*.

77. AB to FB, Boston, December 11, 1795, ING Baring, 7.

78. AB to FB, Philadelphia, February 12, 1797, ING Baring, 1–2.

79. AB to FB, Boston, December 11, 1795, ING Baring, 7.

80. Orbell, "Baring, Sir Francis," *DNB*.

81. AB to FB, Philadelphia, February 12, 1797, ING Baring, 2–3.

82. AB to FB, Philadelphia, May 7, 1799, ING Baring, 5. Emphasis in original.

83. FB to AB, May 20, 1799, ING Baring, 4; FB to AB, February 15, 1800, ING Baring, 1; FB to AB, May 20, 1799, ING Baring, 4.

84. FB to AB, May 20, 1799, ING Baring, 4. Emphasis in original.

85. AB to FB, Boston, December 11, 1795, ING Baring, 1–3, 5.

86. Cathy Matson, "The Revolution, Constitution, and New Nation," in Stanley L. Engerman and Robert E. Gallman, eds., *The Cambridge Economic History of the United States,* vol. 1 (Cambridge: Cambridge University Press, 2000), 395.

87. Robert E. Lipsey, "U.S. Foreign Trade and the Balance of Payments, 1800–1913," in Stanley L. Engerman and Robert E. Gallman, eds., *The Cambridge Economic History of the United States,* vol. 2 (Cambridge: Cambridge University Press, 2000), 687, 723–724. The 30 percent is from a sample of the years between 1798 and 1802.

88. AB to FB, May 5, 1796, ING Baring, 4.

89. Simon Schama, *Citizens: A Chronicle of the French Revolution* (London: Penguin Books, 1999), 733.

90. "Mémoire sur l'etablissement d'une banque indienne à Paris," in Michel Poniatowski, *Talleyrand aux États-Unis, 1794–1796* (Librairie Académique Perrin, 1976), 240.

91. Charles Maurice de Talleyrand-Périgord, "Memoir sent to Mr. Cazenove, June 23, 1794," in *Talleyrand in America as a Financial Promoter, 1794–96: Unpublished Letters and Memoirs,* vol. 2, ed. Hans Huth and Wilma J. Pugh, Annual Report of the American Historical Association for the Year 1941 (Washington, DC: Government Printing Office, 1942), 35; Larry Neal, "A Tale of Two Revolutions: International Capital Flows 1789–1819," *Bulletin of Economic Research* 43, no. 1 (1991): 57–92.

92. Poniatowski, *Talleyrand,* 245. Talleyrand later—and somewhat whimsically—claimed in his memoirs that he tried to get a berth on a ship from Philadel-

phia to Calcutta even before he had sailed up the Delaware. If he did try, he did not succeed. Charles Maurice de Talleyrand-Périgord, *Mémoires, 1754–1815* (Paris: Plon, 1982), 218.

93. Ranajit Guha, *A Rule of Property for Bengal: An Essay on the Idea of Permanent Settlement* (Paris: Mouton, 1963), 175.

94. Talleyrand to Lord Lansdowne, June 15, 1795, in Poniatowski, *Talleyrand,* 299.

95. Talleyrand, "Asiatic Bank," unpublished memorandum, in *Talleyrand in America as a Financial Promoter, 1794–96,* vol. 2, 125–136.

96. Ainslie T. Embree, "Law, Thomas," *DNB,* accessed December 13, 2009.

97. S. Decatur, *Private Affairs of George Washington,* 293, as cited in Embree, "Law, Thomas," *DNB,* accessed December 13, 2009.

98. Lawrence H. Officer, "Exchange Rates between the United States Dollar and Forty-one Currencies," MeasuringWorth, 2009, http://www.measuringworth.org/exchangeglobal/, accessed November 22, 2009.

99. Schama, *Citizens,* 734. No further record of Law's participation exists. The story continues with a different partner. Alexander Baring met Law, though he thought Law's investment in a Washington, D.C. housing lot a bad idea (it was). AB to Hope & Co., Philadelphia, January 10, 1797, ING Baring, 24.

100. Poniatowski, *Talleyrand,* 301, 303, 311. Two notable Holland Land Company figures, Van Staphorst and Schimmelpenninck, were Patriots, providing a Revolutionary connection. Simon Schama, *Patriots & Liberators: Revolution in the Netherlands, 1780–1813* (New York: Knopf, 1977). The Holland Land Company bought another 3 million acres of land from Robert Morris on the hope of its resale in India. Oberholtzer, *Robert Morris,* 303. Beaumetz left Wilmington, Delaware on May 27, 1796, and arrived in Calcutta on November 5, 1796. Talleyrand's departure in June 1796 undermined Beaumetz, Talleyrand later claiming he feared Beaumetz would take his or his own life. Schama, *Citizens,* 735. Talleyrand made one speculation in land—handsomely profitable—while in America. William Chazanof, *Joseph Ellicott and the Holland Land Company: The Opening of Western New York* (Syracuse, NY: Syracuse University Press, 1970). See also Robert Warwick Bingham, *Holland Land Company's Papers: Reports of Joseph Ellicott as Chief of Survey (1797–1800) and as Agent (1800–1821) of the Holland Land Company's Purchase in Western New York* (Buffalo, NY: Buffalo Historical Society, 1937).

101. Schama, *Citizens,* 735. No word on who bought it, how he obtained the clothes, or, sadly, what they were for.

102. Rudyard Kipling, "A Priest in Spite of Himself," in *Rewards and Fairies* (London: Macmillan, 1975), 154. This is a fictional account of Talleyrand's time in America.

334 · Notes to Pages 149–150

6. Beyond the British Empire

1. There is enough material on this period from archives in France, Spain, the Netherlands, Mauritius, Réunion, South Africa, Indonesia, and the Philippines for the shared history among these colonies to merit its own book. It awaits its author.

2. Nicholas Tarling, *Anglo-Dutch Rivalry in the Malay World, 1780–1824* (London: Cambridge University Press, 1962). Walter Ewer, the Commissioner at Bencoolen, suggested Americans might be interested in Sumatran "settlements." Walter Ewer to Governor General Wellesley, August 4, 1803, in J. Kumar, *Select Documents on Indian Trade and Industry, 1773–1833* (New Delhi: Janaki Prakashan, 1981), 39; Lee Kam Hing, *The Sultanate of Aceh: Relations with the British, 1760–1824* (Kuala Lumpur: Oxford University Press, 1995), 263. In one of the few U.S. naval expeditions to East Indian waters during the French Wars, the frigate *USS Essex* convoyed a U.S. merchant fleet from Batavia to the United States in 1800, a sign of U.S. government interest in promoting trade with the archipelago. Perhaps this was the basis for British concerns, or perhaps a scenario in which trade did not follow the flag was unimaginable.

3. Prince of Wales Island (Penang) Factory Records, Political & Secret Consultations, January 17, 1807, OIOC G/34/179, paragraphs 5–6. Officials here were particularly concerned with Americans, going to great lengths to defend against American attack during the War of 1812 as well: overshadowed by Calcutta, Penang officials may have convinced themselves of their importance.

4. Thomas Stamford Raffles, *The History of Java*, vol. 1 (Kuala Lumpur: Oxford University Press, 1978), 217–218.

5. Batavian shipping records survive for some years, often only partially. Since the loss appears random, there is no indication that the data misrepresent any country's shipping. Surviving data are compiled into a list of known arrivals at Batavia Roads between 1793 and 1807. The number of known arrivals varies considerably by year (perhaps an indication of which data survived as much as of actual variation). From 1793 and between 1795 and 1798, 1800 and 1801, and 1805 and 1807, only loose-leaf slips noting individual ships' arrivals survive. From 1803 and 1804 loose-leaf slips and aggregated lists survive. From 1794, 1799, 1802, and between 1808 and 1811, no data survive. When both slips and lists survive, the slips are checked against the lists. From these years, more than 90 percent of slips survive, a rate that may not apply to other years. The 1803 list gives fifty-four arrivals, twenty-five of which were American (46.30 percent). The slips give thirty-six arrivals, fourteen of which were American (38.89 percent). The difference, 7.41 percent, falls within the margin of error (9.52 percent) for a sample of thirty-six from a population of fifty-four. Slips survive from all seasons in 1803. Each vessel is tallied as a percentage of the annual number of known arriving vessels, providing annual sample of the data. Since some samples may be small, the full fourteen-year set should be used for country comparisons.

6. This includes military, Arab, and Aceh vessels, which means the American data is marginally understated. Sources: ANRI HR 2629 (1793); HR 2931 (1795); HR 2632 (1796); HR 2633 (1797); HR 2634 (1798); and HR 2635 (1800–1807). Ships marked "private" have been changed to "Dutch" and ships marked "EIC" have been changed to "English." One "Javan" ship had also been made "Dutch" as implied by ship name and master. "Tosphanhse" was rendered as Tuscan.

7. Joël Eymeret, "L'Administration Napoléonienne en Indonésie," *Revue française d'histoire d'outre mer* 60, no. 218 (1973): 37.

8. The last U.S. vessel in the Batavia-Japan trade was hired in 1809, suggesting that Americans were at Batavia at least until then. E. S. van Eyck van Heslinga, *Van compagnie naar koopvaardij: De scheepvaartverbinding van de Bataafse Republiek met de koloniën in Azië 1795–1806* (Amsterdam: De Bataafsche Leeuw, 1988), 183.

9. The Dutch Republic and the Anglo-Dutch alliance fell in early 1795; news took time to reach Java. The war-and-peace distinction is apparent in 1803; British vessels all arrived by early October of that year, when the last one was confiscated by Dutch authorities apprised of the hostilities. Twelve of the fourteen arrivals in the remaining months were American.

10. Danish merchants were second major carriers at Batavia in this period, trafficking out of Tranquebar and Serampore. Danes, like the Americans, took advantage of their country's neutrality, their trade picking up in 1796. Between 1796 and 1807, 20 percent of known arriving vessels (115 of 586) flew Danish flags.

11. That is, 138 of 166 *non-naval* long-haul vessels. Naval vessels include those classed as HC Brig of War, HC Cruizer, HC Gun Boat, HC Gun Brig, HM Sloop, HMB, HMS, or Transport.

12. The partial shipping data from the 1790s and early 1800s may understate U.S. shipping; alternatively, neutral trade at Java may have remained constrained by the war and structurally unable to reach peacetime levels.

13. "The Arrivals of Ships and Vessels in the Road of Batavia from the 16th of September 1811 to the 21st of April 1812," "The Arrivals of Ships & Vessels in the Road of Batavia in the Month of May 1812," and further monthly reports through September 1812. ANRI Marine, 298. There are no more arrivals from the United States for September–November (no surviving December report), though there are a couple of departures or arrivals from earlier in the year.

14. The other arrivals were sixteen Arab vessels, four Malay, and two Spanish. ANRI HR 2634 and 2635.

15. Cynthia Viallé and Leonard Blussé, *The Deshima Dagregisters*, vol. 10: *1790–1800* (Leiden, Netherlands: Institute for the History of European Expansion, 1997), vii.

16. On the number of U.S. vessels hired for the Japan trade, see van Eyck van Heslinga, *Van compagnie naar koopvaardij*, 183, Neth Nederlandse factorij

in Japan Item 671. See also Allan B. Cole, "The *Mount Vernon's* Voyage from Batavia to Maagzaki in 1807," *American Neptune* 5, no. 4 (October 1945): 255–265.

17. Viallé and Blussé, *Dagregisters,* 152.

18. "Bataafse Republiek. Reguster van aankoms en vertrek van skepe: Tafelbaai en Simonsbaai, Maart 3, 1803–Sept. 19, 1804," CTAR BR 536; "Bataafse Republiek. Reguster van aankoms en vertrek van skepe: Tafelbaai en Simons-baai, Jan. 4, 1805–Jan. 2, 1806," CTAR BR 537. "Likely East Indiamen" here excludes naval, military, cartel, fishing, whaling, and other such vessels. Counting all vessels or merchantmen only reveals similar proportions of American, other neutral, and French-aligned trade.

19. The British merchantmen listed were in port or en route when the Dutch re-occupied the colony, arriving before the end of June 1803. Only four British vessels are known to have arrived after June 1803. Likewise, French vessels departed France before war resumed, largely to reoccupy Pondicherry. Nine of the fifteen French vessels charted made Cape Town by July 1803. Between August 1803 and January 1806, only ten more known French trading vessels stopped at the Cape. Even Dutch shipping at the Cape was constrained by the war. Thirty-three Dutch vessels arrived in 1803; eleven are known to have arrived the following year, and three in 1805. By then, much of the Dutch fleet was bottled in port, sunk, or drafted into Napoleon's invasion flotilla.

20. CTAR BR 537.

21. Nor does Anthony Farrington list more than one English Company vessel making Cape Town in the 1803–1804 or 1804–1805 seasons. Anthony Farrington, *Catalogue of East India Company Ships' Journals and Logs, 1600–1834* (London: The British Library, 1999), 753. However, neutrals likely carried nonneutral cargo in their holds.

22. The Cape Town shipping register is in a continuous run between September 16, 1795, and July 1800. Neutrals included Danish, Genoese, Hamburg, Portuguese, Prussian, Spanish, Swedish, and Tuscan vessels. "A List of the Arrivals of all Ships and Vessels in the Bays of the Cape of Good Hope with their Sailing and other particulars Commencing the 16th of September 1795 the day of Capitulation," First British Occupation, Ships Arrivals, September 1795–July 1800, CTAR BO 194.

23. Archives of the Port Captain and Dock Superintendent Table Bay Harbor, Register of the Arrivals and Departures of Ships, June 1806–January 1824, CTAR PC 3/1. The record does not consider Simons Bay arrivals, which are listed separately from 1809 onward.

24. Auguste Toussaint, *La Route des Iles, contribution à l'histoire maritime des Mascareignes* (Paris: S.E.V.P.E.N., 1967), 216–228. Of those long-distance French vessels that did arrive, most sailed before receiving news of the war in 1793 or during the Peace of Amiens. French long-distance arrivals departed mainly from France (109) but also from India (58), Indonesia (24), and the Indo-Pacific generally (8). Indo-Pacific here refers to the Cape of Good Hope,

Arabia, Ceylon, Burma, and the Philippines. John H. Reinoehl, "Some Remarks on the American Trade: Jacob Crowninshield to James Madison 1806," *WMQ*, 3rd series 16, no. 1 (January 1959): 107.

25. The denominator, taken from Toussaint's data, includes slave vessels, largely French and Portuguese, suggesting that this statistic understates the American share of nonslaving commerce at Port Louis. Toussaint, *La Route des Iles*, 172. Looking at all foreign arrivals rather than all long-distance arrivals yields a different total (789 as opposed to 748) because of several foreign-carried interisland voyages.

26. Auguste Toussaint, *Early American Trade with Mauritius* (Port Louis, Mauritius: Esclapon, 1954), 70–86. Toussaint notes that this larger listing of American arrivals still omits some vessels listed in James Duncan Phillips's study of Salem departures, which is based on newspaper advertisements (James Duncan Phillips, *Salem and the Indies: The Story of the Great Commercial Era of the City* [Boston: Houghton Mifflin, 1947]). Toussaint cites different but overlapping sources for *Early American Trade* and *La Route des Iles*. Reports of arrivals were made orally to either a harbor master or the police. Two separate lists were kept. Each arrival was noted on its own form and not enumerated or tabulated into annual total. Without original totals it is unclear what has been lost. Toussaint's two data sets appear to give conservative estimates of the scale of U.S. trade in relation to other neutral and French shipping and of the relative distribution of ports from which U.S. vessels came. Document degradation makes it unlikely anyone will find more Mauritian archival sources.

27. Maur GB 26. One hundred twenty-five vessels made long-distance stops between January 10, 1811, when the first entry appears in the British records, and April 19, 1815. Eight Portuguese vessels made Mauritius in this period. Long-distance vessels arrived from the Atlantic; South Africa; Middle East; and South, Southeast, or East Asia. "Long-distance" here includes naval vessels.

28. Marina Alfonso Mola and Carlos Martínez Shaw, "Manila: An International Trade Port at the End of the Eighteenth Century" (unpublished conference paper, University of California, Davis, 2006); Marina Alfonso-Mola, "U.S. Ships in the Colonial Spanish Fleet, 1778–1828" (unpublished conference paper, University of California, Davis, 2006).

29. *ASP*, vols. 1 and 2, passim. U.S. customs records contradict the assumption that U.S.-flagged vessels arriving in Manila were actually British vessels in disguise. That disguise would have been distinctively more difficult to pull off in the United States than in the Philippines.

30. Data for 1798–1799 include non-Spanish shipping only. The years 1795–1796 and 1798–1799 begin on June 1. Estado que manifesta las Embarcasiones Nacionales y Estrangeras que con efectos de comercio vinieron al Puerto de Manola des de 1 de Junio de 1795 hasta fines de Mayo de 96, AGI Filipinas, 977. Entrado de las embarcaion extrangeras que entraron en Manila des

Junio 98 Uta Mayo de 99 y sus valores, AGI Filipinas, 978. Del Cargo delos productos del oro de Averia delos anos de 1800, 1801, y 1802, . . . , AGI Filipinas, 969. 1805 Cuenta General del fonds de Averia . . . de Manila. 1806 Cuenta General del fonds de Averia . . . de Manila. 1807 Cuenta General del fonds de Averia . . . de Manila. 1808 Cuenta General del fonds de Averia . . . de Manila. 1809 Cuenta General del fonds de Averia . . . de Manila. 1810 Cuenta General del fonds de Averia . . . de Manila, AGI Filipinas, 970. 1811 Cuenta General del fonds de Averia . . . de Manila. 1812 Cuenta General del fonds de Averia . . . de Manila. 1814 Cuenta General del fonds de Averia . . . de Manila. 1815 Cuenta General del fonds de Averia . . . de Manila, AGI Filipinas, 971.

31. Sumatran pepper was an exception.

32. There were also occasional entries from Malaya, Arabia, and India on native craft.

33. Chinese merchants arriving at Manila likely bought rice, not sugar, as part of the *nanyang* rice trade that Chinese officials encouraged to supply South China's rice deficit. U.S. merchants at Canton eventually thought of bringing in rice from Manila (in addition to specie) to receive the tax abatement on rice ships. Sampans arriving in Manila may well have *also* bought sugar. This requires further investigation.

34. The embargo referred to is the French embargo of U.S. trade, which occurred for roughly a year in the 1790s during the Quasi-War.

35. Ole Feldbaek, *India Trade under the Danish Flag, 1772–1808* (Lund: Studentlitteratur, 1969), 193.

36. Toussaint, *Route des Iles*, 95, relying on William Milburn, *Oriental Commerce*, vol. 2 (London: Black, Perry, 1813), 569. Milburn gives no source for his "data;" prize records extant in the National Archives of Mauritius make it difficult to imagine how anyone in Britain could have reliable information about this in 1813. Milburn's assertion implied that, after the war, his British private trade readers would not face significant U.S. competition in India; this also excused the American success in Indian cloth. Holden Furber, "The Beginnings of American Trade with India, 1784–1812," *The New England Quarterly* 11, no. 2 (June 1938): 235–265, likewise claimed, without evidence, that Mauritius became an entrepôt for Indian goods because of French privateering.

37. Minister Marbois, Philadelphia, 1781, marginal notes by Naval and Colonial Ministry, CAOM C¹13, 216–218.

38. Maur, GB, 21, 23, 47, 50, 53, 61, 66, 70, 80–81, 90–95, 97–98, 103–105, 109–112. Attempts of French Indian merchants to export cloth to Ile de France were sporadic. Some buyers of this cloth had Anglophone names, and may have been Americans. Yet this trade does not appear to have occurred frequently. Eighteenth-Century Documents, vol. 280, "Ile de France. Papiers relaitfs à un voyage à l'Isle de France, 1798–1800," Indian National Archives, Pondicherry Record Centre. The British blockade of Ile de France demanded

a considerable number of vessels. It took seven weeks to get from India to Mauritius, leaving ten weeks on station before a vessel that had set out with a half-year's provisions would have to turn back. The French privateers were dangerous enough to warrant the blockade, but not so dangerous as to warrant committing additional forces. Cyril Northcote Parkinson, *Edward Pellew, Viscount Exmouth, Admiral of the Red* (London: Methuen & Co., 1934), 353.

39. *ASP*, passim. The record for October 1, 1794 through September 30, 1810 gives the portion of the French Wars during which Mauritius was under French control.

40. Henri Prentout, *L'Ile de France sous Decaen, 1803–1810* (Paris: Hachette, 1901), 204. Claude Wanquet notes that Americans supplied the Mascarenes, in part, from British-held regions. Claude Wanquet, "Quelques remarques sur les relations des Mascareignes avec les autres pays de l'Océan Indien à l'époque de la Révolution française," *Annuaire des Pays de l'Océan Indien* 7 (1980): 232–233.

41. Prentout, *L'Ile de France sous Decaen*, 204 Danish neutrals likewise bought sugar and coffee—not Indian cloth—at Mauritius. Ole Feldbaek, "Danish East India Trade 1772–1807: Statistics and Structure," *Scandinavian Economic History Review* 26, no. 2 (1978): 137.

42. van Eyck van Heslinga, *Van compagnie naar koopvaardij*, 183. Java faced similar issues with devaluation. CARAN AF/IV/1325, Governor Jan Willem Janssens to Bonaparte, Batavia, June 11, 1811. Payment in cash might have been, in part, because payment through London banks would have been politically difficult. Stuart Weems Bruchey, *Robert Oliver, Merchant of Baltimore, 1783–1819* (Baltimore: Johns Hopkins University Press, 1956), 182–183.

43. van Eyck van Heslinga, *Van compagnie naar koopvaardij*, 179–182. The renting of American vessels departing from the Netherlands sometimes included a sham sale of the cargo, so that, if stopped, the American captain could claim he was not carrying Dutch property. Such sham sales did not require much U.S. capital, though they did take up shipping space. If a U.S. merchant had the capital, he would prefer to buy the cargo properly for himself, a more-profitable transaction. Hence ship lettings in the Netherlands were outnumbered by Americans buying cargoes directly from Batavia. Ole Feldbaek, "Dutch Batavia Trade via Copenhagen 1795–1807: A Study of Colonial Trade and Neutrality," *Scandinavian Economic History Review* 21, no. 1 (1973): 46. 56.

44. French and Dutch Revolutionary pamphlets and memorials discuss East India monopolies in terms that American revolutionaries would have understood. CARAN AF/IV/1799, Mr. Hogendorp, "Memoire sur les possessions hollandaise aux Indes Orientales," 30 Juin 1806. Links between French, Dutch, and Anglo-American free-trade sentiment in this period needs further investigation.

45. Eymeret, "Adminstration Napoléonienne en Indonésie," 36–37. The mission garnered little, culminating in only one vessel being sent to the Indies, the aptly named *Goldsearcher*. Governor Daendels accused the councilor, Roger Van Polanen, of Anglophilia and (implicitly) of not wholeheartedly encouraging U.S. commerce. On Moluccas: Bernard H. M. Vlekke, *Nusantara: A History of Indonesia* (The Hague, 1959), 245.

46. John H. Reinoehl, "Some Remarks on the American Trade: Jacob Crowninshield to James Madison 1806," *WMQ*, 3rd series, 16, no. 1 (January 1959): 104.

47. O. D. Corpuz, *An Economic History of the Philippines* (Quezon City: University of the Philippines Press, 1997), 39–40; Weng Eang Cheong, "Changing the Rules of the Game (The Indo-Manila Trade: 1785–1809)," *Journal of Southeast Asian Studies* 1, no. 2 (September 1970): 1–19; Weng Eang Cheong, "The Decline of Manila as the Spanish Entrepôt in the Far East, 1785–1826: Its Impact on the Pattern of Southeast Asian Trade," *Journal of Southeast Asian Studies* 2, no. 2 (September 1971): 142–158.

48. Nicholas Tarling, *Cambridge History of Southeast Asia*, vol. 1 (Cambridge: Cambridge University Press, 1992), 608.

49. Corpuz, *Economic History of the Philippines*, 95–96.

50. Weng Eang Cheong, "Canton and Manila in the Eighteenth Century," in Jerome Ch'en and Nicholas Tarling, eds., *Studies in the Social History of China and South-east Asia* (Cambridge: Cambridge University Press, 1970), 239.

51. Nicholas P. Cushner, *Spain in the Philippines from Conquest to Revolution* (Quezon City: Institute of Philippine Culture, 1971), 196.

52. Tarling, *Cambridge History of Southeast Asia*, vol. 1, 607. Many large landholders were in fact mestizo Chinese or Chinese Christians, though it is unclear whether they would have profited from selling sugar in Atlantic markets more than they already did in Asian markets. Thomas R. McHale and Mary C. McHale, *Early American-Philippine Trade: The Journal of Nathaniel Bowditch in Manila, 1796* (New Haven: Yale University, Southeast Asia Studies Monograph Series No. 2, 1962), 20n45.

53. For Manila revenue, see AGI Filipinas, 969–971.

54. Corpuz, *Economic History of the Philippines*, 92.

55. Cushner, *Spain in the Philippines*, 192.

56. Tarling, "Age of Transition," in *Cambridge History of Southeast Asia*, vol. 1, 572–612; Peter Carey, *The Power of Prophecy: Prince Dipanagara and the End of an Old Order in Java, 1785–1855* (Leiden, Netherlands: KITLV Press, 2007), 455, 466, 503.

57. Magallon to Hoche, 15 nivôse 7 (January 4, 1798), CAOM C^4 112, 96, as cited in Claude Wanquet, *La France et la première abolition de l'esclavage 1794-1802: Le cas des colonies orientales Ile de France (Maurice) et la Réunion* (Paris: Karthala, 1998), 472 ; Rapport des bureaux de la Marine sur la lettre au ministre du 26 frimaire an VI (December 16, 1797), CAOM

C^4 112, 16, as cited in Wanquet, *La France et la première abolition de l'esclavage*, 477.

58. The Dutch did hire 300 Swiss soldiers from Spain to help defend Java. Buitenlandse Zaken voor 1813 Nationaal Archief, Den Haag, Netherlands, Inv.nr. 422, April 9, 1800.

59. van Eyck van Heslinga, *Van compagnie naar koopvaardij*, 179–180.

60. Marbot, an official returning from Ile de France, noted his return to France via the United States in a particularly casual way to the French naval and colonial ministers—casually because it was so common. Marbot to Naval and Colonial Minister, September 18, 1806, Paris, CARAN AF/IV/1215.

61. The enclosed Spanish letter gives it as "Apo Bay on the S[outh] W[est] of the Island of Mindoro." Raphael Maria de Aguilar to Drummond, Manila, July 31, 1806, OIOC Mss Eur G92/1, 178; Extract, General Letter from Canton, January 4, 1807, and Extract, Canton Consultations, August 11, 1806, OIOC Mss Eur G92/1, 177. American trade between the Masacarenes and Java also afforded the former additional supplies. See Charles François Tombe, *Voyage aux Indes Orientales, pendant les années 1802, 1803, 1804, 1805 et 1806* (Paris, 1810), 94.

62. Champagny to Napoleon, Paris, November 8, 1808, CARAN AF/IV/1686. For Van de Graaff: Maurice Dupont, *L'Amiral Willaumez* (Paris: Tallandier, 1987), 229. Van de Graaff's vessel was taken by Sercey's squadron. The British took fewer than ten of the nearly 400 U.S. vessels passing through Batavia after 1795, making passage on an American ship an acceptable risk.

63. Amasa Delano, *A narrative of voyages and travels, in the northern and southern hemispheres: Comprising three voyages round the world, together with a voyage of survey and discovery, in the Pacific Ocean and oriental islands* (Boston, 1817), 200.

64. Mauritius was half forest in the 1810s, yet aside from some timbering, economic activity was confined to the deforested parts. Urban artisans, city merchants, and plantation hands—all slaves—were the backbone of the economy. Wanquet, "Quelques remarques sur les relations des Mascareignes," 200, 229.

65. Date: 15 Frimaire An XII. Prentout, *L'Ile de France sous Decaen*, 203–204, citing CAOM C^2 register 102.

66. Charles Decaen, General Report, 1807, CAOM C^2 register 104, as cited in Prentout, *L'Ile de France sous Decaen*, 204–205.

67. Prentout, *L'Ile de France sous Decaen*, 205–206, 224. Napoleon tried, unsuccessfully, to encourage shipping from Ile de France to the metropole in 1808, perhaps in response to the embargo. Decaen did not think Jefferson would go through with the embargo. Decaen, General Report, 1807, CAOM C^2 register 104, as cited in Prentout, *L'Ile de France sous Decaen*, 204–205.

68. Jean Gelman Taylor, *The Social World of Batavia: European and Eurasian in Dutch Asia* (Madison: University of Wisconsin Press, 1983), 111; Carey, *Power of Prophecy*, 278–279.

69. Taylor, *Social World of Batavia*, 78–79, 85, 93. Taylor argues that local Batavian elites were mestizo to the point of not being Dutch. As Anglo-Indians, they preferred "spending on a grand scale, the importance of display" to Dutch "Calvinist, bourgeois thrift" (p. 79). Our understanding of this seems mediated by newly arrived Company employees from the Netherlands; perhaps creoles found such extravagance affordable in Asia. Historians of the French and Dutch East Indies focus on national history or nationally defined imperial history as well as (in Indonesia's case) the *longue durée*. Historians of the French Wars focus on Europe. Both sets of scholars make little of the transimperial commonalities of this period. C. N. Parkinson, *War in the Eastern Seas, 1793–1815* (London: Allen & Unwin, 1954), is the rare volume that considers the French Wars in Asia as an international phenomenon.

70. Taylor, *Social World of Batavia*, 94–95, 111.

71. Kenneth Wyndham Smith, *From Frontier to Midlands: A History of the Graaff Reinet District, 1786–1910*, Occasional Paper No. 20 (Grahamstown, South Africa: Institute of Social and Economic Research, Rhodes University, 1976), 26–34; T. R. H. Davenport and Christopher Saunders, *South Africa: A Modern History* (London: Macmillan, 2000), 39–41.

72. Mémoire du 17 frimaire an V (December 7, 1796) publié par Saint Elme Le Duc 294; Adresse de l'Assemblée aux habitants et pétition à l'Assemblée de la Chaumière de Sainte-Marie, des 6 et 11 nivôse an III (December 26 and 31, 1794), Archives Départmental de la Réunion L 22 and 19/2, as cited in Claude Wanquet, "Les Iles Mascareignes, l'Inde et les Indiens pendant la Révolution Française," *Revue française d'histoire d'outre mer* 78, no. 290 (1991): 40–41.

73. Curtis to Spencer, Cape of Good Hope, October 10, 1800, in Herbert W. Richmond, ed., *Private Papers of George, Second Earl Spencer*, vol. 4 (London: Navy Records Society, 1924), 234.

74. Smith, *History of the Graaff Reinet*, 26–34.

75. R. R. Palmer, *The Age of the Democratic Revolution*, vol. 2 (Princeton: Princeton University Press, 1964), 204–207, finds the evidence for a Jacobin revolt at the Cape intriguing, but little more.

76. Ulbe Bosma and Remco Raben, Wendi Schaffer, trans., *Being "Dutch" in the Indies: A History of Creolization and Empire, 1500–1920* (Singapore: National University of Singapore Press, 2008), 67–103.

77. Taylor, *Social World of Batavia*, 97, citing Thomas Stamford Raffles, *The History of Java*, vol. 2 (London: John Murray, 1830), 270. "European" here takes the broadest possible definition of the term.

78. The 1791 census gives Cape colony as a whole, including several towns in the western districts and some sparsely populated farms in the interior. The Cape had 3,613 male burghers, 2,460 women, and 6,955 children—roughly 14,000 whites. Nonmilitary employees of the Dutch East India Company at the Cape and their dependents numbered approximately 1,500 more. C. W. de Kiewiet gives the population in the western districts as 13,500 at this time. C. W. de

Kiewiet, *A History of South Africa Social and Economic* (Oxford: Oxford University Press, 1957), 30. Whites at the Cape held more than 17,000 slaves. George McCall Theal, *History of South Africa, 1691–1795*, vol. 2 (London: Swan Sonnenschein, 1888), 289–290.

79. Dutch settlements on Java, the Cape, and Ceylon bordered powerful local groups. The so-called Caffre Wars fought after the British conquest of the Cape and the bloody Kandian War waged in 1816 evinced the dangers. The Javan sultanates of Yogyakarta and Surakarta remained antagonistic toward Batavia, especially Daendels's administration, and cooperated with the British in 1811. Yogyakarta rose up in the Javan War (1825–1830). Carey, *The Power of Prophecy*.

80. For Batavia's factions see Wanquet, "Quelques remarques sur les relations des Mascareignes," 223–224.

81. Maur, "Oaths of Allegiance"; Alicia Schrikker, *Dutch and British Colonial Intervention in Sri Lanka, 1780–1815* (Leiden, Netherlands: Brill, 2007), 135, 141–145. Britain defended European whites under its protection. When, on the occasion of the British conquest of Java, the sultan of Palembang executed the Dutch in his domain, the British governor-general in Bengal took the act as a sign of "hostility towards the British Government" in "dissolving the pre-established relation between him the ruling power in Java," and sent a punitive force to "avenge innocent blood" drawn with such "cruelty and treachery" (and to try to expand the empire at Palembang's expense). House of Commons, "Copy of all Diapatches and Documents which have been received by The East India Company, relating to the Acquisition of the Island of Banca, in The East Indies," in *Sessional Papers, 1814–1815, East India Affairs*, 238–241.

82. Roux to Decaen, February 11, 1809, in Papiers du Géneral Decaen, Bibliotheque de le ville de Caen, 104, as cited in Prentout, *L'Ile de France sous Decaen*, 483–486.

83. Governor Daendels on Java was informed of the uprising while he was in Spain in 1808, and received Spanish newspaper clipping enthusiastically narrating the anti-Napoleonic revolt. He forwarded them on to the Spanish governor at Manila, over whom he seems to have assumed some sort of authority. Daendels to Dn. Mariano Fernandez de Folgueras, Buitenzorg, Java, January 23, 1809, ANRI HR, 4071–4072; Ducrest de Villeneuve, *Journal du Voyage de "la Mouche" No. 6, Sous le commandement Du lieutenant de vaisseau Ducrest de Villeneuve, expédiée Pour l'île de France et Manille en 1808* (Paris: Imprimerie Administrative de Paul Dupont, 1857), 9–21.

84. Given Taylor's argument for a distinctly creole, mestizo, and autonomous Batavian elite, this makes their unwillingness to separate from the Netherlands more striking. Taylor, *Social World of Batavia*, 78–113.

85. Taylor emphasizes intensification of Dutch colonial rule and Dutch (rather than local) identity among Batavian elites. Taylor, *Social World of Batavia*, 114–174.

86. In 1819 John Quincy Adams won Caribbean trading concessions partly because they were growing irrelevant.

7. The India Trade

1. For old and new shipping interests see C. H. Philips, *The East India Company, 1784–1834* (Manchester: Manchester University Press, 1940), 80–84 and passim. The shorthand "Shipping Interest" is used here most often in reference to the Old Shipping Interest.

2. Total Company carrying capacity varied considerably by year and with the use of extra ships. David Scott estimated that the Company brought 6,000 to 7,000 tons to London from Calcutta annually. Michael Fry, *The Dundas Despotism* (Edinburgh: Edinburgh University Press, 1992); *Trade Papers,* "Mr. Scott's Paper, with Note from Mr. Scott and 2 Tables, 23 October 1800," appendixes A and B, OIOC L/MAR/C/50, 303–305.

3. Amales Tripathi, *Trade and Finance in the Bengal Presidency, 1793–1833* (Calcutta: Oxford University Press, 1979), 39; John Cochrane to Henry Dundas, Harley Street, March 3, 1799, OIOC H/405, 3. Dundas also enlarged the privilege trade allotted to British Indian residents in order to draw Anglo-Indian remittances to Britain as well.

4. "An Account of all Foreign Ships and their Tonnage, imported & exported at the several Settlements in India, for 5 years last past, 1795 to 1800," OIOC L/MAR/C/547, 9–11. The American figures include inter-Asian and east-west traffic.

5. Smithian free traders held, as Baring later explained, that restrictions or prohibitions on trade "always" create "counteraction and contraband." Edward Parry and Charles Grant (Chairs) to the Court of Directors, East India House, October 14, 1807, OIOC H/494, 21.

6. On Bermuda privateers see Samuel Flagg Bemis, *Jay's Treaty: A Study in Commerce and Diplomacy* (New Haven: Yale University Press, 1962), 294n20.

7. Parry and Grant to Directors, October 14, 1807, OIOC H/494, 17.

8. Company officials did not permanently conquer French, Dutch, and Danish India posts because these posts were created by treaties between the European states and various Indian powers. The Company was, these officials believed, constitutionally obliged to respect their existence. See Robert Travers, *Ideology and Empire in Eighteenth-Century India: The British in Bengal* (New York: Cambridge University Press, 2007).

9. It is unclear who put the East India provision into Jay's instructions. Bemis surmises Alexander Hamilton ghostwrote instructions for Secretary of State Edmund Randolph, perhaps including the East India provision, though this is not completely clear. Bemis, *Jay's Treaty,* 289. It does not appear in Hamilton's April 23, 1794 memorandum to President Washington concerning Jay's negotiating points. Henry Cabot Lodge, ed., *Works of Alexander Hamilton,*

vol. 5 (New York: G. P. Putnam & Sons, 1903), 115–118. Combs notes a parallel letter, Hamilton to Jay, May 6, 1794, in Lodge, ed., *Works*, vol. 1, 124–125. Jerald A. Combs, *The Jay Treaty* (London: University of California Press, 1970), 216. The East India proposal did not originate from the British side. It does not appear in Grenville's intracabinet memorandum, "Project of Heads of Proposals to be made to Mr. Jay," nor does it appear in Hawkesbury's response as President of the Board of Trade. Add. Mss. 38354, f39. Dundas was mute on the subject as well. Bradford Perkins attributes the growth in U.S. trade with India to this concession. Bradford Perkins, *The First Rapprochement: England and the United States, 1795–1805* (Philadelphia: University of Pennsylvania Press, 1955), 5; Bemis, *Jay's Treaty*, 293. Jay's instructions, dated May 6, 1794, can also be found in *American State Papers: Foreign Relations*, vol. 1 (Washington, DC: Gales and Seaton, 1832), 472.

10. Such is Bradford Perkins's interpretation. Holden Furber suggests that Article XIII was Dundas and Pitt's way to undermine the Company's monopoly.

11. Perkins, *First Rapprochement*, 71, citing Dundas to Hugh Inglis, June 14, 1797, OIOC H/MISC/337.

12. Henry Dundas note, June 14, 1797, OIOC H/MISC, 337, 416–417.

13. The *Elizabeth* did this.

14. The *Argonaut* did this.

15. Compare Perkins, *First Rapprochement*, 183. Lloyd Kenyon was appointed master of the rolls after Pitt's ascension to power. He was made lord chief justice created a baron four years later. "Lloyd Kenyon, First Baron Kenyon (1732–1802)," *DNB*, accessed December 13, 2009.

16. Parry and Grant to Court of Directors, East India House, October 1808, OIOC H/494, 209.

17. Parry and Grant to Directors, October 1808, OIOC H/494, 241, 251.

18. Parry and Grant to Directors, October 1808, OIOC H/494, 271.

19. Ole Feldbaek, *India Trade under the Danish Flag 1772–1808: European enterprise and Anglo-Indian Remittance and Trade* (Lund: Studentlitteratur, 1969), 171, 186, OIOC L/MAR/C/535, v–viii. These charges where not unusual. Patrick Crowhurst, *The Defense of British Trade, 1689–1815* (Kent, UK: Dawson, 1977), 215–217.

20. *Minutes of Evidence taken before the Right Honourable the House of Lords in the Lords Committees, appointed to take into consideration so much of the speech of his royal highness the Prince Regent as relates to the Charter of the East-India Company* (London, 1813), OIOC A/2/15, 954–955. More research is needed here into the quality of cloth ordered from India in this period.

21. Parry and Grant to Directors, October 1808, OIOC H/494, 267. Emphasis added. For the zero-sum argument, see also Parry and Grant to Directors, October 14, 1807, OIOC H/494, 43–45, and, on sales of supplies to the European population in India, 85. On tariffs see *ASP*, vol. 1, 47, 599, 615, 619; *ASP*, vol. 2, 33, 225–254, 354, 632–642.

22. Parry and Grant to Directors, October 1808, OIOC H/494, 217.

23. Tripathi, *Trade and Finance*, 80, 117–118.

24. Amasa Delano, *A narrative of voyages and travels, in the northern and south-ern hemispheres: Comprising three voyages round the world, together with a voyage of survey and discovery, in the Pacific Ocean and oriental islands* (Boston, 1817), 236; Feldbaek, *India Trade*, 212.

25. Feldbaek, *India Trade*, 157, 162.

26. Eliza Fay, *Original Letters from India (1779–1815)*, ed. E. M. Forster (London: Hogarth, 1925, 1986), 240–271. The Salem impost book records Jacob Crowninshield and the *Henry* reaching Salem in November 1794. Ten consignees sign for a cargo worth over $60,000. Though the register notes a stop at Cowes, Isle of Wight, it does not note Fay, who could not have signed for it in any case. Crowninshield signed for over $18,000 in goods, likely including Fay's, since he was to sell it for her as well. The impost books thus understate the number of discrete properties on board East Indiamen by including foreign investors, such as Fay, under the merchant handling their business on commission. *Impost Books of the Collector* (Salem, MA), NARA (MA).

27. The Chairs noted to Baring that British investors might also contribute silver to a U.S. venture to India, though apparently they were ignorant of Baring's involvement in that trade. Parry and Grant to Directors, October 1808, OIOC H/494, 323.

28. Funds sent to Britain via the United States in order to save money were larger than they would have been otherwise. This benefited Britain, for the capital holders were successful merchants. The Company, had it taken a cut, would likely have squandered it in India.

29. This argument seems to equate the U.S.-India trade of the French Wars with the Austrian and other European East India Companies that provided a means for British merchants to smuggle into Britain and around the English Company's monopoly before 1784.

30. Parry and Grant to Directors, October 14, 1807, OIOC H/494, 81.

31. OIOC P/339/77, P/339/80, P/339/86, P/339/88, P/339/95, P/339/100, P/339/105, P/339/110, P/339/113, P/339/116, and P/339/121.

32. Parry and Grant to Directors, October 14, 1807, OIOC H/494, 81–83, 87. Following the Chairs' logic, given that specie was a greater share of U.S. sales to India after 1801 than before, and given that Americans brought a greater share of their cargoes in specie than Europeans did, either this growth in U.S. trade did not represent a takeover of the Europeans' trade to India or the Americans were assuming European trade and taking silver to India in cases in which Europeans had found other goods would do.

33. Parry and Grant to Directors, October 1808, OIOC H/494, 317. Emphasis in original. Grant had argued in 1800 that the Americans traded largely with their own funds. Tripathi, *Trade and Finance*, 63.

34. Feldbaek, *India Trade*, 206–207.

35. Tripathi, *Trade and Finance*, 80–81, 105; Feldbaek, *India Trade*, 205.

36. Tripathi, *Trade and Finance,* 118; Parry and Grant to Directors, October 1808, OIOC H/494, 223–225.
37. Reports on External Commerce, Madras, 1804, OIOC P/339/83, paragraphs 6–9.
38. Parry and Grant to Directors, October 14, 1807, OIOC H/494, 63; Parry and Grant to Directors, East India House, October 1808, OIOC H/494, 217, 281–283, 329, 331; Tripathi, *Trade and Finance,* 72, 91, 122. Emphasis in original.
39. Parry and Grant to Directors, October 14, 1807, OIOC H/494, 51.
40. Parry and Grant to Directors, October 14, 1807, OIOC H/494, 67.
41. Parry and Grant to Directors, October 1808, OIOC H/494, 217.
42. Parry and Grant to Directors, October 1808, OIOC H/494, 273.
43. Parry and Grant to Directors, October 1808, OIOC H/494, 319, 323. Emphasis in original. Parry and Grant thought it irrelevant that even American re-exports to Europe might benefit the British economy at large (the remittances were often spent on British manufactures).
44. Robert Grenville Wallace, *Memoirs of India* (London, 1824), 118, 301; Walter Hamilton, *A Geographical, Statistical and Historical Description of Hindostan,* vol. 1 (London, 1820), 49; Delano, *Narrative of Voyages,* 241; R. Heber, *Narrative of a Journey* (London, 1828), 24, 26.
45. Emma Roberts, *Scenes and Characteristics of Hindostan* (London, 1835), 4, 16; T. Williamson, *East India Vade-Mecum* (London, 1810), 161, 163, 166; Hugh Murray et al., *Historical and Descriptive Account of British India* (Edinburgh: Oliver and Boyd, 1833), 428.

   Wallace, *Memoirs of India,* 302; Hamilton, *Historical Description,* 51–52, 55.
46. Hamilton, *Historical Description,* 48, 57; Wallace, *Memoirs of India,* 302, 461; Fay, *Original Letters,* 189; Murray et al., *Historical Account,* 426.
47. Feldbaek, *India Trade,* 187, 187n131; Edward Parry and Charles Grant (Chairs) to the Directors, East India House, October 14, 1807, OIOC H/494, 81; "An Account of all Foreign Ships and their Tonnage, imported & exported at the several Settlements in India, for 5 years last past, 1795 to 1800," OIOC L/MAR/C/547; Pierre Léon, *Histoire économique et sociale du monde,* vol. 3 : *Inerties et révolutions* (Paris: A. Colin, 1978), 311–315.
48. There were 106 U.S. departures (30,662 tons). Reports on External Commerce, Madras, 1802–1812, OIOC P/339/77, P/339/80, P/339/86, P/339/88, P/339/95, P/339/100, P/339/105, P/339/110, P/339/113, P/339/116, and P/339/121, Excludes several U.S. arrivals at the smaller ports in the Madras Presidency that did not stop at the city of Madras itself.
49. "Reports on External Commerce, Madras, 1805," OIOC P/339/88, 20–23; "Reports on External Commerce, Madras, 1811–1812," OIOC P/339/120, 12–14; Quotation from "Reports on External Commerce, Madras for the Year 1803," OIOC P/339/80, 210–212.
50. Tripathi, *Trade and Finance,* 80; Bombay Commercial Reports. OIOC P/419/39 through P/419/47. Further work may be needed on this point.

51. In addition, one U.S. vessel (250 tons) called at Surat in 1804–1805. Bombay Commercial Reports, OIOC P/419/40 through P/419/52. No U.S. trade was recorded from 1811 to 1816. Jacob Crowninshield claimed that Americans carried Bombay cotton to China until the Jay Treaty expired, though the Bombay Commerical Reports do not confirm this. John H. Reinoehl, "Some Remarks on the American Trade: Jacob Crowninshield to James Madison 1806," *WMQ*, 3rd series, 16, no. 1 (January 1959): 109–110. For U.S. trade at Penang, see B. L. Mandal, *India's Trade Relations with Malaya and Indonesia, 1783–1833* (Allahabad: Kitab Mahal, 1984), 132–135.

52. Taken as the sum of tonnage arrived and departed divided by the sum of ships arrived and departed.

53. "A Return of All the Ships Launched in the River Thames for the Service of the East India Company, in each year, from 1770 to 1812, with the Tonnage of each Ship; also the Tonnage of the Ship now building," March 15, 1813, in *Sessional Papers, 1812–1813, East India Company*, 193; Crowhurst, *Defense of British Trade*, 216–217; Directors to Buckinghamshire, East India House, April 15, 1812, Item 64, OIOC A/2/14.

54. Feldbaek, *India Trade*, 160; Mandal, *India's Trade Relations*, 139.

55. C. Northcote Parkinson, *Trade in the Eastern Seas, 1793–1813* (Cambridge: Cambridge University Press, 1937); Cathy Matson, "The Revolution, Constitution, and New Nation," in Stanley Engerman and Robert Gallman, eds., *Cambridge Economic History of the United States*, vol. 1 (Cambridge: Cambridge University Press, 1996–2000), 395; Wellesley to Directors, September 30, 1800. Calcutta, in Montgomery Martin, *The Despatches, Minutes and Correspondence of the Marquess Wellesley, K.G. during his administration in India*, vol. 2 (London, 1836), 384; T. T. Brown, Reporter of External Commerce, Bengal, September 10, 1800. reproduced in J. Kumar, *Select Documents in Indian Trade and Industry, 1773–1833* (New Delhi: Janaki Prakashan, 1981), 36; Thomas Twining, *Travels in America 100 Years Ago* (New York: Harper & Brothers, 1894).

56. OIOC P/339/77, P/339/80, P/339/86, P/339/88, P/339/95, P/339/100, P/339/105, P/339/110, P/339/113, P/339/116, and P/339/121. Morison gives one man for fifteen tons as standard for U.S. vessels of the period. Morison, *Maritime History of Massachusetts, 1783–1860* (Boston: Houghton Mifflin, 1961), 106. Further comparative work on American, British, and European crew/tonnage ratios is needed.

57. Rainier to Spencer, December 10, 1799, in Herbert W. Richmond, ed., *Private Papers of George, Second Earl Spencer*, vol. 4 (London: Navy Records Society, 1924), 202.

58. List of Ships Arriving at St. Helena, 1793–1803, The Archives, The Castle, Jamestown, St. Helena. "Other neutrals" includes Denmark, Hamburg, Genoa, Portugal, Sweden, and Tuscany. For a complete picture of available east-west trade data for the circum-African route, one would need to create a composite

of data at Mauritius, Cape Town, St. Helena, and Rio de Janeiro. This remains to be done.

59. K. N. Chaudhuri, *The English East India Company: The Study of an Early Joint-Stock Company, 1600–1640* (London: Cass, 1965).

60. By contracting in advance, the Company also deprived the open market of significant trading volume. If all trades, including the Company's, went through the spot market, one would expect large purchases to push up prices less.

61. American sailings were sometimes restricted by Company port officers who closed the Hoogly because of French privateers, an action that affected all merchant vessels.

62. Pamela Nightingale, "Scott, David (1746–1805)," *DNB,* accessed May 10, 2005; Fry, *Dundas Despotism,* 149, 195; James G. Parker, "Scottish Enterprise in India, 1750–1914," in R. A. Cage, ed., *The Scots Abroad: Labour, Capital, Enterprise, 1750–1914* (London: Croom Helm, 1985). 204–206; C. H. Philips. ed., *The Correspondence of David Scott Director and Chairman of the East India Company Relating to Indian Affairs 1787–1805* (London: Office of the Royal Historical Society, 1951), 166, 168; Philips, *East India Company,* 97–100. Jacob Bosanquet, then Chair, led the charge. Scott defended himself in *The Debates at the Quarterly General Court Held at The East India House, on Wednesday, March 20, 1799* . . . (London: T. Gillet, 1799), 25–70; *The Debates at the Quarterly General Court Held at The East India House, on Wednesday, June 19, 1799* . . . (London: T. Gillet, 1799); and *The Debate Held at The East India House, on Friday, June 28, 1799* . . . (London: T. Gillet, 1799). See also *Papers respecting illicit trade* [London, April 1799]. Scott's correspondence can be found in OIOC H/404, H/728–731, and H/495–496. Philips, *East India Company,* 98–101; OIOC H/337, 427–514; H/405, 217–221.

63. Tripathi, *Trade and Finance,* 47, 49, 51.

64. In 1809 the Chairs recognized that if their monopoly were abolished only on the *"surplus produce of India"*—which Britons would then be free to bring to London—the Company would be effectively forced to compete in the open market. The logical extension of this—that since Americans already brought the Indian "surplus" to Europe, the Company needed to compete with Americans more effectively—seems not to have been translated into action. Chairs to Robert Dundas, East India House, January 13, 1809, OIOC Mss Eur F/149/102. Emphasis in original.

65. Martin, *Despatches of Marquess Wellesley,* vol. 2, 382, 384, 386; Tripathi, *Trade and Finance,* 40, 52, 93.

66. Feldbaek, *India Trade,* 190; Tripathi, *Trade and Finance,* 78, 117.

67. Feldbaek, *India Trade,* 186, 188–190.

68. Tripathi, *Trade and Finance,* 1.

69. Who made this decision remains unclear.

70. Baring may have been affected by links to the British negotiators for the 1806 Anglo-American treaty; certainly he knew the men. This needs to be investigated.

For Grant's shift see Philips, *East India Company*. Baring and Grant also traded charges of inconsistency. OIOC H/494, 55, 293–297.

71. This debate is carried on through a set of four dueling memoranda. See OIOC H/494, 5–333.

72. Parry and Grant to [Stephen Cottrell?], July 14, 1808, OIOC H/494, 105–121.

73. Parry and Grant to Directors, October 1808, OIOC H/494, 229.

74. Parry and Grant to Directors, October 1808, OIOC H/494, 231.

75. Parry and Grant to Directors, October 1808, OIOC H/494, 229.

76. Tripathi, *Trade and Finance*, 102; H. Bowen, *East India Company: Trade and Domestic Financial Statistics, 1755–1838*, [computer file] (Colchester, Essex: UK Data Archive [distributor], September 2007), SN: 5690. See "imports_textiles."

77. Parry and Grant to Directors, October 14, 1807, OIOC H/494, 15.

78. OIOC H/494, 13–15, 87. The Company also claimed the Americans did not have to pay "War Insurance." Though the Company did not insure its goods, private traders shipping with the Company did (OIOC H/494 57, 315). So did Americans. Work comparing insurance rates for private trade on Company ships, U.S.-carried shipping, and the country trade is needed.

79. Parry and Grant to [Stephen Cottrell?], July 14, 1808, OIOC H/494, 105–121.

80. Parry and Grant to Directors, October 1808, OIOC H/494, 231.

81. Parry and Grant to Directors, October 14, 1807, OIOC H/494, 37.

82. Parry and Grant to Directors, October 14, 1807, OIOC H/494, 61.

83. Parry and Grant to Directors, October 14, 1807, OIOC H/494, 19.

84. Parry and Grant to Directors, October 14, 1807, OIOC H/494, 57, 61. Emphasis in original.

85. Parry and Grant to Directors, October 14, 1807, OIOC H/494, 57.

86. Parry and Grant to Directors, October 1808, OIOC H/494, 321.

8. America's China and Pacific Trade

1. Nor do any good runs of Portuguese shipping records survive from Macau in the archives of the Senato Loyal. Paul Van Dyke, *The Canton Trade: Life and Enterprise on the China Coast, 1690–1845* (Hong Kong: Hong Kong University Press, 2005). Macau's scanty trade records have been mined in A. M. Martins Do Vale, *Os Portugueses em Macau (1750–1800)* (Macau: Institvto Portvgvês do Oriente, 1997); Ângela Guimarães, *Uma Relação Especial Macau e as Relações Luso-Chinesas 1780–1844* (Lisbon: Edição Cies, 1996).

2. Rhys Richards, "United States Trade with China, 1784–1814," *The American Neptune* 54, Special Supplement (1994): 9. Records made in China encompass U.S. vessels' voyages between China and Europe, voyages which would not be encompassed by U.S. customs records. For such voyages see Louis

Dermigny, *La China et l'occident: Le Commerce à Canton au XXIIIe Siècle,* vol. 3 (Paris: S.E.V.P.E.N., 1964), 1170. For the U.S. China trade generally, see Dermigny, *La Chine et l'occident,* 1129–1196.

3. Yen-P'ing Hao, "Chinese Teas to America—A Synopsis," in John K. Fairbank and Ernest May, eds., *America's China Trade in Historical Perspective* (Cambridge, MA: Harvard University Press, 1986), 15.

4. Galabert, Mémoire sur l'Inde An 11, CARAN AF/IV/1211. Emphasis in original. This may have been hyperbole.

5. E. S. van Eyck van Heslinga, *Van compagnie naar koopvaardij: De scheepvaart-verbinding van de Bataafse Republiek met de koloniën in Azië 1795–1806* (Amsterdam: De Bataafsche Leeuw, 1988), 183.

6. The idea that Boston ships went to the Pacific while Salem ships went to the Indian Ocean is misconceived. The error originates with Samuel E. Morison, *Maritime History of Massachusetts, 1783–1860* (Boston: Houghton Mifflin, 1921).

7. Data are derived from the average of 196 arrivals in Canton between 1784 and 1803, in which tonnage and either origin or destination are listed. Richards, "United States Trade with China," 10–39. Fur- and sandalwood-producing areas include Hawaii, the Pacific Northwest Coast, the Marquesas, Mas-à-Fuera, the Falklands, St. Paul, South Georgia, Nootka Sound, the South Seas, New Georgia, and Amsterdam Island.

8. Arrell Morgan Gibson and John S. Whitehead, *Yankees in Paradise: The Pacific Basin Frontier* (Albuquerque: University of New Mexico Press, 1993), 93–130, 155–187, 317–353.

9. John Denis Haeger, *John Jacob Astor: Business and Finance in the Early Republic* (Detroit: Wayne State University Press, 1991), 83, table 2, citing "Statement of American Imports and Exports at Canton, 1808–1818," in "Report by the Lords Committee Appointed Committee to Inquire into the Means of Extending and Securing the Foreign Trade of the Country, and to Report to the House . . . ," *Parliamentary Papers* (1821), vol. 7, 314–315; Jacques Downs, *Golden Ghetto: The American Commercial Community at Canton and the Shaping of American China Policy, 1784–1844* (Bethlehem, PA: Leheigh University Press, 1997), 358–363.

10. Further examination of the changing value by volume of tea, coffee, sugar, and other bulk commodities of this period is required.

11. Axel Madsen, *John Jacob Astor: America's First Multimillionaire* (New York: John Wiley, 2001), 51. How profits from the tea trade compared to profits in other shipping businesses—a crucial matter here—requires further research.

12. Many ships also carried some nankeens, the cotton cloth used to make breeches. On porcelain see Jessica Lanier, "The Post-Revolutionary Ceramics trade in Salem, Massachusetts, 1783–1812" (unpublished MA thesis, Bard College, 2003).

13. For information on the Canton credit market, see W. E. Cheong, *The Hong Merchants of Canton: Chinese Merchants in Sino-Western Trade* (Richmond, Surrey: Corzon, 1997), and Downs, *Golden Ghetto.* For Willing, see Robert

E. Wright and David J. Cohen, *Financial Founding Fathers: The Men Who Made America Rich* (Chicago: University of Chicago Press, 2006), 136.

14. Still, most U.S. ventures to China stopped to trade en route, and the chance for tea re-exports provided China ventures with another way to profit as well.

15. Harold Whitman Bradley, *The American Frontier in Hawaii: The Pioneers 1789–1843* (Stanford: Stanford University Press, 1942), 57, citing Timothy Pitkin, *Statistical View of the Commerce of the United States of America* (New Haven, 1835), 304.

16. James R. Gibson, *Otter Skins, Boston Ships, and China Goods: The Maritime Fur Trade of the Northwestern Coast, 1785–1841* (Seattle: University of Washington Press, 1992), 57.

17. Bradley, *American Frontier in Hawaii,* 18.

18. American merchants also sought North American ginseng. Since this ginseng was often a U.S. product, scholars have tended to overemphasize its importance. Interest in ginseng paled in comparison to interest in Marquesan sandalwood or Pacific fur. Proper quantification of ginseng's importance in U.S.-Chinese trade—particularly in the statistics-poor 1780s, when ginseng seems to have been particularly sought—remains elusive. Jonathan Chu, Program on Early American Economy and Society Post-doctoral Fellow, "Reorienting American Trade: The Origins of the China Trade and the Development of a National Investment Community" (unpublished paper presented to MacNeil Center for Early American Studies and LCP, November 30, 2007).

19. John Richards Child, log of the Ship *Hunter,* 1810–1815, P-326, Part 4, MHS, 19–21.

20. Richard Henry Dana, *Two Years before the Mast* (New York: Harper, 1840), chapter 5.

21. Mary Malloy, *"Boston Men" on the Northwest Coast: The American Maritime Fur Trade 1788–1844* (Fairbanks: University of Alaska Press, 1998), 98.

22. John Meares noted that beaver, martin, river otter, fox, wolf, wolverine, marmot, sable, raccoon, bear, sheep, and various types of seals could be found on the coast. *Minutes of the Committee of Trade from 1 January 1790 to 29 December 1790,* May 27, 1790, PRO BT/5/6.

23. Frank Bergon, ed., *The Journals of Lewis and Clark* (New York: Penguin, 1989), 324–325, 338, 345–346. The *Lydia* of Boston made the Columbia River in November 1805, a fortnight after Lewis and Clark reached its mouth, but the vessel did not appear to meet the American explorers. Bergon, *Journals of Lewis and Clark,* 367, 367n. Lewis and Clark left a letter with the Chinooks that was delivered to the Lydia. Malloy, *"Boston Men" on the Northwest Coast,* 49, 55.

24. Gibson, *Otter Skins,* 299–310; Haeger, *Astor,* 84. Merchants from France, Spain, and Portugal likewise failed to experience a rebirth in trade with the Pacific Northwest after 1815. Gibson notes the late 1820s uptick in Hudson Bay Company (HBC) activity, but it is hard to see how this could have long-

term utility without access to the Canton market; hence the fall of the East India Company's China monopoly was crucial. Gibson, *Otter Skins*, 37, 61. Downs indicates that the Bostonian Thomas H. Perkins traded on behalf of HBC between 1816 and 1821, which suggests that the HBC remained unable to circumvent its lack of access to Canton without U.S. assistance. Downs, *Golden Ghetto*, 106.

25. Gibson, *Otter Skins*, 13. The Spanish Royal Philippine Company also attempted to trade in furs, but the business was confined to a single voyage. Gibson, *Otter Skins*, 20.

26. The Board of Trade forced the Company to relent on this, but the Company still demanded that no ship pass "to the North of the Cape of Good Hope between that place and New South Wales; and shall not pass to the northward of the 30th Degree of South Latitude 'till they shall have passed the one hundred and Eightieth Degree of Longitude," effectively forcing mariners to circumnavigate Africa *and* Australia to reach the Americas, and making the Cape Horn route still more attractive. *Minutes of the Committee of Trade from 2 Jany 1807 to 28 Decr 1807*, February 9, 1807, PRO BT/5/17, 87.

27. Gibson, *Otter Skins*, passim.

28. Michael Fry, "Dundas, Henry, First Viscount Melville (1742–1811)," *DNB*, accessed May 7, 2005.

29. A. V. Venkatarama Ayyar, ed., *James Strange's Journal and Narrative of the Commercial Expedition from Bombay to the North-West Coast of America together with A Chart Showing the Tract of the Expedition* (Madras: Printed by the Superintendent, Government Press, 1928), 1–2, 20, 21, 27. Emphasis in original.

30. Gibson, *Otter Skins*, 24. The two rivals were from Bengal.

31. Ayyar, *James Strange's Journal*, 59, 70. Also OIOC H/605, 78–80. These are extracted from March 18, 1786, no. 9-11, correspondence from Madras Presidency, vol. 5, and March 1, 1788, no. 425-7, correspondence from Madras Presidency, vol 6.

32. "Minutes of the Committee of Trade from January 1, 1790, to December 29, 1790," May 28, 1790, PRO BT/5/6.

33. "Minutes of the Committee of Trade from May 2, 1810, to September 24, 1811," August 2, 1811, PRO BT5/20, 476. Mackenzie first put forth his proposal for intercompany cooperation in 1802 at the end of his account of his *Voyages from Montreal Through the Continent of North America to the Frozen and Pacific Oceans in 1789 and 1793 with an Account of the Rise and State of the Fur Trade* (London: R. Noble, 1801). Dundas may have stopped MacKenkie's lobbying. See Fry, *Dundas Despotism*; Elizabeth Baigent, "Mackenzie, Sir Alexander (1763/4–1820)," *DNB*, accessed March 22, 2006.

34. Gibson, *Otter Skins*, 26. This arrangement lasted until 1822, when new U.S. customs regulations appear to have ruined it.

35. Haeger, *Astor*, 42–46, 63.

36. See *New York Packet*, October 28, 1788, and April 29, 1788.

37. Haeger, *Astor*, 49–51. See also Washington Irving, *Astoria: or Anecdotes of an enterprise beyond the Rocky Mountains* (Philadelphia: Carey, Lea and Blanchard, 1836).

38. E. E. Rich, *The History of Hudson's Bay Company*, vol. 2 (London: Hudson's Bay Record Society, 1958–1959), 290–292, 206; Barry Gough, "The North West Company's Adventure to China," *Oregon Historical Quarterly* 76 (December 1975): 311–315; Wayne Edson Stevens, *The Northwest Fur Trade, 1763–1800* (Urbana: University of Illinois, 1928); Ann Carlos, "The Birth and Death of Predatory Competition in the North American Fur Trade," *Explorations in Economic History* 19 (July 1982): 156–183.

39. Haeger, *Astor*, 59–60.

40. Carl Seaburg and Stanley Patterson, *Merchant Prince of Boston* (Cambridge, MA: Harvard University Press, 1971), 268, 316; Downs, *Golden Ghetto*, 106.

41. On permanent residents at Canton, see Downs, *Golden Ghetto*, 147–156. After the War of 1812, Astor did hire Nicholas Ogden as resident agent at Canton. On the Russians, see Gibson, *Otter Skins*, 76–77.

42. Gibson, *Otter Skins*, 45, 47.

43. Malloy, *"Boston Men" on the Northwest Coast*, 149–150. Tales of sexual availability of Polynesian women were likely exaggerated by sailors who were understandably excitable after having been cooped up for months at sea. Nevertheless, these tales were not simply the product of Western leers but seem to reflect Polynesian comfortability with polyandry. Milton Diamond, "Sexual Behavior in Pre Contact Hawai'i: A Sexological Ethnography," *Revista Española del Pacífico* 16 (2004): 37–58.

44. Bradley, *American Frontier in Hawaii*, 28.

45. Gavan Daws, *Shoal of Time: A History of the Hawaiian Islands* (Honolulu: University of Hawaii Press, 1968), 50, citing Bradley, *American Frontier in Hawaii*, 29–32, and J. Ii, *Fragments of Hawaiian History* (Honolulu: Bishop Museum Press, 1963), 88.

46. Kamehameha's voyage did not turn a profit. The captain, his British advisor Alexander Adams, may have short-changed the Hawaiian leader. The vessel's Hawaiian flag (with eight horizontal red, white, and blue stripes and a Union Jack in the upper left corner, it had both American and British influences) caused trouble at Canton. Bradley, *American Frontier in Hawaii*, 57. Chinese sources regarding Kamehameha's venture have yet to be found.

47. Gibson lists these ships as Hawaiian and they do indeed have Hawaiian names, but it is unclear whether they were, instead, American or British ships in disguise. It seems unlikely that Americans, at least, would have to pretend to be Hawaiian.

48. Child, log of the Ship *Hunter*, December 31, 1810, MHS P-326, Part 4, 25.

49. The two villages are given as "Androgaitor" or "Andougartor" and "Drumdimiear," probably orthographically beyond repair. Child, log of the Ship *Hunter*, December 31, 1810, MHS P-326, Part 4, 25, 46–47.

50. Child, log of the Ship *Hunter,* December 31, 1810, MHS P-326, Part 4, 25, 46–48. Childs's captain appears to have been British. There was nothing exceptionally American about the wanton disregard of crewmen's lives.

51. Other merchants were willing to mistreat their seamen by skimping or cheating on pay. Gibson, *Otter Skins,* 32. The labor history of the American East Indies trade remains to be written.

52. James F. Warren, *The Sulu Zone: The World Capitalist Economy and the Historical Imagination* (Amsterdam: VU University Press, 1998), 29; David E. Sopher, *The Sea Nomads* (Singapore, 1964), 244–246; Ernest S. Dodge, *New England and the South Seas* (Cambridge, MA: Harvard University Press, 1965), 90–95.

53. Warren, *World Capitalist Economy,* 30–31.

54. See, for example, John R. Jewitt, *A narrative of the adventures and sufferigns* [*sic*] *of John R. Jewitt: Only survivor of the crew of the ship Boston, during a captivity of nearly three years among the savages of Nootka sound* (Ithaca, NY: Andrus Gaunfleet, 1851).

55. S. W. Jackman, ed., *The Journal of William Sturgis* (Victoria, BC: Sono Nis Press, 1978), 15. Malloy, *"Boston Men" on the Northwest Coast,* 54–55. Fergurson quote: Malloy, *"Boston Men" on the Northwest Coast,* 48.

56. Bradley, *American Frontier in Hawaii,* 16; Gibson, *Otter Skins,* 39. Kamehameha spared one member from the crew of the *Fair American* and one member from the crew of one of the *Eleanora's* boats, both men advised the king for decades.

57. James Francis Warren, *The Sulu Zone, 1768–1898: The Dynamics of External Trade, Slavery, and Ethnicity in the Transformation of a Southeast Asian Maritime State* (Singapore: Singapore University Press, 1981), 53–66.

58. Raffles to Minto, September 20, 1811, OIOC Eur Mss F/147/7, paragraph 67. The arms-for-trepang trade existed in Fiji as well. Dodge, *New England and the South Seas,* 92; G. W. Hubbell to John Quincy Adams, Secretary of State, December 31, 1823, U.S. National Archives, Consular Dispatches, Manila, 1817–1840, as cited in Warren, *Sulu Zone, 1768–1898,* 52.

59. Tim Flannery, ed., *The Life and Adventures of John Nicol, Mariner* (Melbourne: Text Publishing Company, 1997), 109.

60. Only Kunming and Wuchang also held both levels of officials within their walls. G. William Skinner, "Cities and the Hierarchy of Local Systems," in Skinner, ed., *The City in Late Imperial China* (Stanford: Stanford University Press, 1977), 302.

61. *Fan ch'ung nan p'i.* Skinner, "Cities and the Hierarchy of Local Systems," 317.

62. For the operation and regulation of trade at Canton and Macau see Van Dyke, *Canton Trade,* passim.

63. Max Weber, *The Religion of China: Confucianism and Taoism* (New York: Free Press, 1968), 56.

64. Weber, *Religion of China,* 33–62. H. B. Morse once famously asserted that a customs superintendent serving a three-year term "took the net profit of the

first year of his tenure to obtain his office, of the second year to keep it, and of the third year to drop it and provide for himself." This was, perhaps, an exaggeration and may have been meant more for the Jiaqing and Daoguang periods than the Qianlong. See John K. Fairbank, *Trade and Diplomacy on the China Coast* (Cambridge, MA: Harvard University Press, 1953), 50. For Qing revenue reform see Madeline Zelin, *The Magistrate's Tael: Rationalizing Fiscal Reform in Eighteenth-Century Ch'ina China* (Berkeley: University of California Press, 1984).

65. Max Weber, *Economy and Society: An Outline of Interpretive Sociology*, vol. 2 (Berkeley: University of California Press, 1978), 1047–1048.

66. For a detailed and thorough analysis of the traffic and governance of the Pearl River Delta region. see Van Dyke, *Port Canton and the Pearl River Delta, 1690–1845* (unpublished PhD diss., University of Southern California, 2002), 31–114. Van Dyke adds French, Dutch, Swedish, and Danish sources here to the usual British and American ones.

67. Preston M. Torbert, *The Ch'ing Imperial Household Department: A Study of Its Organization and Principal Functions, 1662–1796* (Cambridge, MA: Council on East Asian Studies, Harvard University, 1977), 98, citing the *Canton Maritime Customs Gazetteer*.

68. For migrants and other social desirables in mid-Qing, see Philip Kuhn, *Soulstealers: The Chinese Sorcery Scare of 1768* (Cambridge, MA: Harvard University Press, 1990); "Public Edict," Canton, 16th d 11 mo. 4th Year, Jiaqing (December 12, 1799), OIOC G/12/195, f114–117. Issued by hoppo, with quoted imperial edict. Translation.

69. "Public Edict," Canton, 16th d 11 mo. 4th Year, Jiaqing (December 12, 1799), OIOC G/12/195, f114–117. Issued by hoppo, with quoted imperial edict. Translation.

70. "Public Edict," Canton, 16th d 11 mo. 4th Year, Jiaqing (December 12, 1799), OIOC G/12/195, f114–117. Issued by hoppo, with quoted imperial edict. Translation.

71. Dilip Kumar Basu, "Asian Merchants and Western Trade: A Comparative Study of Calcutta and Canton 1800–1840" (unpublished PhD diss., University of California, Berkeley, 1975); PRO FO 682/290, "Maritime Regulation and Suppression of Smuggling." Anyone with enough patronage to obtain a degree was unlikely to be punished unless the intent was also to punish his patron.

72. "Public Edict," Canton, 16th d 11 mo. 4th Year, Jiaqing (December 12, 1799), OIOC G/12/195, f114–117. Issued by hoppo, with quoted imperial edict. Translation.

73. Indeed, the main reason behind the edict was probably to let the local clerks and guards know they were being watched. On opium in China see also Frank Dikötter, Lars Laamann, and Zhou Xun, *Narcotic Culture: A History of Drugs in China* (Chicago: University of Chicago Press, 2004).

74. Samuel E. Morison, "Forcing the Dardanelles in 1810: With Some Account of the Early Levant Trade of Massachusetts," *The New England Quarterly* 1, no. 2 (April 1928): 225.

75. Robert Wilkinson to Secretary of State, December 29, 1810, Department of State, Consular Letters, Smyrna, as cited in Morison, "Forcing the Dardanelles," 221n22.

76. Morison, "Forcing the Dardanelles," 209, 215–216. Charles S. Steele, "American Trade in Opium to China, prior to 1820," *Pacific Historical Review* 9, no. 4 (December 1940): 430–431, also notes the American sale of pepper in Smyrna. For the Derbys, see David H. Finnie, *Pioneers East: The Early American Experience in the Middle East* (Cambridge, MA: Harvard University Press, 1967), 243. For the rise in imports from 1806–1812 for "Turkey, Levant and Egypt," as U.S. customs officials termed the region, see James A Field Jr., *From Gibraltar to the Middle East: America and the Mediterranean World, 1776–1882* (1969; reprint, Chicago: Imprint Publications, 1991), 114.

77. Morison blamed "unenterprising" "Levantines," but—considering the precarious state of Ottoman foreign relations—Ottoman merchants may simply have wanted to avoid donating their capital to a foreign prize court. Ottomans, as consumers across the northern Mediterranean, found that their demand for Asian and Caribbean products could be supplied only by the United States. The Ragusans may have attempted the Smyrna-Yemen route. A Ragusan vessel passed from Texel to Cape Town in 1804. CTAR BR 536, 537.

78. Finnie, *Pioneers East,* 25.

79. "Second half" refers to the period from April 28, 1809, to December 1. 1809.

80. Morison, "Forcing the Dardanelles," 215.

81. Morison, "Forcing the Dardanelles, 212. The actual total for the period between August 1811 and June 1812 was $958,446.

82. A. L. Tibawi, *American Interests in Syria, 1800–1901: A Study of Educational, Literary and Religious Work* (Oxford: Clarendon Press, 1966), 2.

83. Jacques M. Downs, "American Merchants and the China Opium Trade, 1800–1840," *Business History Review* 42, no. 4 (Winter 1968): 418–442; Downs, *Golden Ghetto,* 112–125, 355. Yen-P'ing Hao argues that U.S. opium sales in China were not a major part of overall U.S. sales there. However, official data cannot be expected to represent opium sales accurately. Hao, "Chinese Teas to America," 22.

9. The Death of the India Monopoly

1. The revocation of the monopoly was, in the industrial interpretation, the first triumph of industrial capital over mercantile capital, a step on the path to Victorian free-trade liberalism. Marxist historians have emphasized this explanation, though Marx argued that "in 1813 the Anti-Jacobin war … superseded all other political questions." Karl Marx, "The East India Company—Its History and Results," *New-York Daily Tribune,* July 11, 1853. Historians debate to what extent the changes in British economy and society between 1792 and 1815 are attributable to the Industrial Revolution or to the wars with France. A war interpretation of the 1813 charter debate is

explicated in Anthony Webster, "The Political Economy of Trade Liberalization: The East India Company Charter Act of 1813," *EHR*, 2nd series, 43, no. 3 (1990): 404–419. Webster emphasizes that the government saw India as a supplier of cotton and sugar at a time when the wars with Europe and the United States limited access to raw materials elsewhere. It did not see India as an export market. Webster does not, however, make the same argument for the war interpretation as laid out here. The war argument, promulgated in economic circles, has not fully reached historians, who tend to make the industrial argument exclusively. This is unfortunate, for the war argument affects our understanding of free trade in British history and of free trade and British nationalism in nineteenth-century India.

2. P. J. Cain and A. H. Hopkins, *British Imperialism, 1688–2000* (New York: Longman, 2002), 282.

3. Memorial of the Muslin + Callico Manufacturers of Manchester & ca., June 1794, OIOC A/1/85A.

4. Holden Furber also emphasizes how debilitating American competition was for the Company. Holden Furber, "The Beginnings of American Trade with India, 1784–1812," *The New England Quarterly* 11, no. 2 (June 1938): 235–265. The related issue of the China-trade monopoly, which Buckinghamshire ultimately allowed to continue, will not be discussed here.

5. Indeed, recent scholarship has emphasized that the Company—far from being an ineptly managed monopoly—was adept at seeking out and exploiting new business. K. N. Chaudhuri, *The Trading World of Asia and the English East India Company, 1600–1760* (New York: Cambridge University Press, 1978). Hoh-cheung Mui and Lorna H. Mui, *The Management of Monopoly: A Study of the East India Company's Conduct of Its Tea Trade, 1784–1833* (Vancouver: University of British Columbia Press, 1984), xi, present the bizarre argument that "an exclusive right to import tea into England" was not monopolistic.

6. "Two Petitions—of the Mayor and Commonality of the City of *New Sarum*, in Common Council assembled; and of several Merchants and Manufacturers of the City of *New Sarum* . . . ," March 1, 1813, *Journals of the House of Commons*, vol. 68 (Printed by Order of the House of Commons, London, 1813), 245. This argument had been the Company's first line of defense against free traders throughout the late eighteenth century.

7. "A Petition of several Merchants, Manufacturers, and other Inhabitants of the Town and Neighborhood of *Leeds* . . . ," March 1, 1813, *Journals of the House of Commons*, vol. 68, 245. Throughout, emphases are in original.

8. "A Petition of several Inhabitants of *Preston*, in the County of *Lancaster* . . . ," March 4, 1813, *Journals of the House of Commons*, vol. 68, 268–269. This petition refers to the China trade in particular but also the East Indies trade in general. Free traders also contrasted the Company's belligerence in Macau in 1802 and 1808 with the American China-traders' peaceful business. Ironically, after the China trade was opened in 1833, it was private traders who provoked war between Britain and China.

9. "A Petition of the merchants, ship-owners, and traders of King's Lynn," February 9, 1813, Hansard, vol. 24, cols. 416–417.

10. It is unclear who made the American argument standard in anti-Company petitions. The quote from Lynn nearly matches Bridlington's, whose merchants wrote, "the extensive and flourishing commerce of the United States of America with India and the Chinese empire, exhibits a proof that these expectations of advantage from the exertions of private individuals are not unfounded." "A Petition of the merchants, ship-owners, and other inhabitants of Bridlington," February 10, 1813, Hansard, vol. 24, cols. 426–427. The opposition to the Company was highly organized and dominated by mercantile interests from British outports. B. H. Tolley, "The Liverpool Campaign against the Order in Council and the War of 1812," in J. R. Harris, ed., *Liverpool and Merseyside: Essays in the Economic and Social History of the Port and Its Hinterland* (London: Frank Cass, 1969), 98–146. Also D. J. Moss, "Birmingham and the Campaigns against the Orders-in-Council and East India Company Charter, 1812–1813," *Canadian Journal of History* 11 (1976): 173–188.

11. Smith expanded his 1784 edition to address this at length. Emma Rothschild, *Economic Sentiments: Adam Smith, Condorcet, and the Enlightenment* (Cambridge, MA: Harvard University Press, 2001).

12. "A Petition of the chamber of commerce and manufactures of Glasgow," February 5, 1813, Hansard, vol. 24, cols. 386–387.

13. Liverpool merchants charged the Company's unenterprising spirit for accepting an overly expensive crew-to-tonnage ratio. "A Petition of several merchants, ship-owners, tradesmen, and other inhabitants of Liverpool," February 8, 1813, Hansard, vol. 24, cols. 401–405.

14. "A Petition of several Merchants and traders of the City of *Dublin*, was presented," March 1, 1813, *Journals of the House of Commons,* vol. 68 (1813), 245.

15. "A Petition of the provost, magistrates, and town council of the royal burgh of Montrose," February 8, 1813, Hansard, vol. 24, cols. 406–407.

16. The appearance of an American tone is deceptive. In 1813 the language of natural rights was, as far as Parliamentarians were concerned, *French,* hence free traders compensated with resolute patriotism.

17. "A Petition of several Merchants, Traders, and other Inhabitants of the County of the Borough of *Carmarthen*," *Journals of the House of Commons,* vol. 68 (1813), 274.

18. "A Petition of the mayor, burgesses, and commonalty of the city of Bristol, in common council assembled," February 2, 1813, Hansard, vol. 24, cols. 349–350.

19. "A Petition of the royal boroughs of Scotland, assembled at their annual convention," February 2, 1813, Hansard, vol. 24, cols. 347–348.

20. "A Petition of several merchants, traders, and manufacturers of Port Glasgow and Newark," February 5, 1813, Hansard, vol. 24, cols. 388–389.

21. For the American side of this see Pauline Maier, *American Scripture: Making the Declaration of Independence* (New York: Knopf, 1997).
22. For monopolies in common law see Pauline Maier, "The Revolutionary Origins of the American Corporation," *WMQ*, 3rd series, 50, no. 1 (1993): 51–84.
23. "A Petition of the chamber of commerce and manufactures of Glasgow," February 5, 1813, Hansard, vol. 24, cols. 386–387.
24. "A Petition of several merchants, traders, and other inhabitants of the city of Bristol," February 3, 1813, Hansard, vol. 24, cols. 357–360.
25. "A Petition of the merchants house of Glasgow," February 5, 1813, Hansard, vol. 24, cols. 387–388.
26. "A Petition of the bailies and trustees of Port Glasgow and Newark," February 5, 1813, Hansard, vol. 24, cols. 389–391.
27. "A Petition of the merchants, ship-owners, and others interested in the trade of the town of Lancaster," February 11, 1813, Hansard, vol. 24, cols. 438–439. This was in tandem with the general emergence of free-trade ideas and reform sentiments as gentlemanly and respectable policy choices for turn-of-the-century decision makers. Cain and Hopkins, *British Imperialism*, 83.
28. C. D. Yonge, *The life and administration of Robert Banks, second earl of Liverpool* vol. 2 (London: Macmillan, 1868), 416, cited in Norman Gash, "Jenkinson, Robert Banks, Second Earl of Liverpool (1770–1828)," *DNB*, accessed May 7, 2005.
29. The notion that Liverpool espoused a new "liberal toryism" after 1821 misses, as Norman Gash's *DNB* entry points out, the "underlying continuity" of his politics and policies throughout his tenure in office. The revisionist interpretation here of Liverpool as a liberal is taken from Gash, "Jenkinson, Robert Banks, Second Earl of Liverpool (1770–1828)." Other historians have conceded Liverpool's free-trade inclinations. Boyd Hilton, *Corn, Cash, Commerce: The Economic Politics of the Tory Governments 1815–1830* (Oxford: Oxford University Press, 1977).
30. Roland Thorne, "Hobart, Robert, Fourth Earl of Buckinghamshire (1760–1816)," *DNB*, accessed May 7, 2005; Robert Dundas to Chairman of Court of Directors, December 28, 1808, OIOC Mss Eur F/149/102.
31. Amales Tripathi, *Trade and Finance in the Bengal Presidency, 1793–1833* (Calcutta: Oxford University Press, 1979), 106. Particularly striking is Richard Wellesley's role. He was initially in favor of, and in fact abetted, Henry Dundas's plans for free trade, though by 1813 it was against Wellesley's arguments that Buckinghamshire had to vindicate the new charter. This was the result of Wellesley's antagonism toward Liverpool's government. Michael Fry, *The Dundas Despotism* (Edinburgh: Edinburgh University Press, 1992), 316–317; Robert Dundas to George Canning. May 23, 1812, Add. Mss. 37297 f9.
    Ingram, by contrast, argues that Wellesley and Dundas disagreed on free trade. Edward Ingram, ed., *Two Views of British India: The Private Correspondence of Mr. Dundas and Lord Wellesley, 1798–1801* (Bath, UK: Adams & Dart, 1970).

32. For the 1813 vote see C. H. Philips, *The East India Company, 1784–1834* (Manchester: University of Manchester Press, 1961), 182–190.

33. For British patriotism in this period see Linda Colley, *Britons: Forging the Nation, 1707–1837* (New Haven: Yale University Press, 1992).

34. Indeed, the War of 1812 may have strengthened Liverpool's conviction to destroy the Company's Indian monopoly if he thought he could draw in more customs receipts by moving into the now-vacant American share of the Indian export market.

35. Parliament also opened the Indian Subcontinent to Christian missionaries in 1813, and the trade vote cannot be divorced from the ascendance of militant British Protestantism in the Napoleonic period. See Ainslie Embree, *Charles Grant and British Rule in India* (New York: Columbia University Press, 1962). Though Grant was in favor of missions, he opposed Britons settling in India. Evangelicals, however, were usually on the free-trade side of the debate and provided considerable moral suasion for that cause. Boyd Hilton, *The Age of Atonement: The Influence of Evangelicalism on Social and Economic Thought, 1785–1865* (Oxford: Clarendon Press, 1991). British settlement in India—Grants's concern stemming in part from Britain's less-than-salutary experience with her North American settlers in the American Revolution—is further explored in P. J. Marshall, *"A Free though Conquering People": Eighteenth-Century Britain and Its Empire* (Burlington, VT: Variorum, 2003).

36. Philips, *East India Company*, 187, 190. The political efforts to secure these thirty-nine votes by Liverpool and the free-trade press require further study.

37. April 9, 1813. Hansard, vol. 25, col. 703.

38. April 9, 1813. Hansard, vol. 25, col. 703.

39. Previously, the English and Dutch East India Companies kept records of their own trade, but not a full accounting of other merchants' trade.

40. Data from House of Commons, "Statement of the Commerce of British India with London, America and Foreign Europe; from 1802–3 to 1810–11, both inclusive," in item no. 136, "Accounts and Papers relating to the East India Company's Shipping," in *Sessional Papers, 1812–1813, East India Company*, vol. 8, 264–267. Compare H. Bowen, *East India Company: Trade and Domestic Financial Statistics, 1755–1838* [computer file] (Colchester, Essex: UK Data Archive [distributor], September 2007), SN: 5690, which also indicates a falloff in specie exports after 1806. Data from Commons is preferred here as representing information available to Parliament.

41. The Company feared that a U.S. vessel's carriage of "British Manufactures *directly out of the Thames* to British India" would leave "nullified" "a very great commercial argument for the Monopoly of the Company against British Subjects," though, interestingly, British manufactures did not use the example against the Company as much as feared. Parry and Grant to Directors, East India House, October 1808, OIOC H/494, 317. Emphasis in original.

42. Parry and Grant to Baring, East India House, October 1808, OCIC H/494, 285.

43. Study of the post-1813 relationship between free trade, cash-crop agriculture, and industrialization would benefit from U.S. archival research into Anglo-*American* ties, particularly with regard to U.S. cotton, industrialization, and shipping. Tripathi's *Trade and Finance* suggests a way forward.

44. "Statement of the Commerce of British India," in *Sessional Papers, 1812–1813, East India Company,* vol. 8, 264–267.

45. Parry and Grant to Directors, East India House, October 1808, OIOC H/494, 285–287.

46. Tripathi, *Trade and Finance,* 117.

47. House of Commons, "Extract of so much of the Report on External Commerce in Bengal, for 1795–6 . . . as relates to the Trade with *London, Europe, and America,*" in *Sessional Papers, 1812–1813, East India Company,* vol. 8, paper no. 171, April 30, 1813, 433.

48. House of Commons, "Extract of Mr. Brown's Report on the Commerce of British India, in 1802–3; dated 28 December 1804," in *Sessional Papers, 1812–1813, East India Company,* vol. 8, paper no. 171, April 30, 1813, 449.

49. House of Commons, "Extract from Mr. Larkin's Report on the External Commerce of Bengal, as carried on by Individuals in the year 1806–7, or from the 1st of June 1806 to the 31st of May 1807;—dated 1 September 1808," in *Sessional Papers, 1812–1813, East India Company,* vol. 8, paper no. 171, April 30, 1813, 456.

50. House of Commons, "Copy of a Report from the Committee of Correspondence to the Court of Directors of the East India Company, dated 9th February 1813:—On the subject of the Trade with the East Indies and China," in *Sessional Papers, 1812–1813, East India Company,* vol. 8, paper no. 78, March 11, 1813, 15–16.

51. "A Petition of several merchants, ship-owners, tradesmen, and other inhabitants of Liverpool," February 8, 1813, Hansard, vol. 24, cols. 401–405.

52. C. Northcote Parkinson, *Trade in the Eastern Seas, 1793–1813* (Cambridge: Cambridge University Press, 1937), 363.

53. Parry and Grant to Baring, East India House, October 1808, OIOC H/494, 231.

54. Michael Broers, *Europe under Napoleon, 1799–1815* (London: Arnold, 1996), 145.

55. François Crouzet, *L'Économie britannique et le blocus continental (1806–1813),* vol. 2 (Paris: Presses Universitaires de France, 1958), 887, 890.

56. Directors to Buckinghamshire, East India House, April 15, 1812, OIOC A/2/14, Item 64. Particularly with regard to American trade the Chairs seem to have contradicted their previous statements so much by this time that it is difficult to see in them any intellectual coherence—other than an overriding desire to say whatever might protect the Shipping Interest at the moment.

57. "A Petition of several merchants, traders, and other inhabitants of the city of Bristol," February 3, 1813, Hansard, vol. 24, cols. 357–360.

58. Moss, "Birmingham and the Campaigns," 187, 188. Despite this, Philip Harling in *The Waning of "Old Corruption": The Politics of Economical Reform in Britain, 1779–1846* (Oxford: Clarendon Press, 1996), 89–135, devotes a chapter to economic reform in the 1806–1815 period without mentioning the East India Company.

59. B. R. Mitchell, *British Historical Statistics* (New York: Cambridge University Press, 1988), 494–495. These figures include both the China and India trades.

60. *Oriental Herald* 44 (August 1827): 419.

10. American Capital and Corporations

1. Ian W. Toll, *Six Frigates: The Epic History of the Founding of the U.S. Navy* (New York: W. W. Norton, 2006), 374. Toll gives the volume *The Complete East-India Pilot; Or, Oriental Navigator* as American, but various editions appeared on both sides of the Atlantic; the copy at hand was likely an (unauthorized) American reprint of a British version. C. Northcote Parkinson, *War in the Eastern Seas, 1793–1815* (London: Allen & Unwin, 1954), 421–423; Noel Mostert, *The Line upon a Wind: An Intimate History of the Last and Greatest War Fought at Sea under Sail, 1793–1815* (London: Jonathan Cape, 2007), 689; William James, *Naval History of Great Britain*, vol. 5 (1746; reprint, London: Macmillan, 1902), 261–269; James Fenimore Cooper, *The History of the Navy of the United States of America* (Philadelphia: Thomas, Cowperthwait, 1841), 278–301, 438; David Porter, *Journal of a Cruise Made to the Pacific Ocean, by Captain David Porter, in the United States Frigate Essex, in the Years 1812, 1813, and 1814*, 2 vols. (New York: Wiley & Halstead, 1815). For Penang: Lee Kam Hing, *The Sultanate of Aceh: Relations with the British, 1760–1824* (Kuala Lumpur: Oxford University Press, 1995), 220.

2. Historians have recently come to understand the importance of finance in the economy of the early republic. See Peter L. Rousseau and Richard Sylla, "Emerging Financial Markets and Early U.S. Growth," National Bureau of Economic Research Working Paper No. 7448 (Cambridge, MA: National Bureau of Economic Research, 1999); Robert Wright, *The Wealth of Nations Rediscovered: Integration and Expansion in American Financial Markets, 1780–1850* (Cambridge: Cambridge University Press, 2002), 2–4.

3. Andrew Schocket, *Founding Corporate Power in Early National Philadelphia* (DeKalb: Northern Illinois University Press, 2007), 46. Schocket notes that banks' stock issues drew European capital.

4. Schocket, *Funding Corporate Power*, 37, 211.

5. Beatrice G. Reubens, "Burr, Hamilton and the Manhattan Company: Part I: Gaining the Charter," *Political Science Quarterly* 72, no. 4 (December 1957): 581.

6. Definition of "stock" from *OED*, accessed January 30, 2008.

7. Reubens, "Burr, Hamilton and the Manhattan Company: Part I," 586. Hamilton and Burr had been on reasonably good terms socially before this.

8. Bray Hammond, *Banks and Politics in America, from the Revolution to the Civil War* (Princeton: Princeton University Press, 1957), 67.

9. M. L. Davis, *Memoirs of Aaron Burr*, vol. 1 (New York: Harper, 1836), 414, as cited in Hammond, *Banks and Politics,* 153.

10. Charles R. King, ed., *Life and Correspondence of Rufus King*, vol. 2 (New York: G. P. Putnam's Sons, 1894–1900), 597, as cited in Hammond, *Banks and Politics,* 153.

11. Reubens, "Burr, Hamilton and the Manhattan Company: Part I."

12. Burr's actions were judged such a breach of Jeffersonian values that it cost him his seat in the New York state legislature in 1799. Beatrice G. Reubens, "Burr, Hamilton and the Manhattan Company: Part II: Launching a Bank," *Political Science Quarterly* 73, no. 1 (March 1958): 102n7.

13. On limiting corporate activities see Reubens, "Burr, Hamilton and the Manhattan Company: Part I," 600.

14. Donald R. Adams Jr., *Finance and Enterprise in Early America: A Study of Stephen Girard's Bank, 1812–1831* (Philadelphia: University of Pennsylvania Press, 1978), 5–6.

15. For political troubles facing Pennsylvania banks see Schocket, *Funding Corporate Power.*

16. Hammond, *Banks and Politics,* 198.

17. Adams, *Stephen Girard's Bank,* 13–14, cited in David A. Martin, "Bimetallism in the United States before 1850," *The Journal of Political Economy* 76, no. 3 (May–June 1968): 432.

18. Adams, *Stephen Girard's Bank,* 14–15.

19. Adams, *Stephen Girard's Bank,* 17–18. It is unclear whether this law was anti-bank or an attempt to prevent banking bubbles. Indeed, the Pennsylvania state legislature remained so hostile that in 1815 an alliance between Girard's rival banks and anti-bank interests sought to ban unincorporated banks from issuing banknotes. Kenneth L. Brown, "Stephen Girard's Bank," *PMHB* 66 (January 1942): 30, 48. This may have been a result of the numerous bank charters granted in 1814, which widened the interest group opposed to further expansion of banking privileges. See also Hammond, *Banks and Politics.*

20. One wonders whether Girard's decision to fund his bank and finance the U.S. war effort was related to his political leanings (he was Jeffersonian), or if Thorndike's decision *not* to lend to the U.S. Treasury on a scale like Girard's or Astor's was due to his federalism. Boston moneymen were scorned in Pennsylvania for their unwillingness to fund the war effort.

21. Hammond, *Banks and Politics,* 73.

22. Hammond, *Banks and Politics,* 135.

23. Schocket, *Funding Corporate Power,* 26.

24. Secretary Gallatin's newspaper advertisements may have been meant to embarrass reluctant bankers into buying debt. Brown, "Stephen Girard's Bank," 29–55.

25. Paul Cox and Ebenezer Ferguson, respectively. The rest are Theophilus Harris, William Mitchell, William Linnard, Samuel Corswell, Henry Orth, Samuel Williamson, William Jonas Keen, Samuel Smith, Hugh Henry, and Hugh Ferguson. *Constitution of the Philadelphia Society for the Encouragement of Manufacturers. Adopted March 14, 1806* (Philadelphia: D. Hogan, 1806), held at LCP.
26. Schocket, *Funding Corporate Power*, 39–40, 46. Cf. Tony A. Freyer, *Producers versus Capitalists: Constitutional Conflict in Antebellum America* (Charlottesville: University of Virginia Press, 1994), 5.
27. Naomi Lamoreaux, *Insider Lending: Banks, Personal Connections, and Economic Development in Industrial New England* (Cambridge: Cambridge University Press, 1994), 19.
28. N. S. B. Gras, *The Massachusetts First National Bank of Boston, 1784–1834* (Cambridge, MA: Harvard University Press, 1937), 209–212, as cited in Hammond, *Banks and Politics,* 66.
29. Pelatiah Webster, *Political Essays* (Philadelphia, 1791), 439, as cited in Hammond, *Banks and Politics,* 75. Hannis Taylor argues for Webster as the source of many of the ideas bruited about in the Constitutional Convention in *The Origin and Growth of the American Constitution* (Boston: Houghton Mifflin, 1911), for a critique of which see Edward S. Corwin, "The Pelatiah Webster Myth," *Michigan Law Review* 10, no. 8 (June 1912): 619–626; Franklin B. Dexter, *Biographical Sketches of the Graduates of Yale College,* vol. 2 (New York: H. Holt & Co., 1896), 97–102. Webster's subsequent decline into obscurity, provoked by Taylor's debunking, perhaps underestimates his significance.
30. Hammond, *Banks and Politics,* 75, 65; Robert Wright, *Origins of Commercial Banking in America, 1750–1800* (Lanham, MD: Rowman & Littlefield, 2001), 149, 168.
31. Hammond, *Banks and Politics,* 69; Lamoreaux, *Insider Lending,* 6, 13, citing Gras, *Massachusetts First National Bank,* 273–276; Martin, "Bimetallism in the United States before 1850," 440. For difficulties in estimating money supply see Edward J. Stephens, "Composition of the Money Stock prior to the Civil War," *Journal of Money, Credit and Banking* 3, no. 1 (February 1971): 84–101.
32. Lamoreaux, *Insider Lending,* 13; "Note from Lord Melville inclosing a Copy of a Resolution of a Meeting of Persons interested in the Tin Trade," Lord Melville, India Board, March 5, 1812. OIOC A/2/14, Item 30; Hammond, *Banks and Politics,* 67.
33. J. van Festermaker, "The Statistics of American Commercial Banking, 1782–1818," *JEH* 25, no. 3 (September 1965): 400–413; Anna Jcobson Schwartz, "The Beginning of Competitive Banking in Philadelphia, 1782–1809," *Journal of Political Economy* 55, no. 5 (October 1947): 417–431.
34. Winifred Barr Rothenberg, "The Invention of American Capitalism: The Economy of New England in the Federal Period," in Peter Temin, ed., *Engines of Enterprise: An Economic History of New England* (Cambridge, MA: Harvard University Press, 2000), 95.

35. I have eschewed the term "Boston Associates," long used to describe Thorndike, Lowell, and others. The associates were not a rigidly defined group, as some readers have assumed, and Thorndike was more central to the group than previously understood. I refer here and throughout to the BMC and its shareholders instead. Robert F. Dalzell Jr., *Enterprising Elite: The Boston Associates and the World They Made* (Cambridge, MA: Harvard University Press, 1987); Francois Weil, "Capitalism and Industrialization in New England, 1815–1845," *Journal of American History* 84, no. 4 (March 1998): 1334–1354.

36. The original shareholders were Francis C. Lowell (fifteen shares), Benjamin Gorham (three shares), Uriah Cotting (five shares), Patrick Tracy Jackson (twenty shares), Warren Dutton (two shares), John Gore (ten shares), Charles Jackson (ten shares), James Lloyd (five shares), Israel Thorndike Jr. (ten shares), Israel Thorndike Sr. (ten shares), James Jackson (five shares), and Nathan Appleton (five shares). "Articles of Agreement between the Associates of the 'Boston Manufacturing Company' previous to the Organization of the Corporation," September 4, 1813, Boston Manufacturing Company, vol. 1, 7–9, Baker Library, Harvard Business School; "Impost Book of the Collector" (1789–1815), Salem, MA, vols. 1–5, NARA (MA). Jackson's imports from India to Boston do not appear in the "Impost Book" but in Kenneth Wiggins Porter, *The Jacksons and the Lees: Two Generations of Massachusetts Merchants, 1765–1844* (Cambridge, MA: Harvard University Press, 1937). Jackson also corresponded with Lowell, his brother-in-law, from India regarding investments there, suggesting the latter was at least interested in trading there. On installments, see Rothenberg, "Invention of American Capitalism," 97.

37. House of Commons, "Statement of the Commerce of British India with London, America and Foreign Europe; from 1802–3 a. 1810–11, both inclusive," in item no. 136, "Accounts and Papers relating to the East India Company's Shipping," in *Sessional Papers, 1812–1813, East India Company,* vol. 8, 264–267.

38. Porter, *Jacksons and Lees,* 592–594; Patrick Tracy Jackson, Boston, to John Stille & Co, Philadelphia, August 4, 1803, in Porter, *Jacksons and Lees,* 599.

39. J. D. Forbes, *Israel Thorndike, Federalist Financier* (New York: Exposition Press, 1953), 48; David Hackett Fischer, "The Myth of the Essex Junto," *WMQ,* 3rd series, 21, no. 2 (April 1964): 198.

40. "Impost Book of the Collector" (Salem, MA), vols. 1–4, NARA (MA).

41. Florence M. Montgomery, *Printed Textiles: English and American Cottons and Linens 1700–1850* (New York: Viking Press, 1970), 102. American printers stayed with this practice later than English ones, since in the early 1800s English weavers were finally able to produce cloth sufficiently fine and cheap to replace Bengal muslins in the English market (though not, at least right away, for export to India since transport to India increased the cost of the good).

42. Porter, *Jacksons and Lees,* 770; Kishichi Watanabe, "The Business Organization of the Boston Manufacturing Company: The Early Development of Modern Management in the United States," *KSU Economic and Business Review* 1 (1974): 67; Porter, *Jacksons and Lees,* 594. Porter reprints Jackson's correspondence, 595–620.

43. K. N. Chaudhuri, *The Trading World of Asia and the English East India Company, 1660–1760* (New York: Cambridge University Press, 1978), 305–312.

44. James A. Henretta, *The Origins of Capitalism* (Boston: Northeastern University Press, 1991), chapter 6.

45. Sean Wilentz, *Chants Democratic: New York and the Rising of the American Working Class, 1788–1850* (New York: Oxford University Press, 1984); Sven Beckert, *The Monied Metropolis: New York City and the Consolidation of the American Bourgeoisie, 1850–1896* (New York: Cambridge University Press, 2001).

46. The Slater Mill and other mills in the Slater mold typically produced yarn, not cloth. Watanabe, "Business Organization," 49. For the role of treasurer in American textile corporations see Watanabe, "Business Organization," 58–59; "Director's Records," Waltham, November 6, 1815, Boston Manufacturing Company, vol. 2, 18, Baker Library, Harvard Business School; Watanabe, "Business Organization," 57–58.

47. "Boston Mfg Co. Treasurers' Reports, Projects Reports, Estimates, Licenses," Boston, April 22, 1823, Boston Manufacturing Company, Box 1A, Baker Library, Harvard Business School; Forbes, *Israel Thorndike,* 139.

48. Dalzell, *Enterprising Elite;* Rothenberg, "Invention of American Capitalism," 99; Lamoreaux, *Insider Lending,* 19–24.

49. The bank was sold off to Phoenix Bank in 1817. Hammond, *Banks and Politics,* 161.

50. "Manufacturing Corporations," in *The American Jurist and Law Magazine,* vol. 2 (Boston: Freeman & Bolles, July 1829), as reprinted in Robert E. Wright, ed., *The History of Corporate Finance: Development of Anglo-American Securities Markets, Financial Practices, Theories and Laws,* vol. 2 (London: Pickering and Chatto, 2003), 349; Hovenkamp, *Enterprise and American Law, 1836–1937* (Cambridge, MA: Harvard University Press, 1991), 50; Bruce H. Mann, Republic of Debtors, *Bankruptcy in the Age of American Independence* (London: Harvard University Press, 2002), 258; Edward Balleisen, *Navigating Failure: Bankruptcy and Commercial Society in Antebellum America* (Chapel Hill: University of North Carolina Press, 2001).

51. Morton Horwitz, *The Transformation of American Law, 1780–1860* (Oxford: Oxford University Press, 1992), 109–139.

52. Reubens, "Burr, Hamilton and the Manhattan Company: Part II."

53. John Denis Haeger, *John Jacob Astor: Business and Finance in the Early Republic* (Detroit: Wayne State University Press, 1991), 78–81, 136; Jonathan Goldstein, *Philadelphia and the China Trade, 1682–1846: Commercial,*

Cultural, and Attitudinal Effects (University Park: Pennsylvania State University Press, 1978).

54. Astor's investments, like Thorndike's and Girard's, were diverse. Astor even owned shares in the Manhattan Company. Reubens, "Burr, Hamilton and the Manhattan Company: Part II," 103n11.

55. Axel Madsen, *John Jacob Astor: America's First Multimillionaire* (New York: John Wiley, 2001), 53.

56. Haeger, *Astor*, 65, 170, 244–245, 250–251.

57. Haeger, *Astor*, 95. Astor was not the first American to conceive of a permanent settlement in Oregon. In 1810 Jonathan Winship Jr. led a shipload of Americans in building a garden and a log home on the Columbia River, but the Chinooks would not permit such a "Garden of Eden on the shores of the Pacific." Samuel Eliot Morison, *Maritime History of Massachusetts, 1783–1860* (Boston: Houghton Mifflin, 1961), 58. Likewise, though East India captain and U.S. congressman Jacob Crowninshield suggested to Secretary of State Madison that "cessions of territory might be obtained" from Sumatran rajas, Madison was uninterested in following this up. John H. Reinoehl, "Some Remarks on the American Trade: Jacob Crowninshield to James Madison 1806," *WMQ* 3rd series, 16, no. 1 (January 1959): 106.

58. Haeger, *Astor*, 98–99.

59. Haeger, *Astor*, 105–106, 114.

60. Nathaniel Atcheson's *American Encroachments on British Rights* fed off of growing anti-American sentiment in Parliament, largely unchecked after the death of Charles James Fox and particularly strong in some Tory circles. Tellingly, its subtitle included a "Defence of the Shipping Interest," a reference largely to Atlantic shipping, but with favorably citied petitions from East India Company directors like Lushington and Bosanquet as well. Atcheson attacked Baring for his hospitable view toward U.S. trade with the British Atlantic colonies and Continental Europe and defended the East India Company and Canadian merchants against "unfair" U.S. competition, blaming burgeoning Canadian imports of U.S.-carried East Indian goods on an imbalance between American and Canadian tariffs, which "enabled the subjects [sic] of the United States to supply Canada with teas, East Indian goods, of all sorts," and Caribbean, American, and European produce. He also made the standard complaints against Article XIII of the Jay Treaty and the Wilson v. Marryat ruling. Notably, he cites Sir James Eyre's (Chief Justice of the Common Pleas) criticism of Lord Lloyd Kenyon's (Chief Justice of the King's Bench) ruling in this case. Nathaniel Atcheson, *American Encroachments on British Rights; or, Observations on the Importance of the British North American Colonies and on the Late Treaties with the United States* . . . (London, 1808), xi–xii, held at LCP.

61. Haeger, *Astor*, 110, 112, 121, 130.

62. Haeger, *Astor*, 159–160, 162, 165.

63. Schocket, *Funding Corporate Power*, chapter 5, discusses corporate withdrawal from public life. Also Horwitz, *Transformation of American Law.*

64. For the semipublic role of banks in 1790s see Reubens, "Burr, Hamilton and the Manhattan Company: Part I," 602; Hovenkamp, *Enterprise and American Law*, 12.
65. Schocket, *Funding Corporate Power*, 5, 10.

Conclusion

1. Work is needed on how financial capital in the U.S. North and in Britain *together* encouraged the agrarian development of the U.S. South and the British Empire in Asia, forming a new global South.
2. Samuel Eliot Morison, *The Maritime History of Massachusetts, 1783–1860* (Cambridge, MA: Riverside Press, 1961).
3. Cf. Tamara Thornton, *Cultivating Gentlemen: The Meaning of Country Life among the Boston Elite, 1785–1860* (New Haven: Yale University Press, 1989).
4. Robert B. Ekelund and Robert D. Tollison, *Mercantilism as a Rent-Seeking Society: Economic Regulation in Historical Perspective* (College Station: Texas A&M University Press, 1981).
5. David A. Martin, "Bimetallism in the United States before 1850," *The Journal of Political Economy* 76, no. 3 (May–June 1968): 433, 440.
6. Lewis Namier, *The Structure of Politics at the Accession of George III* (London: Macmillan, 1957). The Company's class position allowed directors not only to denigrate the quality of American-carried Indian cloth (accurately or not), but also to denigrate free traders in general as being déclassé. OIOC A/2/14, Directors to Buckinghamshire, East India House, April 15, 1812. Item 64.
7. P. J. Cain and A. G. Hopkins, *British Imperialism, 1688–2000* (New York: Longman, 2002), 4. Cain and Hopkins draw on Douglass North's "new institutional" approach here.
8. The American extension of property rights abroad was more muted, for the United States began with a freer trade. The extension, such as it was, focused for the rest of the nineteenth century on neutral rights for American ships and properties overseas, rather than on empire.
9. On the British government's development of a neutral stance in the economy of empire, see Cain and Hopkins, *British Imperialism*, 11.
10. Cain and Hopkins, *British Imperialism*, 86. Pitt went off the gold standard in 1797. Pomeranz focuses on the issue of industrialization in the West. In his discussion of capital accumulation he considers all forms of capital, including buildings and other fixed capital, and does not address specie separately. Kenneth Pomeranz, *The Great Divergence: China, Europe, and the Making of the Modern World Economy* (Princeton: Princeton University Press, 2000).
11. Amales Tripathi, *Trade and Finance in the Bengal Presidency, 1793–1833* (Calcutta: Oxford University Press, 1979), 111, 131. The significance of the "Far East trade" is often explained as the economic historian Winifred Barr

Rothenberg has done: it is something that "went a long way toward resurrecting New England's maritime economy after the [American] Revolution" but that lost its distinction after 1815 as American "venture capital" went inland. Winifred Barr Rothenberg, "The Invention of American Capitalism: The Economy of New England in the Federal Period," in Peter Temin, ed., *Engines of Enterprise: An Economic History of New England* (Cambridge, MA: Harvard University Press, 2000). 105.

12. Jacques M. Downs, *The Golden Ghetto: The American Commercial Community at Canton and the Shaping of American China Policy, 1784–1844* (Bethlehem, PA: Lehigh University Press, 1997, 143–157.

13. A good many more merchants took up residence in an eastern port for a year or two, engaged in the country trade either so as to club together enough cargo for a return voyage or to amass enough capital, invested in bills on London, to return home with a competence at least. Patrick Tracy Jackson engaged in just this sort of shuttle trade in the first decade of the nineteenth century. One cannot, then, take a merchant's residence in an eastern port for a year or two as evidence of a long-term stay or of a firm's establishing a permanent office in that port. Thomas Lechmere, for example, remained resident in Bombay long enough to become an alderman there, yet it would be too much to assume that he was opening a permanent office in that city based on that indication alone (though he may have). For Lechmere becoming an alderman see Morison, *Maritime History of Massachusetts,* 85. For the overly extensive conclusion drawn from this point see Rothenberg, "Invention of American Capitalism," 103. Growing Asian credit markets also played a role in the decline of freight rental as a business model for the East Indies trade.

14. Includes tea on U.S. and foreign vessels, years ending September 30. *ASP* 2, passim. Specie also continued to comprise an important part of U.S. sales in China. Yen-P'ing Hao, "Chinese Teas to America—A Synopsis," in John K. Fairbank and Ernest May, eds., *America's China Trade in Historical Perspective* (Cambridge, MA: Harvard University Press, 1986), 22–23.

15. Includes pepper on U.S. and foreign vessels, years ending September 30. *ASP* 2, passim.

16. See, for example, "East India Monopoly—Export Trade to India," *The Oriental Herald* 19, no. 59 (November 1828); "East India Company Monopoly—Import Trade from India," *The Oriental Herald* 50 (December 1828); and "American Manufactures—Convention at Harrisburg—East India Monopoly," *The Oriental Herald* (September 1829). See also John Crawfurd, *A view of the present state and future prospects of the free trade and colonisation of India* (London: J. Ridgway, 1828).

17. David Porter, *Journal of a Cruise Made to the Pacific Ocean, by Captain David Porter, in the Unites States Frigate Essex, in the Years 1812, 1813, and 1814,* 2 vols. (New York: Wiley & Halstead, 1815); David F. Long, *Gold Braid and Foreign Relations: Diplomatic Activities of U.S. Naval Officers, 1798–1883* (Annapolis: Naval Institute Press, 1988), 47–48; Greg Dening, *Beach Crossings:*

Voyaging across Times, Cultures, and Self (Philadelphia: University of Pennsylvania Press, 2004), 237–257. Characterizing the U.S. presence in the Pacific as "imperial" by this period is hyperbolic. It blurs the distinctions between the U.S. and British presences in Asia in 1800, the latter being much more overtly imperial than the former. It also leaves little language for distinguishing President McKinley's Pacific empire. In the early republic, private individuals, rather than the U.S. government or any U.S. organization (such as an East India Company) with imperial capabilities, constituted the U.S. presence in Asia. Cf. James M. Lindgren, "'That Every Mariner May Possess the History of the World': A Cabinet for the East India Marine Society of Salem," *New England Quarterly* 68, no. 2 (June 1995): 179–205. Indeed, the early twentieth-century debate over whether French or American vessels sighted the Northern Marquesas first (it was the French) was more revealing of early twentieth-century imperial attitudes than early nineteenth-century ones. Siméon Delmas, "Découverte du groupe Nord-Ouest des Marquises," *Bulletin de la Société des Études Océaniennes* 4, no. 7 (1931): 191–193; Yves Malardé, "Découverte du groupe N.-O. des Iles Marquises," *Bulletin de la Société des Études Océaniennes* 5, no. 1 (1932): 9–11. Compare Porter, *Journal of a Cruise*, vol. 2, 7–9.

18. Spain had had its "Indies"—the Americas, in a perpetuation of Columbus's mistake—and the Philippines had been ruled from there, leaving everyone to agree that the Philippines was in the Indies for quite different reasons. With the loss of Mexico the Philippines came to be ruled more directly from home.

19. Pierre Labrousse discusses the association between the divergent nineteenth-century empires and Europe's new nomenclature for Asia in "Java Classique et le monde maritime, nouvel orient de l'ocean indien," in Claude Wanquet and Benoît Jullien, eds., *Révolution française et océan indién* (Paris: L'Harmattan, 1995), 266–267; Marcello Caetano, *O Conselho Ultramarino: Esboço da sua história* (Lisbon: Agência-Geral do Ultramar, 1967), 13–15.

20. Ironically, by the Gilded Age, monopolies would in fact return to America.

Acknowledgments

This book would not have been possible without funding and guidance from numerous institutions and individuals. Cathy Matson's thoughtful advice and multiple readings were of the utmost importance. The generosity of the Harvard University History Department, the Economic History Association, the Charles Warren Center for American History, the Harvard University Graduate School of Arts and Sciences, the Program on Early American Economy and Society at the Library Company of Pennsylvania, and the Research and Postgraduate Studies Committee at Lingnan University supported both research abroad and writing. The Library Company was especially open minded about research abroad; for this I am grateful. The archivists, librarians, and staff at the following were all extremely helpful: the United States National Archives and Records Administration, especially customs-records experts Gail Farr and Michael Moore; the Oriental and India Office staff at the British Library; the staff of the British National Archives; King's College library (London); the London School of Economics library; the Institute for Historical Research, University of London; the National Archives of Mauritius; the National Library of South Africa; the Cape Town Archives Repository, South Africa; the St. Helena Archives; the Arsip Nasional Republik Indonesia; the Nationaal Archief (Den Haag); the Koninklijke Bibliotheek (Den Haag); the Archivo General de Indias (Seville); the French National Archives in Paris and Aix-en-Provence; the French Naval

Archives in Vicennes; the Library Company of Philadelphia, especially Connie King, Wendy Woloson, Phillip Lapsansky, and Jim Green; and the Widener, Yenching, Houghton, and Baker Business Libraries at Harvard University. Eileen Lohka and Raymond d'Unienville provided insight into Mauritian history. Sirajul Islam provided guidance in the Oriental and India Office Collections; David Armitage gave various suggestions; and Emma Rothschild, Robert Travers, Leonard Blussé, C. A. Bayly, Stanley Engerman, Huw Bowen, and Paul Van Dyke generously read portions of this manuscript in various forms. Colleagues Kris Manjapra, Matthew Mosca, Chie Ikeya, Matthew Cook, Venkat Dhulip, Michael Brillman, Jonathan Eacott, Vanessa Ogle, Michelle Mormul, Thomas Pepinsky, Sandy Polu, Edward Kolla, and Nathan Perl-Rosenthal provided camaraderie in the archives and overseas; the drudgery of copying out statistics was leavened by their good cheer. Fellow early Americanists at Harvard hospitably read and critiqued drafts far afield from colonial American history, and graduate students in history and in East Asian Languages and Civilizations shared their enthusiasm and knowledge. Sven Beckert and Philip Kuhn were immensely helpful with their readings and suggestions, as was Laurel Ulrich, in whose seminar this book first began. Joyce Chaplin provided detailed and thoughtful criticism throughout as well as sound advice; I benefited from her capacious grasp of history and of places far beyond America's shore more than can be expressed adequately here. My colleagues at Lingnan, especially Richard Davis and Mark Hampton, provided support and advice throughout the revision and editorial process. Laura Beardsley, Scott Layton, Frank Menzel, Karine Ramondy, Tristan Stein, and John Wong helped run down last-minute queries in the archives and in the library. Isabelle Lewis drew the map. Despite such open minds and such generous assistance, all errors are of course my own.

Index